AF608070

RELIGION AND EMPIRE IN PORTUGUESE INDIA

ÂNGELA BARRETO XAVIER

Religion and Empire in Portuguese India

Conversion, Resistance, and the Making of Goa

Religion and Empire in Portuguese India: Conversion, Resistance, and the Making of Goa by Ângela Barreto Xavier was first published by Permanent Black D-28 Oxford Apts, 11 IP Extension, Delhi 110092 INDIA, for the territory of SOUTH ASIA. First SUNY Press edition 2022.

Not for sale in South Asia

Cover design by Anuradha Roy

Published by State University of New York Press, Albany

Printed in the United States of America

For information, contact State University of New York Press, Albany, NY
www.sunypress.edu

Library of Congress Cataloging-in-Publication Data

Names: Barreto Xavier, Ângela, author
Title: Religion and empire in Portuguese India : conversion, resistance, and the making of Goa
Description: Albany : State University of New York Press, [2022] | Includes bibliographical references and index.
Identifiers: ISBN 9781438489117 (hardcover : alk. paper) | ISBN 9781438489131 (e-book)
Further information is available at the Library of Congress.

10 9 8 7 6 5 4 3 2 1

Contents

	Preface	vii
	Glossary	xi
	Abbreviations	xvii
	Maps	xix–xxiii
	Introduction	1
1	Reform in the Kingdom, Reform in the Empire	17
2	Designing Conversion	47
3	New Temples and New Priests: The Establishment of Religious Orders in Goan Villages	103
4	Tools of Christianisation: Shaping Memory, Understanding, and Will	153
5	Initial Moves: Discontent, Resistance, Acquiescence	199
6	The Martyrs of Cuncolim and Other Episodes of Resistance	244
7	The Defence of the "Genuine Nobility": Conflicts of Memory, Identity, and Power	278
	Conclusion	328
	Bibliography	339
	Index	399

Preface

THIS BOOK IS a shortened version of *A Invenção de Goa: Poder Imperial e Conversões Culturais nos séculos XVI e XVII*, published in Lisbon in 2008 by Imprensa de Ciências Sociais. It has been adapted to suit the needs of an English-speaking readership.

More than a decade has passed since its original publication, yet *The Invention of Goa* still provides essential clues for the study of Portuguese imperialism and its colonial expressions in India in general, and Goa in particular. The book discusses the multiple agencies at work in the empire, including the hopes and strategies of Europeans and local societies as they faced the challenges of colonialism. As a result, it de-essentialises the categories of coloniser and colonised, making visible instead their inner-group diversity of interests, their different modes of identification, the specificity of local dynamics in their interactions and exchanges – in other words the several threads that wove the fabric of colonial life.

At the same time, this work considers the inhabitants of Goa in the *longue durée*, zooming into Goan society as part and parcel of a long political tradition of dominance, from the Bijapur and Bahmanid sultanates to the Vijayanagar and Portuguese empires. It thus parts company from the assumption that the inhabitants of Goa shared centuries of political culture that had framed their mechanisms for coping with external political domination. I show that their experience allowed locals to occupy *the established* position – to use the vocabulary of the sociologist Norbert Elias – while naturally perceiving the Portuguese as yet another group of *outsiders*. However, since the Portuguese were also competing to be *the established*, conversion policies were devised to allow them to become the point of reference for Goan society.

Religion and Empire focuses not on the city of Goa itself – the usual focus of traditional scholarship – but also on the rural hinterlands that became part of Goa. It contends that the relationship between the Portuguese Crown and the villages of Goa was a crucial factor in the persistence and durability of Portuguese imperial and colonial presence.

Between 2008 and 2022, new insights have appeared to enrich and complement the conclusions of the present book. Besides my own work, and one that I co-authored with Ines G. Županov, *Catholic Orientalism: Portuguese Empire and Indian Knowledge* (2015), various articles and books have been published by Ines G. Županov, Giuseppe Marcocci, Jorge Flores, Paolo Aranha, Sanjay Subrahmanyam, and Zoltán Biedermann, among others, adding new dimensions to the debate, frequently supporting the conclusions of this book and sometimes challenging them. Yet I believe *The Invention of Goa* continues to be of fundamental value to those interested in the Portuguese colonisation of Asia.

Many people and institutions helped me while I wrote the Portuguese version. Besides my PhD supervisors Kirti N. Chaudhuri and António Manuel Hespanha, members of the research group ARACNE – particularly Catarina Madeira Santos, Cristina Nogueira da Silva, and Pedro Cardim – were colleagues with whom I first discussed my work. Conversations with Aldo Mazzacane, António Camões Gouveia, Chandrakant Keni, Cristiana Bastos, Diogo Ramada Curto, Fernando Bouza Alvarez, Iris Kantor, Jaime Reis, Jean-Frédéric Schaub, José Pedro Paiva, Father Joseph Velinkar, Father Nascimento Mascarenhas, Paolo Prodi, Pedro Lains, Peter Ronald de Souza, Ronnie Po-Chia Hsia, Rosa Maria Perez, and Sanjay Subrahmanyam helped me widen my perspectives, understand my limits, and enrich my knowledge of several subjects.

The Ministério dos Negócios Estrangeiros, Fundação para a Ciência e Tecnologia, Fundação Calouste Gulbenkian and Comissão Nacional para a Comemoração dos Descobrimentos

Portugueses of Portugal, and the École Française de Rome, offered me the financial aid to pursue research in libraries and archives across the globe.

This English edition has been made possible by the contributions of many people and institutions. I want to thank Cátia Antunes and Sanjay Subrahmanyam for encouragement to publish it, and Cátia Antunes, Tamar Herzog, and Ines G. Županov for helping me with some of the formal aspects of the book. I am grateful to FCT – Fundação para a Ciência e Tecnologia (Portugal) – which financed the initial translation by Jason Keith Fernandes, and to the V.M. Salgaocar Foundation (Goa, India) for sponsoring the English revision.

I am also deeply indebted to Rukun Advani, editor at Permanent Black, for his refinement of the initial translation. Rukun's queries, observations, and corrections have been crucial to this book's readability.

Sanjay Subrahmanyam was the first reader of the English manuscript. He then gave a huge amount of his time and energy towards its perfection, continuing to re-read and help until the very end. I have no words to thank him for his generosity.

Through all these processes, family and friends have been of fundamental importance with their support and understanding. My husband Steffen and my children, Madalena and João, were my permanent *compagnons de route*.

All footnoted source citations are abbreviated, their full forms are given in the Bibliography. Citations of non-English sources appear in translation.

Parts of Chapter 2 were published in English in "Conversos and Novamente Convertidos: Law, Religion and Identity in the Portuguese Kingdom and Empire (16th and 17th Centuries)", *Journal of Early-Modern History*, Vol. 15 (2011), 255–87; "Empire, Religion and Identity: The Making of Goan People in the Early-Modern Period", in Denis Sindic, Manuela Barreto, and Rui

Costa Lopes, eds, *Power and Identity*, London and New York: Psychology Press, 2014, 13–30; and "Reducing Difference in the Portuguese Empire? A Case Study from Early-Modern Goa", in S. Aboim, P. Granjo, and A. Ramos, eds, *Changing Societies: Legacies and Challenges, Vol. I – Ambiguous Inclusions: Inside Out, Inside In*, Lisbon: Imprensa de Ciências Sociais, 2018, 241–61.

Parts of Chapter 5 were published in English in "Disquiet in the Island: Conversion, Conflicts and Conformity in Sixteenth-Century Goa", *Indian Economic and Social History Review*, 44, 3 (2007), 269–95.

Parts of Chapter 6 were published in English in "Power, Religion and Violence in 16th Century Goa", in Cristiana Bastos, ed., *Parts of Asia, Portuguese Literary & Cultural Studies,* nº 19 (2010), 19–41.

Parts of Chapter 7 were published in English in "Race and Caste: Identity Narratives in Goan Elites", in María Elena Martínez, Max S. Herring Torres, and David Nirenberg, eds, *Race and Blood in Spain and Colonial Hispano-America*, Berlin and London: LIT Verlag, 2012; and in Ângela Barreto Xavier and Ines G. Županov, "Orientalists from Within: Indian Genealogists, Philologists and Historians", in Ângela Barreto Xavier and Ines G. Županov, *Catholic Orientalism: Portuguese Empire, Indian Knowledge, 16th–18th Centuries*, Delhi: Oxford University Press, 2015.

I dedicate this book to my parents, and aunts Carmita and Manuela.

Glossary

Adventícios	Social category attributed by the Portuguese to people resident in the village but thought of as having recent connections to it
Alvará	Permit; grant of permission
Alvarás régios	Royal edicts
Auto-de-fé	A public ceremony of the Inquisition entailing the punishment of heretics and apostates – which could mean burning at the stake
Câmara	Municipality
Câmara Geral	Assembly of the main villages of each region of Goa which decided on matters of common interest
Casa dos Catecúmenos	House of the Cathecumens
Canarim / canarins	Designation, often deprecatory, used by the Portuguese for inhabitants of Goa and the surrounding regions
Carta régia	Document signed by the king to authorise general decision-making, but without affixing the seal of the chancellery
Casados	Portuguese men and South Asian women from the time of Afonso Albuquerque and their descendants

Chatim	or *xette,* usually used by the Portuguese to refer to goldsmiths or merchants
Chaudarim	Workers of the palm groves, or those responsible for the extraction of *sura* (palm oil)
Confrarias	Confraternities and brotherhoods
Cuius regio, eius religio	The idea that inhabitants of a territory should be of the same religion as the ruler
Culacharim/culacharins	Colonists who cultivated lands in the villages, lived there, and followed local custom
Cuntocares	or *khuntkārs,* were investors who owned an important part of *cuntos* (*khunts*)
Cuntos	or *khunt,* shares in the lands of villages available in auctions to people who did not belong to the *gaunkari*
Curumbins	Rural labourers: *kunnbi* or *gaudde*
Estado da Índia	Political entity that, from 1505, organised the Asian and East African territories, fortresses, and factories under Portuguese direct or indirect rule
Fabrica	Legal entity that organised the resources required to build, conserve, and repair Christian churches and pay for the cult
Farazes	The lowest caste in the territories of Goa
Foros	Two types of annual amounts paid to the formal owner of the land, the

	king. They were called *cotubana* when fixed amounts imposed on lands perpetually granted. When imposed on lands granted temporarily, they were called "current" and the amount paid was variable
Gaunkar	Male members of the *gaunkari*, theoretically the first residents of the village
Gaunkari	Village government and administration
Gentiles	Those who were not Christians
Habitus	Concept used by French sociologist Pierre Bourdieu, definable as embodied dispositions that organise the ways people perceive and act in the world
Indiáticos	Sons born of a Portuguese mother and father, sometimes nobles and hereditary *fidalgos*, at other times mestizos
Jonos/jons	Shares in lands of villages available in auctions to *gaunkars*
Lascarim/Lascarins	Soldier/s from Goa or the surrounding regions
Manducar(es)	Paid rural worker(s) who sometimes monitored the work of others
Mestizos	People of mixed Portuguese and South Asian parentage
Mesa da Consciência Consciência e Ordens	Royal court established by King D. João III to decide on matters relating to the king's conscience, as

	well as solve problems relating to the activities of the religious and military orders
Misericórdia	Brotherhood, protected by the Crown, which co-ordinated poor relief and medical assistance
Mocadão	Official of the Sultanate of Bijapur; the title was adopted by the Portuguese administration to name chiefs of different offices
Nemos	Decisions taken by *gaunkars* in meetings of the *gaunkari*
Namoxins	Or *Nāmaśī*. Temple lands in Goan villages which were later transferred to the Church or religious orders in villages
Officium Parochi	Legal capacity to exercise the function of a parish priest with all the rights and obligations it entailed
Padroado	Arrangement between the Papacy and the Portuguese king by which the Papacy delegated to the kings of Portugal the right to nominate bishops and priests, to support and administer churches and the secular and regular clergy (*ius patronatus et praesentandi*)
Pai dos Cristãos	Officer of the Estado da Índia whose job was to protect and control local Christians
Pardao	Currency unit of the Estado da Índia, formerly of Vijayanagar, coined in

	gold, silver, or copper. The silver was equivalent to 5 *tangas* or 300 *réis* and the gold to 6 *tangas* or 360 *réis*
Propaganda Fide	Congregation of the Papacy, founded in 1622, to foster the spread of Catholicism and regulate Catholic affairs in non-Catholic countries. Its mission frequently collided with the Portuguese Padroado
Provisões	Decisions that provided offices and mercies (provisions)
Real/réis	Portuguese copper coin
Reinol	Portuguese person born in Portugal
Relação de Goa	Court of appeal of Estado da Índia
Respublica Christiana	International community of Christian believers
Sede vacante	Condition of a diocese without a bishop, having to be administered by another official of the Church
Tanadar/Tanadar-mor	Superior revenue officer under the Bijapur fiscal administration – an office retained by the Portuguese
Tanga(s)	Silver coin of the value of 60 *réis*
Vangod	Hierarchical divisions within *gaunkars* and caste groups with repercussions in quotidian relations and the spatial organisation of villages
Vedor da Fazenda	Exchequer. Highest officer of the royal treasury of Estado da Índia
Xerafim	Gold or silver coin of the value of 5 *tangas* or 300 *réis*

Abbreviations

AAG	Archive of the Archidiocese of Goa
ACL	Academia das Ciências de Lisboa
AHU	Arquivo Histórico Ultramarino
ARSI	Archivio Romanorum Societatis Iesu
BA	Biblioteca da Ajuda
BNP	Biblioteca Nacional de Portugal
BPADE	Biblioteca Pública e Arquivo Distrital de Évora
BP-APO	Bragança Pereira, *Arquivo Português Oriental*
BPE	Biblioteca Pública de Évora
CC	Corpo Cronológico
Cod.	Codex
CR-APO	Cunha Rivara, *Arquivo Portuguez Oriental*
Cx	Caixa
DHMPPO	Rego, *Documentação para a história das missões do Padroado Português do Oriente*
DUP	Documentação Ultramarina Portuguesa
Fasc.	Fascículo
FU	Filmoteca Ultramarina
Gavetas	As Gavetas da Torre do Tombo
HAG	Historical Archives of Goa
IAN/TT	Instituto dos Arquivos Nacionais/Torre do Tombo

L.	Livro
Mç.	Maço
Monsoon Books	*Documentos Remetidos da Índia ou Livros das Monções*
Mss.	Manuscript(s)
OFM	Ordinis Fratrum Minorum (Franciscan Order, Observants)
OFM Rec.	Ordinis Fratrum Minorum Recollectorum (Franciscan Order, Recollects)
OP	Ordinis Predicatorum (Dominicans)
OSA	Ordinis Sancti Augustini (Augustinians)
QE	Visconde de Santarém, *Quadro Elementar*
S.J. / s.j.	Societatis Jesu (Jesuits)

Goa

16th-17th centuries

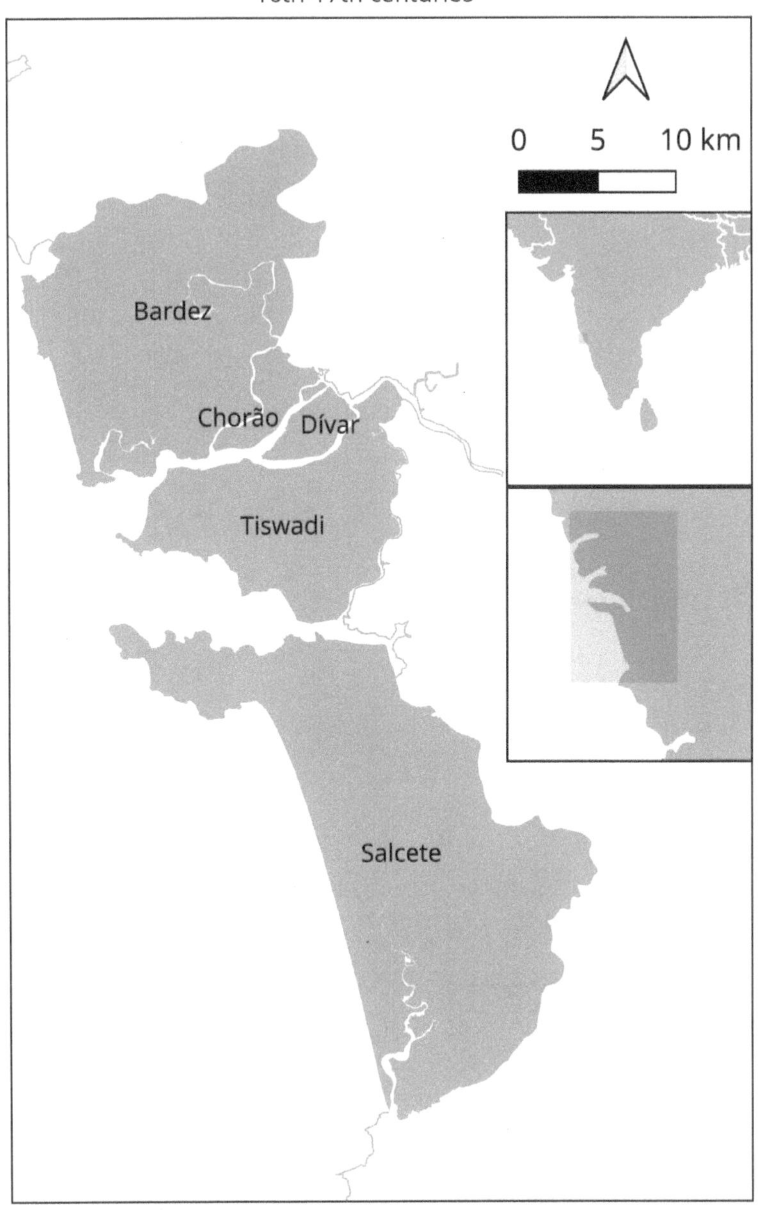

Salcete

Case study villages (bold)

Loutolim
Camorlim
Rachol
Curtorim
Macazana
Margão
Davorlim
Guirdolim
Navelim
Aquem
Dicarpale
Chandor
Cavorim
Dramapur
Talaulim
Deussua
Mulem
Chinchinim
Sarzora
Veroda
Ambelim
Assolna
Cuncolim
0 1 2 km

Bardez

Case study villages (bold)

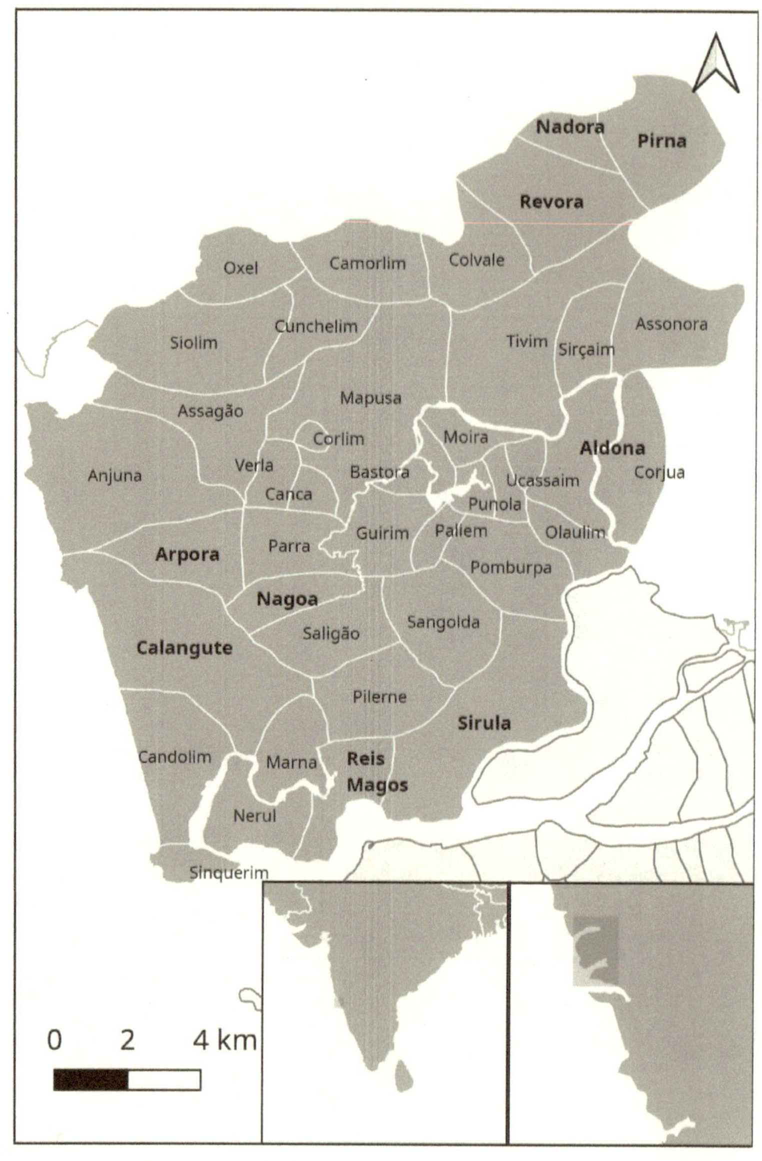

Tiswadi, Chorão and Dívar

Case study villages (bold)

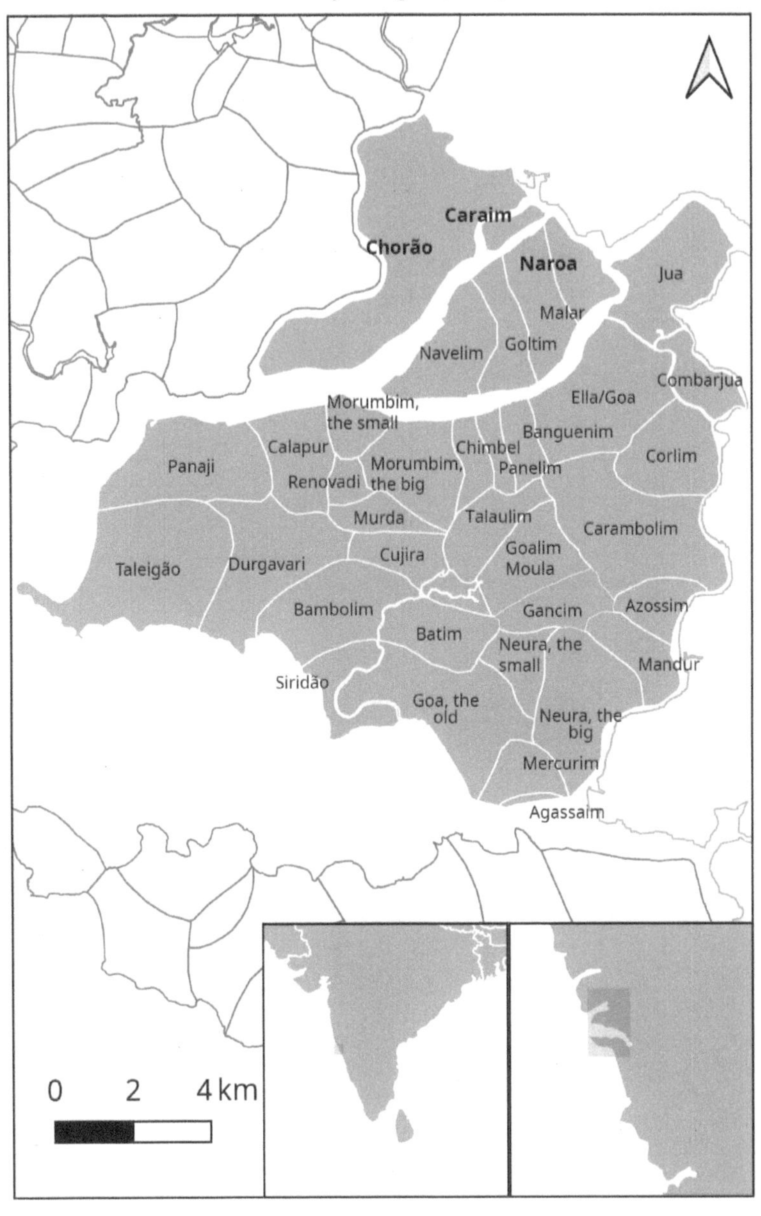

Introduction

TOWARDS THE END of the seventeenth century, António João Frias, parish priest of the Church of Santo André in Goa, completed a treatise. The clergy in this period often employed the art of writing not only to confirm the orthodoxy of the faith but also to express points of view and defend their beliefs. Frias argued that "the nations of India owe to the Lusitanians, who opened the way for the preaching of the Gospel in these territories, the knowledge that they have of the Faith in God, who is the primary cause and the true light that illuminate men with knowledge of the truth." This was a frequent topos in religious writings of Portuguese origin. The intent was to justify not only the imperial presence of the Crown of Portugal in India, but also the hierarchical order of relationship between Portuguese and Indians. Frias' metaphorical interplay drew attention to the semantic proximity of the words Lusos (Lusitanian) and Luzes (light/enlightenment) to underscore that the "enlightenment of the Occident, where they [the Portuguese] live" has taken "to the East the light of the Gospel". Despite being "where the first Sun shines", the regions of India had been in "profound darkness of the ignorance of true Law" until the Portuguese brought it to them.[1]

Frias was not Portuguese. He was an Indian subject of the Portuguese Crown, which makes his discourse particularly symptomatic of the social order that operated in Goa at the end of the 1600s. His words provide a happy metaphor for two *longue durée* processes within the Iberian imperial formations. They serve, first, as a metaphor for the expansion of a historical narrative in which the Occident was the liberating and rationalising agent in other geographies. Frias witnessed the internalisation and dissemination of this narrative by people colonised by Westerners. He was at the

[1] Frias, *Aureola dos Indios*, 159.

crossroads of that grand narrative, since he was part of the Christianised and westernised native elites who conceived of themselves as liberating agents of *other* imperial territories. In his vision he was a colonial agent, the equal of the Portuguese who had been entrusted with bringing the light of the Occident to the East. For Frias and his peers, Ceylon, Africa, and other peripheries of the Portuguese empire emerged as territories where they could expand these enlightening ideas. In time, Frias' descendants too expected they would play similar roles in the centre.[2]

This parish priest's pronouncement was also a metaphor for the transition from pre-modern political systems to modern ones, especially of the articulation between political power and society, as well as the construction of social, cultural, and political identities of members of the polity. To ensure the perpetuation of its political order, the Portuguese Crown instrumentalised various institutions that enabled processes of social and cultural reproduction – such as the family, education, poor relief – through which the Crown aimed to mould its vassals to fit a desired imperial model.[3] Some scholars have pointed out that this transition from pre-modern to modern polities was singularly manifest in imperial situations, making them early laboratories of modernity. For reasons of chronology, locality, and cultural contexts, these laboratories of modernity relied on devices that would today be considered problematic, such as the alliance between political and religious agents. However, the concord alleviated some of the difficulties that the imperial administration faced in the colonies. It facilitated not just the territorialisation of imperial power, but also its inscription in the minds and hearts of its subjects.[4]

As a "model vassal", Frias was an emblem of the success of those

[2] See, for example, Bastos, "The Inverted Mirror"; and Bastos, "Medicina, império".

[3] Bourdieu, "Cultural Reproduction and Social Reproduction".

[4] Charles Boxer had already highlighted this: Boxer, *The Portuguese Seaborne Empire*, esp. Chapters 3 and 10.

two grand narratives and mechanisms of power. Nevertheless, his case simultaneously highlights the tensions provoked by such success in the imperial context. While becoming almost identical to the coloniser, Frias, the colonised, also disturbed the order of imperial relationships, and the hierarchy and difference that such an order necessarily presupposed.

Like Frias, many residents of the territories of Goa similarly constituted multiple (and micro) points of anchorage, not only of those grand narratives but also of the disquiets and contradictions that their imperial manifestations raised.[5] This book invites attention to a double displacement in time and space to understand these processes. It intends to identify the situations that enabled the emergence, reproduction, and persistence of "social types" such as Frias. It also aims to understand how these people contributed to the durability of the Portuguese imperial presence in Goa and other domains.

The present book runs from the last phase of the reign of Dom Manuel I (1495–1521) to the reign of Dom Pedro II (1683–1705) and focuses on the territories that today form part of the state of Goa that – and in the context of the former Estado da Índia – were known as Velhas Conquistas, or Old Conquests. It comprises, therefore, Bardez, Salcete, and the islands of Tiswadi, Chorão, and Dívar.

In the following pages I argue that Goa – that is, the territory today called Goa – was invented in the context of the Portuguese imperial experience. I analyse the role played by the population of Indian origin, which constituted the demographic majority, in this construction, and how this invention was critical for the conservation of the Portuguese empire. Catarina Madeira Santos has, in her study, examined the political and institutional context of how Goa

[5] Cooper and Stoler, eds, *Tensions of Empire*, esp. their Introduction, "Between Metropole and Colony". In the same volume, see also Bhabha, "Of Mimicry and Man"; Comaroff, "Image of Empire, Contests of Conscience"; and Stoler, "Sexual Affronts and Racial Frontiers".

became "the key to the whole of India".[6] She has analysed the construction of the city of Goa as a political centre in the context of the Estado da Índia. In doing so, she has problematised and historicised a taken-for-granted assumption concerning the central political status of the port city of Goa, which sustained most of the scholarship dealing with the subject.[7] The Goa of Madeira Santos is, above all, the city of Goa; and its main characters are almost always of metropolitan Portuguese origin.

The Goa I explore is different. Though linked to the city of Goa, without which it could not have existed, and with which it shared many of its chronologies and spatialities, the Goa of this book is mainly rural Goa and its inhabitants. Teotónio R. de Souza and P.D. Xavier have studied these spaces,[8] but both privilege an analytical and predominantly synchronic description of the various dimensions of their social life rather than a dynamic analysis of their transformation.[9]

Luís Filipe Thomaz's "Goa: Uma sociedade luso-indiana" addresses the question of transformation, attempting to explain the characteristics of the society that resulted from secular interactions between Portuguese and Indians in the context of the imperial colony.[10] Some of the arguments I develop may appear similar to those in the works of Thomaz, as well as in Maria de Jesus dos Mártires Lopes' *Goa Setecentista.*[11] However, my book differs substantially from theirs in moving away from the Luso-tropicalism and Orientalism that inform those works.

[6] Madeira Santos, *Goa é a chave de toda a Índia, passim.*

[7] See, among others, Fonseca, *An Historical and Archaeological Sketch*; Saldanha, *História de Goa*; Aiala, *Goa Antiga e Moderna*; Souza, *Goa Medieval*; M.J.M. Lopes, *Goa Setecentista.*

[8] Souza, *Goa Medieval*; P.D. Xavier, *Goa: A Social History.*

[9] The dimension of "time" is not absent in these works, but the object of analysis is not the process of cultural transformation. In that sense, this book is closer to Mendonça, *Conversions and Citizenry.*

[10] Thomaz, "Goa: Uma sociedade luso-indiana".

[11] M.J.M. Lopes, *Goa Setecentista.*

I argue that the majority of the population of the villages of the Old Conquests consented to live under Portuguese imperial rule. This consent was essential for the invention of Goa, as well as for the conservation of Portuguese imperial power.[12] The manifestations of this consent were not limited to contributing to the economic, financial, and military sustainability of the imperium: the consent was internalised to the extent that the imperial cause became, for many, their own.

Most studies focused on the processes of Christianisation in these territories refer to the existence of local populations but almost always render them as *a priori*, rather than as dynamic subjects who intervened *de facto* in the historical processes within which they were involved. Like Frias, but in the nineteenth and twentieth centuries, some of the authors of this literature were themselves priests. They privileged the actions of actors and institutions of European and Christian origin, often unconsciously ignoring the agency of the converted.[13] This implicit Orientalism – which the continuing use of the adjective "oriental" reiterates – determined the focus, the archive, the sources, the modes of reading, and consequently the interpretations.[14]

In the last few years a significant body of literature has come to

[12] The term is used here in the sense attributed by A.B. Xavier and Madeira Santos, "Cultura Intelectual".

[13] See Manoel, *Missões dos Jesuítas*; Telles, "Ordens religiosas"; F.X. Costa, *Anais Franciscanos*; Lobo, *Memória Histórico-Eclesiástica*; A. Correia, *A dilatação da fé*; Lopes, "A expansão portuguesa"; D'Costa, *The Christianisation of the Goan Islands*; Meersman, *The Ancient Franciscan Provinces*; Meersman, *The Friars Minor*; Wicki, *Missionkirche im Orient*; Wicki, "Kânara und die dortige Jesuitenmission"; J.P.O. Costa, "A colonização portuguesa na Ásia", J.P.O. Costa, *A missão de João de Brito*; Thekkedath, *History of Christianity in India*; Borges, "Christianization of the Caste System"; Borges, *The Economics of the Goa Jesuits*; Velinkar, *India and the West.*

[14] See also, besides the scholarship already cited, M. Dias, "The Hindu-Christian Society of Goa"; M.J.M. Lopes, ed., *O Império Oriental, 1660–1820*; R.S. Brito, *Goa e as Praças do Norte.*

focus on the local population.[15] A good part of this new literature is of Indian, and above all Goan, authorship, with some of it participating in the postcolonial critique of Orientalism and imperialism. Many such writings, however, continue to articulate "nationalist" interpretations.[16] Albeit influenced by the Subaltern Studies school of thought, a number of them deny different types of agency to groups of local origin in the design of the imperial order, drawing attention almost only to the more violent aspects of Portuguese colonialism and Goan resistance.[17] Many of them presuppose the existence of a Goan nation before the arrival of the Portuguese, ironically reinforcing Orientalist assumptions about the organisation of rural life in India and its unchanging nature.[18] Other studies characterise the Goan population as immune to Portuguese influence. In general, the behaviour of the local population is shown within a classic Orientalist scenario dominated by communities, castes, and Hinduism. Moreover, in these studies most "colonised" identities survive the colonial period practically untouched.[19]

While trying to recover the role played by the richly diverse population that lived in the Goan territories over the making

[15] Historical anthropologists have contributed to challenge these images. Besides the already cited work of Bastos, see also Perez, ed., *Histórias de Goa*; Perez, ed., *Os Portugueses e o Oriente*; Robinson, *Conversion, Continuity and Change*; Robinson, "Sixteenth-century Conversions".

[16] Among others, see T.B. Cunha, *Denationalisation of Goans*; Priolkar, *The Goan Inquisition*; Gomes, *Village Goa*; Shirodkar, ed., *Goa: Cultural Trends.*

[17] Panikkar, *Asia and Western Dominance*; Souza, *Goa Medieval*; Shirodkar, "Evangelization by Missionaries"; Kamat, *Farar Far.*

[18] F.N. Xavier, *Bosquejo Histórico*; F.N. Xavier, *Collecção de Leis Peculiares*; Azevedo, *As communidades de Goa*; Baden-Powell, "The Villages of Goa"; Gune, *Ancient Shrines*; Feio, *As Castas Hindús*; Phal, *Society in Goa.*

[19] However, proposals such as those of Ghantkar, *History of Goa*, and Moraes, *Kadamba Kula*, are very important. See also G. Pereira, *An Outline*; R.G. Pereira, *Goa – Hindu Temples*; R.G. Pereira, *Goa. Gaunkari;* Kulkarni, "Marathi Records"; Kulkarni, "Portuguese in the Deccan"; and Mitragotri, *Socio Cultural History.*

of Portuguese imperial rule, I neither attempt to write a history from below nor offer a vision of the vanquished (*Vision des Vaincus*).[20]

The histories outlined above have inspired the ensuing analysis – specially by recognising the centrality of the multiple voices that reflected imperial experiences. Their identification of the languages of dominance, subordination, and revolt is also part of my inquiry. Yet these histories rarely include and consider the "subaltern" population as active participants in the constitution of political power and seldom look at local populations as committed – or even habituated to commit themselves – to power. Instead, they tend to view these populations as accomplices forced into a partnership; as a result they continue to structure their arguments around the fixed dichotomies of "dominant/dominated" and "coloniser/colonised".[21]

The present book suggests that such dichotomies in Goa were less rigid. Its focus draws inspiration from Christopher Bayly's *Indian Society and the Making of the British Empire,*[22] as well as scholarship suggesting, in the wake of Jawaharlal Nehru, that for some people imperial configurations allowed them to become aware that the world was much bigger than they had imagined.[23] However, I do not intend to engage in the kind of revisionism that could be confused with pro-imperialist feeling.

What I argue instead is that there are no durable processes of dominance without the consent, in varied forms, of dominated populations – and that this is also true of Goa. The consent is not merely the fruit of hegemonic supremacy; it can equally be the

[20] Thompson, *The Making of the English Working Class*; Wachtel, *La Vision des Vaincus*.

[21] See especially, the critique by Ruud, "The Indian Hierarchy". The essay by Dipesh Chakrabarty – on who can speak of the Indian past, and the ways in which it is spoken about – is also critical: Chakrabarty, "Postcoloniality and the Artifices of History".

[22] C.A. Bayly, *Indian Society*; C.A. Bayly, *Empire and Information*.

[23] Pagden, *Povos e Impérios*, xxiv.

product of a complex process through which some local groups internalise the imperial narrative. In Goa, these groups comprised pre-existent local elites who adjusted to the demands of the new imperial order to retain their power. Sometimes simultaneously, the subaltern population also recognised a window of opportunity in the imperial order, exploiting it to engender expectations that were not possible within the older order.

The participation of the local population was as varied as were subjects, groups, histories of subordination, and local forms of power. Interactions of these with the imperium depended in good measure on local political culture and other immediate and contingent factors. The different modalities of hegemony resulted from this variety of interactions and negotiations.[24]

From this perspective, the Portuguese colonisers and the Indian colonised mutually constituted each other. The character of their relationship changed over time, depending on the power dynamic and on the ways in which local populations interpreted it. In other words, the material order was constituted as much by the relationships among different subjects, groups, and communities as by the dominant discursive order. This discursive order framed how the Goan "social reality" was textually expressed and meanings attributed to the practices and experiences of subjects. The ways these discourses interpreted reality and its multifaceted meanings contributed to a continuous reinvention of the imperial order and the meanings attributed to it, and in so doing stimulated the making of new imperial realities.[25]

In the case of Goa, the distance between resident Portuguese

[24] This argument is inspired by Foucault, *A Microfísica do Poder*. See also Hespanha, *Panorama da História Institucional*, 19–24, 31–8, on the dispersion of "power" in the Estado da Índia.

[25] Foucault's understanding of the order of the discourse (Foucault, *L'Ordre du Discours*) and its theoretical-methodological implications inspire this book, too. A discussion on these implications for colonial experiences can be found in A.B. Xavier and Madeira Santos, "Cultura Intelectual".

and local population tended to diminish for a complex group of reasons. The discourses produced by Goan elites of local origin show that, to a certain extent, they stopped seeing themselves as the colonised. This reduction of distance between the perceived status of people of Portuguese origin resident in Goa on the one hand, and local elites on the other, became manifest first in the Goan territories and then in the peripheries of the empire, i.e. Ceylon and Africa. In time the same discourses spread elsewhere in the empire, especially in the second half of the eighteenth century, and particularly after the decree of 1761.[26] It was at this time that the colonised began to emerge as key contributors to the metropolitan power sphere, reaching their apogee in the nineteenth century with their appearance in the Portuguese parliament under a liberal monarchy.

What allowed this reduction of distance and caused the transfiguration of the colonised into coloniser? Between *which* colonisers and *which* colonised did this happen? Moreover, how did this imaginary influence the emerging imperial order?

If it were possible to isolate a single variable or instance to explain this transformation, the choice would fall upon the Christianisation and cultural conversion of the local populations.[27] The gradual transformation of local ways of thinking, doing, and being, and of conceiving time and space and the present and the past in the framework of Christianity had long-lasting reverberations. It was not so much the religious conversion as the cultural conversion that ensued – of many of the inhabitants of the 150 villages of the Old Conquests – that was responsible for the conservation of Portuguese imperial power. This cultural conversion was also responsible for the tensions and opportunities that characterised the

[26] This royal decree stated that subjects of the Portuguese king who were original inhabitants of India should be preferred for honours and offices in the Estado da Índia. See Silva, *Collecção da Legislação Portugueza*, Vol. 1, 793–5.

[27] In this book, conversion – more immediate and political – is dissociated from Christianisation, which was a gradual process.

local colonial context and the relation between the metropole and the colony, both of which statuses were, for a variety of reasons and over time, ambivalent.[28]

The Goan elites, in the main, experienced a colonisation of their imagination – *la colonisation de l'imaginaire*, to use the words of Serge Gruzinski about Mexican experiences in the same centuries. Alternatively, it could be said they experienced a colonisation of their conscience – to use the term in Jean and John Comaroff's critical work on nineteenth-century South Africa and twentieth-century colonial experiences.[29]

A variety of strategies that combined military and technological instruments with more amenable tools – such as education and poor relief, associating the agents of political and military power with other powers and other agents – was needed to disseminate the discourse on the supremacy of the Western model (in this case Western *and* Christian). These strategies aimed to mould the social practices of the local populations to ensure that they recognised such supremacy.[30]

In the early-modern period, the relevance of the association of the typical agents of power with other agents to ensure the conservation of the empire was unquestionable. The advice given in 1555 by Dom Luís, brother of King Dom João III (1521–1557), in a letter to the viceroy of India, Dom Pedro de Mascarenhas, for example, is telling. Dom Luís informed the viceroy that the monarch was sending twelve members of the Society of Jesus to Goa, stressing that "they are there to convert the world and it is certain that you should value them more than many of the warriors."[31]

[28] See Rambo, "Theories of Conversion", and the discussion on the different forms of religious conversion and their goals.

[29] Gruzinski, *La Colonisation de l'Imaginaire*; Comaroff and Comaroff, *Of Revelation and Revolution*.

[30] Some of these ideas are already present in Said, *Orientalism* and idem, *Culture and Imperialism*, here in dialogue with Gramsci's concept of hegemony: Gramsci, *Selections*.

[31] Letter of Dom Luís to D. Pedro de Mascarenhas, in 1555, in Wicki, *Documenta Indica* (henceforth DI), Vol. 3, 280.

Dom Luís represented the Jesuits as soldiers of a different order (as did they themselves), as agents of informal power and "soft" violence. This type of analogy demands renewed attention for an understanding of the political role that religious actors had in the construction of early-modern imperial experiences.

But what precisely were the combinations of men and institutions that in effect constructed the hegemony of Portuguese imperialism?[32]

Responding to this question requires knowledge of the attitudes of the inhabitants of the villages of Salcete, Bardez, Tiswadi, Chorão, and Divar towards the missionaries – above all the Franciscans and the Jesuits – as religious and political agents of the Crown who intended to transform "hearts and minds, signs and practices".[33] How did these missionaries convince the local populations that their God and social practices, their ethical references and aesthetics, were better than those that had prevailed indigenously? How did they convince the local communities that the "darkness of ignorance of the true Law" had characterised their history? How did they persuade them that those from the West were their liberators? How did they eventually manage to get local elites to adopt Portuguese as their mother tongue? How did they manage to turn their own political geographies and cultures – of Portugal, Europe, and the West – into the organising frameworks of local consciences?[34] Furthermore, how exactly did local communities appropriate these frameworks? How did the somewhat "egalitarian" discourses, such as that of Frias, fit with them? How did these challenge the relationship between rulers and the ruled – the hierarchy of power that the imperial order presupposed – and the ruptures that such discourses introduced?[35]

[32] The concept of imperialism used in this book follows Loomba, *Colonialism/Postcolonialism*, 29.

[33] Cited from Comaroff and Comaroff, *Of Revelation and Revolution,* I, xi.

[34] About the links between reference and experience, see Quine, *The Roots of Reference*; and Ferry, *Les Puissances de l'Expérience.*

[35] Concerning the contradictions between the Christian discourse and empire, and the tensions conversion to Christianity entailed, see Cox, *Imperial Fault Lines.*

My book remains within the first episode of this history and its vicissitudes, with no promise of a sequel. On the one hand it proposes a history of the profound transformation of the populations that lived in sixteenth- and seventeenth-century Goa, and the impact this transformation had on their descendants' identities and behaviour. It offers a history of the early response of these groups – eventually the holders of visions of new worlds inflected by the discourse and practices of the colonisers – but stops at the beginning of the eighteenth century and does not traverse the colonial order. Moreover, it does not explore contestations of the colonial order in the eighteenth and nineteenth centuries or the liberation movements of the twentieth century. Finally, it does not consider the processes of local identity reinvention in the late-twentieth and twenty-first centuries promoted via the official tourism board of Goa.

Given that the colonial archive is conceived very broadly, the historical sources have multiplied, raising problems concerning the criteria for selecting documents.[36] An enlarged bibliography is a consequence of these epistemological choices too. Studies of the imperial experiences of the British in India, and of the Spanish in the Americas, are relevant to an understanding of the Portuguese imperial experience. The first, because of their playing out in the same geography; and the second, because of a similar cultural configuration, chronology, and other common ground. The theories that emerged from within the anglophone academy – namely, those concerning the critique of Orientalism,[37] *Cultural Studies*, and *Postcolonial Studies*[38] – are also critical to my work. They invite

[36] See the idea of the archive in Foucault, *L'Archéologie du Savoir*. About its relevance to the study of the experiences of the Portuguese Empire, see, *in genere*, A.B. Xavier and Madeira Santos, "Cultura Intelectual".

[37] In addition to Foucault, see Said, *Orientalism* and *Culture and Imperialism*; Inden, *Imagining India*; Trautmann, *Aryans and British India*. These books have, among others, inspired me to rethink the relationship between historical sources and the imperial archive in relation to what concerns Portuguese imperial experiences.

[38] Besides Cooper and Stoler, eds, *Tensions of Empire*, this book was

us to integrate the study of the Portuguese experience into more general synchronic studies and diachronic histories in the colonial and postcolonial register,[39] while adhering to the connected histories method proposed by Sanjay Subrahmanyam.[40]

The impossibility of knowing, in equal measure and with the same depth, both the historiography on the Portuguese Empire and Portugal and on other empires and other places, not to speak of the theoretical debate and methodologies related to them, is reflected in the bibliographic eclecticism of my book. One of the results of my theoretical wanderings within a vast intellectual terrain – as also the need for the book to adhere to a word limit – is that all of the literature directly or indirectly relevant for an analysis of the Christianisation of the territories of Goa has not been brought into play here.[41] But to alert readers to the limits and constraints within which this book – like every other – works should not obscure a larger fact about its purpose: that what it seeks to illuminate – *pace* Frias – are situations that would otherwise remain undocumented.

First of all, I assume that the territories of Goa were not as culturally homogeneous as Orientalist interpretations have suggested. The multiplicity of experiences and histories that characterised the political culture of local populations made them keenly dynamic. These populations were used to external domination; they possessed the intellectual and material wherewithal to manage

---

substantially inspired by the perspectives of Dirks, ed., *Colonialism and Culture*; Breckenridge and van der Veer, eds, *Orientalism and the Postcolonial Predicament*; Prakash, ed., *After Colonialism*.

[39] Comparisons with experiences of Christianisation in other imperial contexts, whether similar (like the Hispanic), or distinct (like the British), are particularly enriching. See, among others, Ballhatchet, *Caste, Society and Catholicism*; and Gruzinski, *La Colonisation de l'imaginaire*.

[40] Subrahmanyam, *Explorations in Connected History*; and Gruzinski, *Les Quatre Parties du Monde*.

[41] One example is the publication of the volumes edinated by M.J.M. Lopes, *O Império Oriental, 1660–1820*. The same happened with Perez, ed., *Os Portugueses e o Oriente*.

situations perceived as reiterations of domination. In other words, the Portuguese presence was perceived, received, incorporated, and filtered through local past experiences and political culture.

The first two chapters chiefly explore the period between 1530 and 1540. In them I suggest that the political and administrative reorganisation of imperial territories conceived of in the reign of Dom João III resulted in a specific *idea of empire*. A reformulation of the relationship established by the kings of Portugal with the people under their rule, with its singular expression in Goa, made this idea material. The first chapter, dedicated to the historiography of the government of Dom João III, analyses the Portuguese presence in mid-sixteenth-century India using the concept of "reform" rather than, as is more common in the scholarship, that of "crisis".

The adoption of "reform" as a theoretical framework has resulted in a reassessment of the scholarship on European cultural and political experiences in the early-modern period, the argument being that the interdependence of political and religious power in the European monarchies (Catholic and Protestant) was crucial to processes conducive to the centralisation of power and a homogenisation of the polity, and thus to laying the foundations of modern European societies. This historiography has not only altered our understanding of early-modern European history but also been critical in creating new understandings of relations between metropole and colony in the Portuguese empire.

In a similar vein, I argue that that the Estado da Índia in the mid-sixteenth century became a kind of imperial refounding inspired by the model of Imperial Rome. This inspiration from ancient Rome then combined with a reformulation of languages and practices of religious and political alterity headed by metropolitan elites. The worldviews of the "reformers", however, did not always coincide with the imaginaries of those credited with having "feito a Índia", i.e. having "made India" – people who believed they had come under a "crisis".

The translation, or implementation, of the practices of political, religious, and cultural homogenisation "planned" in Portugal for the territories most crucial to the Estado da Índia constitute the object of the second chapter. In it I describe the political and administrative implementation of this model and its implications for the relationship between colonisers and the colonised. The chapter also develops the idea that parallel notions of empire coexisted in Portugal and the colony, resulting in an inevitable heterogeneity.

Heterogeneity characterised the clergy – the protagonist of the third and fourth chapters. Both these chapters analyse the strategies and tools developed by Franciscans and Jesuits in order to Christianise and culturally convert non-Christian populations in Goa. The third chapter focuses on the institutional framework implemented in the villages, and the powers accumulated by clerics in these spaces. It also analyses the manner in which missionaries sought to integrate themselves into the local context by manipulating information gathered through ecclesiastical networks, frequently taking advantage of pre-existing local structures of communication. The fourth chapter analyses two mechanisms of social and cultural reproduction: education and poor relief. It discusses how education and poor relief were used by Franciscans and Jesuits to favour distinct modes of cultural conversion.

The fifth chapter inverts the perspective by exploring specific episodes that illustrate the cultural conversion of places and people. Through an analysis of the process of collective conversion of the population of the island of Chorão, this chapter identifies the catalogue of behaviours that characterised the attitudes of local groups facing the mechanics of conversion, ranging from resistance to pragmatism. Inspired by Gauri Viswanathan's work on religious conversions in the context of British India, this chapter also explores the hypothesis that conversion allowed some Goans to express political dissent against the existing order.[42]

Chapter 6 focuses on explicit forms of resistance against the Portuguese imperial administration: for instance, the intense episode

[42] Viswanathan, "Coping with (Civil) Death"; Viswanathan, "Religious Conversion"; Viswanathan, *Outside the Fold.*

which came to be known as the "martyrdom of Cuncolim", but also other less dramatic events and everyday forms of resistance.[43] These revolts and instances of resistance did not annihilate the Portuguese imperial presence. Memories of the repression of the Cuncolim revolt of 1583 were frequently evoked and weaponised by the Portuguese authorities to prevent future uprisings. Furthermore, the concessions made to the "collaborationists" by the Portuguese Crown after these revolts were so enticing that they perpetuated imperial governance. The growing participation of local elites in the imperial administration, and their gradual recognition by the Crown – manifested in the attribution of honours of the Order of Christ and other distinctions – indicate the efficacy of the strategies employed by the Portuguese in Goa.

It is not surprising, therefore, that the final chapter examines forms of conformity and adherence, whether pragmatic or not, to Portuguese rule. Chapter 7 discusses the change of behaviour of local elites which enabled profound cultural conversions in the medium and long term, as attested to by the example of Frias. Similarly, treatises on biblical history and the memory of Christianisation that emerged from the second half of the seventeenth century sought to provide genealogies of Goans as inheritors of pre-Christian and early-Christian traditions. Thus, these genealogies transfigured Goan families and elites into bearers of this spiritual lineage, which then indelibly associated them with the local nobility. These Goan elites assumed that they were those the Portuguese Crown could confide in, and consequently confer on them the principal available roles and appointments. Although the decree of 1761 partially satisfied these aspirations, the "Revolt of the Pintos" (1787) clearly demonstrated the incompatibility between social equality and empire, making it clear that the strategies employed by local elites and the objectives of the Portuguese Crown – but also the liberal monarchy – in the early-modern period had different aims and aspirations.

[43] These events are similar to those referred to in Scott, *Weapons of the Weak*, and Adas, "From Avoidance to Confrontation".

1

Reform in the Kingdom, Reform in the Empire

"TEPID LOVE AND intermittent communication," wrote Gianbattista Confalonieri, a Roman priest who accompanied the papal nuncio Fabio Biondi during the latter's nunciature in Lisbon between 1592 and 1596. The intent of his words was to describe emotions linking the Portuguese settled in distant "colonies" to the king of Portugal.[1] It is difficult to tell how much Confalonieri knew about the relationship of the Crown of Portugal with its subjects. They lived in cities and territories that had once belonged to other kings, and in these the Portuguese constituted but a small percentage of the inhabitants. Perhaps Confalonieri was only theorising in general on the difficulties of empires, based on what he knew and his proximity to the papacy – which, in its own way, also had "colonies".[2] However, Confalonieri's notion also points towards the difficult relationship between the Portuguese Crown and its Asian possessions. The relationship

[1] Apud, *Por Terras de Portugal no século XVI,* 185. About the constitutional importance of the evocation of love in the Portuguese early-modern period, see Cardim, *O Poder dos Afectos.*

[2] Botero explicitly refers to the Portuguese as possessing an empire with scattered territories and elaborates on the difficulties of maintaining this type of empire. However, the Italian author concluded that the Portuguese empire had created conditions favourable for its maintenance: Botero, *Da Razão de Estado*, 6–12.

was in fact so troubled that Gaspar Correia, former secretary to Governor Afonso de Albuquerque (r. 1509–1515) – the conqueror of Goa in 1510 – described the mid-sixteenth century as "*vivos males*" – a living pain.[3]

Confalonieri had touched a raw nerve. Managing, controlling, and maintaining the fragmented territories that constituted the Portuguese empire was no mean task. The archipelagos of Madeira and the Azores were a mere hundred leagues from the shores of Portugal. Lisbon was able to control others less proximate, such as Cape Verde, but those more distant, such as Goa, Malacca, and the territories around Malacca, being very far removed, were another matter. Unlike the Greek and Roman colonies, almost all of which were in the Mediterranean, the Portuguese were spread over various distant seas, requiring tortuous passages and entailing complicated connections.

Other factors of the time also had a bearing on the Italian priest's pithy formulation. The first was the political and administrative architecture of the Portuguese Crown, namely a polysinodal regime that, notwithstanding the political will of the rulers to effect change, would take a long time to transform. A second factor, perhaps even more critical given the diversity of spaces that the Portuguese Crown sought to dominate, was the scarcity of human resources; a third was the character of the imperial agents of the Crown. The complicated nature of its personnel, the territorial diversity of its possessions, and the sheer distance at which they lay from Lisbon meant a formidable compound of difficulties. It made the Portuguese empire an almost impossible proposition.

Lisbon was incapable of the role that classical Athens or Rome – or even to an extent Venice *vis-à-vis* its colonies – had been able to assume.[4] The Portuguese capital had to delegate to other centres some of the co-ordination functions which, had it not been for the distance and the cooling "in love and communication",

[3] Correia, *Lendas da Índia*, Vol. I, 1–2.

[4] On this, see Senos, *O Paço da Ribeira*.

the metropolis would have wanted to retain for itself. Yet in the city of Goa Lisbon managed to found a replica of itself. The Goa of the Portuguese was a material translation of Portugal in the East.[5] The epithet "Rome of the East" suggests the status of Goa as the second pole of an empire that aspired in its dimensions to exceed those of Alexander and Augustus.

Confalonieri was writing in 1593, by when Lisbon had lost its earlier prowess on account of the unification of the Iberian Peninsula by Philip II of Spain. In expressing what he did, the Italian was also conveying the existing situation of dependence in which the Portuguese monarchy was now placed, and thus of an exacerbation in the difficulties of managing its empire.

In this chapter I analyse representations of the Estado da Índia some decades before Confalonieri's report.[6] I argue that the discomfort felt by Gaspar Correia and other imperial agents was the result of a confrontation between "two ideas", "two models", two imperial situations. Over these decades, several Indias were imagined and constructed.[7] In particular, the India idealised by the Crown was different from the India established on the ground in the preceding decades.

India, as imagined by the Portuguese Crown during this early period, had a central role in structuring the imperial experiences of Goa. With the Goan territories having been denominated the most crucial *dominium extra territorium* of the kingdom, the new modalities of imperium that were first experimented with in Goa

[5] Did Francisco de Holanda's *Antigualhas* and *Da fábrica que falece à cidade de Lisboa* have an impact on the imagination and construction of Goa? On the desire to replicate Europe elsewhere, see Alphonse Dupront, "Espace et humanisme".

[6] On this, see M.L.G. Cruz, "As controvérsias", 169–88.

[7] On these "different Indias", see Machado, *O mito do Oriente*; Graça, *A Visão do Oriente*; Flores, "A imagem do Oriente"; Le Goff, "O Ocidente medieval"; Loureiro, "O encontro de Portugal com a Ásia"; Loureiro, O descobrimento da civilização indiana"; Loureiro, "O Humanismo português"; Curvelo, *A Imagem do Oriente*.

could then be replicated in other locations, depending on what was found successful within this initial testing ground.[8]

The chapter's first section discusses negative images of the Estado da Índia and Goa in the bulk of the scholarship on this period.[9] The second focuses on sixteenth-century political and religious experiences in Portugal and its empire, which converge with the argument that this was a period of reform and not of crisis.

The "Crisis of the Asian Empire" and the Political Culture of the Sixteenth Century

Portuguese historiography tends to divide the reign of Dom João III into two periods, the first positive and modernising, the second negative in inaugurating the divergence between Portugal and Europe and bringing about subsequent Portuguese cultural backwardness. In this interpretation the Inquisition and the arrival of Jesuits in Portugal were mainly responsible for the consequent conservative religious and obscurantist nature of the kingdom.[10]

[8] The Goan experience is fundamental to understanding other Portuguese imperial experiences, as argued by Ronald Raminelli, "Império da Fé", 227–47. Probably, the earlier experience with the royalty of Congo was also a source of inspiration for later formulations. However, a comparative analysis of Iberian experiences across diverse territorial possessions during this period is needed, following in the footsteps of Lobo, *Administração Colonial Luso-Espanhola*. Such comparisons are also needed to discuss the "novelty" of some of the methods used later by the British Crown in the Indian subcontinent. For the American case, see Elliott, "Empire and State", 365–82.

[9] For example, João Paulo Oliveira Costa and Vítor Rodrigues consider the reign of Dom João III less interesting than that of Dom Manuel I: Costa and Rodrigues, *Portugal y Oriente*, 161ff.

[10] These authors are indebted to nineteenth-century interpretations, called by Rui Ramos "civic humanism" and "classical republicanism", both critical of imperial expansion. Practically the entire historiography produced in this context (above all Herculano and Oliveira Martins) was critical of the reign of Dom João III and the Indian experience. See Ramos, *Tristes Conquistas*;

In this chapter I propose to substitute the concept of "decline and crisis" with that of "reform". I argue that reform more effectively explains the political culture and events that animated the kingdom and the empire in the middle of the sixteenth century. This argument is directly linked to the work of Adriano Prosperi and other historians of confessionalisation in Europe during the early-modern period. Referring to Italy, Prosperi says: "It is irrefutable that the triad of [Protestant] Reformation-Revolution-Modern World constituted the conceptual network to decipher the historical course, an essential itinerary to guide, evaluate and dismiss, to attribute to each nation its place in the course of civilisation."[11] The same grid substantially conditioned the constructions and historical interpretations of the second half of the sixteenth century in Portugal. The image of Dom João III as "hesitant, but pragmatic, little influenced by the ideology of his father" is dominant in the literature on his governance of the imperial territories.[12]

In contrast, the argument of this chapter is that the combination of normative, political, and administrative transformations, especially those of the imperial territories, was the symptom of *intentional* political, social, and cultural reform. The idea was that these territories ought to resemble the metropole, which was also undergoing substantial transformation at the time. The debates about centralisation, and the application of the principle of *cujus regio eius religio* – by which subjects had to share the religion of their ruler – were part of this process of change.[13] This principle would now substitute the paramountcy of the earlier *convivencia* –

---

also Cruz, *Os Fumos da Índia*. One of the promoters of this thesis was J.S.S. Dias, *Correntes do Sentimento Religioso*; J.S.S. Dias, *Política Cultural*; and J.S.S. Dias, "Cultura e obstáculo epistemológico".

[11] Prosperi, *Tribunali della Coscienza*, xv–xvi, English translation. See bibliography on confessionalisation in footnote 30.

[12] Thomaz, "A política oriental de Dom Manuel I", 205; Thomaz, "L'idée impériale manuéline".

[13] This idea was promoted by Ana Isabel Buescu, in Buescu, *João III*, 224ff.

the argument for tolerance in medieval Iberia – which in effect permitted various religions within the dominion of a single ruler, and which also meant the coexistence of several small communities, ethnic groups, and a plurality of ways of being within the same political space.[14]

Inspired by representations of the late-Roman Empire, the court of Dom João III believed instead that changes were needed to preserve the imperial territories.[15] These changes contested the dominant model which focused on controlling key points on the most favoured routes to India, the China seas, and the African space.

The choice that made Goa the "key to the whole of India" was an expression of the Portuguese determination to move forward with "the effective occupation of the territory and the multiplication of the territorial bases."[16] The fixing of viceregal governance and the institution of central and local administrations, as well as the recognition of Goa as the seat of the Estado da Índia, were part of the process. Somehow, following Albuquerque's project, the political reasons that lay behind this policy were substantially different.[17]

[14] I use the concept of community as developed by Francisco Suárez at the start of the seventeenth century, which reflects, to no small extent, the understanding of community in this period. It included "minor communities" (cities, provinces, small kingdoms) and "big communities" (composite monarchies and empires): Suárez, *Tractatus De Legibus*. The "Old Conquests" were among the "minor communities" that belonged to the Portuguese empire.

[15] On the impact of the Roman empire model in the court of King João III, see among others, J.S.S. Dias, *Portugal e a Cultura Europeia*; J.S.S. Dias, *Os Descobrimentos*; Rodrigues, *Do Humanismo*; AA.VV., *O Humanismo Português*; Aubin, *La Découverte*; Randles, "Peuples Sauvages"; AA.VV., *D. João III e o Império*; Beato, *Rodrigo Sanches*; Carvalho, "As fontes de Duarte Pacheco Pereira"; Diz, *As classes dirigentes*; AA.VV., *Do Mundo Antigo aos Novos Mundos*.

[16] Madeira Santos, *Goa é a chave de toda a Índia*, 148.

[17] From another perspective, Ana Cannas de Cunha calls for a reassessment of the politics of the period: A.C. Cunha, *A Inquisição no Estado da*

This new project entailed different dimensions: the colonisers needed to be Portuguese, which implied an end to the policy of intermarriages, alongside the promotion of marriages with women sent from the kingdom to "whiten" the mestizo colonists.[18] The colonised would be made to submit to Christianisation and westernisation. Various signs would make these territories recognisable extensions of the metropole, such as their new arrangement of urban and rural landscapes, and the Christianising and Lusitanising of both the city of Goa as well as the villages. The villages would need to reproduce the structure of those in the kingdom by being organised around a parish church.[19] A more consolidated power hierarchy replaced the previous autonomy allowed in the governance of the Estado da Índia. Another dimension of these structural changes was the greater control of local land, and in the short term the introduction of new agricultural products and new agrarian techniques of cultivation.

If the Estado da Índia was formally and legally constituted with Viceroy Dom Francisco de Almeida (r. 1505–1509) in 1505 – and influenced by prior experiences in North Africa and the West African coast as well as by the Venetian experience in the Mediterranean and Spanish expansionism – its refoundation dates from the reign of Dom João III. The reconstitution changed the Estado significantly; it went beyond the somewhat fragile and interwoven network established in the preceding decades.[20]

Índia, Chapter 2. Kirti N. Chaudhuri also highlights other chronologies with respect to the development of more complex forms of imperial domination: Chaudhuri, "O estabelecimento no Oriente".

[18] See, in this context, Coates, *Degredados e Orfãs*; and Guedes, "Tentativas de controle". On an older and nationalistic vein, see also A.C.G.S. Correia, *História da Colonização Portuguesa*; and A. Costa, "Órfãs d'el-Rei", 115–24.

[19] On the connections between social memory, cultural identity, the construction of space, and urban and rural landscape, see Harris and Lipman, "Social Symbolism and Space"; Connerton, *How Societies Remember*; Claval, *Géographie Culturel*; Duncan and Ley, *Place/Culture/Representation*.

[20] Costa and Rodrigues, *Portugal y Oriente*, Chapter 5; Madeira Santos, *Goa*

However, various powerful elites in the Portuguese court had different ideas. The crisis of the principal sources of revenue in the Asian empire, the contraction of the value of trade of the Carreira da Índia (the round trip from Lisbon to India and back), and the loss of rights to the customs duty from Hurmuz and Malacca collectively seemed to justify raising questions on the advantages to the Portuguese Crown of maintaining a presence in the Indian Ocean. This questioning was especially intense when other fronts – the traditional African territories – appeared more attractive within the ethos of the high nobility.[21]

For such elites, India was unviable. There were the difficulties of controlling Portuguese officials, the personal projects of governors nominated by the Crown, and the conflicts arising out of alliances that they might stimulate; there were as well the growing military dangers engendered by transformations in geopolitical contexts. The "conquest" in Africa was more in line with the expectations of these echelons of the ruling class.[22] The engendering of similar debates in the Portuguese court in subsequent decades, and between agents *in loco*, contributed to the settling in of the idea that mid-sixteenth-century India was in crisis.

The correspondence of this period between local political agents and the Portuguese court in Lisbon, the reports sent from India, and the requests of the monarch all express the sense of a brewing crisis. For many actors, the transformations they were living through had the "flavour of steel".[23] Terms like "destruction", "help", "necessity", "lack of manpower", "debility", "deplorable

---

é a chave de toda a Índia, 148–9. This happened a little before the viceregal system could begin to operate in Catalonia, Aragon, and Valencia: Elliott, *España Imperial*, 84.

[21] What materialised again was the opposition between two models of expansion – one that was military and noble, and the other mercantile: Subrahmanyam, *O Império Asiático Português*, 113.

[22] M.L.G. Cruz, "As controvérsias"; and M.L.G. Cruz, "As controvérsias (. . .) Compilação de documentos".

[23] Correia, *Lendas da Índia*, Vol. I, 1–2.

state",[24] and "decay" described their perception of the situation in India during the period under study. In 1539 it was Viceroy Dom Garcia de Noronha himself – who in the previous year had requested a substantial loan from the Câmara de Goa to stabilise the financial situation of the Estado da Índia – writing a letter to the Secretary of State, António Carneiro, about "the Government and decay of the state".[25]

If for some the crisis was apparent in the middle of the sixteenth century, for others it became apparent later, between the years 1565 and 1575. Changes in regional geopolitics and problems with some of the institutional structures of the Estado da Índia justified the whole enterprise being rethought during the viceroyalty of Dom Luís de Ataíde (1568–71; 1578–1580). The deviation of the horse trade had undermined the commercial and financial centrality of the city of Goa. For many the so-called battle of Talikota in 1565, the decline of the Vijayanagar Empire, the siege of Goa in 1570–1, and the shift of Portuguese economic interests to South East Asia combined into a cry for either reorganising the

[24] See IAN/TT, Corpo Cronológico, Part I: Mç. 46, nº 21 – "Carta de Nuno Vaz de Castello Branco a ElRey", 16 November 1530; Mç. 50, nº 40 – "Carta de Pedro de Faria dando parte a ElRey do Estado das Conquistas da Ásia", 23 November 1532 ; Mç. 59, nº 109 – "Carta de Pedro de Faria dando conta a ElRey", 20 October 1537; Mç. 64, nº 4 – "Carta de Diogo Pereira a ElRey sobre o deploravel estado", 25 January 1539; Mç. 66, nº 1 – "Traslado de Aggravo que entrepozeram os Moradores da Cidade de Gôa", 11 October 1539; Mç. 66, nº 37 – "Carta de Pedro Faria reprezentando a ElRey a necessidade", 20 November 1539; Mç. 66, nº 99 – "Carta de Diogo Rebello dando parte a ElRey que a India estava exaurida", 24 January 1540; Mss. 71, nº 10 – "Carta de Thomé Rodrigues Soares dando arte a ElRey, do estado em que achava a India", 17 Sept. 1541; Mss. 83, nº 60 – "Carta de Cosme Annes, Ouvidor Geral da Fazenda da India, dando conta a ElRey do deploravel estado daquella terra", 30 Dec. 1549. These letters are evidence of the geopolitical fragility of the Estado da Índia and the fear of attack by Islamic powers.

[25] IAN/TT, Corpo Cronológico, Part I, Mç. 66, nº 12 – "Carta de D. Garcia de Noronha Vice Rey da India ao Secretario Antonio Carneiro", 29 October 1939; Correia, *Lendas da Índia*, IV, 25.

Estado or abandoning it. These proposals contributed to cementing the image that the Estado da Índia was from the mid-sixteenth century in the grip of a crisis which marked the beginning of its decline, with religion being substituted for trade:

> When examining the facts and the documents, one receives the impression that something in the collective mindset had changed: [. . .] as if the commercial imperialism of the initial years had given place to a type of imperialism of the faith that aspired to make the Estado da Índia a powerful Catholic state and Goa a grand ecclesiastical centre, a substantial focus of Christian culture.[26]

These changes are considered more a manifestation of the weakness of imperial power than symptoms of more structural transformations.[27]

There are exceptions to this narrative, such as by Sanjay Subrahmanyam. He believes that a model of expansion more territorial than maritime emerged between 1570 and 1610. The Crown intended to liberate itself from the responsibility of the trade of the Cape Route. At the same time, there were projects relative to new territories, as in the projects of Dom João Ribeiro Gaio, the Bishop of Malacca, between 1580 and 1601.[28]

[26] Thomaz, "A estrutura político-administrativa do Estado da Índia", 252. However, in the same essay Thomaz questions images of the historiography in the second half of the sixteenth century.

[27] On this, see Pearson, *The Portuguese in India,* Chapter 5; Thomaz, "A estrutura politico-administrativa", 250ff.; Thomaz, "Descoberta e Evangelização"; Marques, "A evangelização da Índia", 217ff.; Bouchon, *Afonso de Albuquerque*, 257–9. See also, with regard to this period, the works of Barata, *As Regências*; A.C. Cunha, *A Inquisição no Estado da Índia*; Costa and Rodrigues, *Portugal y Oriente*; Robinson, *Conversion, Continuity and Change.* Nor does Chaudhuri and Bethencourt, eds, *História da Expansão Portuguesa,* vols I and II, advance new interpretations on this subject.

[28] Subrahmanyam, *O Império Asiático Português,* 152, 160. The same may be found in Subrahmanyam and Thomaz, "Evolution of Empire", in which the authors highlight changes in the concept of empire in the Portuguese experience in the Indian Ocean world of the sixteenth century.

Other authors argued that there was a peak in the Cape Route in the period described within the historiography as one of decline. Consequently, the nomination of the viceroy had turned into "a mechanism to co-opt the cream of the Portuguese nobility". Similar changes had occurred at the level of honours bestowed on the military orders, especially the Order of Christ.[29] The growing interest of the higher nobility in the Estado da Índia contrasted with the first decades of the sixteenth century, also bringing into question the view of its decay.

The same question arises when one considers the reign of Dom João III from the perspective of the historiography of confessionalisation.[30] Scholars using the concepts of social disciplining and confessionalisation have argued that an exacerbated religiosity was shared by North and South Europe. The majority of the princes in a fragmented Europe, after the division of Christianity started by Martin Luther, feared that subjects who held a different religious belief were dangerous to their rule.[31] Consequently, politico-religious alliances characterised many European polities. The effort to (re)-Christianise subjects and political society, whether Catholics or Protestants, was normal. This effort sought

[29] Barros, *O Conselho Ultramarino*; M.S. Cunha and Monteiro, "Vice-reis, governadores e conselheiros"; Monteiro, "Trajectórias sociais"; Monteiro, "Governadores e capitães-mores"; Cunha, "Governo e governantes"; Olival, *As Ordens Militares.*

[30] Besides Prosperi, *Tribunali della Coscienza*, cf. Hsia, *Social Discipline in the Reformation*; Schilling; "Chiese confessionali e disciplinamento sociale"; Schilling, "Confessionalization in the Empire"; Reinhard, "Disciplinamento sociale, confessionalizzazione, modernizzazione"; Prodi, *The Papal Prince*; Prodi, ed., *Disciplina dell'anima, disciplina del corpo;* Palomo, "Disciplina Christiana". Apuntes historiográficos"; Copete and Palomo, "Des carêmes après le carême"; Palomo, *Fazer dos campos escolas excelentes*, Introduction; and Bergin, "The Counter-Reformation Church".

[31] Prosperi argues that the process of social disciplining that took place in Italy was not singular: Prosperi, *Tribunali della Coscienza*, xi. Concerning the missionary methods used by the Portuguese in that period, Charles Boxer had already stressed the similarities between the tools used by Catholics and Protestants: Boxer, "A Note on Portuguese Missionary Methods", 89.

to substitute traditional community ties and horizontal solidarities with vertical relations. Each subject, each individual, had a direct relationship with authority, whether terrestrial (represented by the Crown and the Church) or celestial. Such effort ensured a cohesive political community, allowing the ship of state safe passage through a stormy time. In this scenario Dom João III was scarcely distinguishable from other European princes.[32]

Other Images on Old Themes: Refractions from a Confessional Focus

The Portuguese "religious problem" was distinct however from that in other European polities. Instead of the difference between Catholics and Protestants, it was the opposition between Christians and Jews, and in the empire between Christians and Muslims and between Christians and Gentiles, that was dominant. Also, the Portuguese political condition was simultaneously more straightforward and more complex. On the one hand the territory and population of Portugal were relatively small as compared with most European monarchies. On the other its imperial territories and peoples were too considerable to contemplate extending the Portuguese political model to every part of the empire. Despite these differences, the questions faced by the Portuguese monarchy were structurally identical to those in Europe. Federico Palomo has highlighted that the last representatives of the dynasty of Avis – Dom João III, Dom Sebastião (r. 1557–1578), and Cardinal and King Dom Henrique (r. 1578–1580) – took decisive steps to formulate a confessional policy similar to those that obtained in the other religious environments of Western Europe after 1540.[33]

[32] The reign of King João III (1521–57) was contemporary with that of Charles V (1519–56), Francis I of Valois (1515–47), and Henry VIII (1509–47). In the non-European world, it coincided with Suleyman the Magnificent (1520–66), the kings of Vijayanagar, i.e. Krishna Deva Raya (1509–29), Achyuta Deva Raya (1529–42), and Sadasiva Raya (1542–70), as well as the first Mughal emperors.

[33] Palomo, "Disciplina Christiana". Apuntes historiográficos", 57–8; Palomo,

If the papacy was the highest authority responsible for the religious fidelity of people in the Catholic world, each prince was in charge of fidelity within his realm. The addition of several treatises that legitimated reinforcement of the power of the prince – the single apex of the political body – and simultaneously exalted his Christian identity (Catholic, Lutheran, Calvinist, or Anglican, depending on the case) is symptomatic and was replicated in Portugal.

This perspective is not yet dominant in the historiography of the Portuguese imperial experience. However, an increasing number of works have contributed to rethinking the political profile of the government of Dom João III. Ana Isabel Buescu, Rafael Moreira, Sylvie Deswarte, Anne-Marie Jordan, and Joaquim Caetano have, among others, pointed to essential differences in the management of a political image between the reigns of Dom João III (nicknamed O Piedoso, i.e. the Pious) and his father Dom Manuel I.[34] In particular, the forms of representation of the relationship between the prince and society distanced Dom João III from King Dom Manuel, inserting this "pious" king into a classical time that evoked Augustus, Marcus Aurelius, Constantine, and Theodosius.[35]

Fazer dos campos escolas excelentes. The instructions to the Portuguese ambassadors in Rome, the correspondence between them and the kings of Portugal, and the issues discussed are evidence of these processes. The same can be said about the papal bulls and briefs obtained by the Portuguese Crown: Visconde de Santarém, *Quadro Elementar*, hereafter QE, vols X–XIII.

[34] One should remember the respect that the virtue of *pietas* enjoyed in the Roman empire. This virtue was necessary to launch the *utilitas publica* instead of the *utilitas singolorum,* which in Christian terms signified the political obligation to extend Christianity universally: Pagden, *Lords of All the World*, 29ff. Machiavelli, for example, defended piety as one of the principal virtues of the prince and exalted the government which was able to preserve the unity of the faith among its subjects: Machiavelli, *Il Principe*, 72.

[35] Jordan, *Retrato de Corte*, 23. See also Serrão, "Os painéis da Igreja de Unhos"; Serrão, *História da Arte em Portugal*; Moreira, *A Arquitectura do Renascimento*; Moreira, "Arquitectura: Renascimento e Classicismo"; Moreira, "Cultura Material e Visual"; Jordan-Geschwend, "O Maneirismo e o retrato

Dom João III's strategies to control his image are an example. Only one painter, Anthonis Mor, had the official right to paint his image. This constraint evoked Alexander the Great, who had permitted only Apeles to paint him and Lisipo to make statues of him. Ana Isabel Buescu identifies the systematic constitution of a discourse about the prince in this period, "an ideological frame that affirmed the monarchy [which] appears to engage the king himself." Various "Mirrors" and "Regulations" for the prince – treatises on how rulers should comport themselves and reign – fed this ideological frame, converging with those in the rest of Europe. They indicated a constitution of the "figure of the sovereign as the protagonist". The ideal prince was the "vicar of God, just, peaceful and prudent, [the] philosopher prince with platonic roots, surrounded by wise counsellors, who is father and shepherd to his people." The profile of this prince combined biblical models with the classical as well as the Aristotelian medieval models of the good governor, the super-prince, the embodiment of the political community.[36]

In these discourses the actions of the ideal prince found fulfilment in Christian identity and illuminated those around him – in the first place, the royal family; subsequently, the royal court, which was henceforth subject to a growing codification of behaviour;[37] and finally, all members of the *respublica.* If the various "Lives" (biographical literature) and "Imitations" (spiritual and moral guides) of Christ offered the model of the ideal Christian, other literatures developed this model, applying it to

---

de corte"; Deswarte, "La Rome de D. Miguel da Silva (1515–1525)"; Deswarte, *Ideias e Imagens*; Deswarte, "Francisco de Holanda"; Deswarte, "Neoplatonismo e arte"; Caetano, "A identificação de um pintor"; Caetano, "Ao modo de Itália"; Caetano, "S. Silvestre mostrando a Constantino"; Pinto, *A Infanta D. Maria de Portugal.*

[36] Buescu, *Imagens do Príncipe,* 27, 592ff.; also Magalhães, "Os régios protagonistas do poder"; Curto, "A cultura política". On the representations of the prince in this period, see also N.N.C. Santos, *O Príncipe Ideal.*

[37] Buescu, *Imagens do Príncipe*, Conclusion.

every social group and thereby striving towards a harmonisation of the polity.[38]

This literature presented examples intended to mould the behaviour of the prince and his subjects. *Il Cortegiano* of Castiglione – dedicated, significantly, to a Portuguese courtier, Bishop Dom Miguel da Silva – is the best-known example of this literature.[39] Such books ensured that, as announced by Garcia de Resende in his *Breve memorial dos pecados e cousas que pertencem ha confissam*, "each sees the state in which he lives, and should do what he is obliged to."[40]

As indicated earlier, together with the "Mirrors" and "Regulations" for princes, there was, during this period, an increase in theological and moral treatises.[41] These announced the constitution of a Christian society, configuring each political community as a city of God and each subject as the perfect Christian. They insisted at the same time on the supremacy of the Christian road over other life paths. Consequently, idolators, infidels, and heretics became incompatible with the Christian (Catholic, in the Roman-influenced countries) political identity. The integration, and legal

[38] Gil Vicente's theatre, represented in Portuguese court, materialised these ideas: Cruz, *Gil Vicente e a Sociedade*.

[39] On the role of the treatises on the ideal price and other such literature in the constitution of a good society, see, among others, Prodi, ed., *Disciplina dell'Anima, disciplina del corpo*; Continisio, "Il principe"; Frigo, "Tradizione aristotelica"; Frigo, "Disciplina rei familiar"; Frova, "Disciplina e ruoli sacrale"; Buescu, *Imagens do Príncipe*; Fernandes, "As artes da confissão"; Fernandes, *Espelhos, Cartas e Guias*.

[40] Resende, *Breve memorial dos pecados*, 3v. Though it was written before the start of the reign of Dom João III, the book ran into three more editions during his reign.

[41] This was the case of Manuais de Confessores (Guides for Confessors), inventoried and analysed by Fernandes, "Artes da confissão", the "Vidas . . ." of saints and other people highlighted by their sanctity which expanded the tradition of the medieval *exempla* (Geremek, "L'exemplum et la circulation") and offered models of behaviour: Fernandes, *Espelhos, Cartas e Guias*; Carvalho, "D. António, Prior do Crato"; Crispim, "O Espelho de Cristina".

and political exclusion, of members of Jewish communities was also part of this new political culture.[42]

Another dimension in this scenario was the interdependence of knowledge and power. This allowed the bridging of unrelated discursive fields, such as moral theology, ethics and politics, law, history, medicine, geography, cartography, and instrumental knowledge (such as arithmetic and engineering).[43] Such interdependence stimulated the invention of institutional tools that could promote the efficacy of both spheres: that of knowledge of territories and their peoples, and the politics of ordering them.[44] The complexity of political and administrative mechanisms that aimed at homogenising the political community was part of this design. Schools, the Inquisition, censorship, confession, as well as institutions oriented toward the fixing of a social norm were among these mechanisms.[45]

[42] Asensio, *Estudios Portugueses*; Baroncelli, "Contro la carità discreta"; Baroncelli and Assereto, "Pauperismo e religione"; and also A.B. Xavier, "De converso a novamente convertido".

[43] Foucault, *As Palavras e as Coisas.*

[44] The Cadastro do Reino of 1527–1532 (an enumeration of the people living in the kingdom of Portugal) provided, for the first time, an overview of the number of vassals and households, allowing, consequently, the reorganisation of the territory: T.F. Rodrigues, "As estruturas populacionais", 197–211; J.J.A. Dias, *Portugal do Renascimento,* 11–26; Magalhães, "O enquadramento do espaço nacional". It revealed a new understanding of the relationship between king and kingdom; also, the growing connection between the tools of knowledge and the mechanisms of power. Surprisingly, not a single study exists of the political and administrative characteristics of the reign of João III. On that, see general works, such as Magalhães, "Os régios protagonistas do poder", 530–40; and J.J.A. Dias, *Portugal do Renascimento.* On the impact of these policies on ecclesiastical organisation, see Paiva, "Dioceses e organização eclesiástica", 187–91; and Paiva, *Os Bispos de Portugal e do Império.*

[45] There is a vast literature on the transformation of institutions and reformation of society in the sixteenth and seventeenth centuries. For a general overview on changes in the poor relief institutions space in the Catholic and Protestant worlds, see Pullan, *Rich and Poor*; Gutton, *La Societé des Pauvres*; Geremek, *Inutiles au monde*; Geremek, *Poverty. A History*; Rijs, *Aspects of Poverty*; and Jütte, *Poverty and Deviance.*

The establishment of new tribunals was part of this reform effort too. Among those that stand out are the Mesa da Consciência e Ordens (Board of the Conscience [of the king] and Orders, an institution which still awaits a substantial study), and the Inquisition, established in 1536.[46] Reform of the diocesan and parochial organisation was seconded by the entrusting of new roles to bishops and parish priests. The reform of religious and missionary orders, complemented by the royal incorporation of military orders, went hand in hand.[47] Finally, the quick adoption of the Tridentine decrees as a law of the kingdom witnessed the early confessionalisation of the Portuguese monarchy.[48]

Other forms of regulation of social life multiplied too. The garment laws of 1536, the sanitary laws of the next decades, the laws against begging, and penal laws testify the Crown's will to control all forms of social life.[49] Naturally, an educational strategy was part of all this. The Crown established primary schools and

[46] Besides the conscience of the king, the tribunal had competence over matters of reform of religious orders, of hospitals, rest-houses, other places of pious works, the release of war prisoners, and so forth: De Witte, *La Correspondence des Premiers Nonces*; M.R.T.B. Cruz, *As Regências*, Vol. 2. Other tribunals were also reformed, with new rules and new offices. This period witnesses, as well, an explosion of officials trained in bureaucratic skills: Subtil, "O governo e a administração", 78–90; Curto, "A cultura política", 130–1 and 145.

[47] On this, see IAN/TT, Col. de São Vicente, L. 2 – Matérias várias do tempo do rei D. João III e da rainha D. Catarina, fls 33–41; L. 6 – Cartas da Embaixada do Comendador–Mor em Roma, fls 294–5; L. 10 – Cartas e papéis variados da rainha D. Catarina, fls 321v.–322.

[48] Despite many such initiatives having been originated during the previous reign, they materialised during the reign of João III. On the legal reception of the Tridentine decrees, see Caetano, "Recepção e execução dos decretos"; A. da Silva, *Trent's Impact*; Fernandes, "Da reforma da igreja à reforma dos cristãos".

[49] Carvalho e Paiva, "A evolução das visitas pastorais"; Soares, "A missionação na arquidiocese de Braga". About these processes, see also Sá, "Os hospitais portugueses"; Sá, *Quando o rico se faz pobre*; Sá, *As Misericórdias Portuguesas*; and Abreu, "Padronização hospitalar"; the introductions to vols 3, 4, and 5 of the collection *Portugaliae Monumenta Misericordiarum* as well as the state of the art published in the first volume of the same collection.

reformed the university in 1537 by establishing a College of Arts.[50] All such decisions reveal the intent to reconstitute the subjects of the Portuguese monarchy.

João de Barros has highlighted the attitude of "continued vigilance", "sometimes inventing", "at other times correcting" as being a characteristic of the governance of Dom João III.[51] These signs indicated new modes of governance which collided with the traditional constitution of the *respublica*. The originality of this initiative cannot be attributed only to Dom João III. However, the growing complexity of the political and administrative apparatus, the attempt to concentrate political power, and the establishment of another model of political relations were characteristic of this period.

The alliance between political and religious power resulted from a consciousness of the gap between political projects and their effectiveness. This alliance took Nicolas Clenardus, the Flemish humanist and teacher of Dom Henrique of Avis – the future King Dom Henrique – to say: "Today, it is the Theodosians who direct the Ambrosian." This pronouncement evokes the spontaneous connections that these historical actors established between the Portuguese experience and the Roman Christian Empire. In this case, the link was between the Emperor Theodosius, who was responsible for the Edict of 380 CE (which made Christianity the official religion of the Eastern Roman Empire), and King Dom João III. It also evokes the different relationship between political and religious power in these two periods. Clenardus referred to the controversy between the Emperor Theodosius and his former teacher Ambrose, one of the most important fathers of the early Church. Ambrose, Bishop of Milan, had criticised and excommunicated the emperor for a massacre in Thessalonica. His reprimand expressed a relationship between religious power and

[50] Dias, *A Política Cultural*; Curto, "A cultura política"; Mendes, "A vida cultural".

[51] Magalhães, "O enquadramento do espaço nacional", 61; Magalhães, "Os régios protagonistas do poder", 18–32.

political power where the former was not subservient to the second. Clenardus' sentence – "it is the Theodosians who direct the Ambrosian" – meant precisely the opposite.[52]

Francisco Bethencourt labelled this alliance between the Portuguese Crown and the Church an "étatisation" and "naturalisation" of the Church. In contrast, José Pedro Paiva opted to qualify it as a "clericalisation of the state".[53] Despite the distinct designations, their content is similar. Both refer to the political and institutional proximity between hierarchies of political power and religious power, eventually articulated in the figure of Cardinal Dom Henrique.[54] Through his lifetime, this brother of Dom João III accumulated the most important ecclesiastical and political responsibilities in the realm: he was Archbishop of Braga, Évora, and Lisbon, legate of the Holy See, inquisitor-general, regent, and finally king. He was also the chief propagandist for the most critical confessional norms of the Portuguese Crown and was later succeeded, during the Philippine period, by Cardinal Archduke Alberto de Áustria.

To what extent did this alliance benefit the interests of the Crown?

There is no doubt that, through this alliance, the central administration was able to extend its reach, both territorially as well as within the political community, into remote locations. Ecclesiastic and monastic administrative networks covered practically the whole kingdom, urban and rural. Ecclesiastical agents alone

[52] Anthony Pagden highlighted the omnipresence of the imperial Roman experience, and in particular that of the Christian empire, in the configuration of the European empires: Pagden, *Spanish Imperialism*; Pagden, *Lords of All the World*; Pagden, *Povos e Impérios*. In this period many books that invoked this Roman past circulated in the Portuguese space, such as that of Francisco de Holanda – for example, Holanda, *Da Fábrica que falece* – but also Halicarnasso, *De origine Urbis Romae*; Goltz, *Fastus Magistratuum*; Laeti, *De magistratibus et sacerdotijs romanorum,* among others.

[53] Bethencourt, "A Inquisição"; Paiva, "A Igreja e o Poder".

[54] On Cardinal Dom Henrique, see A.M.P. Silva, *O Cardeal D. Henrique*; A.M.P. Silva, "O Cardeal Infante D. Henrique"; A.M.P. Silva, *D. Henrique.*

could physically reach every subject as well as access their inner dispositions and intimate convictions – in order to reorient them along the Christian canon. In this sense, ecclesiastical agents concentrated in themselves the capacities necessary to lead (or, at the very least, to second) the political and social reforms that were under way.[55]

As early as 1988, Bethencourt offered an exciting interpretation of the connections between this will towards social control and the intensification of certain religious instruments. While confession operated as a tool to control the personal ethos by repressing divergent consciences, the inquisition was a tool of collective control. These two institutions were symptoms of the attitude that characterised the new forms of political relationship as they came to be conceived by the Catholic monarchies. Bethencourt also highlights the involvement of Dom João III in the development of these mechanisms as indicative of royal intent.[56] The very king who protected the arts and connected the Portuguese monarchy with the models of classical antiquity was also promoting the inquisition, that most oppressive of institutions.

The process identified by Bethencourt corroborates the conclusions of José Pedro Paiva, who reinforces the opinion that, already in the middle of the sixteenth century, there was an increase in social control. The methods included the inquisition as well as pastoral visits. Paiva argues that the information network which sustained pastoral visits was more refined than those of the Holy Office, allowing access to windows into the soul that even inquisitors

[55] In the religious and cultural dimension, the (re)Christianisation of every subject purified their relationship with God through his principal mediator, Jesus Christ. In the political dimension, the perception of the monarch as representative of the same God supported the idea that the subject should develop and maintain an analogous relationship with him. It is in this context that the epithet the "Pious" attributed to Dom João III should be understood, as a manifestation of force/power, and not as a representation of political weakness.

[56] Bethencourt, *História das Inquisições*, 23–4. See also Bethencourt, "Inquisição" (1993); and Bethencourt, "Inquisição" (2000), 95–134.

could not know. The episcopal courts were part of the same set of disciplinary tools, demonstrating that the interpenetration of Church and State was frequent. The fact that the interests of both spheres were more compatible than antagonistic favoured the cementing of this alliance.[57] All of these surveillance tools enabled, at least in theory, the Crown to gain in-depth information about its subjects, which thus allowed it to secure society by thwarting social dissension.

The Inquisition, episcopal courts, pastoral visits, and confessions existed in Portugal before the conclusion (in 1563) of the Council of Trent, demonstrating a remarkable similarity between the Portuguese case and that of the Italians as presented by Adriano Prosperi. Federico Palomo's work reinforces the same idea. It stresses the image of a sixteenth-century society in which the annihilation of political, religious, and social deviance, and the Christianisation and salvation of subjects of the king appear to constitute a veritable obsession for political and religious power.

Palomo has analysed internal missions undertaken by Jesuits in southern Portugal during the sixteenth and seventeenth centuries. These missions combined preaching, confession, and spiritual guidance and were expressions of the alliance between missionaries and diocesan structures. Through them the prince was able to access the most intimate details about subjects who lived in the farthest reaches of the kingdom – the "rustics", the "barbarians", the "internal Indians". The work of these missionaries was to discipline the consciences of these subjects, "reconstituting them" as faithful subjects and perfect Christians.[58]

The prosecution of this project, whether by political or religious power, was anything but linear. The negotiation between agents of power and communities was critical for its efficiency. While

[57] Paiva, "Inquisição e visitas pastorais"; Paiva, "Uma instrução aos visitadores"; Paiva, "A Igreja e o Poder".

[58] Prosperi, *Tribunali della Coscienza*. In Palomo's opinion, these transformations point to the sedimentation of vertical political linkages between the Crown and subjects, in contrast with the horizontal linkages typical of medieval society: Palomo, *Fazer dos Campos escolas excelentes*.

these processes unfolded, unspoken secrets, unexpected perceptions, and misunderstandings were apparent. The actual position of the various actors involved in the process was not always evident. From the outset it was never clear who could embody the idealised Christian and who could then be guided towards the path to salvation.[59] Also, due to the still-dominant political culture of those involved in the process, what initially emerged as a delegation of royal power came not infrequently to transform itself into a counterpower.

Inquisitorial cases involving the king's friends, including religious figures, reveal the difficulties of the Crown in disciplining its agents. At another level, jurisdictional conflicts between those representing the Crown and the Church express other inherent difficulties.[60] Agents contested the functionalisation of religion that Machiavelli extolled and which Giovanni Botero included in his *Reason of the State*.[61] Simultaneously, the maintenance and consolidation of religious power, amplifying its ability to operate in parallel as an alternative power, or even as a counterpower, created a situation that a wise prince would certainly have wanted to avoid. The concentration of a royal power that simultaneously sought both the aid and the subordination of other powers was one of the structural contradictions inherent within this process.[62]

To assess the extent to which this political configuration impacted imperial space is the principal object of the pages that follow. The imperial dynamics in the Goan situation were quite

[59] Peter von Moos defended, for example, that women wholly embody these projects. This would explain the tendency to "feminise" emotions and religious practices: von Moos, "Kirchlische Disziplienierung".

[60] Paiva remembers that the sixteenth-century Church cannot be understood as a single and homogeneous entity: Paiva, "A Igreja e o Poder", 135ff.; Paiva, *Os Bispos de Portugal e do Império, passim.*

[61] Machiavelli, *Il Principe*; Botero, *Da Razão de Estado.*

[62] During the Iberian Union, the monarchs had more success in submitting the eclesiastical structures to the Crown: Palomo, *Fazer dos campos escolas excelentes*, Chapter 1.

similar to those in the kingdom. The translation of strategies experimented with in the kingdom required, however, the conversion and systematic Christianisation of the colonised populations. António Hespanha has pointed out that "a single administrative model did not structure the Portuguese empire. Instead, there coexisted extremely varied institutions in agreement with local conditions (and influences)."[63] In the case of the Estado da Índia, this institutional diversity was explained by Luís Filipe Thomaz in a classic study, "Estrutura político-administrativa do Estado da Índia", which laid the ground for other analyses of the diversity of the imperial space.[64] The sharing of power, legal pluralism, and the polysinodal regime organised political and institutional space in coherence with a multiplicity of forms of imperium, as emphasised by the titles of the kings of Portugal.[65]

Vasconcelos e Saldanha has highlighted the forms of incorporation of new territories in the Portuguese empire, especially in comparison with the expansionist routines of the European monarchies. "The rights of conquest and first acquisition of uninhabited territories understood as *res nullius*" was the main instrument, besides royal marriages and alliances.[66] This form of expansion ensured that the new spaces were Portuguese Crown

[63] Hespanha, *Panorama da História Institucional*, 11.

[64] Thomaz, "Estrutura político-administrativa"; Madeira Santos and Hespanha, "Os poderes num império"; Hespanha, *Panorama da História Institucional;* Hespanha, "A constituição do império português"; Bethencourt, "Configurações do Império"; Villiers, "The Estado da Índia".

[65] Saldanha, "Conceitos de espaço e poder", 109; and, *in genere,* Saldanha, *Iustum Imperium.*

[66] Saldanha, "Conceitos de espaço e poder", 106; Hespanha, *Panorama da História Institucional*, 12. The legitimacy of this expansion was primarily founded by the papal bulls and the Treaties of Alcáçova, Tordesilhas, and Saragossa. However, it was also founded upon the symbolic marking of these domains through the erection of *padrões*, which were being built in stone since the reign of Dom João II, a practice followed in later "discoveries" in Africa, as well as in Asia and Brazil, as well as other signs of Portuguese presence: the *feitorias* and forts, churches and hospitals.

territories in which the king could exercise direct control. The tentative character, the improvising and invention of a new imperial architecture – in short the process of learning colonialism (to use an expression glossed by Luiz Felipe de Alencastro) were characteristics of the initial period.[67]

Why did an empire not concerned "so much with persons as it was with the relationship between persons" become concerned with people? [68] If one turns to the political imaginary of King Dom João III's reign, it becomes easier to understand why the model of domination that had characterised the empire until then did not satisfy the new king. With Dom João III the Crown established a new relationship with the peoples under its direct rule. Political and administrative reforms initiated in this period are evidence of a time when the Portuguese imperium begins to present itself as "the organizer of productive work, the dispenser of social privileges and the guardian of religious orthodoxy."[69] As Alencastro has noticed, the Portuguese Crown tended to centralise and exercise ever-increasing control over the political, social, and moral destinies of its subjects everywhere, as well as the productivity and economic viability of their territories. A growing desire for a territorial continuum and new attention to the economic potential of rural spaces become evident.[70]

The Portuguese empire would grow from a thalassocracy, which had inspired its start, to that other imperial model – the classical

[67] Guerra, "L'état et les communautés"; Alencastro, "The Apprenticeship of Colonization".

[68] Thomaz, "Estrutura político-administrativa", 210, 216.

[69] Alencastro, "The Apprenticeship of Colonization", 93. A thick reading of the sources of the period, such as in Andrada, ed., *Relações* de *Pero Alcáçova Carneiro*, the writings of António Pinheiro (Pinheiro, *Colleçam das Obras Portuguezas*), or even the *Anais de D. João III* by Friar Luís de Sousa (Sousa, *Anais de D. João III*), is elucidating.

[70] Sanjay Subrahmanyam identifies Martim Afonso de Sousa as one of the champions of this new attitude, influenced by his familiarity with the Spanish court, where he would certainly have heard talk of the feats of Cortez and Hernandez in Mexico and Peru: Subrahmanyam, *Penumbral Visions*, Chapter 2.

and late-Roman empire.[71] Numerous poets and chroniclers were already extolling this latter model, each paean more ornate than the next. These would in time constitute the frames of reference of the Portuguese kingdom, replacing the medieval concept of an empire.[72] A rational political-administrative organisation, as well as instruments of integration and differentiation of legally governed populations in the language and religion of the prince, were characteristic of the new model.

Replicating in imperial territories – to the extent possible – institutions, laws, and Christian practices created the condition for the empire's political conservation. For this reason João de Barros defended the teaching of "Luso" manners and the Portuguese language to "conquered peoples" in imitation of the Roman practice, arguing that "surely good practices and language will endure longer than a memorial pillar."[73] Explicit networks of communication between colonies and metropole could transform the Atlantic and Indian oceans into a new *mare nostrum.*[74] It became possible to club diverse geographies, societies, and cultures into a similar politico-administrative structure, thereby constituting diverse territories into a unified space where "the whole did not

[71] The mid-sixteenth-century treatise of António Galvão (Galvão, *Tratado dos Descobrimentos),* as well as the history of the Portuguese in Asia by João de Barros (Barros, *Décadas da Ásia*), are indicators of the constrution of the imperial memory along this model.

[72] On the structural features of Augustus' empire, see Tulard, *Les Empires Occidentaux* (Vol. 1), as well as the classic works of Pierre Grimal (Grimal, *O Século de Augusto*; Grimal, *O Império Romano*). See also MacCormack, "Sin, Citizenship and the Salvation of Souls", 622–73. See also the manner in which the English monarchy launched a variety of strategies of internal colonialisation, many of which evidence the attempt to recover the form of the Roman Empire, the most perfect political model: Ohlmeyer, "Civilizing of those Rude Parts", 130ff.

[73] Introduction of Maria Leonor Carvalhão Buescu to Barros in Barros, *Gramática da Língua Portuguesa*, LI–LII; see also J.V. Serrão, "João de Barros".

[74] Ferreira, *Problemas Marítimos*, 118. See also Seed, *Ceremonies of Possession,* 140ff., 180ff.

consume the parts."[75] The strategy meant the empire could integrate local authorities, constituted after conversion to Christianity, as intermediaries.

The circulation of political models between the court of Charles V – whose most prolonged residence in Castile occurred between 1522 and 1529[76] – and of Dom João III (married to Catarina of Austria, sister of the Emperor) is part of this process. [77] Establishing connections between the two Iberian experiences is even more critical.[78] The reason is that it was this period that saw the start of reforms in the Habsburg court, which had the effect of restructuring the relationship between the Spanish kingdom and its American empire.[79]

In the imperial territories, Goa was the first location where these ideas were systematically experimented with. For some decades,

[75] Hespanha, *As Vésperas do Leviathan*, 33.

[76] The dates which, continuing into 1539, marked the rise of the empress Isabel, sister of the Portuguese king.

[77] The cases of António de Guevara, António Moro, and Friar Sebastião Toscano are emblematic. On this, see Rodriguez Sanchez, "Carlos V y Portugal", 21–8; Bouza, *Portugal no Tempo dos Filipes*; but also Jordan, *Retrato de Corte*; Jordan-Geschwend, "O Maneirismo e o Retrato"; and Terra, "Espagnols au Portugal".

[78] The similarities that one finds between the Jesuits' settlements in Paraná, in the sixteenth century, and those that the Jesuits had in Bassein and Thana, led Correia-Afonso to suggest that the implantation of missionaries in India served as an inspiration for experiments on the other side of the Atlantic: Correia-Afonso, "Ignatius de Loyola, Portugal, and the Indian Missions", 40. Adriano Prosperi also identifies similarities between the formulae used in different territories, in particular the similarities between the American "*reducciones*" and the "*missões*": Prosperi, "Otras Indias"; see also, in this regard, Schallenberger, "Conflitos coloniais".

[79] It was during the reigns of Dom João III and Charles V that the Spanish monarchy stabilised and began to expand. Following John H. Elliott, the creation of the Consejo de las Indias, in 1524, initiated a complex of reforms that structurally altered the organisation of the empire: Elliott, *España Imperial*, 184; Gil, "A apropriação da ideia de império"; Fernandez-Alvarez, *Carlos V*, 135ff.

there was a spatial reconceptualisation of the Estado da Índia. Descriptions in administrative documents complement the situation on the ground regarding fortification of these territories and the greater control of crossings between these various territories. The need for fortification developed into a special obsession. In response to a request to the king dated 1523, António Fonseca provided details of the state of rents, forts, hospitals, and ships that he had encountered while in Goa. In the subsequent year residents of the city petitioned the king to fortify the city. The letters of Friar Lourenço de Goes and Pedro Faria from the same period speak of the construction of fortifications in Cranganore, Diu, Bassein. In others the subject is the state of disrepair of these forts. Some letters also refer to the need to change the methods of construction. From 1530 the construction of forts followed Italian models, gradually substituting the earlier Manueline form. Still, some forts that had served as protection from enemy attacks when first constructed were not destroyed because they constituted a symbolic statement of the chronology of possession by the Crown, as well as an affirmation of royal power and the extension of its forces.[80]

Making the city of Goa the capital of the Estado da Índia is part of this context. The event represented an institutional change with crucial constitutional significance. Catarina Madeira Santos defines it as the first moment of shift – because of the decision's significance in terms of political options in the present and potential options in the future. The establishment of similar

[80] IAN/TT, Corpo Cronológico, Part I, Mç. 30, n. º 36 – "Carta de Antonio Fonseca dando conta a ElRey", 18 October 1523; Mç. 31, nº 83 – "Carta da Camara de Goa, dando parte a ElRey, chegar o Conde da Vidigueia", 31 October 1524; Mç. 59, nº 109 – "Carta de Pedro de Faria dando conta a ElRey", 20 October 1537; Mç. 66, nº 37 – "Carta de Pedro Faria reprezentando a ElRey a necessidade", 20 November 1539; Mç. 66, nº 99 – "Carta de Diogo Rebello dando parte a ElRey que a India estava exaurida", 24 January 1540. See also Moreira, *História das Fortificações*, 150; and Correia, *D. Francisco de Almeida*, 57–62.

political-administrative institutions that existed in metropolitan Lisbon flowed naturally from the new vision of the imperial space. These institutions included the Viceroyalty, the Conselho de Estado (Council of State), the Relação de Goa (Court of Appeal), the extension of the privileges of the municipality of Lisbon to that of Goa, collectively making the latter the most important municipality in the Estado da Índia. Subsequently, in the course of the sixteenth century, Goa also saw the institution of the Conselho da Fazenda (Council of Finance), the Mesa da Consciência e Ordens, and ecclesiastical institutions that enjoyed a political status similar to that in Lisbon. The elevation of the bishopric to an archbishopric and the institution of the Inquisition are good examples.[81]

At this level, there were other consequences related to the city of Goa's new status. The establishment of the viceregal government rested on the assumption of "the *regalia* [rights and powers of the king] which one traditionally associated with the exercise of the *officium regis*", and the viceroy being "a magistrate invested with the same royal powers who would represent the king of Portugal and his sovereignty *extra territorium.*"[82] It was not merely the *regalia maiora* or the *imperium maximum* that the viceroy or even the governor could hope to exercise. The viceroy also had the power to punish (*imperium maius*), to deport (*imperium magnum*), and to exile and expropriate (*imperium parvum*). His status comprehended other minor imperial powers, even though these were reduced as the bureaucracy grew in complexity.[83] The

[81] Madeira Santos, *Goa é a chave de toda a Índia*, Chapter 2. For example, the acquisition of the same privileges and competencies as the city of Lisbon did not reduce the power of the viceroy, nor of the municipal council. This was similar in the ecclesiastical world: cf., for example, IAN/TT, Corpo Cronológico, Part I, Mç. 72, nº 155 – "Carta do Chantre de Gôa dando parte a ElRey", 31 October 1542.

[82] Madeira Santos, *Goa é a chave de toda a Índia*, 35.

[83] On the powers and attributes of the imperium, see Hespanha, *Panorama Histórico*, 108–10.

powers of the viceroy, like those of the bishops, were so vast that in 1548 the rector of the college of the Jesuits, António Gomes, reported to Simão Rodrigues, provincial of the Jesuits in Lisbon, that "here the bishop is pope and the governor king." Three years later Gomes made a similar suggestion, though with somewhat different nuances. Praising the friendship of Afonso de Noronha with Governor Jorge Cabral (r. 1549–1550), Gomes justified this friendship, saying "the virtuous and honourable men are all friends to the Governors, and seek to aid him, seeing him as the king, our Lord."[84]

The political and legal status of the inhabitants of Goa changed too. Until about 1540, and because the systematic conversion of local populations had only just begun, the ambit of the viceroy's jurisdiction over these populations was relatively marginal.[85] However, if the initial decades of Portuguese domination were marked by a normative plurality, by the third decade of the sixteenth century the need to Christianise the population of Goa had begun to materialise.[86]

Many signs suggest the decades between 1530 and 1540 as the moment when these aspirations began to look concrete. Terms such as "idolatry", "demons", "unfaithful", "service of God", "care

[84] These letters can be found in DI, Vol. 1, 408ff.; Vol. 2, 140. In contrast with the Spanish Empire, where, since the beginning, the viceroys were above all governors, empowered only with administrative power (judicial power was vested in the Audiencias), in the Portuguese Empire the viceroy assembled an enormous diversity of power: Madeira Santos, *Goa é a chave de toda a Índia*, 177ff.

[85] In order to articulate a single state structure that would be compatible with a variety of diverse juridical (and social) orders, the solution was to apply the doctrine of common law, according to which each "nation" or "community" had its own laws: see Hespanha, *Panorama Histórico*, 102–10; and Tau Anzoátegui, *Casuismo y Sistema*, 84.

[86] Encompassing a population of around 200,000 persons, this constituted a major demographic change. M.N. Pearson calculated the poulation of Tiswadi, Salcete, and Bardez, in 1630, to be around 250,000: Pearson, *The Portuguese in India*, 92–3.

of and desire for conversion" invaded the preamble of several *cartas régias, alvarás, provisões*, and other norms, always guided by the need to justify the transfer of benefits – whether political, religious, economic, or social – from the hands of non-Christians to Christians.[87] Through the equation of *regeneratio* (or baptism, the second birth) with *generatio* (biological birth), the integration of the local population into the Portuguese juridical system became a possibility. This then allowed for an ever-increasing number to convert and become in the process the most common category of political identification for the local populations in the territory of Goa. Other mechanisms accompanied this new attitude: in the year 1540 Father Miguel Vaz, the vicar-general of India, initiated a process involving the demolition of all non-Christian temples on the island(s) of Tiswadi. Three hundred of these temples were destroyed by 1541 and their rents transferred to the Catholic cult. The destruction of these local religious structures went hand in hand with the implanting of a parish network and other religious structures (crosses, churches, hospitals, schools) in the urban world, i.e. in the city of Goa, as well as in the rural, i.e. the villages of the islands of Tiswadi, Divar, Chorão, and Jua; and after 1543 in the villages of Bardez and Salcete as well. There was, simultaneously, the systematic establishment of religious orders – above all of the Franciscans and the Jesuits – with parish duties, and the creation of the Holy Office. Initially established for New Christians – meaning converted Jews – who had travelled from Portugal to these newly conquered territories, this last institution would rapidly grow to address itself to the "newly converted".

[87] See, for example, the norms included in Cunha Rivara, *Archivo Portuguez Oriental* (henceforth CR–APO), Fasc 5, Part I, 161–70 and 223–5.

2

Designing Conversion

In 1537 Dom João de Castro, governor and viceroy of the Portuguese possessions in India between 1545 and 1548, wrote:

> If I could be a seal, I would stamp decrees and lodge them in the Torre do Tombo, in order to affirm that the Portuguese should not enter even a handspan into the interior of India. Nothing else preserves peace and friendship with the kings and lords of India than having them believe and knowing for certain that our only interest is the sea, and that no purpose nor imagination of ours could lead us to desire their lands.[1]

Over this period the territorial ambitions of the Portuguese Crown seemed absurd to Castro, and even a danger to the conservation of the Crown's interests in India. He was not wrong in observing that local princes considered control of the land much more valuable than control of the sea and its domains.

Some years later, however, he argued that the Portuguese king could become "Emperor of the East". His belief that 10,000 men would be enough for the king of Portugal to become one of the "leading rulers of the world and Emperor of the East" was, nevertheless, utopian. What prompted his change of mind?

The Portuguese military success in Diu and potential alliance

[1] L. Albuquerque, ed., *Cartas de D. João de Castro*, 12. (Parts of this chapter were published in A.B. Xavier, "A organização religiosa do primeiro Estado da Índia".)

with Vijayanagar against the sultanate of Bijapur appeared to be a good sign for future military success. Also, Castro's surmise was voiced at a time when Portuguese territorial dominions in India had more than doubled. In 1534 the Portuguese annexed some provinces of the Gujarat sultanate, and in 1543 Salcete and Bardez, which had been possessions of the sultanate of Bijapur. The territories of the Estado da Índia had thus doubled, and this perhaps led Castro to foresee a Portuguese future in India at odds with his reckoning of it eight years earlier.

In Castro's opinion a good army was necessary for the conservation and expansion of Portuguese conquests. To capitalise on their military success, he suggested conquering "one or two places, yet to be determined; either in Bassein and Manorá, or the mainland of Goa" and stationing 4000 men in each.[2] These places would then serve as bases from which to defend territories already acquired. And eventually, military contingents responsible for future territorial expansion might swell the ranks of those already in position.[3]

Castro's suggestions were similar to those sent to the Portuguese king in this period, revealing that his ideas were neither singular nor limited to his vision of the future. There was a general belief that securing the future of the existing Portuguese presence required an urgent reorganisation of the dominion based on other foundations. Luíz Martins, for example, had made similar proposals twenty years before Castro. Later, Cosme Annes did the same.[4] But, by contrast with them, Castro wanted his ideas to take proper effect.

[2] L. Albuquerque, ed., *Cartas de D. João de Castro,* 129. Two years before, Salcete and Bardez had been integrated into the territories of Goa under the rule of the Portuguese Crown. With regard to the increasing attraction of the "hinterland" of India among the Portuguese, see Subrahmanyam, *Penumbral Visions*, 21–8.

[3] The letters exchanged between Dom João de Castro and his sons show not only the governor announcing his project but that he had begun implementing it. See L. Albuquerque, ed., *Cartas de D. João de Castro.*

[4] IAN/TT, *Gavetas*, nº 15, Mç. 17, nº 19, 89–104. In 1555, Annes argued

The Portuguese Crown chose paths different from those proposed by all three. In addition to reinforcing military contingents, evangelising and converting local people became a critical strategy and the linchpin of a sounder plan of defence to maintain the Indian possessions. Instead of bringing in 10,000 soldiers, the evangelisation of Indians allowed a multiplication of forces, making conversion an instrument for guaranteeing the conservation of imperial power.

Evangelisation came to be not just the *object* but also the *objective*. In 1553 the Castilian Julião de Alva, Bishop of Portalegre, counsellor and spiritual adviser to Queen Dona Catarina, presented the dynamics of evangelisation in India – as well as in Brazil and Guinea – as being of the utmost importance for Portuguese Christianity. He claimed that "all must take this path, and there is an increasing necessity to use the tools at our disposal to encourage others to mend their ways and create a new world."[5] The need for this policy was also evident in a letter sent by Friar João Pereira to members of the Portuguese court in the course of the Council of Trent. Pereira argued that Lutheranism "is a laugh [for] although there is evil lurking around indeed, they have faith in the crucified Christ and confess to the trinity, and yet think nothing of disapproving the gospel!"[6] To Pereira, the Council of Trent was frittering away time on subjects far less urgent than those he believed necessary. He thought it crucial to assemble a council to discuss the evangelisation of overseas territories, as well as the selling of Church properties and the raising of money from monks, New Christians, and noblemen to meet the costs of such a project. All of this had the objective of challenging Islamic domination in India. At the end of his letter the friar lashed out – "What remains of

---

that Dom João III could reign over all of India as long as he succeeded in checking the forces of the 'Adil Shah and Nizam Shah: Mç. 12, nº 35, 414.

[5] *Apud* Terra, "Espagnols au Portugal", 488. At the same period, this bishop tried to reform his diocese: Paiva, "Dioceses e organização eclesiástica", 242; Dias, *Correntes do sentimento religioso*, Vol. 1, 165, fn. 4.

[6] Colecção de S. Lourenço, Vol. 1, 118.

Christianity if the Turk enters India?" He argued that an alliance between religious, political, and military interests was the only way to defend Christianity when facing Islam.[7]

Writing to Francisco Borgia in 1555 from Goa, the Jesuit Melchior Carneiro indicated that "Using all human means and favours as the initial impulse, even if not the final cause" was essential for achieving the Christianisation of overseas territories. He stressed that the Portuguese Crown had to be more involved in this process than it had been.[8]

These proposals to convert and baptise the indigenous population, and the means to achieve these ends, will be discussed in the first part of this chapter. Later I focus on the legal framework and the creation of institutional mechanisms, concluding with an analysis of the opposition to these policies.

"Apparatus and Disposition to Reform and Create a New World"[9]

Dom João III was the recipient of a significant number of letters on the evangelisation of India even before Goa had become a bishopric. Until the second creation of a capital for the Estado da Índia – that is to say, until the moment when Goa became a bishopric – these territories were framed by a scattered religious order.[10]

From the time of the papal bull *Inter caetera*, issued by Calisto III in 1456, the *ius patronatus* (the right of patronage) of land conquered, or yet to be conquered, by the Portuguese Crown belonged

[7] The circulation of anti-Islamic sentiment reiterating such messages was characteristic of this period. See, for example, Chinchón, *Libro llamado AntiAlcorano*, 1532.

[8] Letter of Melchior Carneiro, 1555 (DI, Vol. 3, 355–8).

[9] *Apud* Terra, "Espagnols au Portugal", 488.

[10] Madeira Santos, *Goa é a chave de toda a Índia*, regards this institutional gesture as one of the most significant in the process of transforming Goa into the capital of the Estado da Índia.

to the Order of Christ under its master and vicar.[11] The spiritual health of Christians was the end sought, and to this end the Order of Christ had extensive jurisdiction. It nominated bishops and clerics. It provided for the foundation, conservation, and repair of churches, monasteries, and holy places. It offered temples and monasteries with the objects necessary for the celebration of the cult.

These privileges and obligations confronted a parallel reality. The administration of military orders had since the beginning of the fifteenth century been granted to members of the royal family. The destinies of the Order of Christ and the dynasty of Avis were intertwined because the ideals and culture of this military order informed royal policy, and conversely the jurisdiction of the Order of Christ depended on the Portuguese Crown.

During the reign of Dom Manuel I, Master of the Order of Christ since 1484, Vasco da Gama had reached the shores of India. Theoretically, the Order had then received the *ius patronatus et praesentandi* concerning the Asian territories. However, in 1500 Alexander VI issued the brief *Cum Sicut maiestas* asking Dom Manuel, in his role as the king of Portugal, to nominate an apostolic commissioner for territories between the Cape of Good Hope and India.[12]

The commissioner had episcopal powers, was under the secular hierarchy of the Church, and did not have to be a member of the Order of Christ.

The papal bulls of 1514, *Dum Fidei constantiam* and *Pro excellentis praeeminentia* by Leo X, tried to solve the ambiguity created

[11] This bull extended the old right of patronage: a cluster of privileges granted to those that constructed, reconstructed, or offered money to any given church. See, among others, De Witte, *La Correspondance des Premiers Nonces*; I. Godinho, *The Padroado of Portugal*; Rego, *História das Missões*; Xavier, "Aparejo y disposición"; N.S. Gonçalves, "O Padroado", 364–8.

[12] The names of these bulls are the first words of the document and frequently do not denote anything concrete. *Cum Sicut maiestas*, thus, translates roughly as "To the majesty . . ."

by the brief of 1500. A first bull granted the Order of Christ full jurisdiction over the churches already built and those yet to be built in North Africa. Five days later a second bull suppressed the right of the Order of Christ concerning other imperial territories. These rights were given to the new diocese of Funchal. The Order of Christ continued to nominate minor offices and the chapter of the See of Funchal. It also had the right to the tithes collected by agents of the Crown, and the maintenance of churches in this vast diocese was part of its responsibility.

Vasco da Gama's voyage was connected with this change. From this point on, the king tried to directly control the ecclesiastic structure of the Asian domains, nominating prelates, vicar generals, and candidates for the most important offices. Significantly, the monarch nominated the principal offices in his capacity as king of Portugal, and not as Master of the Order of Christ. From this period, prelates and vicars, or commissioners with similar tasks, were supposed to report to the king of Portugal. The Order of Christ kept the right of nominating parish priests, clerics, and other minor offices.[13] This blend of royal patronage of the Church with reduced jurisdiction for the Order of Christ in the overseas territories organised the initial ecclesiastic framework of the Estado da Índia.

The papal bull *Aequum reputamus* of 3 November 1534 elevated Goa as the seat of a diocese. On the same day, the pope created the dioceses of the Azores and São Tomé. With this bull the Bishop of Funchal obtained the title "Primate of the Indies" and began exercising jurisdiction over an extensive territory. Dom Martinho de Portugal, a humanist prelate, was nominated its bishop. Meanwhile, the king nominated Francisco de Melo as Bishop of Goa. Diplomat, mathematician, philosopher, and theologian, teacher of the princes Dom Fernando and Dom Luís, as well as an official

[13] De Witte, *La Correspondance des Premiers Nonces,* 11–13; 30–1, 49ff., 66, 78ff.; Vieira, "As constituições sinodais", 457–8; Sorge and Fasa, *India tra Occidente e Oriente*, 603.

orator for the Crown, Melo was the type of cleric idealised by Dom João III.[14] In 1535 Francisco de Melo opened the Cortes of Évora with an eulogy linking Neoplatonism and Erasmianism to evoke the model of the *respublica* of the king of Portugal. The basis of this *respublica* was order, diligence, and harmony. If Martinho de Portugal was a critical humanist, so was Francisco de Melo.[15]

Melo died before taking up his position in India. His death delayed the arrival of the first resident Bishop of Goa by about five years. During the period of the Spaniard Juan de Albuquerque, Goa became the biggest diocese of the empire, including Japan, Ceylon, the Maldives, China, Korea, Arabia, Persia, and India. Until 1551 it was a suffragan diocese of Funchal. The Order of Christ continued to have financial responsibilities relating to churches and their cult objects. However, the *ius patronatus et praesentandi* concerning major and minor benefices of the diocese was with the king of Portugal, who nominated the prelates, delegating to them the nomination of those in lower offices. One of the aims was to raise the See of Goa to a stature equal to that of Lisbon. Goa became a metropolitan diocese in 1551 and an archbishopric in 1558. Thereafter, Malacca and Kochi became its suffragans.

However, between 1514 and 1534 – or more likely 1539, when the bishop actually arrived – a power vacuum existed in relation to Goa. There was no bishop or similar prelate permanently resident in Goa, therefore no one really responsible for the spiritual health of the Christian inhabitants and the conversion of non-Christians in the Asian territories. Instead, a vicar-general, some subordinate vicars, as well as a few clergymen performing the tasks of curates, priests, and chaplains constituted the secular hierarchy. As for the regular clergy, there were several mendicants, especially Franciscans, dispersed through the territory who from very early on settled down in residencies, afterwards in convents, and finally in a cus-

[14] Paiva, *Os Bispos de Portugal e do Império*, 277ff.

[15] A detailed interpretation of this speech has been undertaken by Rafael Moreira in his PhD thesis: Moreira, "A Arquitectura do Renascimento", 198–210, 236–7.

tody;[16] and there were in addition some Dominicans.[17] And, from time to time, one could count on the presence of apostolic commissioners.

In the absence of a prelate, vicar-generals and vicars constituted the most important ecclesiastic authorities. Until 1539, there were four vicar generals. Little is known about Domingos de Sousa, a Dominican friar (1513–1517), and not very much more about João Pacheco (1518–1522), Sebastião Pires (1522–1532), and Miguel Vaz (1533–1547).[18] Pacheco was the target of much criticism, as was Pires; Pires and Vaz, on the other hand, complained about the religious situation in Goa, attaching blame either to inaction by the Crown or lack of interest among its local agents.[19]

[16] A Custody was an institutionalised agglomerate of Franciscan convents, dependent on a Province, which was hierarchically superior and assembled several Custodies.

[17] Many documents attest to the work accomplished by the Franciscans in this time period. See, among others, IAN/TT, Corpo Cronológico, Part I, Mç. 23, nº 133 – "Carta do Commissario Guardião a ElRey", 4 November 1518; Mç. 58, nº 23 – "Carta de Frei Lourenço de Goes, Guardião de Convento de S. Antonio de Cochim", 28 December 1536; Mç. 81, nº 59 – "Carta de Fr. Antonio do Porto, dando parte a ElRey", 7 October 1548; Part II, Mç. 77, nº 108 – "Mandado de Diogo Lopes", 25 Sept. 1518; Mç. 154, nº 47 – "Recibo de Frei Francisco de Alenquer", 8 March 1528; Mç. 165, nº 3 – "Recibo de Fr. António, Guardião do Convento de São Francisco de Goa", 9 Sept. 1530; BPADE, "Fundo Rivara, r 5e, 6–14 – Fundação do convento de S. Francisco". There is also interesting documentation on the construction of the first Dominican buildings in these lands and their protection by the king: IAN/TT, Corpo Cronológico, Part I, Mss. 81, nº 101 – "Carta de Fr. Diogo Bermides dando parte a ElRey", 6 December 1548; Mç. 82, nº 5 – "Carta dos Mestres da Casa dos Vinte e Quatro de Goa"; Mç. 83, nº 59 – "Carta de Rui Gonçalves Caminha", 30 December 1549; Mç. 100, nº 122 – "Carta de frei Estêvão de Santa Maria", 25 February 1557.

[18] Costa and Rodrigues, *Portugal y Oriente*, 265.

[19] Castilian friar Vicente de Laguna also warned Dom João III at the start of the 1530s on the effects that bad vicars could have on the state of Christianity: IAN/TT, Corpo Cronológico, Part I, Mss. 30, nº 76: "Carta do Bispo de Cochim dando conta a ElRey do mao governo daquella terra", 28 Dec. 1523; Mç. 45, nº 127 – "Carta de Fr. Vicente de Laguna a ElRey",

The few testimonies that exist about the doings of apostolic commissioners – Dom Duarte Nunes at the start of the 1520s, and Dom Fernando Vaqueiro in the following decade – refer to these problems. Both Nunes and Vaqueiro were tasked with identifying local religious problems and communicating them to the king.[20]

In 1520, however, the Franciscan Friar António Louro lamented that they had very little power. The Franciscan contingent was the most significant in this first period. More than converting the locals, it was concerned with the Portuguese. However, there was an explicit missionary intent among Franciscans settled in the Malabar Coast to reintroduce the Christians of St Thomas (or Syrian Christians) to the Roman Church.[21] Some correspondence refers to 6000 Christians converted in 1514, and to between 10,000 and 12,000 by 1518 in Kochi. In contrast, various other testimonies point to a much smaller (and more credible) number of conversions.[22]

---

25 Sept. 1530; Mç. 50, nº 45 – "Carta de Fr. Vicente Laguna a ElRey sobre o grande descuido", 29 Nov. 1532.

[20] On the state of Christianity in the first period, see also IAN/TT, Corpo Cronológico, Part I, Mç. 12, nº 39 – "Carta para ElRey sobre o que ordinariamente sucede na India", 7 Dec. 1512; Mç. 23, nº 5 – "Carta de Sebastião Pires, Vigario de Cochim", 8 Jan. 1518; Mç. 25, nº 55 – "Carta do Juiz da Confraria de Nossa Senhora do Rozario de Gôa", 25 Oct. 1519; Mç. 27, nº 93 – "Carta de Sebastião Pires Vigario Geral de Cochim", 10 Jan. 1522; Mss. 27, nº 95: "Carta do Bispo Dumuense dando conta a ElRey de suas Missoens", 12 Jan. 1522; Mç. 28, nº 122 – "Carta de Pedro de Faria, dando parte a ElRey", 25 Oct. 1522; Mç. 50, nº 52 – "Carta do Bispo D. Fernando, dando parte a ElRey", 12 Dec. 1532; Mç. 78, nº 101 – ; BPADE, CIX/2–3, Mss. 3, nº 22 – " Carta de Fr. Lourenço de Goes, Guardião do Convento de Santo Antonio de Cochim", 28 Dec. 1536.

[21] Schurhammer, ed., *Orientalia*, 207–12; J.M. Correia, *Os Franciscanos em Cochim*; J.M. Correia, *D. Francisco de Almeida*, 140ff.; M.P. Gonçalves, "A presença franciscana".

[22] These numbers arise in letters from Pero Mascarenhas and Vicar Sebastião Pires: Mundadan, *History of Christianity in India*, I, 359.

In 1519, the same year as Hernando Cortez began the Mexican campaigns, António Louro wrote a letter to the king, following another more detailed one (unfortunately lost), giving an account of the state of Christianity in India. By that time there was the convent of São Francisco (St Francis of Assisi) in Goa and of Santo António (St Antony) in Kochi. The construction of two other smaller monasteries, one in Cannanore, the other in Cranganore, had also begun. The friar wanted permission to welcome the converted into the Franciscan residencies. The aim was to teach and instruct them to prevent their "having a Christian name without knowledge of the doctrine." After being instructed and converted, the new Christians were to be distributed in neighbourhoods and separated from the Gentiles.[23] Louro also argued that the "*jogis*, which is what they call beggars," had to be physically separated from Christians. They could not enter Goa "because they bring scrolls and relics from their pagodas, as well as devils that will restore the gentileness of these men."

Louro seemed to have taken inspiration for these last two solutions, i.e. segregation and the restriction of communication between Christians and non-Christians, from the model that operated in Iberia in relation to Jews and Muslims.[24] However, by contrast with Portugal, Christians were the demographic minority in the Indian territories. Segregation and communication restrictions were intended to protect the new and fragile community of Christians and enable it to grow. The relevance of instruction before conversion seems to spring either from the Franciscan tradition of St Bonaventure or from Christian humanism influenced

[23] IAN/TT, Corpo Cronológico, Part I, Mç. 23, nº 133 – "Carta do Commissario Guardião a ElRey sobre o Estado", 4 Nov.1518; BPADE, CIX/2–3, M. 3, nº 13 – "Carta de Frei Antonio a ElRey Dom Manoel sobre a conversão dos Gentios", 4 Nov. 1518, fl. 8; also cited in Meersman, *The Ancient Franciscan Provinces*, 63.

[24] Ferro, *Os Judeus em Portugal*; Ferro, *Inquisição e Judaísmo*; Glick, *Islamic and Christian Spain*; Moreno, *Marginalidade e Conflitos Sociais*; Moreno, "Exclusão e marginalidade social", 37–51; Antunes, "Acerca da liberdade de religião", 64–83.

by Erasmus, which was very much in vogue at the time. Louro's response to the question on the "land's capacity to be converted" suggests the influence of classic Franciscan doctrines which stressed the importance of grace rather than "human means". "This kind of work is divine, and therefore it is for God alone to call them to receive the true faith," Louro wrote. Nevertheless, his actions demonstrate a tension between the need to create institutional conditions favouring conversion and recognition of the action of "divine grace". For example, he proposed the offer of rice for the "Gentiles", arguing that it would persuade them to convert.

Aligned with the "reformists", Louro wrote another letter to the king in 1520, insisting that the vicar instruct the converted at least once a week since the Franciscans did not have "any more rule other than for them to preach publicly [and] no more power beyond the front door of the convent." He refers as well to the presence of *naturais* (natives) and mestizos in the convent of São Francisco waiting to receive sacred orders. Louro was undoubtedly aware of the brief *Exponi Nobis super* by which the pope Leo X conceded to the Bishop of Lamego the power to grant sacred orders to Ethiopians and other Africans, notwithstanding any "blood taint".[25] He wished to see the same applied to the Indian territories. The arrival of "twenty monks and confessors, and three preachers" would be of the utmost importance, for "now, Sire, it is time for your Royal Highness to help this sacred work more than ever, which I hope in the passion of Christ you shall do."[26]

The letters written by Dom Duarte Nunes are even more eloquent. In them it is possible to find some of the best descriptions of the struggle to establish Christianity in these early years.[27] A

[25] QE, X, 250.

[26] Between 1530 and 1532, the Dominican friar Vicente Laguna also asked for ministers to "plant the Evangelical word", and for their protection by the vicars: cited in fn. 148. See A.S. Pereira, "Intenções catequéticas"; I.R. Pereira, "O ensino da doutrina cristã".

[27] BNP, Cod. 176 – Notícias do arcebispado de Goa, fls 97–97v. Information on these apostolic commissioners is unclear. One knows, however, that Duarte Nunes professed his vows in 1489, being promoted to Bishop of

Dominican friar, Nunes was appointed Bishop of Dume and left for India in 1520, eventually returning to Portugal where he died in 1528.[28] His first letters are from 1518 and 1519, before he departed for India. They indicate that Nunes was part of a group of people who formed the entourage of the Archbishop of Lisbon, Dom Martinho da Costa; that he was an apostolic commissary of the Bishop of Funchal; and that he was unhappy with his appointment to India. "Lord, send me anywhere you wish, but to the Indies," St Thomas had said, and after being in India awhile the Portuguese Nunes agreed with him.[29] His project was to "always pray . . . always give the Episcopal Sacraments [and be] very clean, and with servants." Besides, he wanted "that all the clergy obeys me wherever I go, and that I have the jurisdiction to punish them if they do not respond when called up to deliver any Sacrament." He also believed it necessary that the captain not interfere with his jurisdiction. The secretary of the Crown, António Carneiro, thought his requirements exaggerated, while the friar Louro estimated them as "no power whatsoever".[30]

Other missives sent to the king between 1522 and 1523 describe the condition of Christianity in India. They register Nunes' visits to Kochi, Calicut, Cranganore, and Goa, indicating that the churches were in terrible shape, the secular clergy nonchalant, and the post of vicar denigrated. Nunes was shocked by the greed of

---

Laudiceia: BPADE, CXVI/1–39, nº 21 – "Memorias Sepulcraes da India", fls 1–2.

[28] IAN/TT, Corpo Cronológico, Part I, Mss. 27, nº 95: "Carta do Bispo Dumuense dando conta a ElRey de suas Missoens", 12 Jan. 1522; Mç. 30, nº 76 – "Carta do Bispo de Cochim dando conta a ElRey do mao governo daquella terra", 28 Dec. 1523.

[29] These thoughts and proposals were expressed at the same time in Mexico: Bernand and Gruzinksi, *Histoire du Nouveau Monde*, I, 398.

[30] BPADE, CIX/2–3, Mç. 3, nº 9 – "Carta do Bispo Dumiense ao Secretº Antº Carneiro", 5 Oct. 1518; nº 10 – "Carta do Bispo Dumiense ao Secretº Antº Carneiro sobre a sua viagem", 5 Dec. 1519; and nº 11 – "Carta do Bispo Dumiense a Antonio Carneiro", 16 Dec. 1519.

the clergy, their refusal to baptise without receiving fees, and the facility with which they divorced Portuguese couples. "All is lost due to the ignorance of those in charge," he said, holding Vicar-General João Pacheco entirely responsible for this sorry state of affairs. Pacheco had gone to Goa after doing "terrible crimes" on the island of Terceira. Since he "had undergone the acts of penitence awarded to him," he arrived in India with the title of Vicar General, "poisoning in the process all of Christianity with his evil way of living and bad example." Nunes was clear that the secular clergy dispatched to Goa did not possess the required virtues.

The regular clergy was a problem too. Many of the friars had concubines and lived away from convents. Nevertheless, the prelate hails the work of the Franciscans and tells the king that Vicar-General João Pacheco expelled four Franciscan brothers from Kochi without having the authority; Pacheco's attitude had defamed "Episcopal Dignity". He had even argued that Nunes "should be suspended, among many other matters."

Christians frequently did not receive the sacrament, some were married several times, others were continually fighting, and many oppressed the newly converted. Besides, they participated openly in non-Christian religious festivals that took place on the island of Goa. Denying Christ, some soldiers worked for Muslims or sold them arms.[31]

After listing the problems afflicting Christianity, the Dominican outlined ways to improve this state of affairs and persuade the locals to convert. To begin with, funds were required to restore

[31] BPADE, CIX/2–3, Mç. 3, nº 12 – "Carta do Bispo Dumiense em que dá conta a ElRey", 12 Jan. 1522; IAN/TT, Corpo Cronológico, Part I, Mss. 27, nº 95 – "Carta do Bispo Dumuense dando conta a ElRey de suas Missoens", 12 Jan. 1522; Mç. 30, nº 76 – "Carta do Bispo de Cochim dando conta a ElRey do mao governo daquella terra", 28 Dec. 1523. Unfortunately, Carlos Mercês de Mello's study on the recruitment of the native clergy does not go back to this period, but only deals with the time after the establishment of the Congregation of the Propaganda Fide: Mello, *The Recruitment and Formation*.

churches and provide them with the necessities. Subsequently, it was vital to send out more secular and regular clergy to invest in the education of local converts. If well taught, the newly converted might some day take on ecclesiastical and missionary roles themselves. However, a reform of the clergy was of utmost importance, for it had become impossible to control the laxity with which the Portuguese behaved and practised their faith. "The Portuguese change in quality and nation on arriving in this land," says Nunes, and "adjust their lifestyles according to the manner of the land, desiring nothing more than to follow lust." He recommends the destruction of temples and Gentile idols in order to build up "churches with Saints". It was wrong to allow the locals to continue in their idolatry, which had resulted in the Portuguese taking part in temple festivals and contributing to their financial sustenance. The Christianisation of locals would prevent these un-Christian practices. The bishop argued: "whosoever desires to live on this island and desires to keep their lands and their houses must be Christian, and if not, leave the island."

Bishop Nunes' conclusion reveals his ideas on the future of the imperial order in such places:

> Your Highness should believe that nothing will survive if they do not turn towards Christ, our Lord, for they have no other way to live if they are taken off the island. Furthermore, if these are not good Christians, their children will be. Their obstinacy would be removed as well, and they would not have to leave the certain for the uncertain, and God would be served, as well as Your Highness, for having been the reason for the salvation of so many lost souls. They would have no difficulty in converting to Christianity, and it is only out of respect for their forefathers, and because of their ancient customs, that they neither believe in nor worship anything. They are easy to manipulate, but I believe that if they do not convert, it is because of our scandalous lifestyle and that we do not practice what we preach.[32]

[32] BPADE, CIX/2–3, M. 3, nº 12 – "Carta do Bispo Dumiense em que dá conta a ElRey", 12 Jan. 1522, 8–9.

The phrases "they neither believe in nor worship anything" and "are easy to manipulate" reveal Nunes' ignorance of the devotional and socio-cultural reality of Tiswadi.[33] Conversion was far more complicated than he believed.

In the 1530s the Franciscan Dom Fernando Vaqueiro occupied the same institutional position.[34] He had arrived in India in 1532, spent some time in Hurmuz between 1536 and 1537, and was a member of the Franciscan Province of Piety. This Franciscan province was the result of a Spanish spiritual reform which split into several branches at the beginning of the sixteenth century. The branches were called "Discalced", "Friars of the Gospel", "Friars of Piety", "Friars of Our Lady of Light", "Custodians of the Estremadura", and so on. Eleven of the "twelve apostles" that went to New Spain, charged with the responsibility of converting Amerindians, were natives of the province of St Gabriel and shared the spirituality of the friars who departed for India in 1532.[35]

The Portuguese branch of this spiritual order originated in Spain's Trujillo, the city of Francisco Pizarro, conqueror of Peru. In Portugal they settled in the lands of the Duke of Braganza.[36]

[33] On this devotional context, see Heras, "Pre-Portuguese Remains"; Pissurlencar, *Goa pré-portuguesa*; G. Pereira, *An Outline of Pre-Portuguese*; R.G. Pereira, *Goa – Hindu Temples*; Vasantamadhava, "Gove–Karnataka Cultural Contacts"; Mitragotri, *Socio Cultural History*. See also Chapter 4 of the PhD dissertation that served as a basis for the present book: A.B. Xavier, *A Invenção de Goa*, PhD Thesis; also A.B. Xavier, "Katholischen Orientalismus".

[34] IAN/TT, Corpo Cronológico, Part I, Mç. 50, n°. 52 – "Carta do Bispo D. Fernando, dando parte a ElRey", 12 Dec. 1532.

[35] This idea was put forward by Andrés Martín, "Primeros pasos comunes"; Andrés Martín, "La espiritualidade franciscana". Quiñones instructed the "twelve apostles" to follow the rule of the Provinces of Los Angeles, St Gabriel, and of the Piety: Andrés Martín, "Primeros pasos comunes", 879. On this subject, see also Phelan, *The Millennial Kingdom,* 44ff.; Duverger, *La conversion des Indiens,* 33ff., 154; Bernand and Gruzinski, *Histoire du Nouveau Monde,* I, 157ff., 357ff.

[36] The Bragança family in Portugal had matrimonial links with families of this region: Rosa,"D. Jaime, Duque de Bragança", 325.

Dom Jaime, the Duke, intended to become a friar too, against the will of King Dom Manuel, himself a partisan of the Observant Franciscans, whom he expected would unify the Franciscan family. His son, King Dom João III, would instead support the reformed branches of the Franciscans – such as those of the Province of Piedade – helping them found new monasteries and select members of the province for prestigious ecclesiastic honours.[37]

Friar Fernando Vaqueiro received high praise in the *Chronica da Provincia da Piedade* (Chronicle of the Province of Piety). During his stay in India he attempted to reform the Portuguese, convert idolaters, and reduce the number of "schismatics".[38] In the *Memorias* by Bravo de Morais, we are told that this bishop acted "with much zeal in reforming the practices and conversion of the faithless."[39] Nevertheless, by 1530 a good part of his functions had been transferred to Vicar-General Miguel Vaz. Vaz was the vicar chosen to carry out the work of the first Bishop of Goa, Francisco de Melo,[40] and his arrival in Goa – which coincided with the elevation of the city of Goa to the head of the diocese – marks the beginning of the second phase of this first period.

Vaz occupied his position between 1533 and 1547, the year in which he was, apparently, assassinated. Given Francisco de Melo's

[37] These were the cases of Dom Diogo da Silva, Bishop of Ceuta, future Archbishop of Braga and General-Inquisitor, as well as of three bishops sent to India: Fernando Vaqueiro, Juan de Albuquerque, and Gaspar de Leão, despite the last having done his duty after the monarch's death and adhering only then to the Reform. On this question, see Rosa, "D. Jaime de Bragança"; and Strathern, "O papel da Província da Piedade". Rosa refers, for example, to the dialogue between Carlos V and Friar Francisco da Gatta, of the convent in Borba, Portugal, whom the emperor would ask for advice during the campaign in Tunes: Rosa, "D. Jaime de Bragança", 325.

[38] Monforte, *Chronica da Provincia da Piedade*, 397.

[39] BNP, Cod. 176 – Notícias do arcebispado de Goa, fls. 97v–98. See also IAN/TT, Corpo Cronológico, Part I, Mç. 50, nº 52 – "Carta do Bispo D. Fernando, dando parte a ElRey", 12 Dec. 1532; Schurhammer, *Orientalia*, 157, 159.

[40] Dias, *Correntes do Sentimento Religioso*, Vol. 1, 187–8; Moreira, *A Arquitectura do Renascimento*, 236–7.

death before he had even left for Goa, and Vaqueiro's destitution, Vaz enjoyed a wide range of powers until the arrival of the first resident bishop in Goa in 1539.

Little is known about Vaz's life before India. The *Memorias Eccleziasticas* affirms that he was a clergyman of São Pedro. Other testimonies suggest he studied Canon Law at the University of Salamanca alongside the best doctors of that school, notably Domingos de Soto and Francisco Vitoria. This provides an insight into his spiritual universe. He, as well as the other clergymen who travelled with him to India, were "disciples of the spirit of Father Master Avilla". The other clerics of note with him were Father Simão Vaz, martyred in 1535 on the island of Moro; Father Gaspar Coelho, who went to Mylapore; and Father Vicente da Veiga, who went to Malacca. These clergymen were entirely abreast of the spiritualities developed in the Spanish monarchy, tied mainly to the Grenadan experience.[41] These small indicators point to the existence of a rather well-knit group that the monarchy wanted to send to such places, their leader being almost uniformly complemented by representatives of the Portuguese Crown.[42]

What was Vaz's role in the project of converting the locals to Christianity? The most important report he sent to the king of Portugal is lost, but there is a résumé of it in the Portuguese archives. In it Vaz asked the monarch that his proposals be taken up with the bishop so that, when the latter settled down in Goa, he was already armed with determination to execute the wishes and powers of the Crown.[43]

[41] The spreading of Ávila's spirituality is generally attributed to Friar Luís de Granada, who was in Portugal in 1550. Cf. Dias, *Correntes do Sentimento Religioso,* Vol. 1, 173–4; M.I.R. Rodrigues, "Fray Luis de Granada", 728ff.; M.I.R. Rodrigues, "Frei Luís de Granada".

[42] Schurhammer, *Francisco Xavier*, Vol. 3, 202–3. This would be a constant until the end of Dom João III"s reign. A group from the Piety was also sent to evangelise Ceylon: F.F. Lopes, *Os Franciscanos*, 7–74.

[43] Published in *Gavetas*, Vol. 20, 87–192. The codex with this report also contains the decisions made relating to the requests made by the general vicar. Next to each request, one can find the answer by Pedro Alcáçova Carneiro.

Vaz explained his plans of reform and the baptisms he had performed.[44] Like Duarte Nunes a decade earlier, he linked the fates of the "newly converted" with those of the Estado da Índia. He requested that the king appoint an official who would be "like a father to these Christians and takes special care of them," protecting them from the vexations of landowners,[45] but also from other kinds of oppression. He drew particular attention to the arrest of "new Christians . . . for being found around town after the curfew bell rang, and other things of this sort," leaving them "very poor for reasons of the penalties".[46]

The Pai dos Cristãos – or Father of Christians, an official authorised to protect and control the new Christians of Goa – would also have the right to take "the children of these Christians and put them in jobs such as caulkers, of which there are supposedly no more than ten or twelve . . .". Besides, Vaz proposed that converted Indians take on other jobs, such as those of blacksmiths, turners, and carpenters.

Protect, integrate, and guide. Guide the way towards proper behaviour. The brotherhood of the spirit that the Pai dos Cristãos evoked was a community that allowed for the establishment and consolidation of bonds between the locally converted and the colonising community. It also put in place vertical links between the recently converted with the Portuguese official who protected them. It was the overlap of this new spiritual community with the pre-existing one – the effort to replace the former with the latter – that was the objective of evangelisation. In time this

[44] He had already visited Cannanore, Kochi, and Goa, noting the need for more alms and wages. The first were given to him, and the second sent to the captain-general.

[45] A recurring theme can be seen here and everywhere where evangelisation was going on: the clash of interests between missionaries and the laity.

[46] Another "vexation" was perpetrated on the Christian women of the land – forcing them to go to prayer even when there was no need. To avoid this situation, Vaz compiled a roster of all those who already knew the doctrine, then let them "go about their business": Schurhammer, *Orientalia*, 173.

overlap would allow the entry of the Indian community into the "*curral católico*", the Catholic stable – to use a widely understood metaphor of the time.

Vaz's proposals were adjusted with the constitutions *Altitude* by Paul III in 1537, and later the brief *Misericordiarum patur* by Pius V in 1567. Both defended the view that the converted be treated as "children of God" and cared for with "paternal affection".[47] There was also a convergence between papal decisions concerning the New Christian and the legal framing of "children" within the Portuguese realm. As António Manuel Hespanha has highlighted, the authorities assumed the protection of those who, on account of their incapacity for independence, could not personally defend their own interests.[48]

The analogy with the New Christians in Portugal also put the Christians of India in a state of perennial transition. They were eternally on the path of the acknowledgement of their independence, or, to use Victor Turner's concept, in a state of liminality.[49] The role of the Pai dos Cristãos was essential to fortify the relationship between the colonists and the colonised, assuring the "permanent infantile treatment" of the latter, and, as a result, the former's legitimacy and right to govern them. From 1537 the Estado da Índia could count on this office, the only one of its kind in the Iberian empires, to work as an interface between the political and ecclesiastic orders and the neo-Christian community.[50]

The problems posed to the demographic minority in the Estado da Índia could explain the immediate establishment of the office

[47] The House of the Catechumens appeared at more or less the same time with a similar intent: to enable the transition of identity to be softer.

[48] Hespanha, "A família", 180.

[49] Turner, *The Ritual Process*. About an enforcement of this over the new Christians, see Kriegel, "De la question des 'nouveaux-chrétiens'"; on the relation between the new Christians and the newly converted, see A.B. Xavier, "De converso a novamente convertido".

[50] On this office, see *O Livro do Pai dos Cristãos*; R.R.L. Fernandes, "O 'Pai dos Cristãos'"; D'Costa, *The Christianisation of the Goan Islands*; Araújo, "O Pai dos Cristãos".

of the Pai dos Cristãos. A testament to this possibility comes from a petition by Rui Barbudo, *vereador* (councillor) of the Municipal Council of the city of Goa, the first Pai dos Cristãos.[51] Barbudo, one of the few laymen to occupy this office, asked the Câmara of Goa to concede a neighbourhood where the new Christians could "be taught and accustomed to the things that are necessary for them to learn and know of our faith, [which is necessary] for their salvation."[52] He also asked the king for provisions to verbally adjudicate ongoing conflicts between Christians and non-Christians.[53]

Besides this, Miguel Vaz desired that "by their own will" the local natives should want "to become Christians and ask for their baptism." The king was in favour of free will conversions, revealing that a kind of Erasmian Christian humanism characterised this monarch's spirituality. Diogo Teive, a humanist, said the king took "great pleasure" from this.[54]

Nevertheless, one senses in Vaz's words a tension similar to António Louro's. Both were troubled by the divergence between the ideological commitment to the principle of conversion as a result of divine grace, and the reality of human interventions to facilitate the same. While defending the principle of voluntary conversions, the Vicar-General simultaneously initiated other strategies that aimed to persuade Indians to convert. "Well-trained" vicars and priests were fundamental to the effort. They were the "weapons" needed to "subjugate the land" and to "have access to

[51] In 1547, Dom João III was informed that Rui Barbudo, the Pai dos Cristãos, encountered many obstacles thrown in his way by the king's officials while trying to do his job.

[52] The Goa Municipal Council would grant some lands for the realisation of this proposal: HAG, nº 7737, fls 72–4; see also S. Gonçalves, *Primeira Parte da História*, Vol. 1, 75–6. In 1550, it was the viceroy who granted a piece of land administered by the church of the Chorão for poor Christians: D'Costa, *The Christianisation of the Goan Islands*, 145.

[53] IAN/TT, Corpo Cronológico, Part I, Mç. 81, nº 116 – "Carta de Rui Barbudo dando conta a ElRey", 6 Dec. 1548.

[54] Costa, Discurso de Diogo de Teive, 108.

many bodies and souls". The autonomy of the ecclesiastic structure was crucial to the success of conversion as well.[55]

In 1539 the arrival of Bishop Juan de Albuquerque, also a Franciscan of Piety, allowed the project of conversion to bear fruit. Coming from the small town of Albuquerque in Spanish Extremadura – site of the central convent of the province of St Gabriel – the future bishop was part of a group of monks that included João de Guadalupe and Pedro Melgar, progenitors of the Province of Piedade. He held the office of Provincial twice, in 1526 and 1532, and in that capacity took part in the General Congregation of Assisi (Italy) in 1526, subsequently visiting the provinces of Portugal and the Algarve. Three years later, Albuquerque was the confessor of Dom Jaime, Duke of Braganza, who would recommend the friar to the king, so that he became the monarch's confessor too in 1535. In 1537 Albuquerque was nominated the Bishop of Goa and in 1538 was "consecrated" – i.e. officially received the office – in the convent of São Francisco in Lisbon. He departed the same year for India in the fleet of Viceroy Dom Garcia de Noronha. With him travelled a priest, Diogo Borba, of the Province of Piety, with the status of a preacher, and Friar Vicente Lagos who was from the same province.[56]

The *cursus honorum* (career) of Dom Juan de Albuquerque accompanied a set of ongoing changes at the very heart of the Franciscan family in Portugal under the tutelage of Dom João III. The king was interested in making the Portuguese Franciscans independent of the larger family to which they belonged, connecting them directly with the minister-general in Rome. He aimed to

[55] Schurhammer, *Orientalia*, 174.

[56] BNP, Cod. 176 – Notícias do arcebispado de Goa, fl. 98v.; IAN/TT, Corpo Cronológico, Part II, Mç. 221, nº 172 – "Certidão do juramento que prestou D. João de Albuquerque", 30 Feb. 1538; Monforte, *Chronica da Provincia da Piedade*, 398. Also Paiva, *Os Bispos de Portugal e do Império*, 49, 213ff. For Félix Lopes, Father Diogo Borba was also in the circle of Father João de Ávila, having probably studied theology in Salamanca: see Trindade, *Conquista Espiritual do Oriente*, Vol. I, 269, fn. 5.

reduce the privileges of the religious orders, reform their monasteries, and improve the behaviour of their friars. It is unknown to what extent sending this Franciscan to India – at a time when the king was negotiating the arrival of an Italian general commissioner to visit the provinces of the kingdom – was part of a co-ordinated strategy. However, reorganisation of the Franciscan missions of the Estado da Índia took place during Friar João Calvo's stay. The Custody of São Tomé is of that period too.[57]

The episcopal duties of Dom Juan de Albuquerque started with the constitution of the church of St Catherine as a See. A serious jurisdictional conflict arose immediately as the bishop refused to recognise Fr. Diogo de Morais, Vicar of the See, as the dean of the chapter.[58] The Order of Christ nominated the canons of the chapter of the See. However, Juan de Albuquerque wanted to establish his supremacy and clarify the jurisdictional hierarchy.

Albuquerque was unable to rid himself of the Vicar-General, Miguel Vaz, as quickly as he had Father Diogo de Morais. Vaz himself nursed the hope of being named a bishop. This possibility is evident from a letter sent in 1539 by Dom João de Castro to Dom João III, where Castro says Vaz is "abounding with virtues", concluding "that I know of no head in these current times where a mitre would be better suited."[59]

[57] In this context, see Félix Lopes' study on Friar André da Insua: F.F. Lopes, *Colectânea de Estudos,* Vol. 2, 158ff., 165–6. Many letters sent by Dom João III indicate the monarch's efforts to try and "organise" the order of San Francisco. Cf. IAN/TT, Col. São Vicente, L. 6 – Cartas da Embaixada do Comendador-Mor em Roma, fls 292ff.; L. 9 – Várias Cartas e Provisões do rei D. João III e da rainha D. Catarina, fls 402ff.; L. 10 – Cartas e papéis variados da rainha D. Catarina, fls 46ff.

[58] IAN/TT, Corpo Cronológico, Part I, Mç. 64, nº 138 – "Auto de Protesto que o Bispo de Gôa mandou fazer", 6 June 1539; Mç. 65, nº 72 – "Instrumento de testemunhas que mandou tirar o Bispo de Gôa", 6 Sept. 1539; Mç. 66, nº 53 – Inquirição que se tirou conta o Padre Diogo Moraes Vigairo", 16 Sept. 1539.

[59] *Apud* Correia, *D. Francisco de Almeida,* 349–51. Also the chapter of the See of Goa held the vicar-general in high esteem: IAN/TT, Corpo

Despite their similarity in perspective on conversions, the relationship of these two was not amicable.[60] Some testimonies insinuate that the prelate had been behind Vaz's death by poisoning in Chaul in 1547. This account is, however, denied by others who pin the blame on locals.

Albuquerque fulfilled his obligations through preaching, administering sacraments, reforming practices, and defending the integrity of the faith. It was in this context that an assembly formed by Franciscan theologians and Dominicans, as well as by a representative of the secular clergy, asked for the establishment of a Goan inquisition that could solve minor cases. The more pressing matters went to Lisbon directly under an entirely different institutional structure.[61]

Albuquerque's arrival also witnessed a series of measures to forge the "tool[s] . . . to reform and create another new world". The plans he conceived were similar to ongoing processes in the Iberian kingdoms and the Spanish colonies on the American continent.[62] By incorporating previous proposals, Albuquerque proposed smooth options as well as darker ways to persuade a more significant number of people to convert. The easy paths included the award of "prizes and honours" to those who converted. Punishment could be expected by those who "persisted stubbornly in their ideologies".[63]

Cronológico, Part I, Mç. 75, nº 109 – "Carta do Cabido da Sé de Gôa expondo a ElRey o grande zelo, e virtudes do Vigario Geral", 3 Dec. 1544.

[60] IAN/TT, *Gavetas*, nº 15, Mç. 12, nº 35, 414.

[61] Monforte, *Chronica da Provincia da Piedade*, 400–1. On the period immediately before the foundation of the Inquisition, Priolkar, *The Goan Inquisition*; and Cunha, *A Inquisição no Estado da Índia*.

[62] Bernand and Gruzinski, *Histoire du Nouveau Monde*, Vol. 1, 357ff., 373–401; Gruzinski and Wachtel, "Cultural Interbreedings", *passim*.

[63] HAG, Livro 4º of the *Registos da Casa dos Contos*, fl. 236v.; Livro de Alvarás, nº 1–A, fl. 67v.; *O Livro do "Pai dos Cristãos"*, fls 39v and 106. Statements like, "because it is part of our duty to persuade them to have our Catholic faith" (HAG, Leis a favor da Cristandade, fls 12v.–13), and "as such

The intellectual and spiritual deprecation of local peoples underlay the two methods and was made explicit in the preambles of the norms relating to conversion.[64] These legitimised destruction of the existing religious order, such as its buildings, books, and deities. They also justified the juridical differentiation and distinction between local Christians and those that persisted in their non-Christian beliefs. As a result, the former received substantial privileges aimed at the eventual physical separation of Christians and non-Christians. The latter were to live on the outskirts of the city of Goa, and, if necessary, be expelled from places within the Portuguese jurisdiction. In particular, there were punishments for Brahmans who opposed the new Christians; and those who remained Gentiles had to support members of their family who had converted.

The destruction of all temples on the island of Tiswadi happened in this period.[65] It is not clear whether this was Miguel Vaz's idea, nor if it was he who came up with the idea of transferring to the Christian cult the revenues that had sustained local places of worship. This transfer destroyed the means of survival of the local religious order, and with it part of the social order. The

---

they would incite others to become Christians as well" (HAG, Livro 4.º de Registos Antigos, fl. 105), structured decrees, *cartas régias*, and royal orders.

[64] In 1541, this preamble says: "I let it be known to those that read this, wishing to worship God, remember these people and their land, that for so long had been subject to the devil and his idols": published in CR-APO, Fasc. 5, Vol. 1, 161. The same idea would later be crystallised in the decrees of the First Provincial Council, published by Cunha Rivara in his *Archivo Oriental Portuguez.* The 9th decree of the first Action said that Christians were ordained by God to "completely destroy all the idols, temples, and places that offered worship to false Gods": CR–APO, Fasc. 4, *1st. Council*, 1567, Action 2, d. 9, 12–14.

[65] Paulo da Trindade claims that the Franciscans played a leading role in this project: Trindade, *Conquista Espiritual do Oriente*, Vol. 1, 266, fn. 1. Sebastião Gonçalves accredited Father Borba with the initial idea, after discussing with Miguel Vaz, Pero Fernandes, Cosme Annes, and, finally, with the bishop and the vedor da Fazenda – the governor being absent at the time: Gonçalves, *Primeira Parte da História*, Part I, 120–1.

rents from lands dedicated to temples now funded the building of Christian churches, the purchase of cult objects, and the payments to priests. Once such lands had been attached, the older system gave way to a Christianised order. Now, the *fabricas* – a legal entity that assembled the resources required to build, conserve, and repair a church and pay for the cult – managed properties and brotherhoods and chapels, as was customary in the Christian order, and contributed to the dignity of the Christian cult. The construction of new temples and the restoration of old temples was prohibited.

The Confraria da Santa Fé (Confraternity of the Holy Faith), the homonymous seminary and college, and the Casa dos Catecúmenos (House of the Catechumens) complemented the processes under way. This confraternity came to be the place where the conversion of the local populations was conceived, argued, and promoted. Probably an idea espoused by Miguel Vaz and Diogo Borba, the Confraria da Santa Fé was the driving force behind the conversion process. New Christians were to be protected by the Crown, given jobs, and rendered exempt from taxes. Their orphans would be protected, their dead buried.[66] Finally, Christian slaves could not be sold to Muslims.[67] The brotherhood built a school where new Christians were taught and instructed, and a seminary.[68] In the long term this seminary contributed considerably to the increase in and reproduction of Christianity.[69]

[66] A normative similarity can be seen between the laws relating to Jews and the new Christians, found in the *Ordenações Afonsinas e Manuelinas* and the laws sent to Goa relating to the "Gentiles" and to the newly converted: see A.B. Xavier, "De converso a novamente convertido".

[67] *Documentação Ultramarina Portuguesa* (hereafter DUP), Vol. 1, 542ff.; IAN/TT, Corpo Cronológico, Part I, Mç. 71, nº 31 – "Carta da Confraria da Conversão da Fé", 14 Dec. 1541; D'Costa, *The Christianisation of Goan Islands*, 138ff.

[68] The orphanage of Our Lady of the Light had been founded by Franciscans a year earlier. Near Baçaim, this institution aimed to instruct forty orphan children, expecting them to be, later, assistants to the missionaries: D'Costa, *The Christianisation of Goan Islands*, 138.

[69] Five years before, in Tlatelolco, Mexico, another Franciscan bishop, Juan de Zumárraga, and the viceroy, António de Mendoza, established a school

All these spaces institutionalised conversion, enabling the expansion of the Christian faith to other parts of the Estado da Índia where the Franciscans had already established churches, convents, residencies, schools, and brotherhoods.[70] Later called Apostle of the Indies, Francis Xavier now disembarked in Goa.

The figure of Francis Xavier, nobleman from Navarre and member of the circle of Ignatius of Loyola, inevitably crosses the path of those who study conversion processes in sixteenth-century Asia.[71] Even though Alessandro Valignano was, in many ways, more critical than Xavier, Valignano did not have the same kind of social impact on collective memory. [72]

---

with similar duties. At around the same time, Vasco de Quiroga founded the Santa Fé hospitals in the same places. See Phelan, *The Millennial Kingdom,* 47; Bernard and Gruzinski, *Histoire du Nouveau Monde,* Vol. 1, 392ff. A comparison of the processes ongoing in the Spanish possessions of Mexico and Peru, at the same time, makes it crucial to be able to understand the Goan experience: see also, Wachtel, *La Vision des Vaincus*; Gruzinski, *La colonisation de l'imaginaire*; Mills, "The Limits of Religious Coercion"; Gruzinski and Wachtel, "Cultural Interbreedings".

[70] In this context, at least six churches, three convents, and two colleges were built outside the territories of Goa (in Kochi, Cannanore, Mylapore, Nagapattinam, Bassein, Thana, Chaul); and nine churches, one convent, and one seminar in the territories of Goa. All were under the charge of the Franciscans or secular clergies: cf. Farinha, *A Expansão da Fé,* 70ff. The conversion of the Parava community on the Fishery coast added to these projects.

[71] On the role Xavier played in the Portuguese national memory, see the interesting reflection by Alonso Romo, "A 'lusitanização' de S. Francisco Xavier".

[72] The best biography of Xavier is still Schurhammer's, *Francisco Xavier.* The fact that Xavier visited all those that he knew to be "responsible" for the local political life suggests his personal sensitivity to these realms of jurisdiction: Schurhammer, *S. Francisco Xavier,* Vol. 2. From 1545 on, Xavier spent more time outside the Estado da Índia than inside its borders. His trips to the capital of the state were of an administrative character (1542 arrival in Goa; 1542/1544 Fishery Coast; 1545/1548 Malacca and Moluccas; 1548–1551 Japan; 1552 to the borders of China). Xavier's mission developed

As a member of a religious institution that had just been officially recognised by the pope, and nominated Apostolic delegate to India by Pope Paul III himself, Xavier arrived in Goa when the religious structures previously mentioned had already begun to consolidate. Given the jurisdictional culture dominant at the time, he had to negotiate with the established authorities. It is questionable, therefore, to suggest – as is dominant in the scholarship – that it was with Xavier's arrival in India that the missionary process began.[73] The memory of his travels, his pragmatism, and his proximity to the Portuguese Crown contributed to this image. (Which is not to underestimate the ability of the Jesuits to construct memory.) By going beyond the "borders" of the Estado da Índia – forging not only into Indian territory but also Japan and even the Chinese hinterland, Xavier developed the basis for new missionary areas, marked this time by the priority of the Jesuit order. His acts were heroic, contributing to the aura of singularity that was rapidly developed around not only Xavier – who would come to be proclaimed a saint – but also his companions.[74]

The sympathy of the Portuguese royal family on the one hand, and that of the Papacy on the other, was of considerable assistance to the Jesuits in navigating jurisdictional conflicts with the secular

---

primarily in these other places: see also J.F. Marques, "A evangelização da Índia", 231–59. On the rivalries with other religious orders, see Leitão, "Os primórdios das rivalidades".

[73] Manoel, *Missões dos Jesuítas*; Plattner, *Quand l'Europe cherchait l'Asie*; Souza, *Goa Medieval*; Souza and Borges, *Jesuits in India*; Borges, *The Economics of the Goan Jesuits*; Lach, *Asia in the Making of Europe*, Vol. 1. For a critical analysis of this pre-understanding, see A.B. Xavier, "Itinerários franciscanos".

[74] The letter that Cosme Annes sent to the king on 30 November 1547 provides a glimpse that the Jesuits who were going to India (with the exception of Francis Xavier) were not up for the challenge: IAN/TT, *Gavetas*, nº 15, Mç. 12, n.º35, 414. The following year, Tomé Lobo let the king know of the great work that Xavier was doing with his sermons and doctrinal catechism: IAN/TT, Corpo Cronológico, Part I, Mç. 81, n.º62 – "Carta de Thome Lobo dando conta a ElRey", 13 Oct. 1548.

and regular clergy,[75] as also with other administrative-political bodies. This apart, these Jesuit missionaries had about them the ardour of neophytes, so that they searched tirelessly for solutions that would make the conversion process more efficient. They encountered and overcame problems relating to communication, memory, and the construction of identity. They developed an image of themselves in contrast with those of other religious orders whose goals were similar to their own but who, from the Jesuit perspective, had achieved nothing as much as the Jesuits.[76] This Jesuitic self-representation has seduced many historians into according the Society of Jesus a primacy in the sixteenth century that needs to be nuanced.

In this respect, the Goan case is emblematic. While Francis Xavier wandered through lands outside the Estado da Índia, those who organised and carried out conversions remained in the capital. This means that while Xavier reflected on the conversion process, and wrote and communicated his thoughts, a trio comprising Bishop Juan de Albuquerque, Miguel Vaz, and Diogo Borba did much of the work alongside Franciscans and laypersons such as Cosme Annes and Castelo Branco. There had already been complaints for decades on the lack of foot soldiers in the task of conversion. Therefore, the arrival of the Jesuits was welcomed. However, those already *in situ* did not await Jesuit guidance. Thus, if some were happy, others felt threatened. Among the latter were the Franciscans, whose privileged position had till now been entirely uncontested.

The Franciscans had already sought to fortify and solidify their position locally. In 1537 the pope granted them several privileges. At the beginning of the 1540s, a brief of Paul III recognised them

[75] Strathern highlights the competition between the Jesuits and the Franciscans of the Piety: Strathern, "A Província da Piedade".

[76] On how the Jesuits developed their identity construction, along with their relations with the Asian missions, see Ines Županov's excellent studies: Županov, "Le repli du religieux"; Županov, *Disputed Mission*; Županov, *Missionary Tropics*; Županov, "A História do Futuro".

as the Custody of São Tomé, renewing privileges granted by Adrian VI in the Papal Bull *Omni Moda* in 1522.[77] However, the Friars of Piedade wanted to constitute separate Custody too. In a letter of 1547 they requested privileges and exemptions identical to those enjoyed by the Observants and the Jesuits. They did not manage to obtain these concessions.

Alongside a secular hierarchy, Franciscans and Jesuits came to be the frontrunners of evangelisation. The processes they set in motion were not limited to conversion. They entwined political with religious power along with the secular hierarchy and the regular clergy. In this context the importance of Juan de Albuquerque's role is undeniable.[78]

In 1544 a pastoral letter of Albuquerque divided Goa into four parishes, each with a children's school.[79] Four years later another pastoral letter prohibited all Gentile rituals and urged the exclusion of any idolater from gaining access to public office. Furthermore, in a provision of 1550 the bishop underlined that his job was to "work toward the annihilation of this evil idolatry," commissioning the Franciscans and Jesuits, as well as Father Belchior Gonçalves and Vicar Simão Travassos, to demolish the "public pagodas" and "secret ones". He added that "no others can be built, not from stone, copper, or any other kind of metal." These officials had to ensure "that all over the island, there shall be no kind of public

[77] Almost all of these were confirmed in 1567 with the permission granted by Pope Pio V for the exercise of the *officium parochi*, against the Council of Trent (session XXIV, C. 13: session XIV, C. 11; session VII, CC. 6 and 7). See F. Coutinho, *Le Régime Paroissial*; also Trindade, *Conquista Espiritual do Oriente,* Vol. 1, Chapter 63.

[78] Friar Diogo de Bermudes, for example, was of the opinion that the prelate did not do enough: IAN/TT, Corpo Cronológico, Part I, Mç. 81, nº 101 – "Carta de Fr. Diogo Bermudes dando parte a ElRey do deploravel estado", 6 Dec. 1548; Mç. 87, nº 45 – "Carta de Fr. Diogo Bermudes expondo a D. Bernardo Bispo de S. Thomé o deploravel estado em que se achava a India", 31 Dec. 1551.

[79] F. Coutinho, *Le Régime Paroissial*, 36; C. Figueiredo, *As Communidades de Goa*, 105.

gentilic feasts, nor may residents [of the city] welcome in their home Brahman preachers from the mainland." They also had to undertake searches "in the homes of all Brahmans and Gentiles when there is the slightest inkling that they are idolatrous." Worth noting is that this pastoral letter identifies private spaces as locations where idolatry could continue discreetly, and thus merited control.[80]

The suppression of visual signs of Gentileness led to the expulsion of the principal Brahmans, the destruction of temples, a prohibition on the construction of new temples and the repair of old ones, as well as to the forbidding of "*festas gemtilicas pubricas*" (public Gentile festivals). The inspection of homes in search of wrongdoers became frequent. Finally, several laws limited non-Christians from holding certain offices.

Another group of decisions defended other solutions favouring Christianity. Vaz suggested that converted women be permitted to receive their parental inheritance. The idea appealed particularly to a group with reduced succession rights in the local order. Christians had to make "sacrifices to help and favour this spirituality [of conversion]," for the newly converted lost "all the help and support of their family," who "are enemies to them. If they are unable to find help, they will lose themselves."[81] In addition, baptism and attending the principal sacraments (outward manifestations of adherence to the Christian order) were encouraged not only in the territories in Tiswadi but also in Salcete, Bardez, Bassein, Chaul, and Kochi.[82]

[80] *Colecção São Lourenço*, Vol. 2, 391–4. On the same topic, see some of the decrees of the Provincial Councils defending similar measures: CR–APO, Fasc. 4, *1st Council*, Action 2, d. 6, 11; d. 9, 12–14; *3rd. Council*, Action 2, s. 4, 123; *4rd Council*, d. 7, 189.

[81] On this, see the report of Father Miguel Vaz published in DI, Vol. 1, 63–89. From the late-Roman period, when conversion and baptism implicated changes in inheritance rights: MacCormack, "Sin, Citizenship", 659ff.

[82] The external dimension of conversion, expressed through practising Christian rites, is separated from its internal form, the faith itself: Asad,

In this respect, the bishop was in harmony with the vicar-general.[83] The king continued to spur Vaz on towards effecting more conversions, saying that "in all that pertains to conversion, you should take great care and diligence to ensure that they proceed well." Dom João III did also suggest that the vicar-general engage in conversions "without scandal, if possible".

Despite the substantial support that they received from both the monarch and the viceregal government, the ecclesiastical authorities in Goa considered it insufficient enough to complain that "one cannot maintain the body without support from the head." More than once, they accused the government of not being severe enough with the non-Christian population. The bishop complained to the effect that had he received the necessary support, "the fathers of the Congregation of Jesus and I as their companion . . . in one year, or the very latest two, would make this whole land Christian."[84]

The truth is that the conversion of the locals would pick up a more intense rhythm in the 1550s, when the Society of Jesus arrived in the empire armed with exemptions and privileges.[85] In the previous decades, the few conversions that had happened were in the socially marginal groups. Now, the elites were the goal. These elites did not have many options – they could either

---

"Comments on Conversion", 263–74. The attempt to achieve both was the ultimate goal of the missionaries, but only accomplished after a long process of Christianisation.

[83] Instead of responding directly to the points enumerated by the vicar-general, the *Instructio* contains materials related to the Christian cult: the state of Christianity, the priests' provisions, and the construction and upkeep of religious buildings – in addition to building colleges and schools that would guarantee the training and reproduction of the Christian ideal: *Instructio* of King Dom João III to Miguel Vaz, 1546, DI, Vol. 1, 90–107.

[84] Responding to another letter by Dom João III at the end of 1549, the bishop praised the Jesuits, going so far as to say, "I give them all my authority and power, as such they can go wherever they please": DI, Vol. 1, 300–5.

[85] Costa, "A diáspora missionária", 274–5.

convert or risk losing their privileged social status (more on this in Chapter 5). Social downgrading and expulsion applied to the defiant. Conversely, those who converted retained their honours and privileges.

From this perspective one can see why the bishop wrote to the king in 1548 detailing the conversion of Loqu, one of the most important men in the city of Goa.[86] The text distinguishes itself by its metaphoric style. First, it compares Loqu to Paul in Damascus, "lavishing the Gentiles with alms, doing this since they had not yet made themselves Christians." The writer establishes the same comparison to describe the moment of conversion: "God arrives, casts him down from his horse, which was the honour on which he rode, and gives him some lashings," and then "some blows inside his heart". Furthermore, according to Juan de Albuquerque, Loqu had shed the scales of idolatry, pagodas, ceremonies, stubbornness, and unfaithfulness, ensuring that his eyes had turned to see the "potency of the soul, knowledge, memory, and will." The transition from the state of blindness to sight heralded that total conversion in which "understanding occupies itself with learning the articles of the faith; memory in learning them, and desire in loving its precepts."

Although the bishop invited the monarch to protect (or punish) the local elites, believing this the best way to encourage them to convert, the prelate did not hesitate to insist on the role of divine grace as the ultimate cause for all conversions. Grace was the cause for Paul, painted on the altarpiece of the Confraria da Santa Fé,[87] and likewise for Loqu.

[86] IAN/TT, Corpo Cronológico, Part II, Mç. 241, nº 90 – "Carta o Fr. João de Albuquerque Bº de Goa dando parte a ElRey bautizar hum gentio chamado Loquce", in DI, Vol. 1, 325–7. There are other letters to Dom João III. In one from 1548, Albuquerque told the king that Friar João de Villa do Conde had gone to Lisbon with news of Christianity in Ceylon and its conversion: IAN/TT, Corpo Cronológico, Part I, Mç. 81, nº 99 – Carta de Fr. João de Albuquerque, Bispo de Gôa", 6 Dec. 1548.

[87] DUP, Vol. 1, 542.

Concerning the conversion of the king of Tanor (in Kerala), who refused Portuguese dress, the same prelate would back up the argument presented by this king, who had indicated that he could maintain his dress "until he converts the leaders of his nayres [Nairs . . .] to the faith of Jesus Christ." Albuquerque thought that the king of Tanor would, one day, break "the Brahman line, and would destroy the old garments, and remain dressed in Christian ones, just as the knight Saint Sebastian did."[88]

These episodes demonstrate the constant tension between theological rigour and pragmatism even in the Franciscan territory. Awareness of the ubiquity of this tension helps us understand the variations, bad timing, and even the evident contradictions in the conversion processes.

The eventual realisation that the conversion of the native populations was taking longer than expected or hoped for resulted in greater pragmatism – the Jesuit strategy. One assumption was that conversion was the preliminary step that would lead to the real and immediate objective: Christianising the newly converted. In what follows I demonstrate that this pragmatism became apparent in the escalation of violent options, as against softer ones, culminating in the physical separation of Christians from non-Christians, and the attempt to expel all families that chose to remain non-Christian.[89]

[88] IAN/TT, Corpo Cronológico, Part I, Mç. 77, nº 12 – "Carta de D. João, Principe do Ceilão", 15 Nov. 1545. On a report on the topic, Dom Juan de Albuquerque was favourably inclined to this conversion because of the impact that it could have: BA, Cod., 51–VII–22, fls 179–181v. In his opinion, this king was "extremely powerful in number of subjects". See this bishop's letter in DI, Vol. 1, 532–48. For a synthesis on this process, see L. Albuquerque, *Alguns Casos da Índia Portuguesa,* II, 7–55.

[89] The inferfaces between the anti-Jewish and anti-Gentile discourses have already been studied: A.B. Xavier, "A Invenção de Goa", PhD thesis, Chapter 2. See, also, the *topoi* that circulated in the anti-Semitic literature of this period: Azpicuelta Navarro, *Relectio cap.*; Arrais, *Diálogos* – the dialogue on Jewish people; Aragão, *Doutrina Católica*; Aragão, *Extinçam do Judaísmo*; IAN/TT, Armário Jesuítico, Mss. 18 – Pareceres sobre a Gente da Nação; BPADE, Col. Manizola, Cod. 48, nº 11 – *Das fábulas de Talmud.*

Incentives for Conversion and the Legal-Political Framework

The project of converting the native populations gained force after it acquired juridical expression. The laws of the period demonstrate a fine-tuning of proposals suggested since the third decade of the sixteenth century. The whole array of laws that emerged between 1540 and 1570 sought to realise more extreme ideas, as against the more harmonious management of social situations earlier.

There were two categories of laws. The first comprised laws aimed to dissuade locals from remaining Gentile. A refusal to convert had all kinds of negative consequences entailing economic, social, political, and cultural marginalisation. They included impoverishing those who resisted, withholding from them the means for survival and access to resources; disruption of family ties; exclusion from cultural practices such as preventing the performance of specific prayers or the practice of various traditions; and prohibition from holding traditional offices.

One of the most effective ways of convincing people to convert had to do with access to property and rights over land – the principal source of wealth among the residents of the villages of Tiswadi, Salcete, and Bardez. The wealthy feared the loss of their lands and the impact such losses would have on their status. In contrast, this was an opportunity for the underprivileged. The new context was their opportunity to escape their ascribed social fate.

Also worth highlighting is the rupture that took place with what had happened during the reign of Dom Manuel. At that time, while affirming that "the lands of Goa are nobody's patrimony, if not of the king and master of the land", the Crown had also confirmed ownership of village lands by locals as long as they were

---

On this literature and its circulation in the kingdom and empire, see M.I.R. Rodrigues, "Literatura e anti–semitismo"; Feitler, *O catolicismo como ideal*; Feitler, "A circulação de obras anti-judaicas". The ubiquitous presence of the New Christian population in the Estado da Índia, primarily studied by José Alberto Tavim, *Judeus e Cristãos-Novos*, sheds some light on this topic.

not Muslim, guaranteeing the continued existence of local institutions.[90]

The Portuguese who married in Goa, to "live there forever", received lands owned by the "Moorish enemies of our holy faith," which permitted them "to have and enjoy the land to better sustain them and their children." The following year another law explained that this decision was to apply only to the lands of Muslims who had abandoned the city.[91] Establishing a homestead and cultivating land were among the most traditional ways of asserting rights of occupation and stimulating the economy.[92] Likewise, in the Portuguese kingdom there was a practice of endowing *casais*, i.e. providing newly-weds with land to settle them where population densities were low. This not only helped increase the population but also to remedy scarce agricultural production.

The first decade of Dom João's reign did not change this arrangement to any particular degree. The Foral de Mexia, 1526 (a Charter of Uses and Customs that assembled a selection of rules and customs that organised the villages of Tiswadi), was part of this kind of policy. By recognising the right of the existing elites to run the villages, the Foral protected the foundations of the local order. The same applies to the meeting in 1541 that united the *gaunkars* of Tiswadi and the Vedor da Fazenda (Exchequer), Fernão Rodrigues de Castelo Branco, after the destruction of the island's temples.[93] The aim was to redirect the revenues previously

[90] The confirmation of the property of the village land, made by Albuquerque, was based on the assumption that these lands already belonged to the king of Portugal by virtue of conquest. This assumption also justified the handing over of lands found in Muslim hands to the *casados*. On this, see Bragança Pereira, *Arquivo Portuguez Oriental* (hereafter BP-APO), Parte I – 3, Part I, 152, and CR-APO, Fasc. 5, Vol. 1, 170–2, n. (A).

[91] A printed version of this law can be found in CR–APO, Fasc. 5, Vol. 1, 12–16, 41–43.

[92] See Seed, *Ceremonies of Possession*, 17–18.

[93] The *gaunkars* occupied the highest positions in the institutional framework of the village. Literature on the *gaunkari* is vast: F.N. Xavier, *Bosquejo Histórico*; F.N. Xavier, *Collecção de Leis Peculiares*; Cunha Rivara, *Brados a favor*

entrusted to the Gentile cult toward the Christian. Declaring that "the rents of the land . . . belonged to them alone," and not "to the king, our Lord," the *gaunkars* agreed to support the Christian cult, but of their own volition. Castelo Branco agreed and guaranteed that there would never be oppression because of "the revenues of said lands".[94]

However, the premises of this system were changing. Governor Martim Afonso de Sousa (1542–1545) transferred such rents to the Jesuits, and in 1550 the Jesuits benefited from "any other estate" that had belonged to the temples.[95] The decision resulted in a substantial backlash from the village elites.

In 1595, the meeting in 1541 and the transfer of the land of the temples to the *gaunkars* came under critique. The Vedor da Fazenda Francisco Paes noticed that it was against the principle that said: "the offers to the divine may not divert to the human." Besides, Paes added, the *gaunkars* had divided the land among themselves, contradicting what Afonso de Albuquerque had declared: "we shall not concede to them more than that which they possess."

The meeting in 1541 is exemplary of the paradoxes of a transitional period. The first three decades of Portuguese presence defended the sanctity of property ownership. In the subsequent period the Portuguese king considered the lands of Tiswadi, Salcete, and Bardez his "property". He claimed the power to

---

das Communidades; Guimarães, *Communidades Indianas*; Baden-Powell, "The Villages of Goa"; Baden-Powell, *The Origin and Growth*; Saldanha, *História de Goa*; Kosambi, "The Village Community"; Kosambi, *An Introduction*; G. Pereira, *An Outline of Pre-Portuguese*; Kulkarni, "Marathi Records"; Gomes, *Village Goa*; Souza, *Goa Medieval*. On the longevity of the corporate institutions in Indian territory, see Majumdar, *Corporate Life*.

[94] That the destination of these revenues was not a matter of consensus is made evident by the legal reports offered in 1625, in which the subject was taken up again. On those discussions, see CR–APO, Fasc. 5, Vol. 1, 65, 161–70.

[95] Cited by Pissurlencar, *Agentes da Diplomacia Portuguesa*, 65.

expropriate and redistribute them as he saw fit and according to criteria he identified as just.[96]

The destruction of the temples and reallocation of their properties and revenue to the Christian cult had multiple effects. They were symbolic in the sense of asserting that the "divine winner" was he to whom their wealth should be dedicated. The political significance was that it established the right of the Crown to intervene in religious matters whenever it so desired.[97] Furthermore, the expulsion of priests and other servants of the temple resulted in a transformation of the social landscape.[98]

The transfer of properties, lands, and money from villages did not stop here. Other *provisões* (provisions) and *alvarás régios* (royal charters) demonstrate that this became a recurrent concern for many reasons. There were changes in the succession regime, in the annual auctions of village wetlands, and in relation to orphans' inheritance – not to mention the resumption of lands of people and villages considered rebellious, such as Carmona, Cuncolim, Assolna, Ambelim, Navelim, Veroda, Velim, Cola, Anjuna, Revora, Nadora, Pirna. In addition, viceroys offered village lands to the *casados* and Crown officials.[99]

[96] On this meeting and its consequences, see CR–APO, Fasc. 5, Vol. 1, 212, 230–4, 336–7; also HAG, nº 7737 – Senado da Câmara – Acórdãos, fls 50, 52, 56, and 75–6.

[97] On this, see CR–APO, Fasc. 5, Vol. 1, 182–3; and HAG, nº 824 – Provisões do Colégio de Rachol, 1596–1680, fls 3–5. The same discourse – that everything conquered belonged to the Crown, which could do with these conquests as it wished – is found among the colonisers in Mexico and Peru, too: Bernand and Gruzinski, *Histoire du Nouveau Monde*, Vol. 2, Chapter 7.

[98] The locals had to declare all properties that belonged to "the priests, the *pernis*, the single women, *joshis*, and goods of all other quality, such as gold and silver jewels, men and women slaves, cows", enumerating, as well, who were servants of the temple: *jogis*, *farazes*, carpenters, painters, *gauris*, trumpeteers, *bhandaris*, and others: CR-APO, Fasc. 5, Vol. 2, 643–5.

[99] CR-APO, Fasc. 5, Part I, 199–202; Vol. 2, 841–2, 903–3. The legitimacy of these confiscations was a recurrent theme in treatises written in defence of the interests of the villages and their inhabitants. For Diogo,

Governor and Viceroy Dom João de Castro (1545–1548), for example, was exceptionally liberal. In a letter about the Diu campaigns to Dom João III he exalted the support given by the *casados* in Goa, describing them as more outstanding than what one read about the Romans. Unsurprisingly, therefore, as governor he wished to express his *liberalitas* in the face of the exertions of these citizens.[100] The "Livro das Mercês" records this. Some of these grants were the allocation of paddy fields, palm groves, areca groves, and other wetlands in the villages of Calata, Talaulim, Benastarim, Curtorim, Utorda, Vanelim, and Seraulim in the Salcete region. Under Castro's ruling around a hundred Portuguese received one or more properties in the Goan villages. A well-known humanist, Castro possibly saw these concessions as a way to create "colonies", as the Romans had once, in the territories of Salcete and Bardez.[101]

The right of inheritance was also critical for the balance of power in the village. For example, a law of 1557 concerning "the inheritances of those that converted to the Catholic faith" was extremely detrimental to those who had not converted.[102] Invoking

---

nicknamed "of the Fort", the result of destroying the idols and temples was positive. As a reward for his actions, he received wetlands in the village of Curtorim: CR–APO, F 5, II, 872–4.

[100] Luís de Albuquerque, co-ord., *Portugal no Mundo,* 87 and 102–3. See also, for a previous period, IAN/TT, Corpo Cronológico, Part I, Mss. 58, nº 7 – "Carta da Câmara de Gôa expondo a ElRey os relevantes serviços que seus Moradores sempre fizerão", 15 Nov. 1536.

[101] In 1585, Viceroy Dom Duarte de Meneses (r. 1584–1588) granted a coconut grove to João Saldanha and João Berreira; the year before, the rector of Salcete received nine parcels of land; he in turn sold these parcels to Francisco Barreto, a local Christian. Barreto received other lands in Benaulim, "for three lives", that is to say, for three generations. Other local Christians, like Salvador Moura, referred to their poverty to request land – in his case, in the village of Carmona. Similar situations were also recorded in the villages of Talaulim, Chinchim, Calata, Orlim: HAG nº 3071 – Foral de Salcete, cópia feita de 1585, fls 520, 530–2, 546, 548, 555, 580, 582, 600.

[102] This law is included in CR-APO, Fasc. 5, Vol. 3, 1572–4.

a compilation of the royal laws, the *Ordenações Manuelinas* (1514), the law now favoured the converted and disfavoured those who had not. In the absence of other male children, the former would end up receiving "a third by right" of their parents' property.[103]

Such methods, dissuading Indians from persisting in their Gentileness, were quite obviously invitations to conversion, often opportune. They made land accessible to the converted. António Costa, for example, received "half of the property in the village of Margão, in Salcete" that had belonged "to a yogi by the name of Samjanato absent in Moorish lands." Other times, grants that had passed from local to Portuguese hands could go back to the earlier (or other) local owners if the locals had meanwhile been converted. This was how António Rodrigues, a local Christian, received lands in possession of the heirs of Diogo Fernandes, "*o do Forte*" (of the fortress), who had been granted these lands as reward for the destruction of the temples of Salcete.[104]

The land issue had a massive impact on conversion. The legal changes in wedding contracts and the succession regime concerning women, widows, and orphans were no less critical.[105] In this

[103] There was an "economic" transfer from the non-Christians to the Christians. A Brief of Paul III, of 1547, said that the properties of New Christians and their descendants that were seized by the Inquisition were not to be lost or confiscated but allocated to the "Catholic family members" of the convicted: IAN/TT, Col. São Vicente, L. 10 – Cartas e papéis variados da rainha D. Catarina, fls 275–275v.

[104] HAG, nº 7583–5 – Foral de 1622, L. I, fl. 43, 10v., 25ff.; CR-APO, Fasc. 5, Vol. 3, 1095–99nn. A similar process occurred in the Mughal empire. As John F. Richards has shown, conversion to Islam was also a tool of social mobility and a way to obtain political privileges: Richards, *The Mughal Empire*, 177.

[105] In Goa, inheritance was a right available only to men and through the male line. Change of this opened the door for others to participate in the *gaunkari*, as clearly expressed by Bento Baena Sanchez, the Ouvidor-geral of the Estado da Índia. Baena informed the monarch of the village council's impotence in relation to the succession rights of widows who had converted under the new legal regime. Sometimes, these rights would be taken on by

context the Crown issued the first two *alvarás* relating to widows. The law signed by Queen Dona Catarina, which had been preceded by an *alvará* by Governor Francisco Barreto (1555–1558) written at the instance of the Jesuits, declared that, if they were Christians, women and their daughters could inherit should the father die without leaving a son. If they did not convert, their right of inheritance would pass on to the closest relative who had converted. Such rights went against the local laws of inheritance.[106]

The fact that women were converting changed one of the foundational aspects of local life: marriage and reproduction processes. Intervening in the status of orphans and women within the local order, and expanding their say in matters, had long-term effects and unsettled the previously established balance of the order.[107] It was a reconfiguration by fiat of social cohesion and the traditional community.[108]

Something analogous happened in relation to orphans with the suppression of the rights of local families in order to favour Christian interests.[109] The law signed by Dona Catarina on 23 March 1559, continuing an earlier trend, allowed for the separation

---

the Portuguese themselves: Azevedo, *As communidades de Goa*, 58, 60, 68, 69; R.G. Pereira, *Goa – Gaunkari*, 101.

106 See norms from 1542 to 1544, from 1557, and from 1559: CR-APO, Fasc. 5, Part I, 171–3, 175–8, 381–3, 392–4, 410; Vol. 3, 1570–1.

107 See IAN/TT, Corpo Cronológico, Part I, Mç. 97, nº 27 – "Carta de Baltasar Lobo", 12 Oct. 1555; Mç. 106, nº 121 – "Minuta dos apontamentos (. . .) para o bom regímen das órfãs", 20 Feb. 1564; Mç. 106, nº 122 – "Carta de Fr. André Torneiro", 20 Feb. 1564. On orphans, see also CR-APO, Fasc. 4, *1st Council*, 1567, Action 2, d. 13, 16.

108 John Bossy's thoughts on this subject: Bossy, *A Cristandade no Ocidente*, 34–42; Bossy, *Dalla Comunità all'Individuo*, 37–58, are suggestive in relation to what was at issue when one intervenes in the foundational aspects of social life.

109 This was a problem of great political and symbolic importance in the kingdom since the orphans were the most fragile among those that were legally considered "minors". Besides, they could be the *locus* of social reproduction in the absence of another male heir.

of Hindu orphans – boys younger than fourteen, girls under twelve – from their families if they did not have grandparents or parents. In these circumstances, the Colégio de São Paulo (College of Saint-Paul) had the custody of orphans and responsibility for their education. If the college were unable to take them in, any other convent or fortress in the Estado da Índia could. Upon their majority – even if they had a mother, grandfather, or grandmother – they would be entrusted to the care of a Christian tutor who would teach them proper manners and take care of their properties.[110]

In 1567 zealous participants in the first Provincial Council of Goa congratulated themselves "for the results that we see every day following the laws that Your Excellency has set out for us." In 1575 the second Council recommended intensifying the measures already taken, arguing that mothers lost custody of children whose fathers had departed in their infancy. It was vital for conversion to keep such orphans in Goa within protection since their life was sometimes under threat. Some locals were known to cast their infants to the beasts if they happened to be "born on a day deemed inauspicious". This kind of inhumanity urgently needed reform. The assembly suggested that the monarch effect legislation separating children from their mothers – not convert them immediately, but to raise them in line with Christian customs. This suggestion, however, found no echo among the political authorities.[111]

Other examples indicate the options available to those who chose to accept or deny conversion.[112] Other changes altered the

[110] Cf. those norms from 1559, 1564, 1575, 1581, and 1582: CR-APO, Fasc. 5, Part I, 385–6ff.; Vol. 2, 577–8, 904–5; Vol. 3, 982–3, 990–1. These norms continued to be reproduced in subsequent years.

[111] CR-APO, Fasc. 4, *2nd Council*, 1575, Action 2, d. 4, 92–3.

[112] Similarly, there were certain norms that forbade Gentiles from presenting themselves with dignity. This was the case of the *alvará* of 1574 which prohibited the pandits and Gentile physicians from riding on horseback, or being borne in palanquins: *O Livro do "Pai dos Cristãos"*, 190–2. In addition, some rules forbade Brahmans from wearing the sacred thread that marked

very form of the social order: access to positions in imperial governance, either in the village or in the city,[113] and exemption from specific taxes and penalties.[114]

The persistence of discussions about the best means to achieve conversion into the middle of the sixteenth century demonstrates just how vital a religious identity was for a political one. This importance is neatly clear within a law by Dom João III in 1542 which gave Christians resident in the city of Goa a juridical identity independent of their ethnic one. A provision of 1559 confirmed this law, and another of 1571 expanded it to all Christians in India.[115]

---

their distinction, forcing them to cover them up, as stated in a decree of the 3rd. Provincial Council: CR-APO, Fasc. 4, *3rd. Council,* Action 2, d. 5, 124. There were exceptions for those who were financially close to Portuguese power.

[113] In 1566, Viceroy Dom Antão de Noronha forbade the scribes of the villages and non-Christian *gaunkars* from participating in assemblies where there were more Christians than Gentiles. Noronha's order repeated a well-known argument: "I am informed that by depriving them of this honour it would be easier for them to convert to our holy Catholic faith." Four years later, Governor António Moniz Barreto (r. 1573–1576) issued a decree prohibiting the existence of *gaunkaris* without Christians: Priolkar, *The Goan Inquisition*, 126. In 1582, any Gentile was forbidden from exercising a public office: Rego, *Documentação para a história das missões*, Vol. 12, 752, hereafter DHMPPO. It was still preferred, however, for the newly converted to occupy jobs where they spoke the local languages. These offices were granted for just three years "because during this time they will have to serve many Christians, and this will be a reason for which they and others become Christians." See the *alvarás* on these issues in DHMPPO, Vol. 11, 67; Vol. 12, 406.

[114] The rules of 1561, 1570, 1581, 1597, 1598, and 1613 related to these matters are published in CR-APO, Fasc. 3, 724, 870–2; Fasc. 5, Part I, 473; Vol. 2, 733; Vol. 3, 976–7, 1301–4; and *Documentos Remetidos da Índia ou Livros das Monções*, hereafter *Monsoon Books*, II, 340–2.

[115] "Any Portuguese person, as well as from any other nation, descent, and quality that is married in the city, or founds a new household, if they are Christian, as soon as they are married or found the said households, may at once enjoy and use all the rights and freedom that I grant them, and from

Despite the violence inherent in the majority of the strategies mentioned, none imposed any kind of physical separation between Christians and non-Christians. However, some of those involved in the conversion process promoted the idea. António Louro, Duarte Nunes, Miguel Vaz, Pero Fernandes de Sardinha, and Martim Afonso de Mello believed in one way or another in the advantages of physically separating the two groups.[116] In the middle of the century the same idea continued to be promoted, this time by the Jesuit provincial Father Gonçalo da Silveira, who defined the Brahmans as "malicious people and most zealous to plant their sect and to attract all to it, most inimical to the Christian name, and through diabolic dissimulation, they are the bankers of Hell, of usury and evil spells . . ."[117] For which reason

---

here onwards grant to the inhabitants there, notwithstanding the ordination of the Book 2 of my orders, title twenty-one": CR–APO, Fasc. 2, 115–16. In order to limit the effects of this law, the king issued another in which the offices of the governance of the city were to be reserved exclusively for "casados and residents, who are Portuguese of nation and descent, and for no other nation, descent or quality": CR-APO, Fasc. 2, 115–16. See for the laws of 1569 and 1571, CR-APO, Fasc. 5, Part I, 386–7; DHMPPO, Vol. 11, 78. On this legal levelling in the Hispanic monarchy, see Herzog, *Vecinos y Extranjeros.*

[116] Miguel Vaz was substituted by Pero Fernandes Sardinha, the future Bishop of Bahia. His time in India did not last long and he was criticised by Governor Garcia de Sá, who disliked the manner in which he treated the newly converted. Pero Fernandes wrote a report to the king in which he supported Vaz's proposals. He also insisted on physically separating the "Christians" from the "Gentiles", and further separating the Brahmans. In his opinion, the converted should not take sacred orders, nor the "mulattos and Portuguese that are born there". On Sardinha and others who defended the physical separation, see DI, Vol. 1, Memorial of Father Miguel Vaz, 1545; Letter of Father Pedro Fernandes de Sardinha to King Dom João III, 1547; Letter of King Dom João III to Dom Pedro de Mascarenhas, 1539, DI, Vol. 1, 63–89; 744–7; 752–5.

[117] Letter of Father Gonçalo da Silveira, 1557, DI, Vol. 4, 3. By the end of the seventeenth century, Juan Martinez de la Puente, in a chapter dedicated to "origin and customs of the Indian people", argued that there was a

this Jesuit argued that the best solution was to separate Brahmans from any contact with Christians.

An initial refusal to take this route, and subsequently a reversal of the decision demonstrates that there was a change in the way the Portuguese perceived the local populations. They were the "most malicious" people, the "most inimical to the Christian name", and they showed "diabolic dissimulation". These were tropes that became increasingly frequent, reminding one of the Moors and the Jews, two other communities that experienced similar treatment in Portugal.[118]

Early anthropological optimism gradually gave way to pessimism, melancholia, and even scepticism. These feelings ensured discourses postulating the destruction of all religious symbols from non-Christian religions became routine, idolatry being "gravely sinful". The religious argued they had been ordered by God that "in the promised land in which they would live, they had to eradicate all idols, temples, and places in which they worshipped the false gods, to annihilate idolatry [. . .] among the unfaithful. Then, they had no longer any occasion for idolatry and veneration of the Demon."[119] Rigorous methods had therefore become prevalent.

A letter of 25 October 1549 by the rector of the Jesuit college in Goa, Father António Gomes, revealed to Dom João III that the

---

clear link between the origin of the Jews and the Brahmans of India. They were also equivalent in their "greed, changing opinions, fallacies, apostasy, diverse and corrupted superstitions." This was justification of Brahmans being treated similarly to the Jews in Europe: Martinez de la Puente, *Compendio de las Historias,* 57. In 1724, Veyssière de La Croze too had no doubt, that Brahmans were the descendants of Semitic people: La Croze, *Histoire du Christianisme des Indes.*

[118] A.M. Xavier, "De converso a novamente convertido", attempts to demonstrate the similarities (as well as the differences) that existed between the two conversion processes and the legal status of both the converted, Jews and Indians. The ease with which in the medieval ages links were established between lepers, Jews, and Muslims was also characteristic: Ginzburg, *História Nocturna,* 43ff.

[119] CR-APO, Fasc. 4, *1st Council,* 1567, Action 2, d. 9, 12–14.

expulsion of some members of the local community had already begun. However, it was a decade later, during the government of Dom Constantino de Bragança (1558–1561), that this process reached its apex. The viceroy became a great ally of the Society of Jesus and Queen Dona Catarina de Áustria. This second trio initiated a more coherent and systematic strategy to discriminate against non-Christians. The Inquisition was established in this period. Not only a method for suppressing the errors of new Christians, the Inquisition was also, as Maria José Ferro has highlighted, an instrument of "catechism through fear". A *provisão* from 1560 provided a list of Brahmans who had to leave the city of Goa immediately, being allowed to go to Bardez and Salcete. If they were from there originally, they had to "live in their villages" where they would remain captive forever. Failure to comply would result in being sent to the galleys without remission and the loss of their estates, half of which would go to those who had denounced them, the other half to those the king indicated.[120] Three years later, Viceroy Dom Francisco Coutinho (1561–1564), the Count of Redondo, passed a similar *provisão*, this time in compliance with an order from Lisbon. Given that the Count contested the policy's utility, his *provisão* restricted the expulsion of Brahmans to those who were not essential to the economic order, allowing those that worked on the land with their own hands to stay in the territories because "they cannot do any harm . . . Since they have been useful for working the land, I do not want them to be expelled." In contrast, Brahmans who occupied positions that could better be in the hands of "Portuguese Christians and *naturaes da terra*" were expelled.[121]

The constitutions of the Archbishopric of Goa and the first Provincial Council of Goa insisted in 1567 on the model of physical separation. Through a *provisão* of Dom Sebastião that recognised

[120] CR-APO, Fasc. 5, Part I, 35. Something similar had previously happened with the Jews in the kingdom: Ferro, *Os Judeus em Portugal*.

[121] CR-APO, Fasc. 5, Vol. 2, 543–5, 612, 903–4; on this, see M.S. Cunha and Monteiro, "Vice-reis, governadores e conselheiros", 97.

these tools as laws of the kingdom, this model received the status of law applicable in the Estado da Índia in 1569.[122] The constitutions proposed that non-Christians had to identify themselves; at the same time, Brahmans were forbidden to show the caste marks that defined their status, and consequently their social pre-eminence. This measure ensured not just the identification of non-Christians from a distance, but also symbolically the setting up of discrimination against all non-Christians with no distinction, local elites included. For the Brahmans, this was disastrous. Now, because of contact with people whom they considered impure being imposed on them, they stood to lose their caste identity and become like the "untouchables".

Christians could not share their homes with non-Christians – Gentiles, Muslims, Jews. And non-Christians were prohibited from living on the same streets as Christians, ensuring that the former were forced to live – as were foreigners – in areas located even beyond the lazarettos. Women considered "fallen" were also meant to live in specific neighbourhoods, though even in their case it was "Christians in one, infidels in another".[123]

Participation, or any form of collaboration, in non-Christian festivals was consequently strictly prohibited. In order to enforce this obligation, non-Christians could not pass through Christian lands when they went on pilgrimages: the authorities were not to grant the *cartazes* (safe-passes) necessary for such journeys. Nor could non-Christians build new temples "with the money that they earn from us" or take "false relics" with them when they used Portuguese ships for pilgrimage, or used ships which brought them into Christian territory via alms that they had received "for the pagodas of their lands".[124]

122 CR-APO, Fasc. 4, *1st Council*, 1567, Action 2, d. 24, 22–23.; BA, Cod., 49-II-48 – Leis e Provisoes que elRey Dom Sebastiao fez, fl. 203.

123 CR–APO, Fasc. 4, *1st Council*, 1567, Action 2, dd. 7 and 8, 38–40; *3rd. Council*, 1585, 124–5.

124 CR-APO, Fasc. 4, *1st Council*, 1567, Action 2, d. 13, 40; *3rd Council*, 1585, Action 2, dd. 4, 6, 9, 123–7; 5th Council, 1606, Action 2, d. 10, 210.

These ideas were repeated and expanded in the subsequent Councils: the repetition in them of norms, decrees, and so forth reveals the persistence of practices they wanted to control or deny. Phrases often repeated, such as "one has information" and "it is said that", justified the repetition of norms and are also evidence of the difficulty in eradicating un-Christian practices.

After recognising the failure of previous decrees, the third Provincial Council sent a request for a new roster of non-Christians considered "harmful to the conversion of Christianity"; this was intended to enable the viceroy to have them "expelled from the lands of the king". In the fourth Council, at the end of the sixteenth century, the prohibition of cohabitation was extended to denote from the "cottage" to the "kitchen garden", suggesting the numerous ways in which, more than thirty years after the first prohibition, Christians had managed to sidestep the restrictions to continue living alongside "infidels". A decree of the fifth Council from the seventeenth century prohibited "any person, be he ecclesiastic or secular" from employing the services of an "infidel barber".[125]

Dissenting Voices, Mismatched Interests

These decisions made by the Portuguese Crown concerning the Goan territories from the 1530s onward were in large part guided by a political pragmatism made all the more evident as the complexity of the project increased.

I focus here on the opinions of those who in general disagreed with the politics of conversion. The two groups identified as most opposed to the process of conversion of locals were the Portuguese

---

Conforming to the will of the ecclesiastics, Dom Sebastião declared in 1570 that only Christian kings or those that favoured Christianity be granted safe-passes, "to understand what they gain by being Christians, and by following the Christian path": CR-APO, Fasc. 5, Vol. 2, 732.

[125] See these decrees in CR–APO, Fasc. 4, *3rd Council*, 1585, Action 2, d. 6, 124–5; *4rd. Council*, d. 4, 187–8; *5th Council*, Action 2, d. 10, 210.

settled in these territories (i.e. the *casados*),[126] and the Brahmans. Many *casados* and the captains of the fortress, at times including the viceroy and governor as well, disagreed on the conversion of locals. Some of these had been established in various places around India since 1500 and identified with the ways of life of the resident populations. Among these, many had ended up renouncing their political loyalty to the monarch and had established new political ties.[127] Others remained under the jurisdiction of the Portuguese Crown and continued to obey the king of Portugal and his local officials, or even act in his name – though without disregarding local business considerations or the other relationships established among the Indian, Arab, and other communities that they had encountered. The strongest reactions against the conversion process emerged among members of this second group.[128]

In 1550 Father Nicolao Lancilloto wrote a letter evaluating the fifty years of Christian presence in India. One of the most intelligent observers of the Portuguese imperial presence in India, Lancilloto was highly critical of the period. Over these fifty years the Portuguese had not just negotiated with Gentiles, Jews, and Muslims, frequently making them incur excommunication penalties in the process, each of them had also bought anywhere between ten and twenty slaves for sex, thus adopting local polygamous practices. The following year, Luís Fróis condemned the sin, scandal, greed, and "illicit traits" of the Portuguese, both men and women, settled in India. Six years later he pointed out that the *casados* mistreated local Christians. They had refused to accept "that the Christians should so suddenly have names and be honoured and recognised." They said that once the locals converted,

[126] About this group and its positions and aspirations, see A.M. Xavier, "Pensare la nazione partendo dell'impero".

[127] On this point, see Coates, *Degredados e Órfãs*; Couto, "Quelques observations sur les renégats"; M.A.L. Cruz, "Exiles and Renegades".

[128] On the political coexistence and integration among groups verified in the previous period, and the changes that conversion brought on in their ways of relating with each other, see Madeira Santos, *Goa é a chave de toda a Índia*.

they had "a better opinion of themselves than previously, and they do not suffer treatments as had been done to them while Gentiles." They themselves, by contrast, "were discredited and their authority and honour diminished."[129]

In 1561 Father António Quadros conveyed other explanations. In a letter to the king of Portugal he condemned the opposition of some of the Portuguese regarding conversion. Their opposition, he said, was motivated by their commercial relations with expelled Brahmans.[130] The most unsettling factor, however, was that the governor himself frequently opposed conversion. In a letter, Dom Juan de Albuquerque, wrote describing the collection of a large box of books with sacred Indian writings destined for destruction and narrated how the governors had impeded the process of conversion. At this time the bishop had received a visit from an official of Dom João de Castro, who had been accompanied by Dadagi, son of the powerful Krishna.[131] In the course of this visit the official sent by Castro had asked Albuquerque to return the sacred books. In his letter to the king the bishop said he chased Dadagi, threatened him with his cane, and expelled him from the house. Dom Juan de Albuquerque would make it clear, however, that "these endeavours that I do, and for quite some time now, in times of past governors, was out of kindness, to let the Catholic faith of Jesus Christ flourish . . . I came to this land for no other reason than that which was mandated by our Lord the king."[132]

[129] Letter of Father Nicolao Lancillotto, s.j., to Inacio de Loyola, 1550; Letters of Father Luís Fróis, s.j., 1552, 1560; Letter of Father António Quadros, 1561; Report of Fathers Francisco Henriques and André de Carvalho, 1561: DI, Vol. 2, 123–31, 445–91; Vol. 4, 719–20; Vol. 5, 63–7, 160–88.

[130] Quadros' letter and other similar letters have been published in DI, Vol. 5, 63–7, 160–88.

[131] Krishna had been involved, for example, in the incorporation of Salcete and Bardez into the Portuguese Crown: IAN/TT, Corpo Cronológico, Part II, Mss. 241, nº 24: "Carta de Chrisna expondo a ElRey o serviço que lhe fizera persuadindo ao Idalcão largar ao mesmo Snr. as terras de Salsete, e Bardez", 6 Dec. 1546.

[132] This description can be found in DI, Vol. 1, 328.

Although the king's mandate was clear, its interpretation and adjustment to reality depended on various factors, as the episode mentioned above demonstrates. The episode shows the influence of some local groups over political power – a power that ensured the multiplicity of such episodes.

The governors' opposition to the conversion process became a *topos* of religious correspondence. Some governors sinned by default – by not favouring conversion openly, or by creating expectations without results, as was the case with Pedro Mascarenhas. Others were directly opposed to Christianisation. A letter penned by Father Melchior Carneiro to Francisco Borgia suggests that the disenchantment reached unusually high levels: "As the situation stands, Christianity shall not grow, for as Your Reverence well knows, there is not the abundance of miracles as in the early Church, so it is necessary to use all human strength and means to push the cause until the very end. If the king does not send a zealous governor who favours Christians to these parts, we can do little in comparison with what we could do." Carneiro criticised the governor, Dom Francisco Barreto, "a friend of the blind, the lame, the one-armed, and one-eyed" – in the words of another priest. Two years later, however, the same priest was more optimistic. He said that "the way the Church goes about its business, and if it goes on as such, we can expect that the whole island of Goa shall receive the Gospel quite soon. This governor now favours Christianity in what it requires to be, and this is one of those reasons why it is growing, for this is the righteous path to continue to let Christianity grow."[133]

On account of the sheer number of conversions he achieved, the viceroy Dom Constantino, the brother of the Duke of Bragança, was showered with identical compliments. The Jesuits even compared him for obvious reasons to the Roman emperor Constantine. The second half of the 1550s saw many governors transformed from obstacles to genuine supporters. Some of them did nearly all

[133] These letters of Carneiro were published in DI, Vol. 3, 297–302.

that the Society of Jesus asked them to do. The absence of a resident bishop between 1553 and 1560 favoured such men.[134]

Gaspar de Leão, bishop and archbishop of Goa from 1553 to 1567, and again from 1572 to 1576, arrived in Goa only in 1560.[135] Juan de Albuquerque had died in 1553, and Viceroy Dom Constantino de Bragança (who, some said, took on the role of the bishop) had been in power since 1558. Leão arrived at the precise moment at which the viceroy was protecting and encouraging the collective conversion of Indians, publicly expressed through ostentatiously celebrated baptisms. Known for his spiritual inclination, Leão thought that there was an excess of "human means" in the business of conversion, and little space for the grace of God to manifest itself.[136] He said he had provided for "converting Christians as they should be, and as the Church mandates."[137] It is worth thinking about this statement. What did

[134] On this alliance between Jesuits and governors, see Letter of Father Balthasar Dias, s.j., 1555; Letter of Father Gonçalo da Silveira, 1557; Letter of Father Melchior Carneiro, s.j., 1557, DI, Vol. 3, 402–9, 620ff.; Vol. 4, 5–13.

[135] Friar Paulo da Trindade dedicates a compliment to Gaspar de Leão regarding his "saintly" personality, and his status as a founder of the Custody of the Mother of God. However, he says little about his activity as prelate and about this conflict which set him against the viceroy Dom Constantine and the Society of Jesus: Trindade, *Conquista Espiritual do Oriente*, Vol. I, 214–18.

[136] Leão arrived in Goa with ample powers, including that of providing and confirming the local ecclesiastic benefices. The monarch trusted the archbishop to nominate "competent people, able to serve in the See and the churches, and in doing, as he is supposed to alleviate my conscience and his": CR-APO, Fasc. 5, Part I, 436–8. In this way the king accepted the suggestion of the Dominican Friar Diogo Bermudes, who had requested that the bishops and not the governors appoint ecclesiastic benefices in Indias: an extract from Friar Diogo Bermundes' letter in IAN/TT, Col. São Vicente, L. 9 – Várias Cartas e Provisões do rei D. João III e da rainha D. Catarina, fl. 290.

[137] Two months before, in September, the archbishop had sent a letter with the same contents to Father Miguel Torres, provincial of the Jesuits: see also *Gavetas*, Vol. 3, 190–1; DI, Vol. 5, 224–7. The human means that Leão seemed to prefer were of another kind: namely, books that invited Jews and Muslims to convert, and the Christians to be perfect, as was the case of the

the Church mandate? Moreover, what precisely was the standard of conversions? Leão's discomfort was mainly towards the mass conversions of Gentiles by the Jesuits, which he felt an ethical obligation to monitor.

Gaspar de Leão arrived at a time which was, thus, once again a time of transition. The enthusiasm of the first two decades of systematically converting local peoples had already begun to wane, privileging punishment as a means to correct and convert. Almost simultaneously, and primarily among the Italian missionaries, there emerged the idea that "adapting" to the local cultures was another way of getting around the problem and increasing success. Leão himself was against conversion obtained by fear of punishment instead of the love of God and free will. Even though the archbishop did not use the expression "force", its spectre overshadowed every conversion.[138]

António Quadros contested this interpretation of the Jesuit methods in a letter of February 1561. Each Sunday, two priests taught "in chapels and in the villages where there is no church." There they retained "the baptized ones" and brought in "those who were not". Instead of using force, the Jesuits used compassion, "giving to them the holy baptism that they ask for."[139] A council of scholars and theologians had already inquired into the legitimacy of conversion strategies, prohibiting the use of methods considered particularly violent.

The letters of Father Herédia were more explicit. In his first letter he described the processes of conversion adopted by the Jesuits in a very different way. A Jesuit himself, Herédia explained that

---

Tratado . . . contra os judeus, of Jerónimo da Santa Fé, published by Leão in 1565, with a pastoral letter – Leão, ed., *Tratado . . .*

[138] In a letter of 1552 to Dom João III, Simão Botelho also told him that some missionaries wished "to make Christians forcedly and wipe out the Gentiles which is the reason why this land is becoming less populated": Botelho, *Textos sobre o Estado da Índia*, 70–1.

[139] Letter of Father António Quadros, 1561, DI, Vol. 5, 63–7.

the Jesuits had forged documents and *alvarás* to imprison those they considered a danger to Christianity, acting more as agents of justice than representatives of God. Another letter, from the provincial of Portugal, did away with the sophistries and the register of language was smoother. Miguel Torres explained to Diego Lainez, the *geral* or "general" of the Jesuits, that the reason underlying the archbishop's reprimands was the "extraordinary" behaviour of the Jesuits who, "among them and other similar persons . . . put Gentiles in prison as they performed Gentile rituals against the law and ordinances of the king of Portugal." Although Torres presented such means as legitimate, he considered them inappropriate for the image that the Society of Jesus sought to cultivate.[140]

The letters exchanged between the Papacy, the Crown of Portugal, the Archbishop of Goa, the Viceroy of India, the Jesuit general in Rome, the Provincial in Lisbon and Goa, and the Jesuits *in loco* suggest that Jesuit methods were under critique. This correspondence also demonstrates the divisions among the religious about the methods of conversion.

At the very foundation of these differences was a simple question: to figure out to what extent "human means" were acceptable for ensuring conversion. Only the right balance between "human means", "God's grace", and "free will" guaranteed that Christians were "made as they ought to be".[141] Despite all these contestations,

[140] Herédia's and Torres' letters can be found in DI, Vol. 5, 150–2, 192–202. A message not very different from Torres' was conveyed by Francisco Henriques and André Carvalho in September 1561. However, these Jesuits argued that coercion had been used only three or four times, and had been necessary to reach the intended goal. They argued, too, that since Christians already numbered more than non-Christians, the fear of violence would cease: DI, Vol. 5, 160–88.

[141] At the very outset of the conversion activity there were voices against certain methods of conversion. In 1545 Father Antonio Criminali was scandalised by the fact that "Gentiles, Muslims, unfaithful come to the church, and are allowed to attend the mass, for they say that many of them become Christians by listening to the divine offices [. . .] But the *Rationale Divinorum Officiorum* says that these people could only stay in the church until the

some decades later the clergy of India could pride itself on having made Goa "entirely Christian".[142]

"If they will not be good Christians, then at least their children will be," proclaimed Bishop Duarte Nunes at the beginning of the sixteenth century. It was this conviction that inspired the establishment of missionaries in each of the villages of the Old Conquests, resulting in an evangelism that increasingly sought to turn the newly converted into proper Christians. The methods used by them to further Christianise the converted will be the focus of the subsequent chapters. By itself, conversion was a political instrument with delayed effects. It was in the second phase that the cultural conversion of locals was attempted. Only by looking at village life is it possible to reconstruct some dimensions of these experiences.

The regular clergy – the missionaries – of this second phase were different from those of the 1530s and 1540s. Franciscan spirituality was characteristic of the first, where "the strictest observance" in which "grace", "love", and the "example of poverty" played a crucial role in the mechanics of conversion. A mixed spirituality imbued the second phase. On the one hand missionaries were not insensitive to changes in the spiritual order effected by the Council of Trent in the political, institutional, and religious spheres. On the other, from 1580 onward these religious communities also had to take into consideration the insertion of the Estado da Índia into the Spanish monarchy, and the crisis of the Estado that followed some decades later.[143]

---

offertory, even the cathecumens. But here, neither the cathecumens nor the unfaithful are monitored. Everybody comes and listens to the mass when it pleases them." DI, Vol. 1, 7–10.

[142] Cf. BNP, Cod. 1119 – Repertorio . . ., "Casos Notáveis"; IAN/TT, Conselho Geral do Santo Ofício, nº 462.

[143] There are few systematic studies on this impact from the perspective of the colonial order. The most important works have privileged the geopolitical retraction of the Estado da Índia: Boxer, *Portuguese India*; Boxer, *The Portuguese Seaborne Empire*; Disney, *A Decadência do Império*. See also, for

After 1640, and especially after 1668, a Portuguese dynasty again controlled the monarchy. The royal family, the Braganzas, had had deep links with the Estado da Índia in the previous century. However, to win the Restoration wars between 1640 and 1668, aid to Brazil superseded the needs of the Estado da Índia – as confirmed by documents produced by the Overseas Council.[144] Besides, the interregnum in the nomination of Asian bishops that the movement of 1640 implied resulted in the Goan diocese remaining in *sede vacante* between the death of Dom Frei Francisco dos Mártires in 1652 and the nomination of Dom Frei Cristóvão da Silveira in 1670, as well as the creation of the Junta de Missões (Board of Missions). The Junta was to be the central administrative organ of the kingdom of Portugal. It resulted in new jurisdictional situations, either because of the absence of a local prelate for two decades or the administrative delegation of missionary activities in the empire to a new institution.

The implications of these changes on the geopolitical, political, and institutional scale, and on the micro level within the daily lives of local people, are still not widely known and have only summarily been addressed in this book.[145] For example, how the Overseas Council, founded in 1541, affected relations between the kingdom and the Estado da Índia in matters ecclesiastical remains to be studied. These matters required the Council to engage with the Mesa da Consciência e Ordens, which was responsible for most religious affairs in India. Edval de Souza Barros has demonstrated that one of the most frequently referred subjects in the Council's meetings throughout the 1640s was how Christianity

---

a more general idea of the Habsburg period, Bouza, *Portugal no Tempo dos Filipes*; Schaub, *Portugal na Monarquia Hispânica*; Palomo, "Para el sosiego y quietude".

[144] Barros, *O Conselho Ultramarino*, 155–6.

[145] On the effects of these geopolitical contexts in Goa and in the Estado da Índia following 1640, see Ames, *Renascent Empire?*; Valladares, *Castilla y Portugal*; Barros, *O Conselho Ultramarino*; Lopes, ed., *O Império Oriental.*

could be protected. The councillors said that, despite this evident concern, the matter did not particularly resonate in the circles around Dom João IV.[146]

Besides these critical changes in the context of the relationship between the colony and the metropolis, it is necessary to mention the impact of interactions in the other local contexts on the local populations, such as in South India, the Konkan, and the Indian Ocean in general. The sieges of Goa in the sixteenth and seventeenth centuries left traces of destruction, as did the military attacks by the sultanate of Bijapur and the Maratha confederation. The rivalries between the Portuguese, the English, and the Dutch ended in a substantial reduction of the Estado da Índia. All this challenged the centrality of the city of Goa, its financial autonomy, and life in the villages of Goa.

[146] Barros, *O Conselho Ultramarino,* 114ff., 138ff.

3

New Temples and New Priests

The Establishment of Religious Orders in Goan Villages

ALESSANDRO VALIGNANO, a Jesuit visitor to the missions of the Estado da Índia at the end of the sixteenth century, did not share the opinion of the local Jesuits, Fathers Pina and Melchior Carneiro, about Christianity. Both priests had high expectations of the local Christians. Father Pina was said to obtain spiritual consolation from the confessions of his "madanellas" (Magdalenes), while Father Melchior Carneiro believed that before long the "Christians of the land" would become its true apostles.[1] In contrast, Valignano had his doubts about the nature of such converts. In one of his most important reports, the Jesuit explained that to instil the idea that conversion was something "supernatural" and not "something human" was necessary for the conversion to be thought genuine.[2] Conversion did not mean changing "caste and way of life, leaving behind the caste of the Gentiles and becoming part of the Christian one," Valignano said. Locals needed to convert not merely to obtain "human favours".

[1] Letter of Father Melchior Carneiro, 1557, in DI, Vol. 4, 5–13.

[2] This text is a precious source of information on the position that the Italian Valignano occupied in the Asian missionary world, as well as a register of the effects of almost a century of Portuguse presence in the Indian world: Valignano, *Sumario de las cosas que pertenecen a la Yndia Oriental,* in DHMPPO, Vol. 12.

He felt that for most Indians conversion was still an event external to their interior selfhood.

Ironically, what bothered Valignano were the conversions achieved by his fellow Jesuits over the decades before his arrival, which they had considered a success. As argued in the previous chapter, a distinction between conversion and Christianisation was part of the "official strategy" of the religious orders *in loco.* Conversion was a formal instrument allowing people to move from one political status to another. As a result, baptism, the Christian rite that enabled this passage, was, essentially, a political act.[3] Because of this, almost all tactics ensuring baptism were thought legitimate, even those that relied on the offer of "human means". Baptism created new relationships among subjects who could now be politically and socially regulated. Sabine MacCormack has illustrated how, in the first centuries of Christianisation in the Roman world, "secular dispositions were conditioned by the meaning of baptism," justifying changes at a legislative level.[4] John Bossy has also emphasised the importance that the ritual of baptism gained in the medieval period. He points out that during the Middle Ages baptism constituted a way of enabling community cohesion. This had the effect of either intensifying, extending, or at times challenging pre-existing blood ties.[5] The process of conversion in Goa, which began in the decades of the 1530s and 1540s, was based on similar assumptions.

The members of the religious orders understood that Christianisation was the second step – that this was the real conversion, the internal conversion, the cultural conversion. They reasoned that this second stage would be easier to achieve by integrating native populations into the Portuguese juridical and political order, and,

[3] MacCormack, "Sin, Citizenship", 655. On the ways in which baptism was conceived by the reformers, see Prosperi, *Il Concilio di Trento*, 137ff. On the political role played by baptism, see Herzog, *Vecinos y estrangeros*, 179ff.

[4] See MacCormack, "Sin, Citizenship", and her analysis of changes in inheritance rights in the late-Roman Empire: 657ff.

[5] Bossy, *Dalla communitá all'individuo*, 43ff.

as such, place them under the tutelage of the Portuguese Crown in both private and public spheres. From this point of view the adoption of "human means" was essential to achieve the desired end: to enable local people to change their entire way of living, including how they perceived their past, present, and future existence, their entire sense of themselves. The interior metamorphosis, which implied informed consent to the Christian project and the civility that it represented, was possible only through the slow and time-consuming process of Christianisation.[6]

Valignano himself seems to have recognised the impossibility of achieving Christianisation before baptism. "However much the fathers work, they are unable to inform or teach them appropriately before baptising them," he wrote. This impossibility was in his view because of the spiritual and intellectual incapacity among the locals: "these brown people have only a small capacity for understanding issues relating to God, and it seems they cannot lift their spirits up from the ground, and for this reason they are unable to learn the ways of our law which is wholly spiritual."[7]

Notwithstanding his scepticism, Valignano insisted on investing in other "human means" which would enable the Christianisation of people in the medium and long term. This chapter as well as the next focus on the means used to achieve the cultural conversion of locals.

The Jesuit visitor believed that fluency in the local languages was necessary among those who "teach them what is necessary . . . administer them the sacraments," and "instruct them in worship". Mastering the local languages was the only way to communicate the mysteries of the faith, while also hearing and controlling

[6] Again, the Christianisation of Mexico follows similar patterns: Duverger, *La conversion des Indiens*, 132ff.

[7] A hundred pages earlier, Valignano considered that the Indians, besides being "of black colour", had "little distinction and low capacities". Citing Aristotle, he concluded that "their nature is to serve": Valignano *Sumario de las cosas que pertenecen a la Yndia Oriental,* in DHMPPO, Vol. 12, 596–7. This is also cited in Boxer, *Relações Raciais,* 64–5.

how Indians received and interpreted these mysteries. Besides emphasising the mastery of local languages, many of his proposals were similar to those suggested in the first decades of the sixteenth century by Friar António Louro and Dom Duarte Nunes. Valignano also made similar suggestions about the flow of communication between Christians and non-Christians, ". . . which mixture and communication are very often sufficient to pervert the Portuguese themselves with their vices and superstitions, leave alone the Christians who are so powerless and so young [in the faith]." Concerning proposals for the daily "pauses" during which the locals were to be catechised, Valignano observed that "since they are many and penniless and are [spread out] in so many different villages, and those that do not work during the day will have nothing to eat, they are hardly able to come together to be catechised as would be necessary." In order to overcome these obstacles, "these measures, if used simultaneously, will gradually enter into them, and they will profit from them; this will take a lot of work and sweat from the fathers because the results will appear very slowly."[8]

"Very slowly," wrote Valignano, expecting that "their children and grandchildren born Christians, and unaware of the superstitions and ceremonies of the pagodas of their ancestors" would be genuine Christians. The same idea of a conformist inertia formed by their *habitus* (in Bourdieu's terms) that led men to follow "the law and customs of their forefathers" can be found in the words of Sebastião Gonçalves in his *História*. Moreover, for him, this tendency was much more robust in Asian society than in the rest of the world.[9]

One should be attentive to the meaning of these words, and especially the conclusions of Valignano. It is possible that, subconsciously, he did not really believe in the possibility of conversion.

[8] Valignano, *Sumario de las cosas que pertenecen a la Yndia Oriental,* in DHMPPO, Vol. 12, 609.

[9] For the concept of *habitus*, Bourdieu, "Cultural Reproduction and Social Reproduction".

What he proposed instead was the making of Christians by educating them from the day they were born. A broad understanding of education – encompassing doctrine, teaching the alphabet, and controlling local custom – informed his proposals. The Jesuits and religious orders were meant to undertake this pedagogy. He envisioned inscribing all that Christian civility entailed onto the hearts and minds of the local population from their very infancy. This would effectively allow the children of locals – future adults and subjects of the king of Portugal – to identify with their own selves, with the world, and with the transcendent as true Christians.

Christianisation had, in a sense, to be embedded in the physiognomy and entailed what are now called "structural effects" involving the cognitive order and human understanding. In sum, the cultural conversion of local communities came down to the education of each subject in fundamentals that, in many aspects, were radically different from those of the previous order.

This culturalist perception of Christianisation is central to any proper understanding of the attitudes of the Goan populations during the sixteenth and seventeenth centuries, and their ways of living and being in the subsequent centuries. A systematic investment in schools and colleges was crucial to achieving these goals. The growing presence of missionaries in the countryside, made possible after the Brief of 1552 – which made the Jesuits, Franciscans, and Dominicans responsible for the villages and future parishes of Tiswadi, Salcete, and Bardez – becomes all the more meaningful when one realises how the missionaries were to evangelise.

However, the success or failure of Christianisation did not depend entirely on how well each religious order or its members fulfilled their tasks. The unique situation of every village that they sought to convert was equally important.[10] The response of

[10] In his *Breve relação das principaes ordens*, BNP, Cod. 58, Spinola holds the parish clergy responsible for the superficial Christianisation of the local populations. He refers mainly to the island of Tiswadi, where many parishes had been put in the charge of secular priests.

the local populations that, based on their history or future expectation either received, refracted, conformed to, or refused the proposals that the religious sought to impose was as fundamental as the missionaries' initiatives. In any case, the social order which operated in these territories by the end of the seventeenth century diverged significantly from that of the two centuries prior, when the conversion process and Christianisation had started.

The Christians were unable to wipe out "idolatry" and completely Christianise the local population, but the locals were not impervious to the Christian message. After the regular clergy settled in the Goan villages, their landscape was visually transformed with the presence of a church and neighbourhoods containing "Portuguese houses". Besides, the Christian intervention in what was a (re)construction of identity implied a readjustment of the forms of local cohesion and the mechanisms of reciprocity that guaranteed social equilibrium. It also led to different ways in which the local populations related to the transcendent. In a way, the Christianisation of the Goan villages ensured what Remi Clignet, quoting Paulo Freire, defined as a double alienation. The first alienation was the result of the exposure to cultural and educational stimuli which were aimed at wiping out the local past. The second alienation which flowed from such stimuli, provided the Goan population with a distorted image of the metropole, and thus contributed to the shoring up of colonial power.[11]

In order to understand the unfolding of this process, a detailed analysis of the devices used to achieve Christianisation is needed. The institutional status of the religious orders that had settled in the villages represented a critical condition enabling this presence.[12] The first section below deals with some of the implications of the presence of the new religious institutional framework in the villages; what tasks were carried out; and to what extent they

[11] Clignet, "Damned If You Do", 84ff.

[12] See, on this, the observations of A. da Silva about the relevance of the institutional framing of the new Christian communities: A. da Silva, *Trent's Impact*, 29ff.

succeeded. Subsequently, the second section analyses certain cases to understand religious interventions relating to communication, family, and perceptions of time and space.

The Political, Institutional, and Economic Status of the Religious Orders

Assigning Jesuits, Franciscans, and Dominicans to the parishes in Tiswadi, Salcete, and Bardez had critical consequences for the future of the populations there. However, until the eighteenth century only Franciscans and Jesuits were put in charge of the parishes of Bardez and Salcete, since the Crown and archbishop were able to replace the regular clergy of Tiswadi with the secular clergy in compliance with the Tridentine decrees.[13] This substitution aided the Crown's ability to gain control over the central territories of Goa. At the same time, some defended the view that the regular clergy was more effective in certain places than in others. In the seventeenth century some theologians of the Mesa da Consciência e Ordens argued that it was "more convenient to give the churches of the city and ports of the sea to the [secular] clergy, and only those of the interior to the friars, since the latter were usually better at caring for their souls." The truth is that, at the beginning of the seventeenth century, clergymen born in Goa headed eleven of the seventeen churches on Tiswadi Island (excluding those in the city of Goa). In contrast, until the eighteenth century Bardez and Salcete had regular clergy.[14]

[13] Only in 1777 were the Franciscans obliged to abandon the parishes of Bardez: F. Coutinho, *Le Régime Paroissial*, 50. On their settlement in India, see Meersman, *The Ancient Franciscan Provinces*; idem, *The Friars Minor*; F.X. da Costa, *Anais Franciscanos*; G. Couto, "Acção missionária dos franciscanos"; Catão, "The Reformed Franciscans"; F.F. Lopes, *Os Franciscanos no Oriente*; Telles, *Os Franciscanos no Oriente*. For the Jesuits, see F. Coutinho, *Le Régime Paroissial*, 51; Lopes, *Goa Setecentista*, 173; Mascarenhas, "The Church in Eighteenth-century Goa", 83. The Jesuits were expelled from Salcete in 1760: Moraes, *A History of Christianity*, Vol. 2, 331.

[14] S. Gonçalves, *Primeira Parte da História*, Vol. 3, 292–3. The Dominicans

Despite being separated from the territory of Tiswadi by the Mandovi and Zuari rivers, Bardez and Salcete constituted a substantial territorial continuum. They were the most populated regions of Goa and constituted altogether almost 10 per cent of the sixteenth-century Portuguese population. Military units and fiscal agents whose roles were to collect taxes from the residents were the first signs of Portuguese rule over these territories. An analysis of the initiatives undertaken by Viceroy Dom João de Castro, via a detailed look at the correspondence between him and his sons, was published by Luís de Albuquerque and offers an insight into the role played by the humanist governor in that process. In 1547, for example, Castro supervised the construction of a fortress in Bardez, and in relation to the fortress in Rachol, in Salcete, he asked his son Dom Alvaro "to write down how the land is, and the size of the hill, with all of the most vital things necessary." Castro's use of the phrase "write down" demonstrates how he associated writing with taking political decisions, an association increasingly frequent in the politics of the time.[15] Nevertheless, it was only after the establishment of parishes in these territories that colonisation started effectively.[16]

These parishes gained an importance beyond their mission of managing the religious life of believers. They became the primary administrative cells, with tasks that went beyond the religious. The parish was the political-administrative headquarters of imperial power in these lands, critical when the Crown lacked institutional and human resources for those projects that were neither fiscal nor military.[17] If the Portuguese Crown saw the village as the primary fiscal and military unit of its empire, the parish was superimposed

arrived in India in 1548 and worked principally among the Portuguese. The Augustinians arrived much later, in 1572.

[15] L. Albuquerque, *et al., Os Portugueses no Mundo,* Vol. 3, 45–7.

[16] See, in this context, the case study by van Oss on a parish in Guatemala in the period of the Spanish monarchy: van Oss, *Catholic Colonialism.*

[17] Allegra, "Il parroco", 895–930.

on other administrative structures which combined objectives that were distinct from one another yet complementary.

This superimposition made concrete the shift in the relationship between the Portuguese Crown and the local people, and the Crown's intent to exercise firm control. At first glance, this alliance between the Crown and the regular clergy allowed the latter to extend its power. However, the Crown sought, not much later, to withdraw the powers initially bestowed on the religious orders and parish priests. The withdrawal resulted in strong reactions from those who had pioneered the establishment of Catholic structures in the rural Goan world and taken control of these territories on the assumption that they were the final authorities.[18]

This territorial appropriation began in 1552 with the formal division of Salcete and Bardez into parishes. The papal bull *Exponi Nobis* and the canonical procedure of *incorporatio* enabled a process that had begun in the city of Goa in 1543 and 1544.[19] The Franciscans and Jesuits received the parishes of Bardez and Salcete. The parishes of Tiswadi were divided among Jesuits and Dominicans. The Augustinians got only one.

This distribution did not meet the objectives set by the Society of Jesus. At a meeting convened by Dom João III in Lisbon on

[18] The conflicts that pitched the bishops against the religious orders established in Goa suggest that their relations were informed by the bull *Omnimoda* of Adrian VI of 1522. This bull conceded great autonomy to the religious orders, whose superiors enjoyed an almost episcopal jurisdiction: F. Coutinho, *Le Régime Paroissial*, 66.

[19] The administrative divisions enabled offering assistance to the population in the course of the choleric epidemic that raged during this period, killing dozens of people each day: see Županov, "Drugs, Health, Bodies". Regarding "*incorporatio*", from the Middle Ages, the juridical regime of *incorporatio* allowed for the religious orders to incorporate parochial faculties into the Conventual regime. After the Council of Trent, this possibility was reduced, giving the bishops the power to annul previous situations or decide on new ones. Bishops had judicial power to visit churches and monitor the lives of all priests belonging to the religious orders: F. Coutinho, *Le Régime Paroissial*, 65–6.

27 February 1550, it was decided that "all things about Christendom should be given to the priests [the Jesuits] and their counsel followed." The Jesuits wanted to have full control over the parishes of Goa, a desire not shared by Dom Juan de Albuquerque and Viceroy Dom Pedro de Mascarenhas, who, three years later, sanctioned the division of these territories between all the religious orders settled in Goa.[20]

These decisions were contrary to the desires of the ambitious Society of Jesus. However, Francis Xavier had passed away, and in Portugal Simão Rodrigues had lost credit. In Goa they were now not only bereft of their most emblematic symbol but also led by the divisive figure of Father António Quadros. Simultaneously, with the death of Bishop Albuquerque in 1552, the diocese lay *sede vacante*, and its governance was temporarily handed over to Sebastião Pinheiro from the Relação de Goa.[21] To accede to Jesuit desires meant handing over immeasurable power to the Society of Jesus, as well as possibly running the risk of Goa becoming a kind of Ignatian *respublica*.

The decision to distribute the territories among the different religious orders was confirmed by a decree of Pope Paul IV on 23 March 1567, the year of the first Provincial Council of Goa, and of the publication of the Constitutions of the Archdiocese.[22] The papal decree gave the religious orders in India permission to perform the *officium parochi* as well as the power to celebrate all the sacraments and the right to preach. The pope also urged

[20] The Jesuits revealed their incomprehension when the viceroy divided the parishes among different religious orders instead of giving all to them. Many of them expressed expectations that had been nursed with the departure of Dom Pedro de Mascarenhas as Viceroy to India in 1555. On this, see the Letter of Father Balthasar Dias, s.j., 1555; Letter of Father Gonçalo da Silveira, 1557; Letter of Father Melchior Carneiro, s.j., 1557, DI, Vol. 3, 402–9, 620ff.; Vol. 4, 5–13.

[21] IAN/TT, Corpo Cronológico, Part I, Mç. 95, nº 26 – "Carta de ElRey ao Dezembargador da Relação da India", 23 March 1555.

[22] Initially, this did not substantially alter the local order established by the Portuguese Crown.

them to follow the Tridentine regulations. Several chapters were about the regulation of ordinary jurisdiction, the jurisdiction of the curates, and the learning of local languages.[23] Dispensations and privileges from Rome, which made an exception for these territories, accompanied these decrees. They allowed the religious clergy to exercise powers that had not been granted to them in the parishes of Europe.[24]

In the previous decades, the fifth session of the Council of Trent (1546) had discussed the role and relevance of parishes. The Council considered their centrality in the administration of the *Respublica Christiana* while submitting them to the authority of the bishop.[25] However, as underlined by A. da Silva, even though the Council of Trent was under way at the historical moment of mission expansion, it was very much a non-missionary Council.[26] The discussions in Trent were restricted to Europe and

[23] F. Coutinho, *Le Régime Paroissial*, 66. On the attempts made by the missionaries to increase their religious powers, see Silva, *Trent's Impact,* 99–109. On the privileges of the Franciscans, see Trindade, *Conquista Espiritual do Oriente*, Vol. 1, Chapter 63.

[24] Before this, in 1563, Pius IV, in a *Suprema dispositione*, exempted bishops of the overseas dioceses from *ad limine* visits on account of the dimensions of these dioceses. He simultaneously gave prelates the power to nominate the religious as presbyters: QE, Vol. XIII, 440.

[25] Bernhard, Lefebvre, and Rapp, *L'Époque de la Réforme*, 382. This topic was resumed in the sessions of 1562. These sessions also discussed other questions, such as those relating to the power of the bishop, the nomination to offices, the insufficiency of the clergy. For a synthesis on the Council of Trent, see Adriano Prosperi, *Il Concilio di Trento*. On the adoption of these decisions in Portugal, see M. Caetano, "Recepção e Execução"; Paiva, "A Igreja e o Poder"; Palomo, "La autoridade de los prelados;" Palomo, *A Contra-Reforma em Portugal.*

[26] Silva, *Trent's Impact*, 40. On the concept of mission that circulated in early-modern Portugal, here is Bluteau: "Mission is also the territory, Province, or Kingdom, where the missionaries preach the Faith, and cultivate the vineyard of the Lord. The mission of Malabar, in Asia, of Maranhão, in America, of Congo, in Africa, etc." Bluteau also speaks of "The mission of the Apostolic men, preachers of the gospel, that the pope and the bishops

did not contemplate overseas missions. Nevertheless, Goa felt the effects of Trent immediately. Not only was Portugal among the first monarchies to adopt decrees from the Council as the law of the kingdom, but, as has been pointed out, the diocese of Goa organised its first Provincial Council simultaneously with those of the other principal dioceses of the kingdom.[27]

Taking Trent's decisions seriously, Gaspar de Leão and his successors tried to submit the missionary clergy and their practices to their authority, applying their decrees to the imperial territories. The echoes of Trent resounded across the rest of the Estado da Índia as well. Trent's legislation also applied to all the secular clergy wishing to travel to India: they had to submit themselves to an elaborate examination by the Mesa da Consciência e Ordens, which assessed the candidates' suitability.[28] In keeping with the Tridentine reforms, the examination which determined whether or not the candidate met the profile of the ideal parish priest followed the constitutions *Sanctum et Salutare* of Sixtus V (1589) and the *Cum Sancrosanctum* of the same year.[29] At the same time, the bishop of the diocese was given more power to facilitate his command of the institutional and official networks of regular and secular priests,[30] complementing the rules that had already been

---

and the prelates of the religious orders send to the conversion of the Heretics & the *Gentios,* or for the instruction of the people", and of other more theological understandings of the term: Bluteau, *Vocabulario,* Vol. 5, K–N, 511–12. On stricter uses of the word in this period, see Palomo, *Fazer dos Campos escolas excelentes.*

[27] In this context, see Paiva, *Os Bispos de Portugal e do Império.*

[28] F. Coutinho, *Le Régime Paroissial,* 52ff.

[29] Silva, *Trent's Impact,* 89–92. The Council of Trent was concerned with the formation of the secular and regular clergy. The concerns were expressed in several chapters and provisions. They travelled all the way to imperial territories and found expression in the establishment of seminaries. Their aim was to train clergymen to fulfil their apostolate *ad infidelem.*

[30] *Vide* Paiva, *Os Bispos de Portugal e do Império.* The bishops made constant efforts to obtain privileges, especially concerning confession. Such privileges

pointing in that direction. For example, a royal provision granted Dom Gaspar de Leão the power to fill and confirm ecclesiastical benefices in the diocese of Goa. This provision indicated that the monarch trusted the "archbishop who shall elect wise and competent persons to serve in the Church and do as the king commands." All this signals the confidence that the Crown had in the Archbishop of Goa making suitable choices not just for pastoral but for political and administrative positions as well.[31]

However, the actual practice of the powers of the archbishop was challenged by the religious orders. The conflict between Gaspar de Leão and the Society of Jesus in the 1560s illustrates this, but it was not the first conflict that arose, for tensions had grown between the secular and regular clergy in India.[32] Nevertheless, the support of the Crown was critical to the Goan appropriation of Trent. As laid out in Chapter 3 of the session, "Bishops and Cardinals", the Council expressed the desire that these prelates take up in earnest the task of introducing the faithful to sound doctrine, promoting good customs, and rousing the hearts of the people through proper guidance in other aspects of the faith. As such, the pastoral visits became more frequent, and this in turn allowed a higher "control" of some of the more critical aspects

---

gave them greater authority and liberty when carrying out their episcopal duties. This clashed with the regulars who wished to maintain their prior autonomy: Silva, *Trent's Impact*, 94–7. On these conflicts, see Prosperi, *Tribunali della Coscienza*, 270ff.

[31] Paiva, *Os Bispos de Portugal e do Império*, 147ff., 191–3.

[32] The opposition between the Crown and the Franciscans is one of the aspects of this conflict. References can be found in Trindade's *Conquista Espiritual do Oriente.* Trindade discusses the identical privileges enjoyed by the Franciscans of America and India, which were based on the idea of *communicatio privilegiorum*. Other sources are Miguel da Purificação, *Relação Defensiva,* as well as the documentation produced in the context of the conflicts with Friar Simão da Nazaré: IAN/TT, Col. São Vicente, L.19 – Cartas de Filipe IV sobre as matérias da Índia, fls 61, 42, 317; *Monsoon Books*, Vol. 1, 16–23, 80–90, 296–305; CR–APO, Fasc. 6, Vol. 2, 1211–12.

of theology, pastoral guidance, and Catholic liturgy. There were several limits to the Trent prescriptions, in any case. For example, even though knowledge of the local language was a supposed prerequisite for exercise of the office of a parish priest, in practice this was not an impediment. Further, despite the various powers allowed to the prelate, his control over religious believers in Bardez and Salcete was insufficient.

As it was for the other religious orders, for the Franciscans in Asia the city of Goa was the centre of activity. The Franciscans were divided into the Observants and the Recollects. The former were a branch of the Province of Portugal. The latter, coming from the Province of Nossa Senhora da Piedade, later also included people from the Portuguese Province of Arrábida. The former was given charge of the conversion of Bardez. Recognised as the Custody of São Tomé da Província Oriental and subject to the Province of Portugal in 1543, they had a significant network of convents and colleges spread through the subcontinent, from the Malabar coast to Gujarat. In 1583 they were given the right to become a separate Province, as decided by the Council of Toledo. However, it was only in 1619 that this decision took effect. In the ensuing decades the Province of Portugal tried unsuccessfully to limit their autonomy, reducing them to the level of a Custody once again. The convent of São Francisco in Goa centralised their activities. This convent was critical to the other convents, schools, rectories, and residences which followed its command. A Franciscan friar headed the affiliated institutions and was until 1619 responsible first to the Custody and then to the Province of Portugal. Thereafter, the Province of St Thomas was directly answerable to Cismontane authority and Rome.[33]

After 1622 the Recollect friars of Madre de Deus also obtained the status of a Province, resulting in a rivalry between the two Franciscan groups settled in the Estado da Índia. Apart from

[33] On the institutional architecture of the Franciscans and the relationship between the headquarters in Rome and distant provinces, custodies, and rectories, see Lemoine, *L'Époque Moderne*, Chapter 4; Penco, Battista, Matanic, D'Urso, and Sommavilla, *Gli Ordini Religiosi*.

these internal tensions, the human resources of the Province of São Tomé da Província Oriental were substantially more significant than those enjoyed by Madre de Deus, which resulted in a kind of hierarchy between the two Provinces.[34]

Information is scarce on the Franciscan institutional network in these territories, and on the organisation of the rectories in the villages. Very few original documents survive, and texts such as *Conquista Espiritual* by Friar Paulo da Trindade pay little attention to the institutional aspects. Nevertheless, Trindade tells us that the friar with the *officium parochi* shared his rectory with one or two other friars. He was the vicar, another the curate, and a third the *custos* – a lay brother who handled the finances. Often, however, these officials were not the only residents of the rectory. Sometimes, the residence or monastery associated with a church had more than twelve members, the vicar being their guardian.[35]

Although the Franciscans were the first order to establish themselves in the Estado da Índia, they did not enjoy the papal protection that the Jesuits did. Francis Xavier founded the Jesuit mission when he disembarked in Goa in 1542 as a papal nuncio, becoming in 1549 the first provincial of one of the first Provinces of the Company anywhere in the world. The jurisdictional architecture of the Jesuits was much more straightforward than that of the Franciscans. From Rome to the farthest points in the globe, the hierarchy of command was clear. Nevertheless, the founding of the Provinces of Portugal and Goa, in 1546 and 1549, had consequences for the relationship between the two. Later, the Province of Malabar of 1605 (Vice Province from 1601), the Province of Japan of 1611 (Vice Province in 1583), and the Vice Province of China (1623) became divisions of the Province of Goa. All of them hosted novitiates, seminaries, schools, residences, and all the other Jesuit institutions. They were part of the Assistancy of Portugal, the oldest in the Company. Rome hosted the Assistancy, allowing the Assistant to be the principal intermediary

[34] This time there were the Observants of Goa who tried to reduce them to the status of Custody.

[35] Lemoine, *L'Époque Moderne*, 97–8.

between the general of the Company and the Provinces of the Assistancy.[36]

A few decades after the first regular clergy had settled in Salcete and Bardez, several of the villages already had stable institutional structures, many of which continue to mark the material and symbolic presence of Christians in these areas to this day. As mentioned, some of the parishes encompassed more than one village, suggesting the scale of implantation of ecclesiastic structures and religious orders in these areas. In 1621 the Archbishop of Goa, Cristóvão de Sá e Lisboa, reported the existence of twenty-seven parochial churches in Tiswadi, ten in Bardez, and more than twenty in Salcete. Another list at around the same time refers, however, to the existence of thirteen churches in Bardez.[37] Some years later the Franciscans had seventeen parochial churches in Bardez (which served thirty-four villages), in addition to a college, a seminary, two hospitals, and several other services provided by the churches. In contrast, in Salcete the Jesuits had more than twenty-two churches, the hospital of Margão, and the college of Rachol. In 1640 the Archbishop Dom Francisco de Mártires reported the existence of seventy-nine parochial churches in the Old Conquests, twenty more than those that existed two decades prior, a number that persisted until the following century.[38]

In general, the king of Portugal was responsible for the construction and funding of these churches through tithes.[39] Besides the Crown,

[36] The best overview on this organisation and its connection with the Province of Portugal is Dauril Alden's, *The Making of an Enterprise*, Vol. 3, Chapter 10. On the Province of Portugal, see F. Rodrigues, *História da Companhia de Jesus*, or for a quick overview of its institutional architecture, see Lemoine, *L'Époque Moderne*, Chapter 6.

[37] "Relatio de Statu Ecclesiae Goanae ab Archiepiscopo Cristophoro de Sa e Lisboa, Goa (1621)", in ASCPF, S. Congregatio Concilii; Meersman, *The Ancient Franciscan Provinces*, 95–6; F. Coutinho, *Le Régime Paroissial*, 40–1.

[38] F.X. Costa, *Anais Franciscanos*; Borges, *The Economics of the Goa Jesuits*, 161–7.

[39] Frequently, the Crown spent the tithes on other needs. A decree by the Mesa da Consciência e Ordens reiterated "the tithes of the aforementioned Provinces destined for this purpose . . . [should] uphold this first as an

they could receive funding from the charitable brotherhood of the Misericórdia, private donations, village communities, and pious legacies. The construction of some of these churches had been paid through alms collected in the villages or donations by private parties. Of this type were two churches in Bardez. The Jesuit General Poulanco said the same of churches established on the island of Chorão in Goa and Thana in the Northern Province. "They are our churches" became a Jesuit universal statement. It implied that the Archbishop of Goa did not have jurisdiction over them.

The most significant funding for these churches came from rents received on lands transferred from non-Christian temples to the Christian cult. In Tiswadi the College and seminary of São Paulo led the process of accumulating funds as well as immoveable and moveable property. This college was given the properties of all the temples, divinities, and priests of the villages of Tiswadi, which it managed together with *confrarias* that were charged with building churches. In Bardez and Salcete, the provision of 23 March 1569 allocated these properties to the Franciscans and the Jesuits.[40] This legislation delimited the conditions associated with the usufruct of these properties: to endow the communities with the necessary means for their spiritual sustenance (conversion and worship, for example); to build and repair churches; to maintain the House of the Catechumens, the *confrarias*, the curates, vicars, chaplains, and chapter; and to encourage Christian devotion in general. The provision also specified that the sacraments had to be given freely, in line with the precept *gratis accepistis, gratis date* (you have taken freely, give freely), although the priests could still accept alms given through free will.[41]

---

obligation, as stated in the Bull of 26 September 1565": IAN/TT, Mesa da Consciência e Ordens, nos 302–6 – Aranha, Meza das Três Ordens, Vol. 2, 20.

[40] On the financial power of the religious orders, see a *provisão* of 1591 and an *alvará* of 1611: CR–APO, Fasc. 5, Vol. 3, 1280–1; IAN/TT, Cartório Jesuítico, mç. 57, nº 2 – "Alvará sobre os mosteiros"; as well as several royal letters asking for information on the holdings of the religious. See CR–APO, Fasc. 3, 98, 192, 204, 274, and 286.

[41] F. Coutinho, *Le Régime Paroissial*, 97–8. Despite this prohibition, the

With the necessary financial conditions established, the arrival of missionaries complemented the institutional implantation of the religious orders. The *Livro do Estado da Índia Oriental* (1635) by António Bocarro and Pedro Barreto Resende is essential when considering the effects of this. Fourteen years after Cristóvão de Sá e Lisboa reported on the state of Christianity in the Estado da Índia, their report gives the reader an idea of the number of "Europeans" living in the city of Goa. Sanjay Subrahmanyam has comprehensively analysed these numbers. His analysis reveals the presence of around 800 *casados brancos* (of Portuguese origin), 2200 *casados negros* (local Christians), and 639 classified as religious. Among the last category 220 were Franciscans (Observants and of Madre de Deus), 149 were Jesuits, 125 were Augustinians, and the Dominicans accounted for 102.[42]

When compared with the total of Portuguese subjects in the Estado da Índia, these numbers reveal the religious centrality of the city of Goa. The number of regular clergy living there represented about 40 per cent of all missionaries spread through the Estado da Índia and outside it. If only for this reason, Goa could justly be considered the Rome of the East. In any case, these numbers prove the imposing presence of the regular clergy in the territories. This presence was more substantial than in Portugal, where the religious presence was already higher than in the other European monarchies.[43] This inflated presence was the result of the human

---

practice of charging for the sacraments was frequent. The § 14 of the register of the pastoral visit of Archbishop Dom Frei Aleixo de Meneses in 1596 criticises it and the practice continued to be denounced even in 1748. By that time, the archbishop was informed that the parish priest of Sancoale (Sankval, in south Goa) refused to celebrate the mass without payment of two and a half xerafins, or, if the devotee was poor, two xerafins: AAG, Livro 1 de Visitas Pastorais, 1747, Salcete, 36.

[42] Unfortunately, Bocarro does not explain if these categories included just the city or the other surrounding areas of Tiswadi, Salcete, and Bardez: Subrahmanyam, *Portuguese Empire in Asia*, 232–5.

[43] Subrahmanyam, *Portuguese Empire in Asia*, 234–5; Palomo, *Fazer dos campos escolas excelentes*, 76.

resources required for the project of conversion and Christianisation of local populations. The ratio between converted and non-Christians proved that the main objective of the missionary presence had been achieved.

Mira Mascarenhas has stated that the proportion of the converted vis-à-vis non-Christians in the Tiswadi, Bardez, and Salcete villages at the beginning of the eighteenth century favoured the former. Information collected on request by the Academia Real da História (Royal Academy of History), compiled in the codex *Notícias do arcebispado de Goa,* confirms this. At the time, Salcete, considered by many to be the "bouquet of the Church of God", had about 100,000 converts and merely 3000 non-Christians. The same applied to other Goan territories, except the city of Goa, where the situation was different.[44] The city of Goa was exceptional, given that non-Christian communities were allowed to live in the capital for financial and commercial purposes, these being deemed necessary for the upkeep of the Estado da Índia. The circumstances of the city were not representative, however, of the hinterland.

At the beginning of the seventeenth century, the numbers were quite different. According to M.N. Pearson, around 50,000 converts inhabited the Goan territories, representing between a fourth and a third of the local population, whereas in the city of Goa, where conversion had been more intense, converts comprised two-thirds of the population. A letter of 1579 by Father Duarte de Sande says there were at most 8000 converts in Salcete out of a total of approximately 80,000 residents. Considering how much the situation was reversed a century later, these numbers speak for themselves.[45]

[44] Mascarenhas, "The Church in Eighteenth Century Goa", 84. A Jesuit source from 1666–8 refers to the presence of 80,000 Christian souls: *Lista das rendas e despezas da Província de Goa,* 356. See, for the rest of the seventeenth century, M.J.M. Lopes, *Goa Setecentista*, 83ff.

[45] Pearson, *Portuguese in India*; DHMPPO, Vol. 12, 448. These numbers suggest that during the seventeenth century there was also a concerted push towards converting the locals.

The conjunction of the mission and parochial structure, and of the apostolate and curacy, ensured the establishment of structures necessary to enable the transition from nominal conversion to the desired cultural conversion. The regular clergy became the leading intermediaries between the cultures and societies of Christians and locals. For this to happen, access to the parochial structure was essential, since the parish, as Luciano Allegra has noted, was the privileged institutional space among various "cultures". It was mainly through these parishes that conversions and baptisms took place, and through them the converted were Christianised – equipped with a new consciousness and new beliefs.[46]

As in other places, from the moment they established themselves in the villages the regular clergy launched several strategies to achieve their goals.[47] They used their power either in strictly religious tasks such as celebrating Christian holidays, or in more mundane aspects such as debts, property distribution, and the payment of taxes.

In sum, the regular clergy had substantial powers. They held a monopoly over the sacred institutions in the villages, which meant control over visible relationships among subjects, groups, and the idea of the transcendent. However, if these efforts were to achieve significant success, they had to carefully craft their actions and their reception by the local communities. They had to intervene at many different levels in local life: in forms of communication, the family, notions of time and space, systems of production and the circulation of goods, the dispensing of justice. This was the

[46] However, this author differentiates between the success of the administrative structure and the potential failure in the prosecution of certain goals, especially when they tried to impose ideologies that were too alien to the community: Allegra, "Il Parroco", 879.

[47] Delumeau, *Catholicism Between Luther and Voltaire*, 25ff.; Allegra, "Il Parroco", 897ff.; Copete and Palomo, "Des carêmes après la carême", 20. The most sophisticated strategies and regulations were developed in the parishes. Through them, the parish priest gained a further, and personal, insight into his flock, registering the most important events of Christian life from birth to death.

second stage in the implementation of Christianity. The initial model of action was almost always the same: substituting local religious symbols – temples, priests, and rituals – with Christian ones.

In Tiswadi, the allocation of the clergy to the parishes followed the destruction of the material signs of idolatry. The same process happened with the transfer of rents of the temple properties to the Christian cult, first to the Confraria and Colégio da Santa Fé and later to its new administrators, the Jesuits. Economic conditions favourable for conversion had been established before Tiswadi was divided into parishes. Simão Botelho had systematically collected information on the revenues due to the lands now subject to the king,[48] and the *tanadar-mor* had compiled information on lands and properties "of all sorts" that "belonged to the pagodas of the village and its servants" of Tiswadi, Chorão, Divar, and Jua.[49] In contrast, the destruction of the temples in Salcete and Bardez happened *after* the Jesuits and Franciscans received their parishes.

The year 1567 saw the destruction of the temples of the territories of Salcete and Bardez, and transfer of the property, rents, and revenues of temples to the Christian cult. Again, the aim was to pay the "vicars, curates, and beneficiaries" and fund the workshops attached to the churches (the *fabricas*), as well as their maintenance and repair. In Salcete the college of the Jesuits received such funds. Other royal decisions complemented these privileges. The donations established the financial basis and economy of the

[48] In 1548 Botelho had begun with the Foral of the lands of Diu, and in 1552 he confirmed in a letter to the King to have almost finished "the general register of affairs in these parts". See Botelho, *Textos sobre o Estado da Índia*, 74; cf. IAN/TT, Núcleo Antigo, Tombo de Simão Botelho, 1554.

[49] The revenues of the temples included not just the ground rents, but all of the properties that belonged to the *gurus*, ascetics, single women (or devadasis), and temple-servants, and included the gold and silver jewellery, the male and female slaves of the temples, their herds of cattle, and other goods; also the possessions of the carpenters who made the banners, those that tended the areca groves, the soothsayers, the trumpeters, the *bhandaris*, and others: HAG, nº 7604, Foral das Ilhas de Goa, 1553–1562, fls 37v–38.

new religious order. The economic power of the regular clergy was further reinforced by receipts from ground rents and royal grants, donations from the Crown and other subjects, the purchase of properties and their development, commercial enterprise, and the imposition of "taxes" on the local people.[50]

The transfer of rents to the Christian cult inaugurated a process of not merely financial but overall economic intervention in the life of the villages, resulting in the Jesuits being able to accumulate vast riches.[51] The same was true for the Franciscans, though in their case the arrangements were more complicated given that the statutes of the Franciscans prevented them owning property, and permitted only usufruct rights.[52]

The grant of village properties, which in some places consisted of substantial swathes of arable land, complemented such

[50] On this, see HAG, nº 824 – Provisões do Colégio de Rachol, 1596–1680, fls 3–6v; HAG, nº 3071 – Foral de Salcete, copy of 1585; HAG, nº 7583–7585 – Foral of 1622; HAG, nº 7604 – Foral de Salcete, Summary of 1635 of the Foral of 1622; HAG, nº 7587 – Foral Antigo de Bardez, 1649. One also finds multiple references to these transactions in HAG, nº 4469 – Provisões, leis e alvarás, 1558–1567.

[51] On the Jesuit properties, see IAN/TT, Corpo Cronológico, Part I, Mss. 107, nº 38 – "Carta de D. Antão de Noronha [. . .] razoes que teve para não dar Igrejas, e aforar algumas Aldêas aos Padres da Companhia", 30 Dec. 1564. The vast documentation, from the "Tombo dos Namoxins" to the "Provisões do Colégio de Rachol" and uncountable decisions witness this process of accumulation of riches: CR–APO, Fasc. 5, Part I, 182–3, 212, 230, 234, 249, 254, 330, 489, and 993. For a bibliography, see Moraes, *History of Christianity*, 395ff.; Borges, *The Economics of the Goa Jesuits*; A.T. Matos, "The Financial Situation". On forms of the economic power of the Jesuits in general in the Assistancy of Portugal, see Alden, *The Making of an Enterprise*, Part IV.

[52] A petition by the *gaunkars* in Bardez in 1613 provides information on the Franciscans' revenue: "forty years ago they demolished our temples and built up thirteen churches intended to sustain their ministry. The villages that were applied to the sustenance of the temples generated more than three thousand pardaos each year . . .": *Monsoon Books*, Vol. 2, 323–5. A viceregal provision of 1568 had already increased their income "for the betterment of Christians in these parts": CR–APO, Fasc. 5, Vol. 2, 687–9.

revenues. This process of accumulation, which began under Governor Martim Afonso de Sousa, went on through the subsequent decades and centuries. By the end of the century, the College of São Paulo, for example, also benefited from the transfer of the *foros* – rent paid to the Portuguese king for the right to cultivate his land – of the villages of Assolna, Velim, and Ambelim. Dom Pedro de Castro had donated these *foros* to them.[53]

A list of the revenues and expenses of the Jesuit Province of Goa reveals the riches of the Jesuits at this time. Despite many attempts by the Crown to reduce their economic power, the Jesuits were able to accumulate substantial property, including double-storeyed houses and lands; coconut groves in Quelossim, Carmona, Benaulim, Dramapur, Chinchinim, Betalbatim, Majorda, Calata; orchards in Chorão; the estate of Sant' Anna; the island of Lovarim; the land of Rachol; revenues from the Assolna, Velim, and Ambelim lands; and revenue from the Rachol fair. A survey in the *Tombo dos Namoxins* described the economic power that the religious enjoyed, especially in Salcete. And, as Dauril Alden has noted, it was not just in the countryside that the Jesuits had properties. The buildings they owned in the urban centres generated substantial income for the Company. In the Goan case, however, the properties were generally sold off, owing to the massive number of problems that they brought with them.[54]

In addition to accumulating property, the Jesuits intervened in the modes of cultivation. From constant references to increases in the rents that could be paid "on account of our industry and labour", it appears that the interventions made the lands more productive, increasing their value. The establishment of seed banks to store seeds was one such productive measure. When needed, they distributed the seeds to the more impoverished farmers.[55]

[53] Alden, *The Making of an Enterprise,* 392–3.

[54] Borges, *The Economics of the Goa Jesuits*; Alden, *The Making of an Enterprise*, 398.

[55] The *"Lista das rendas e despezas da Província de Goa"* frequently uses this phrase to explain the increase in the revenues of the Jesuits. For an

More controversial was the process through which rice-paddy fields were converted into coconut groves, probably because the latter offered better returns than rice farming. The Crown was against this and discontinued the practice. There were critiques of other activities, too. A letter from the Câmara de Goa to the king in 1602 protested and criticised a toll imposed by Jesuits to increase their income. This toll applied to non-Christians who went to the mainland (the *terras firmes*) to celebrate rituals prohibited in Goa. "Through this tribute," the Jesuits sought to enable "conversion [. . .] saying that since the infidels do not convert, let them pay for the costs of the converted." The Provincial Councils forbade such practices, as did several royal decrees. Nevertheless, the Jesuits justified them as their means for securing a higher end, namely conversion.[56]

That an economic sensibility structured the Jesuit presence in the villages of Goa is evident in the *Modos de falar em Canary* (Forms of Speech in Canarim), composed by Father António Saldanha in the second half of the seventeenth century, and included in the volume entitled *Prasse Pastoral.* This book was an essential companion for Jesuits recently arrived in the parishes of Salcete. The dialogues included in the lexicon frequently concern the fruits of the land and their quality:

Tem mangas?	Do you have mangoes?
A como rendem?	How much do they sell for?
Cento a pardao	Hundred for a *pardao*
Mandaime huas poucas	Send me some
He vos de prender, se não pagais	I will imprison you if you do not pay

approximate idea of their wealth, see HAG, nº 824, Provisões do Colégio de Rachol, 1596–1680, 824. On this, see Souza, *Goa Medieval,* 96.

[56] HAG, nº 9530 – Assentos do Conselho da Fazenda, fls182v–183; HAG, nº 1160 – Assentos do Conselho da Fazenda, fl. 38v; IAN/TT, Mesa da Consciência e Ordens – Aranha, Meza das Três Ordens, Vol. 2, fl. 40; CR–APO, Fasc. 1, Vol. 2, 91–110; see Borges, *The Economics of the Goa Jesuits,* 41ff.; A.T. Matos, "The Financial Situation", 151ff.; Godinho, "Les finances"; Alden, *The Making of an Enterprise,* 415.

De quem he este palmar?	Whose is this coconut grove?
São estas varzeas?	Whose are these paddies?[57]

These examples show the fundamental interests of the fathers *in loco*, often matters that had little connection with conversion.

Besides the labour contracts with villagers, the use of slave labour – referred to in the codexes found in "*Conventos extintos*" from the archives of Goa – also indicates that the religious orders were substantially involved in the village economy. Other accounts too are far from positive – we know that the Pai dos Cristãos of Bardez organised workers among the converts under his charge by offering a meagre amount of rice, while there were parishes that engaged local Christians "in their service for half the day as if they were slaves".[58]

Eventually, the success of these economic activities was so overwhelming that the accumulation of wealth by missionaries became a moral problem. Texts by missionaries written to legitimise their high level of prosperity give us access to these controversies. Father Francisco Rodrigues reflected on contracts, loans, and the sale of forbidden products to non-believers when legitimising them.[59] In other texts Jesuits presented themselves as victims of the Crown's unjust persecution. Valignano, for example, argued that prohibiting commercial activity would result in all-round poverty. The consequences of impoverishment jeopardising the interests of Christianity were argued as being more harmful than the possession of "illicit" property. To counter the critiques against them, the Jesuits appealed to papal authority and obtained permission to continue with the majority of their activities.[60]

[57] IAN/TT, Manuscritos da Livraria, Cod. 757 – António de Saldanha, s.j., Prasse Pastoral, fls 11v., 18v.

[58] See, e.g., HAG, nº 2789, "Conventos extintos, Papéis, 1619–1810". Borges, *The Economics of the Goa Jesuits*, 47–8; Araújo, "O 'Pai dos Cristãos'", 312. About Goan slaves, see J. Pinto, *Slavery in Portuguese India*; Pescatello, "The African Presence in Portuguese India".

[59] *Apud* Wicki, *Problemas morais*, 257–63.

[60] See, on this topic, IAN/TT, Armário Jesuítico, Mss. nº 8 – Livro de Pareceres do Pe. António Soares, fls 619–41, in defence of the lands acquired

The Franciscans sought to justify their transgressions too. In his *Breves Resoluções Morais,* Friar António da Graça, Commissioner General of the provinces of São Tomé and Madre de Deus, dedicated a chapter to religious poverty in which he discussed several delicate situations. He highlighted the subtle difference between the legal concepts of property and *dominio* to defend the *domínio útil* (usufructuary rights) that Franciscans enjoyed over specific properties. In such cases, he argued, Franciscan control of property did not violate their vow of poverty. Elaborating on the appropriate use of these rents, Graça argued that Franciscans ought to be able to receive the right to perpetual rents directed towards supporting the cult for their necessities – books and medicines – as well as annual grants from princes and kings and other forms of rent for a maximum period of ten years. Such means enabled them to spend money "for personal use which prudent judgement would not deem superfluous, such as dress, food, books, which require to be purchased." Beyond the money given to those with "*arbítrio do prudente*" (prudent judgement), thirty further situations were shown as exceptions; these Graça justified by recourse to a tenet that was becoming increasingly familiar: "necessity surpasses the law".[61]

Nevertheless, complaints brought against the religious orders by officials of the Crown increased. Besides the economic aspects, a certain laxity was noted in terms of the disciplinary mechanisms of the clergy. The "*anos benevolentes*" (happy years) that Alden speaks of gave way to a progressive reduction in the power of the religious orders.[62]

---

by the religious orders; nº 14 – Livro com vários pareceres de Pes. Jezuitas sobre várias matérias resolvidas pelo Pe. Diogo de Areda, fls 39ff.; Cartório Jesuítico, Mç.57, nº 26 – Informaçam por partes dos Religiosos da Cª de IESU sobre os bens de raiz".

[61] Central Library of Panaji, Breves Resoluções Morais, M – 4.

[62] See some of these complaints in *Monsoon Books*, Vol. 1, 296–305; CR–APO, Fasc. 3, 568, 581, 610, and 618. See also Alden, *The Making of an Enterprise*, 432ff.

The Crown was now able to count on the support of the secular clergy, besides the Mesa da Consciência e Ordens and the Inquisition, to cope with the religious needs of its empire. Besides, the Council of Trent had been clear about the submission of the regular clergy to the secular hierarchy. The religious order could no longer argue that it was exempt from diocesan jurisdiction when exercising *officium parochi* by special papal dispensation. Furthermore, the Habsburg reforms included a growing control over Church structures.[63] Other variables, such as the rise in Rome of the Propaganda Fide, were important, too. From 1622, with the foundation of the congregation of the Propaganda Fide, the secular and regular ecclesiastic jurisdictions began to be substantially reorganised. Right from the fifteenth century, successive papal bulls had granted the missionary task of *extra territorium* to the Iberian kingdoms. This situation changed as Rome sought to denationalise these jurisdictions wherever possible and establish its supremacy. To a large extent this change redefined the Portuguese rights of *padroado* (patronage) too, and the role of the religious orders in it.[64]

The challenges faced by the Goan missionaries were undeniable, and all was not smooth sailing. In a letter to the viceroy of India dated 1588, the secretary, Miguel de Moura, referred to an Augustinian petition that pleaded poverty as a reason for alms. Not only did Moura not respond to this request, he instead initiated an inquiry into the holdings of the order which snowballed to cover

[63] Dom Philip II of Spain (Dom Philip I of Portugal) started the reform of the religious orders in Spain, which he considered essential pillars in the spiritual renovation of Christianity. The systematic nature of disciplining strategies and reform of the religious orders in the Portuguese realm are part of this context: Novalin, *Historia de la Iglesia*, Vol. 2–2°, Chapter 2; Vol. 3–2°, 20ff. Palomo, *Fazer dos campos escolas excelentes*, Chapter 1. Something similar also started to happen in the "American empire" since the mid-sixteenth century: see, among others, Phelan, *The Millennial Kingdom*; and van Oss, *Catholic Colonialism*.

[64] Still worth reading in this context is Boxer's *A Igreja e a Expansão Ibérica,* 98–106.

other religious orders and continued over the following decades.[65] One of the targets was the convent of Santa Mónica in Goa, the second biggest women's convent in the Portuguese world (the biggest being the one in Odivelas, near Lisbon).[66] The attraction of the convent for women was among the major reasons for the growing depopulation of the city of Goa, people said. Others said its attraction translated into an excessive accumulation of wealth, making the institution excessively rich and powerful at a time when the Estado da Índia was financially fragile.

Moura also received a letter from the Jesuits requesting "the payment of all the grants and alms that they are owed from the treasury in the Estado from the taxes that are paid to the said treasury from the villages and other properties that can be found in those parts." The secretary responded that they would have to wait for him to complete the inquiry initiated on account of their request. Eventually, in the following year, rather than extend grants, the viceroy revoked the donations made to them by Dom Pedro de Castro of the villages of Assolna, Velim, and Ambelim in Salcete that had been confiscated from the "gentiles" after violent incidents. The Crown argued that Castro did not have the authority to make such a donation. Moreover, the Jesuit claim to the 8000–10,000 *pardaos* they had in these villages did not apply in relation to sovereign rents – as stated clearly in the *Ordenações*.[67]

In 1591 a new royal order forbade future acquisition of *bens de raiz* (realty; property). There were two reasons for this order: the first was non-payment of the tithes on these properties, which

[65] CR–APO, F.3, 98. About the continuity of the process during the reign of Dom Philip IV, see IAN/TT, Col. São Vicente, L. 19 – Cartas de Filipe IV sobre as matérias da Índia.

[66] On this aspect, see Nunes, "D. Frei Miguel de Rangel"; Bethencourt, "Os conventos femininos".

[67] A document of the mid-seventeenth century mentions the same villages as part of the society's rents, which seems to suggest that the king had given up the revocation: *Lista das rendas e despezas da Província de Goa,* 354; CR–APO, Fasc. 3, 110–20, 192–204. See Borges, *The Economics of the Gòa Jesuits*, 72ff.

had resulted in setbacks for the king; and the second, the "general and common scandal".[68]

Thirteen years later the Duke of Vila Nova referred specifically to the scandal that had followed from missionaries getting "hold of properties to return with riches to these kingdoms, and us[ing] them to support their relatives and other obligations, [which go] against the principal vows they have professed." To avoid such situations, Vila Nova proposed that missionaries who travelled to India should not be allowed to return to the kingdom unless they were called back for reasons of the common good. This would restrict their focus to "converting Gentiles, and in the exclusive exercise of their religious calling, as ministers of promoting the holy gospel," replacing their immersion in terrestrial affairs. Within five years, a *carta régia* pointed in the same direction. It prohibited the clergy of the Estado da Índia from engaging in commerce. Again, "scandal" was the expression used to convey displeasure at the situation. The king recalled that "their example should be more excellent, considering the proximity they have with the Gentiles." Their will to convert, he added, "cools as a result of the enormous scandal that this provokes, not just among them, but also the Christians."[69]

Given its inability to deter the religious orders, as Viceroy Miguel de Noronha attested later, political power tried to resolve the problem differently: the king forbade all Christians and locals from trading in goods belonging to the ecclesiastics. The matter would, nevertheless, surface again in 1610. In that year the king prohibited, once again, the donation of any more villages to the Jesuits, alleging that they already possessed properties valued at more than 10,000 *pardaos*. The king added that "The people of the villages are usually impoverished and weak, but nearly each

[68] CR–APO, Fasc. 5, Vol. 3, 1280–1.

[69] CR–APO, Fasc. 6, Vol. 2, 760–1. This was a common practice, as one can infer from the vast number of petitions that the Crown received from both sides of the empire: Cod. 47–VIII–7 – Decreta s. congregationis episcoporum & regularum, fls 586–98, 633–4.

has four monasteries, and because of it, it is impossible to support so many religious."[70] Two years later the Crown would encourage the denunciation of offenders by promising the informants half the impugned property. In 1615 the Crown referred to the *Ordenações* to support its decisions. In 1630 it was the Conselho de Estado's turn to criticise the religious orders by saying that "the missionaries have a reason to be in India, and it is not to build up grandiose convents for which there is little need." The Council underlined that, given the state of material poverty in India, it would be better to decrease the number of the regular clergy. They insisted, in any case, that the authorities take "particular care to pay the prelates, inquisitors and religious people."[71]

Running contrary to these tendencies, however, was the position of the *Junta sobre materias tocantes as Religiões deste estado*, a meeting held in 1636 in Goa, on matters pertaining to the regular clergy of the Estado da Índia. This assembly rejected previous criticisms and defended the religious orders, regarding both their properties and the number of the regular clergy. While not making direct reference to the riches of the Jesuits, the inquisitor Jorge Seco de Macedo said the Franciscans did not own estates, and that "those of Saint Dominic [the Dominicans] and Saint Augustine [the Augustinians] were not just poor but miserable."[72]

Whether poor, miserable, or rich, what is certain is that the power of the missionaries in the Goan villages was unrivalled in the first decades of the seventeenth century, at least in the sphere of religion, law, and the economy. Their power would not have been possible without support from the local elites, who were essential both for their presence to be accepted, and for them

[70] On these royal orders, see *Monsoon Books*, Vol. 1, 281–3, 308–11; CR–APO, Fasc. 6, Vol. 2, 1259.

[71] Cunha Rivara's *Archivo Portuguez Oriental* is full of these orders and decisions (see CR–APO, Fasc. 3, 568–81; Fasc. 6, Vol. 2, 892–3, 1117). On the decisions of the Council of State, see Pissurlencar, ed., *Assentos do Conselho de Estado*, 517–18. The same criticisms continued to be made until the eighteenth century: Ames, *Renascent Empire?*, Chapter 3.

[72] CR–APO, Fasc. 1, Vol. 2, 34.

to be able to have any success in changing the lifestyles of the local populations. Inside the village, the missionaries knew that an amicable relationship with the *gaunkari* (assembly of village notables) would allow for easier access to all sectors of village life.

After they distanced and replaced the caretakers of the local temples, the symbolic uprooting of the spaces where the *gaunkari* would meet was an explicit manifestation of the new order. Earlier, the *gaunkari* met under the shade of mango or banyan trees. If it rained, they would retreat into the house of a *gaunkar*. In the new order, *gaunkars* increasingly met in the houses of imperial agents, so that imperial power not only framed and protected but also legitimated local practices. At the same time, it used these acts of legitimation to secure the new geography of power that the empire had put in place. The proceeding of several other *gaunkaris* demonstrate the approximation between the empire and the village. In February 1608 the *gaunkari* of Azossim decided to give rents to the *gaunkars'* widows, in line with the village vicar's desire. Some years later, the same village referred to a debt owed to the same vicar, Father Estevão de Ataíde, suggesting a somewhat dubious relationship. In fact, the intimacy between priests and local elites became so intense that it ended up causing tensions and conflicts. According to the account of a *gaunkar* in Carambolim, Father Simão Araújo had ordered some farmers to be arrested.[73] In the region of Bardez, Friar Simão de Nazaré, a controversial Franciscan, had factions of supporters and rivals in various villages.[74]

The powers of the missionaries and parishes included, as mentioned above, those in the administrative and judicial spheres. During the government of Francisco Barreto, António Martins, the Pai dos Cristãos, could solve civil conflicts involving a fine up to five xerafins. His decisions had no right of appeal, the same

[73] HAG, nº 10020 – Comunidades, Azossim, Deliberações e contas correntes, 1608, 41; HAG, nº 10023 – Comunidades, Azossim, Deliberações e contas correntes, 1614, 26v. On that, see Souza, *Goa Medieval.*

[74] See, e.g., Borges, "Foreign Jesuits and Native Resistance".

applying to his jurisdiction over criminal cases in which there had been no bloodshed. Some years later, in 1562, the Count of Redondo attributed the same powers to the rectors of churches to determine cases involving both native Christians and non-Christians, with fines up to three tangas. Once again, there were no rights of appeal against their decisions.[75] In the following decade, a clause required that if the rectors knew "the people in those lands and islands worshipped idols, or engaged in other forms of Gentile acts prohibited by the Council," they were obliged to inform the competent judge of these. This second provision ensured that the rectors were endowed not only with religious power to resolve matters of minor import but were also required to denounce the ritual activity of those who had not yet converted via other judicial authorities.[76]

However, after the initial period of high interdependence between the Crown and regular clergy in judicial matters, the former tried to revoke the priests' judicial authority. In 1581 their judicial functions were extinguished through the creation of the office of Conservador e Juiz dos Cristãos da Terra (Judge of the Christians of the Land). This official had to investigate and resolve all cases among the newly converted. When this official was not present, his functions were handed over to the captains of the forts.[77]

[75] In 1560, Pius IV's bull, *Pro salubri regnorum*, renewed for Dom Sebastião the rights of the monarchy to hire ecclesiastics and Christians in civil affairs, such as judging cases of crime. These rights had initially been conceded by Pope Paul III to Dom João III: QE, Vol. XIII, 124. A provision of Viceroy Dom Francisco Coutinho explicitly said: "I order that one of the *mordomos* of the parishes and confraternities of the churches, whoever is present, should listen to the Christians of the land and to the Gentiles, in their conflicts, deciding about them up to the value of three *tangas*; and his decision be executed without appeal or interference": CR–APO, Fasc. 5, Vol. 2, 512–13.

[76] There are several provisions concerning these issues. Another provision of Viceroy Dom Francisco Coutinho says, for example, that the new Christians and the Gentiles were punished if they worked on Sundays and holidays: CR–APO, Fasc. 5, Vol. 2, 510–12, 903–4; Vol. 3, 1429–31nn.

[77] CR–APO, Fasc. 5, Vol. 3, 974–5. In the following years, there was a similar legislation: CR–APO, Fasc. 5, Vol. 3, 1427–8 n., 1430–5; HAG,

All this indicates the power that missionaries had in the villages of Goa. The lexicon of Father Saldanha is evidence of this power too. The lexicon includes many dialogues in the imperative form exemplifying how this power operated in daily life:

Tornay a levar isso.	Return this.
Mandastes ja chamar?	Have you sent for them?
Fizestes ja o que vos disse?	Have you done what I told you?
Chamastes loja?	Did you call the shop?
Chamai os gancares co o escrivão.	Call the *gaunkars* and the clerk.
Fazeis devação ao anjo da guarda?	Do you make your devotions to the guardian angel?[78]

It is crucial to see how this power was exercised to change beliefs in the transcendent, but also conceptions and perceptions of time and space as well as how these subjects perceived themselves, their family, and society. The case of the Brahman Manuel, of the village of Sirula, illustrates some of these aspects.

Methods of Implantation: A Case in the Village of Sirula

Sirula, or Serula (close to Mapusa) was reputed to be the principal village of Bardez. It was one of nine villages represented in the Câmara Geral, which denoted an assembly of the main villages of the territory that decided on matters of common interest. The Brahmans dominated the *gaunkari*, but other villagers were of different ethnic and social extraction.[79] After 1565, Sirula hosted the Church of Salvador do Mundo, as well as a Franciscan rectory.

---

nº 8779 – Assentos da Relação de Goa, nº 70, nº 79. See also the documentation published by Abranches, *Arquivo da Relação de Goa*, related to this jurisdiction.

[78] IAN/TT, Manuscritos da Livraria, Cod. 757 – António de Saldanha, s.j., Prasse Pastoral, *passim*.

[79] R.G. Pereira, *Goa – Hindu Temples*, 80.

According to Paulo da Trindade's *Conquista Espiritual do Oriente*, the buildings attached to the church were where the friars learned the local languages before 1606. Thereafter the newly built Colégio de São Boaventura (College of Saint-Bonaventure) in the city of Goa assumed that mission. The ruins of a local temple destroyed around 1567 lay below the church and its buildings. Possibly the main temple of the village,[80] the temple was part of a complex of the seventeen temples of Sirula. These were divided among the Vaishnavites devoted to Vitthala, Narayana, Dakti Vanadevata, and Mahalakshmi (Malcumi); the Shaivites meanwhile were devoted to Siddhanatha, Bhagavati, Mahakali, and Gopeshwar.[81] There were devotions to divinities of Dravidian or regional origin, too, like Ravalnath, Khetrapal, Santeri, or Vir; to the founders of the village (Garam-Purusha); and to the forefathers of the ancient *vangods* (Kul-Purusha). There were cults to other gods, too, like Somanatha and Mallinatha. At the time of the destruction of the temples, these divinities were transferred to Mulgaon, a village in the sultanate of Bijapur.[82]

The several temples of Sirula indicated a socio-culturally diverse settlement. The place represented a fragile social balance, with rival groups coexisting. Later conflicts among them allow us to trace networks of solidarity and tensions in the village. These networks included Shaivites and Vaishnavites who were not only members of different social groups but also represented different castes. This pre-existing tension enabled the intrusion and establishment of new powers.

Following Trindade's account, it would seem that in the first

[80] A letter of donation of lands of 1580, through which King Dom Henrique gives to the church of Reis Magos of Verem a paddy field in Sirula that had previously belonged to the temple "Vitula", seems to indicate that the temple to Vitthala was the main temple of Sirula. On the temples of Sirula, see Pereira, *Goa – Hindu Temples*, 89–90.

[81] Some of these deities were part of what has been considered the classical pantheon of Hindu deities: Daniélou, *Mythes et Dieux de l'Inde*.

[82] Sen, *Medieval Mysticism of India*; Shirodkar, "Influence of Nath Cult in Goa".

decades of the seventeenth century Sirula had 81 Christians of communion, 2170 of confession, and 530 children. Many converted via a general baptism performed in the third quarter of the sixteenth century by Archbishop Dom Gaspar de Leão. Given that in M.N. Pearson's estimate of this time only a third or a quarter of the Goan population had been converted, and considering that the larger part of the village must have remained non-Christian, Sirula emerges as a rather populous village.

The Franciscan friar Tomé Toscano was the rector of the village at the time of Trindade's account. In 1585 Toscano was a missionary in Nagapattinam, and in 1595 he was guardian of the convent of São Francisco in the city of Goa; subsequently he became Rector in Sirula. This means that the episode in view took place during the transition between the sixteenth and the seventeenth century, three or four decades after the Franciscans had settled down in Bardez.[83]

The protagonist of the narrative was a "Brahman from the principal families of the village," possibly a *gaunkar* aged about a hundred years (no doubt an exaggeration). Three of his sons were already Christian while one of them, like the father, had refused conversion. Valignano would probably have liked to visit Sirula since the Franciscans used a method of conversion similar to his. There was also there a "continuous and wide-ranging conversation of the priests [which] they engage in slowly in a manner that they enter into the person and make use of the opportunity."

Given that the old man spoke Portuguese,[84] and that he was able to converse with Franciscans who "worked much with him to turn him, telling him many things of our holy faith," the non-Christian son feared his father would convert to Christianity in the final years of his life.[85] To thwart the possible conversion, the

[83] Trindade, *Conquista Espiritual do Oriente*, Vol. 1, 310–11.

[84] Neither Friar Toscano nor his helper seemed to know the local language well. Otherwise, the fact that the older man spoke Portuguese would not have been presented as an additional danger that his son had to cope with.

[85] Conversions of elderly people on their deathbeds are a recurring topic

son transported the father to neighbouring lands that were under Bijapur rule, leaving him in the care of a temple in the hope that he would pass away following the faith of his forefathers. According to Trindade, the Christian God himself inspired the old man to return to his village, with the man pleading that he could not bear separation from his family.[86] Unhappy at his father's return, the son hid him in the second storey of the house so that no one in the village knew of his presence there. Nevertheless, despite his best efforts, the rector of the parish, Father Tomé Toscano, knew the old man had returned and sent one of his companions to fetch the man. However, because he was hidden, the companion could not find him, until the old man, moved by God, revealed himself, crying out in a loud voice: "Father, here I am, make me Christian [for] that is what I wish to be, and give me the name Manuel, which is the name of God."[87]

After giving expression to this desire for conversion, and because he was already familiar with the tenets of the Christian faith, the old man was baptised immediately and died some days later. At his death, Trindade says, angels dressed in white came down "from the sky in search of his soul". Viewing this supernatural event, other members of the family expressed their desire for baptism.

Beyond the symbolic meanings of this story, one can read the narrative against the grain. Right at the start, it reveals how critical knowledge of the details of daily village life was for the project of conversion and Christianisation. To gather this information was part of a "politics of space", of the attempt to appropriate the physical space within which the religious establishment and the local people interacted.[88] Through the constitution of networks of

---

in the texts of these missionaries. For a Jesuit counterpoint, see, e.g., the cases referred to by Guerreiro, *Relação Anual*, Vol. 3, 2.

[86] Trindade said he would tell the friars that, when he stayed at a certain temple, an "old friar" (perhaps St Francis) appeared to the old man and ordered him to become Christian: Trindade, *Conquista Espiritual do Oriente,* Vol. 1, 310–11.

[87] Trindade, *Conquista Espiritual do Oriente,* Vol. 1, 311.

[88] Comaroff and Comaroff, *Revelation and Revolution,* Vol. 1, 199ff.

information, or their control over pre-existing ones, missionaries accessed the news that allowed them more effective control over the residents of the villages – whether converted, Christianised, or not.[89]

Besides establishing trusting relationships with the villagers, it was necessary to classify them. Hence questions like, "Where do you come from?", "Where is your house?", "In what neighbourhood?", "Are you married?", "How many children?", "How old are your children?", "How old are the boys?", "Are they grown? Or still young?", "Who is the one there?", "Who lives here?", "Of what caste is he?", "Whose child is it?" – were some of the first expressions learned in the local language.[90]

These dialogues, in turn, were based on knowing the terrain. It was only after such initial steps that a network of information became possible. Friar Simão de Nazaré provides an account of the existence of such a network in Bardez. Nazaré was the Pai dos Cristãos in Bardez in the first decades of the seventeenth century, as well as a commissary of the Holy Office. A man of ill repute – who was "publicly known to have [fathered] many children in Bardez" and accused of various things that were later proven true during the "visit of the Inquisition of Goa" in 1632 – he was also known as a New Christian.[91]

[89] Even though there are no studies about this aspect in the case of Goa, it is known that various information networks existed in other political spaces in India, as was shown by Christopher Bayly, *Empire and Information.* See also Guha, "The Politics of Identity". To what extent did already existing networks create a reference point for the local implantation of these missionaries?

[90] Again, the lexicon of Father António Saldanha is enlightening: IAN/TT, Manuscritos da Livraria, Cod. 757 – António de Saldanha, s.j., Prasse Pastoral, fls 3, 5v., 9v., 11v. and 31v. Questions such as "Have you already had lunch?", "What are you having for lunch?", and "What are you having for dinner?" were equally important for mapping the rhythms of local life.

[91] "He sent presents of fruit, kid goats and other similar items to the inquisitor João Delgado," said António Faria Machado in denunciation when asked about the role played by Simão da Nazaré in the Inquisition: IAN/TT, Conselho Geral do Santo Ofício, nº 184, fl. 14; see also the testimony

Accused by the Inquisition, in his written defence entitled "*Arezoado sobre a nullidade dos libellos falsos infamatorios que contra mim fizerão* [. . .]" (Account of the nullity of the infamous and false libels that they accuse me of) there is a list of the "Defects of the people who have signed the false libel against me, in the name of the people of Bardez, who are about 40,000 souls in 48 villages." The principal objective of this list was to discredit those who had criticised him. However, its title suggests how the Christians and local groups mobilised their solidarity and perhaps client networks. The "*Arezoado*" reveals the practice of registering information about the people targeted as an obstacle to Christianity. Furthermore, it shows that non-Christians also kept lists of those that had converted to Christianity.[92]

It was about these non-Christians that Nazaré collected information. He said that a certain Santu Parbu was fat and welcomed sorcerers, yogis, and gurus in his house "to the great scandal of the Christians". Nazaré admonished Santu Naique and his brother for engaging with these groups. Vantu Santo was arrested "for hiding some of his nephews" who had been made Christians by Nazaré. Two Christians who lived in Sirula were also involved in the same affairs. Through him, the Holy Office condemned for his heresy Fernão Martins, a *gaunkar* responsible for the fire that had destroyed the Church of Nagoa; as also André Furtado, another *gaunkar* of Sirula and cousin of Martins, described as his co-conspirator.[93]

Despite the drama of the episode, which it is necessary to highlight here, it is clear how easy it was for Simão de Nazaré to identify his enemies. Commissary of the Goan Inquisition, the Franciscan

---

of Mateus Gomes, fls 35v–6. It was also said that Friar Simão was the judge in charge of the tax that the New Christians had paid in Macau and that he had several New Christian relatives in Goa: fl. 7, fl. 21v.

[92] IAN/TT, Manuscritos da Livraria, Cod. 1777 – "Relação de papeis autênticos jurados".

[93] IAN/TT, Conselho Geral do Santo Ofício nº 184, fl. 101v.; Manuscritos da Livraria, Cod. 1777 – "Relação de papeis autênticos jurados", fls 42–3v.

was able to establish a network of informants across the forty-eight villages of Bardez, obtaining from them precious information on the "defects" and virtues of its residents.[94]

The fact that he was Pai dos Cristãos enhanced Nazaré's power in Bardez; the position gave him a different kind of access to local people. The Franciscan rectors of the parishes in Bardez certainly provided a great deal of the information that was included in the "*Arezoado*". In 1631, for example, the Holy Office received information that the rector of the parish of São Cristovão in Bardez wanted to denounce certain matters that impinged on the faith. To collect the information he required, Simão de Nazaré mandated a new commission to go to that Province and ended up interrogating five people whom the parish priest accused of Gentile activity.[95]

Condemnation was expected by people who resisted conversion. This happened with Vantu Santo, who, according to Nazaré, prevented his nephews from converting; the same happened with the Gentile who had hidden his father to prevent conversion. A violation of privacy was obvious in Father Toscano sending his companion to the house of the old Brahman. After 1550, such intrusion into the homes of locals was made legitimate. That year, Bishop Dom Juan de Albuquerque authorised the Jesuits and the Franciscans to search the "homes of all Brahmans and Gentiles in which they suspected the existence of idols." There were so many searches that in 1561 Father Herédia accused the fathers of doing "terrible things, both night and day, with weapons and threats, visiting houses in the night by torchlight, looking for women, and at times seizing them even in the dark." These dissonant voices

[94] It is also known through this codex that this friar celebrated autos-de-fé in which it was not known how many people were punished because nobody else was present: IAN/TT, Conselho Geral do Santo Ofício, nº 184, fl. 14; see also the testimony of Mateus Gomes and the reference to nine letters of the same friar in the Book of Secrets of the Inquisition: fl. 36, fl. 111v.

[95] IAN/TT, Conselho Geral do Santo Ofício, nº 184, fl. 105. This rectorate consisted of four villages – Tivim, Pirna, Assonora, and Sirçaim – all located in the northern part of Bardez, at the frontier with Bijapur.

did not reach very far. Several decrees of the Council of 1606 repeated previous dispositions and issued new ones. Making lists of non-Christians was one of its aims. The idea was to find new ways of persuading locals to convert.

An example of these new strategies is visible in the conclusion of Decree 14: "The said vicars will find out how many Gentiles are sick, so that they may exhort and persuade them to our holy faith with charity, and without force; and no Christian nor Gentile will hinder the vicar in this activity so necessary for the salvation of the sick . . ."[96]

Between 1550 and 1606 a series of royal provisions established severe penalties on non-Christians and encouraged missionaries to develop strategies allowing them to get around the obstacles to conversion. In such a context, the creation of a network of informants ensured an efficient understanding of the reality of local society.

The information collected from existing networks did not always coincide with the truth. The informants were not necessarily of the same persuasion as those they were informing on, and the strategies of missionaries were often at odds with the information provided. There is no way of ascertaining if rumour and denunciation were frequent practices in the daily life of the local people before the arrival of the Portuguese; what can be confirmed, however, is that after the mid-sixteenth century these practices were a part of daily routine.

The variety of situations and tensions that invaded each village, challenging the equilibrium between groups, favoured the mixed use of solidarities, information, silence, and defamation. The implementation of these strategies depended on the favour or opposition of the various powers in the village. They included traditional powers, represented by the *gaunkars*, and the rising power, expressed as the alliance between missionaries and Christian *gaunkars*, other Christians, or expressed in the shape of groups who were not pleased with their circumstances.

[96] CR–APO, Fasc. 4, *5th. Council*, 1606, Action 2, d. 14, 211–12.

Returning to the episode narrated by Trindade: despite the son's best efforts to hide his father in an uninhabited house, the Franciscan friars were able to obtain news of his arrival. Sirula was an "extensive [village] that extended over many valleys," and most houses were not near the parish church.[97] The case demonstrates the breadth and scope of the friars' control and supervision of the villagers. Their control had the support of residents for whom denouncing members of a local family was not a problem.

The increasing awareness that idolatry continued in the privacy of homes stimulated the missionaries to try gaining access to, and control of, domestic life.[98] As the Dutchman Jan Huyghen van Linschoten wrote, Indians "secretly do in their houses what they want, to not cause any trouble or scandal." Based on his notions of clandestine behaviour, Linschoten revealed that the *visibility* of idolatry was the cause of scandal. There were misunderstandings about what idolatry in fact was. Both Linschoten and the Portuguese *did not see* other idolatrous practices because they were not included in their concept of idolatry.[99] At the end of the sixteenth century, few missionaries understood that doing away with the universe of idolatry was not easy. In contrast, the majority of them still believed that annihilation of the visible signs of idolatry was the method of eradicating it.

These intertwined parochial and inquisitorial networks allowed the clergy to identify the families persisting in their idolatry, even as they improved their ability to intrude and intervene in their daily lives. It was only through these networks that the regular clergy was able to decipher the "secret" of idolatrous practices. Deciphering them was crucial to making Christianisation successful.

Interventions in the lives of the resident populations went beyond forced entry into the homes of non-Christians. The Chris-

[97] Trindade, *Conquista Espiritual do Oriente*, Vol. 1, 293.

[98] On the concept of idolatry adopted in this period, see Bernand and Gruzinski, *De l'idolâtrie*.

[99] Linschoten, *Itinerário*, 187.This could be the case of a series of questions related to the preparation of food, for example: Khare, *The Hindu Hearth and Home*.

tianisation of individual members of families, orphans and widows included, was also crucial. Conversions carried out in socially powerful families – as was the case with the earlier mentioned Loqu – were specially prized. Opting for Christianity, as Loqu did, meant a renunciation of the old order and acceptance of the new. The conversion of Loqu's family ensured others would follow suit.

Even the conversion of one or two people within a family disturbed the local order. Families were thereby made culturally and religiously mixed and differentiated. In a cultural group marked by pollution taboos of various sorts, such conversion had a negative impact on daily life in a non-Christian home. A physical separation was introduced between the converted and the non-Christian, meals were often segregated, and the situation made routine.[100]

Everything came to have different meanings, ranging from devotion to commensality to daily activity, whether at home or in the fields. Individual difficulties increased when the eldest son, who had to continue the lineage and the household, converted. Similarly the conversion of the *pater familias*, perceived and assumed to be head of the family unit, was more significant than that of the mother.[101]

Sometimes a single conversion could shift the links of a domestic group and the community to which it belonged, stigmatising the family and jeopardising its future. Conversion affected the reputations of families accustomed to marrying within particular

[100] In this context, there were several references to the mistreatment that converted family members were subjected to. See, e.g., though not for the case of Goa, a letter of 1548 from Friar António do Porto about the fate of the Christians of Bassein: IAN/TT, Corpo Cronológico, Part I, mç. 81, nº 59 – "Carta de Fr. António do Porto, dando parte a ElRey", 7 Oct. 1548.

[101] This topic also concerned issues relating to orphans. From a Christian perspective, the education of orphans within Christian society was a form of guaranteeing, in the medium run, a population that adhered wholly to the Christian model and was politically loyal to the Portuguese Crown. However, this policy had dramatic effects in the interior of the local social system, in particular when the orphans were boys.

social groups, and of those using strategies to maintain or improve their positions. Conversion of a single member in a family interfered with the transmission of land and inheritance, changing the pattern of organisation and hierarchy in such families.[102] Conversions within families entailed fragmentation, not just in their own eyes, but also in those of the village community. Which is to say that losing one of its members to conversion could be devastating, especially if he was of significance within the family, as were Loqu and one of the daughters of Meale, or Ali bin Yusuf Khan (a prince from Bijapur exiled in Goa).[103]

Material consequences naturally followed. As mentioned in the earlier chapters, several of the new norms resulted in mortal wounds to the traditional order. Inheritance and succession to the *gaunkari* now favoured Christian sons. Similar legislation opened up new social horizons for orphans and widows: widows could now inherit as well as remarry. The introduction of monogamous marriage as a norm, too, had no small impact on the power and status of the married woman.

Changes to names, and to titles that identified one's caste, family, and lineage, also came to be new imperatives. Let us look again at the old man of Sirula. Trindade says he requested "the name Manuel". Trindade's effort in noting this is to demonstrate that the man was not only familiar with Christian principles, he knew them so well that he had chosen a name for himself that was no less than the name of God. For Trindade, this choice was clear sign of an interior transformation.[104] Names defined and explained the nature of things, and, as Louis Châtellier reminds us, at that

[102] About the relevance of these practices on the forms of social identification in Asia, see Chaudhuri, *Asia Before Europe,* 152, 180, and 190ff. See also Ludden, *An Agrarian History of South Asia*, 97ff., in particular on the role of matrimony as a means of social reproduction.

[103] The importance of this event is attested by a letter written by Father Luís Fróis in 1557, dedicated exclusively to registering it: DI, Vol. 4, 735–50.

[104] See, also, the theorisation about naming in Friar João Cardoso, *Jornada*, fl. 193v.

moment in religious history pronouncing the name of God "was also an appeal to a supernatural force, capable of making enemies of God flee in a moment, whether it be the Devil or someone in your community."[105]

Perhaps the Franciscans held this belief when they heard, or imagined they had heard, such a cry. It was the symbolic meaning they wished to register. It may also have been the result of a spontaneous Christianisation of widespread local practice – attributing to men the names of God. To say "Manuel" could have several meanings, all of them interpretable both by those who spoke it and those listening. In any event, the choice of a Christian name, if accompanied by changes in dress, food, and marital and familial behaviour, was a clear and definite sign of having opted for a new history – a history that entailed new notions of terrestrial time, personal time, and sacred time.[106]

The collection *Livros das Comunidades* indicates, for example, the Christianisation of the cycle of village feasts. As was common in the rural world, these feasts entwined the agricultural cycle with the ritual cycle of devotions. Before Christianisation, these local festivities were concentrated in the period between August and November, while the marriage season was between November and May. Examining the Christian ritual calendar in the villages of Salcete, Rowena Robinson suggests that there was a homology between the new calendar and the pre-Christian devotional calendar.[107] This overlap ensured that feasts which had only minor importance in Western Europe gained greater importance in local Christianity, while those that were significant feasts in the West diminished in relevance – the feast of Christmas being one example. The spread of a theology of saints contributed to replace local non-Christian devotions, taking advantage of a calendar full

[105] Châtellier, *A Religião dos Pobres*, 118.

[106] An excellent discussion of these conceptions of time and their variations can be found in Trautmann, "Indian Time, European Time".

[107] Robinson, *Conversion, Continuity and Change*, 130ff.

of festivities, rituals, and ceremonies in times of hunger, epidemics, and tempests.[108]

Robinson's argument illustrates other situations, such as in the maintenance of social practices of patronage and organisation of the religious world. On 17 April 1612 the *gaunkari* of Carambolim auctioned ground rents and deeds for the feast of Santa Catarina, Easter, and Corpus Christi. The following year auctions similar to those held earlier to celebrate local festivities took place to celebrate the feast of Nossa Senhora da Guia. Even the *farazes* (untouchables) received money for use in the feast of São João. On 18 December 1614 the *gaunkars* of Azossim met under a mango tree belonging to João Pereira to decide how many arecanut trees they should contribute to the feast of St Catherine, Christmas, Easter, Corpus Christi, São João, and the feasts of São Tiago, and São Matias.[109] The calendar of these feasts frequently duplicated those in honour of local divinities. Though the form of the divinities may have changed, many of the older practices remained.

Although Robinson makes an appealing argument, she does not discuss the opposition between Christian and local matrimonial periods. Christians could not marry in December, February, and March, a time in which – especially during Lent – it was a grave and even a "mortal" sin to hold wedding feasts. These feasts led "to scandals to all the prudent Christians as was seen from experience." Such was the prohibition that permission given to the Gentiles to celebrate weddings in Goan territories caused enormous problems and aroused much controversy, especially at the start of the seventeenth century.[110]

The records of the *Livros das Comunidades* also demonstrate the permanence of a routine that was critical to maintaining the local social order: the interdependence between political power, i.e. the *gaunkars* and *gaunkaris*, and religious power, in this case

[108] Mosse, "Catholic Saints and the Hindu Pantheon", 304–7.

[109] HAG, nº 10041 – Comunidades – Carambolim, 1612, fls 15–16v.; HAG, nº 10042 – Comunidades – Carambolim, 1613–14, fls 51 and 60.

[110] CR–APO, Fasc. 4, *3rd Council,* 1585, Action 2, 127–8.

the missionaries.[111] In Carambolim the registers of the *gaunkari* mention regular contributions to the administration of religious life. Several records refer to the needs of the Church of São João Baptista. Construction of the last portion of the chaplaincy required more money, as did the roof beams. Also, the *gaunkari* had to choose people to watch over Christian buildings.[112] The obligation extended to guarding against possible petty theft. This became increasingly frequent, as is evident from the record of a meeting in Cortalim where the theft of a cauldron and two candlesticks from the Church of the Santos Apóstolos was discussed. The items, according to a Jesuit father, were worth fifteen xerafins, a sum that the *gaunkars* promised to reimburse.[113]

In supporting the administration and processes of religious life in the village, the *gaunkars* contributed to the Christianisation of daily routines. It was not just the perception of religious time that changed with missionary intervention; the perception of work hours changed as well. The regular tolling of church bells, religious instruction, and religious chants now governed daily time. The daily lives of residents of the villages in the Old Conquests – at least those involved in agricultural labour – was marked by men leaving for work in the rice paddies each morning. It was there that they would lunch or snack on food prepared by their wives, returning home when it got dark. Women could also go to the paddy fields, heading there around lunchtime and staying until nightfall.[114] Artisans and other craftsmen who made up the rural world had different routines. However, after a time these routines too were punctuated by church bells announcing activities that

[111] See the books that record the decisions taken by the *gaunkars* of Azossim in 1614 and 1615: HAG, nº 10023–4 – Comunidades, Azossim, Deliberações e contas correntes, 1614, 1615; as well as those of the village of Carambolim, 1612–1615, cited in fn. 407.

[112] HAG, nº 10041 – Comunidades – Carambolim, 1612, fl. 21; n.º 10042 – Comunidades – Carambolim, 1613–14, fl. 36v.

[113] HAG, nº 10226 – Cortalim – Corrente, 1629, fl. 18.

[114] Brito, *Goa e as Praças do Norte*, 66.

the religious had introduced into village life. In practice, such activities likely translated into less uninterrupted time during the course of each day.

The Christianisation of labour routines is evident in a letter from Viceroy Dom Miguel de Noronha (r. 1629–1635), Count of Linhares, to the king. In it the Count refers to problems in the village with the conversion of residents who then began going to church, listening to sermons, and attending catechism. In this context, the viceroy said:

> no village landowner impedes his tenants from becoming Christians. However, there is no doubt about what he would feel for reasons to do with the impact on his purse, because the moment one becomes a Christian he loses a worker who was earlier almost his captive. With the teaching of the doctrine they are always occupied in their private activities, and this is something that I cannot solve, since I do not fail to warn and remind the ecclesiastical ministers about this.[115]

In other words, the interests of Christianity ran counter to the economic interests of village landowners. This tension characterised the Christianisation of people in these territories over the next several centuries.[116]

Another variety of tension pertained to the clergy. Repeated requests to send virtuous clergy to India reveal that those actually sent could become obstacles. In 1545 Father Antonio Criminali expressed regret at how many missionaries wanted to get rich. In the following year Henrique Henriques urged that only "suitable" persons be deployed. Father Lancilloto suggested training Jesuits

[115] This letter has been published in CR–APO, Fasc. 6, Vol. 2, 1257.

[116] Once again, Father Valignano's 1579–80 report to Jesuit General Mercuriano offers an excellent synthesis of this situation. Among the obstacles to conversion existing in India, he underlined the resistance of landowners: "when the priests try to convert some of them to Christianity or try to educate their orphans, as decreed by the King, these Gentiles resist. They say that they want to abandon the country, not wanting those that converted to Christianity to live among them": Valignano, *Historia Indica*, Vol. 12, 593.

in the natural sciences. In 1552 Francis Xavier argued for missionaries who were between thirty and forty years old. He expected men "of great mortification" and "experienced and tested in all kinds of work, and challenges whether of body or mind." Local Christians were excluded. Five years later, it was time for Father Gonçalo da Silveira to summarise the profile of a missionary in India: perfect, wishing to mortify himself *ad gloriam Dei*, healthy, of good judgement, zealous, knowing languages, a good preacher, a good confessor, a man of letters, an ascetic.[117]

Similar correspondence concerning the Franciscan friars in India does not exist. Nevertheless, the ideal Franciscan parish priest had to have all the necessary virtues, and before departing be selected by the authorities of the Province. Writing in 1627, but reproducing an ideal drawn from earlier centuries, Frei Dâmaso da Apresentação, a friar of the Province of Santo António of Portugal, indicated that the ideal candidates for the role were "those with more than just physical strength, but also spiritual, whose soul is very pure, and whose faith very constant. They must be exercised in patience, proven in life, impeccable in conversation and very honest in their practices."[118]

In the sixteenth century the Portuguese version of the treatise *Da Composição dos Costumes* of St Bonaventure suggested that every imitator of Christ should carry in his heart "his customs

[117] Xavier's letters are referred to by S. Gonçalves, *Primeira Parte da História*, Vol. 1, 462. Three years earlier, Francisco Xavier wrote to Ignatius Loyola, suggesting that the Indians did not have the right profile to perpetuate the Society of Jesus: Moraes, *History of Christianity*, Vol. 2, 403. Loyola answered by proposing that he chose those who were most suited and dedicated time to them: DI, Vol. 1, 510–15. On the alternative proposals, see DI, Vol. 1, 8–22, 148–56; Vol. 2, 127; Vol. 3, 610–20. While the majority of letters exchanged between Goa, Lisbon, and Rome criticised missionaries who went to India, in other letters these same missionaries were described in a very positive light. See, in this context, the letters of Lancilloto and of Raimundus Pereira, of the years 1551 and 1552: DI, Vol. 2, 144–9, 506–9.

[118] Apresentação, *Obrigaçam do Frade Menor*, fl. 549. See also the *Manual de las cosas essentiales a que son obligados los frayles menores* of 1571.

and works". Franciscans should show a humble exterior, be affable, benign, and mild in what they ate and drank, and be modest. Good health was emphasised, and caution urged against contagious disease and bodily defects. The missionary ought not to have Jewish blood; he needed to be capable of celebrating the sacraments of baptism, Eucharist, and confession. The same profile was believed ideal within the monasteries of India as well.[119]

Nevertheless, the missionaries established *in loco* were *"homens imperfeitos"* for *"campos muito dificeis"* (imperfect men, in challenging terrains). The exceptions were people like Francis Xavier, Henrique Henriques, Alessandro Valignano, Robert de Nobili, Matteo Ricci, and João de Brito. The average cleric, whether parish priest or missionary, was considerably less heroic. The average missionary fulfilled his tasks by mimicking models created by others, or appropriating models and adapting them to the circumstances. Missionaries in the European world had been enjoined certain necessary steps that they needed to follow. These included visiting the local church and getting to know the parish priests who, in turn, would describe the manners and ways of the locals. Only after this foundational work could they engage in preaching the doctrine, catechism, and confession.[120] In Goa, the missionary was frequently himself the parish priest. When they first arrived at a village, they encountered not a local church but only the ruins of local temples. There they would find that the vast majority of people were not Christian, and sometimes populations whose *fides implicita* (implicit faith in Christ) was rudimentary.

The role of these missionaries was quite literally to "create a new world" by building over the ruins and subsequently aiding, protecting, and reproducing the new order. This could only happen after the religious established themselves institutionally, while educating themselves about the groups in the village in order to

[119] São Boaventura, *Alguns Tratados*, fl. 22; Deos, *Caminho dos Frades Menores,* 166–79, 230.

[120] Prosperi, "O missionário"; Prosperi, *Tribunali della Coscienza,* 210–11.

get closer to residents, and to then take control of the physical space within which they could develop a relationship. Only by a rigorous following of these processes could missionaries arrive at routines leading to genuine Christianisation. It is these routines that are the subject of the next chapter.

4

Tools of Christianisation

Shaping Memory, Understanding, and Will

THE CODEX *Memórias Ecclesiásticas do Estado da Índia* (Ecclesiastical Memoirs of the State of India) from the eighteenth century makes reference to the hermitage of Nossa Senhora do Monte on Tiswadi Island, offering thereby a fleeting illustration of how the construction of a Christian order led to conflicting interpretations.

The *Memórias* refers to an existing female-deity temple destroyed by Afonso de Albuquerque to which the locals prayed every 8th September. Despite the erasure of this temple and the construction of a Christian hermitage in its stead, many Gentiles continued to gather on that day and "brought gifts of oil, wax, and money. They believed they were cured of their afflictions whenever they sought out this Lady's aid. They are so blind that, in this way, they fail to leave behind their idolatry."[1]

The erasure which Albuquerque and other Christians aimed to achieve by replacing pagan signs and locations with Christian ones was in line with European understandings of the day, where the preferred model of conversion focused on changes to memory, understanding, and will. According to the dominant culture of the time, the external acts of individuals transformed their inner

[1] BNP, Cod. 176 – Notícias do arcebispado de Goa, 131.

being. As such, the alteration brought about by external action would, through repetitive acts, create a new *habitus* which in turn would be conducive to the construction of a new spiritual architecture. In other words, the hope was that Gentiles would come to appreciate "Senhora", or the Virgin Mary, instead of "Deosa" or the "Goddess", because of having witnessed miracles by the former. The process was intended to result in a general acceptance of the "infallible and certain" superiority of Christian divinities, of Christianity, of Christian power.

As seen in the previous chapter, the Franciscans and Jesuits were quite aware of the variety of tools at their disposal to push the local populations toward conversion and Christianisation. Although at the start both orders shared apostolic cultures which were not very distinct, they soon came to be marked by significant differences. These differences resulted from their anthropological beliefs, as well as from the instruments of conversion that they selected and combined. Their decisions brought about changes not only in their relationships with each other but also influenced how they interacted with the populations among whom they lived.

The Franciscan method was primarily directed at the heart (sensibility), as they believed that *impressions* at this level affected memory, enabling subsequent dispositional changes in understanding and will. This affective way – in which divine grace was manifest more visibly – was at odds with the intellectual way, which was more culturalist. The Jesuits favoured the more intellectual and culturalist path, which called upon memory (and not the heart) to ignite understanding. As such, the Jesuits made great use of intellectual disputations to convince the converted.

In other words, for the Franciscans Christianity was something actively done and felt, whereas for the Jesuits intellectual work was critical to transforming and perfecting each person. In order to achieve perfection, Loyola proposed five stages in his *Exercises*:

> *First point:* The first step is coming to terms with sins, to acknowledge, and remember all sins committed throughout life, and looking back at them from year to year, or from period to period . . .

Second point: Secondly, ponder over your sins, confronting the ugliness and evil that each mortal sin has in and of itself, on the condition that it not be concealed.

Third point: This being to observe who you are and make yourself humble by taking into consideration the following questions. For example: What am I in comparison with other men? Secondly, what are men in comparison to all the angels and saints in Paradise? Third, gaze upon Creation in comparison to God, then ask yourself, "What can I be?" Fourth, consider all corruption and corporeal ugliness. Fifth, view yourself as an ulcer and abscess from which so many sins, evils, and poison have emerged.

Fourth point: Fourth, ask yourself who is God, against whom you have sinned, then with all his attributes in mind, compare them to all that is contrary in yourself . . .

Fifth point: Admiration along with growing affection for all creatures on this world, as we are all part of this world and in it conserved . . .

Discussion: We end this discussion on compassion, praying and giving grace to God, our Lord, for the life he has given, proposing modifications with his grace thenceforth. Our Father.[2]

How did the missionaries transform these beliefs into action in the villages of Bardez and Salcete? In addition to the methods mentioned in the previous chapter – i.e. the blending of *officium parochi* with missionary activity, the destruction of temples, the expulsion of priests and other servants, the building and control of networks of communication – what other means did they use to transform locals into true Christians?

These missionaries believed that after destroying the external landscape of idolatry they could (re)construct the landscape of the soul among the converted. Preaching, confession, and communion, in addition to schools for orphans, young children, and instruction for adults stand out in the spectrum of tools used

[2] Loyola, *Exercícios Espirituais*, 2. A century later Father António Saldanha replicated this same method, adjusting it to the cultural conditions of Goa, in his *Prasse Pastoral*: IAN/TT, Manuscritos da Livraria, Cod. 757 – António de Saldanha, s.j., Prasse Pastoral, 1st part.

to achieve this ambitious goal. Schools provided instruction on Christian doctrine and teaching people how to read texts was fundamental. Furthermore, confession allowed control of the souls of new Christians, and, when necessary, alterations to them. As Father Pina reported the situation, "it seems that they knew all their lives how to confess" since they reported all their sins – every last one.

Charity complemented these tools. In contrast to disciplinary institutions like confession and the Inquisition, charity was an expression of Christian mercy. Missionaries established charities, brotherhoods, and hospitals in the villages. On the one hand, these helped the locals. On the other, they integrated the new Christians, the intention being to transform them as well into agents of Christian mercy.

When Christianisation started, the relationship between the Christians – almost always Portuguese – and the non-Christians was one of polarisation. According to the Franciscan and Neoplatonist João Cardoso, it was a relationship where one side was civilised, wise, honourable, and peaceful, while the other was barbaric, ignorant, degraded, warlike, and miserable.[3] In this set-up the Old Christians embodied the positive side of a binary while the locals were the other pole. Rulers and ruled, colonisers and colonised – these dichotomies were the pillars of the institutions established and the tools chosen. The difficulty lay in reducing the cultural gap between the two communities, transforming the locals, from the perspective of the missionaries, into "civilised, wise, honourable and peaceful Christians".

As in the previous chapter, the focus here is on the strategies employed by the missionaries, albeit in relation to different issues. The typical apostolic tasks – preaching, confession, and maintaining the peace, along with the instruction of Christian doctrine and teaching of Portuguese – are addressed in the first section. The second concerns the "supplementary" devices, namely works of charity and poor relief.

[3] Cardoso, *Jornada*, fls 1, 5v., 12v., 19v., 23, and 42v.

"This will cost the Fathers much work and sweat, So that they may reap the fruit over much time"

The principal aim of this section is to discuss how doctrine, preaching, and confession, the three critical tools in Christianisation, were developed in the territories of Salcete and Bardez. Unlike the internal missions taking place in Portugal, studied by Federico Palomo, which were temporary, in India the missionaries found themselves faced with a different kind of apostolate.[4] A daily relationship with the local population characterised the apostolate in Goa. The missionary parish priest exercised his activity within a defined jurisdiction, a framework of spatial and temporal stability.[5] Another difference is also visible in the missions to kingdoms beyond the boundaries of the Estado da Índia. The missionaries there, especially the Italians – as has been demonstrated by Ines Županov – viewed the mission as a kind of endurance test.[6] Albeit in a diverse way, the missionary parish priests established in Bardez and Salcete also experienced this endurance test in their extended conversations with local populations.

One "identity practice" applied more in Goa than elsewhere in the empire was the teaching of Portuguese to locals. As stated by the humanist João de Barros, "good habits and vocabulary last longer than a monument in stone." This project of linguistic and cultural colonisation structured many of the techniques adopted

[4] Copete and Palomo, "Des Carêmes aprés la Carême", 365–7; Palomo, *Fazer dos campos escolas excelentes*; Morán and Andrés-Gallego, "O Pregador", 142ff.

[5] In 1562 Father Francisco de Pina revealed that the Jesuit fathers would fan out in groups of two to preach in the several villages that constituted the parish of Nossa Senhora de Guadalupe in Batim. Thereafter each parish came to be constituted by two or three villages, reducing the geography the missionaries had to cope with: DI, Vol. 5, 548–3.

[6] The efforts of Roberto di Nobili are emblematic of this tendency, but the histories of all the martyrs and their motivations are equally notable: Županov, "Le répli du religieux"; Županov, *Disputed Mission*; Županov, *Missionary Tropics*; Županov, "A História do Futuro".

by the Portuguese in the first phase. The belief that knowing a Christian language was fundamental to comprehending the teachings of Christ and the Christian code inspired this initial moment.[7]

In 1539 Barros published his *Cartinha*, which aimed to teach non-Christians and bring them into God's realm. Barros wrote his text after hearing of the "conversion of fifty-seven thousand souls in the land of Malabar" by the Franciscans. In this context, "four of the princes of these people" had gone to Lisbon, where they learned "the notions of the faith". Barros insisted that the greatest glory was the learning of Portuguese by the children of Ethiopia, Persia, India, "and those beyond the Ganges"; by learning it they had been enabled to understand "the precepts of our faith".[8]

How did the educational network spread? What were the chief features of the schools of Goa? What books were used when teaching the villagers? How did missionaries cope with "students" who neither knew Portuguese nor shared the same cultural codes? Did these schools somehow replace the local *pathasalas* and *parishads*, usually open only to higher-caste groups? What was the effect of this "replacement"?[9]

The first reference to the teaching of Portuguese dates back to the time of Afonso de Albuquerque. There are references to 50 different *cartilhas* of Christian doctrine sent to the Estado da Índia (of which 200 copies were received), as well as 5 *Flos Sanctorum* and 4 gospels for the school in the city of Goa; 1000 of these booklets were sent to Prester John, the ruler of Ethiopia. In 1517 Dom Manuel sent another 150 booklets, the final destination being the city of Goa. Ten years later there were two schools for boys in Goa and a few others in the rest of the Estado da Índia. In 1532

[7] See Barros, *Gramática da Língua Portuguesa*, "Introduction", by Maria Leonor Carvalhão Buescu, LI–III; Curto, "Práticas de identidade". The dilemmas that accompany translations, where one is not always able to convey certain concepts, can be seen in Konkani translations of the time, where sacred terms almost always appear in Portuguese.

[8] Barros, *Gramática da Língua Portuguesa*, 239–40, 405.

[9] For more information on this pre-Christian network in the territories of Goa, see A.M. Xavier, "A Invenção de Goa", PhD thesis, Chapter 4; and Mitragotri, *Socio-Cultural History of Goa*.

the Vicar of Malacca used the *Cathecismo Pequeno* (1504; Little Catechism) of Diogo de Ortiz e Villegas, to teach the fundamental aspects of the Christian doctrine.[10]

According to a Franciscan chronicler, the Franciscans had also begun these practices. In the second decade of the sixteenth century, the friar António do Louro asked the king to send him books and preachers. Later, the College of Santa Fé systematised these needs. Father Diogo de Borba, a secular priest who had studied at the Franciscan convent of Piedade in the town of Borba in Portugal, had founded the college in 1541. With this institution, the connection between conversion, education, and Christianisation became evident.

The College of Santa Fé aimed to instruct locals in the fundamentals of the Christian faith before their baptism. It had "two classes, one in which some learn to read and write Christian doctrine, the other in which they learn Latin." The college complemented the activities of the Casa dos Catecúmenos, created at the same time.[11]

Three years later the city of Goa had four more schools, all associated with parishes established by Bishop Dom Juan de Albuquerque. In 1546 the king, Dom João III, confirmed this decision, which was later expanded to include the new parishes of Salcete and Bardez. This translated into Goa what had transpired in Portugal and elsewhere in Europe. As in Portugal, parish priests in Goa were obliged to instruct urban parishioners and rural residents, providing them basic literacy and Christian doctrine. By the end of the 1540s more than a dozen schools taught Portuguese and the basics of Christian doctrine in Goa. A document of 1666 claims that "each church has its own [school]", though it provides no details.[12]

[10] Azevedo, ed., *Dicionário de História Religiosa*, Vol. A–C, 305; A. da Silva, *Trent's Impact*, 113–17; A.S. Pereira, "Intenções Catequéticas", 360–3, 369–70.

[11] Trindade, *Conquista Espiritual do Oriente*, Vol. I, 268.

[12] Moraes, *History of Christianity*, Vol. 2, 395; *Lista das rendas e despezas da Província de Goa*, 351–8.

Jesuit correspondence brims with references to the effect that "everywhere there is someone who teaches the prayers and assists them: girls in the morning and the boys in the afternoon, men on Sunday and women on Saturday." Though this example is drawn from the Fishery coast of southern Tamilnadu, i.e. a periphery by comparison with Goa, Goa followed a related model.[13]

Friar Paulo da Trindade provides a similar description of Franciscan pedagogical activities before 1636. He says Franciscans gathered "in the morning all the boys and girls in each rectory." The boys were up to fifteen years old and the girls up to twelve; they came to the church with "their raised crosses". There they learned "the Christian doctrine and other devotions and prayers" in the language of the land.[14] In line with Trindade's description, which tried to converge with the Trent Council's decisions, the Franciscans taught in the local languages instead of Portuguese. However, they rarely taught the *doctrine* in the local languages – they communicated it in Portuguese with the help of an interpreter.

One of the methods of teaching the language and the doctrine was by associating each letter with a different image. Already present in the *Cartinha* of Barros, this technique was found particularly apt for the Asian territories by Francis Xavier as well. Not only did he use this method, writing down a catechism between 1546 and 1547, but he inspired others, such as Father Henrique Henriques. In 1579 Henriques published from Kochi a *Doutrina Christam por modo de dialogo* in the Tamil language. Following the grammatical form and the "many lives of Saints", Henriques' project may have followed the catechism of Xavier, later published in 1557 by Joham de Bustamonte. The other three possible sources are two other catechisms of Jesuit authorship printed at the press of the College of Saint-Paul between 1556 and 1561, or the *Cathecismo Pequeno* of Villegas from a later publication in Kollam.[15]

[13] Letter of Father Manuel de Morais, s.j.,1547, DI, Vol. 1, 240–9.

[14] Trindade, *Conquista Espiritual do Oriente*, Vol. I, 353.

[15] Letter of Father Nicolao Lancillotto, s.j., 1550, DI, Vol. 2, 145–6. On the productions of Henrique Henriques, see Županov, "Esperimenti linguistici

Like Barros' *Cartinha* – which was probably not as popular as he may have hoped – the publication of similar texts was frequent in the Iberian world. In all of them the dialogical method was characteristic. As Federico Palomo points out, "the biggest novelty that the sixteenth century produced concerning the pedagogy of catechism was the introduction of dialogical formats."[16] These happened with the catechisms of Juan de Valdés, Constantino Ponce de la Fuente, and Juan de Ávila of 1529, 1547, and 1554, as well as with the *Cartinha*. The *Doutrina Christam* of the Jesuit Marcos Jorge, first published in 1566 and widely used in India, was the apex of this tendency. The text saw translations into several South Asian languages. The Jesuit Thomas Stephens translated it into Konkani under the title *Doutrina Christam em lingoa bramana canarim* (1622). Earlier, its 1616 edition contained illustrations.

The dialogical form, an essential mechanism in the reform of the Church,[17] was of particular significance in Indian Christianisation. Already in use before the middle of the sixteenth century, it remained the preferred method for the next century. The catechisms written by Robert de Nobili, Diogo de Sant' Anna and the *Doutrina* of Thomas Stephens are three other examples of the popularity of this model.[18]

Owing to their inability to impose the Portuguese language, the learning of local languages became crucial to achieving the Christianisation of locals.[19] The twenty-fourth session of the Council of Trent in 1562, which regulated the transmission of

---

dei gesuiti". The production of texts would naturally be associated with the means necessary to publish them. The Colégio de São Paulo and the Colégio de Rachol had printing presses, which printed grammars, doctrines, and booklets in local languages, as well as texts of doctrinal refutation: Županov, "Esperimenti linguistici dei gesuiti", 49–54.

[16] Palomo, *Fazer dos campos escolas excelentes*, 207.

[17] Prosperi, *Tribunali della Coscienza*, 611ff.

[18] Central Library – Pangim, Nobili, Catecismo; BA, 49-I-77, Sant' Anna, *Cathecismo*; Estêvão, *Doutrina Christam*.

[19] Županov, "Esperimenti linguistici dei gesuiti", 45.

the *rudimenta fidei*, defended linguistic diversity given that it was necessary for the dissemination of Christianity. Each Sunday, priests were expected teach their parishioners the fundamentals of the Christian faith in the language they understood.[20]

The *Catecismo Romano* (1566) assembled these pillars of the Christian faith. The idea was to have only one text taught to all Christians, whether adults or children. The *Catecismo* standardised Catholic practices and knowledge to ensure their easy transmission in Europe and elsewhere. It aimed to ensure a universal Catholic orthodoxy and the assertion of a shared cultural code that went beyond spatial, social, and linguistic borders.[21]

The Provincial Councils of Goa adopted many of the Tridentine and Roman decisions. In 1592 the fourth Provincial Council deemed as necessary the production of a compendium of Christian doctrine and instruction, and its translation into the "most common languages of the Province". All priors, curates, and vicars had to teach them in their entirety, or else in part, to local Christians on feast days and Sundays throughout the year. To facilitate this process the Provincial Council mandated that four confessors and four preachers "go to the churches and, according to the Ordinary [Book], preach, and confess the Christians of the land, as assistants to the vicars."[22]

However, the Estado da Índia was not an inert receptacle for diktats from Europe. Even as doctrines and catechisms in Portuguese – such as a package of Mártires' *Catecismo* – were sent to India, and even as the College of São Paulo printed Jorge's *Doutrina,* Alessandro Valignano initiated local projects. In 1575 he insisted that another catechism, another Christian doctrine, a confessional, and a *Flos Sanctorum* should receive Tamil translations, and the

[20] A. da Silva, *Trent's Impact*, 107–9. By this time, the Jesuits had successfully petitioned Viceroy Dom Constantino de Bragança to issue a provision which compelled the Brahmans of Goa to attend Christian indoctrination in churches every Sunday, from 3 to 4 p.m. The same was decided in the 1st Provincial Council: CR–APO, *1st Council, Action* 2, d. 5, 10.

[21] Prosperi, *Tribunali della Coscienza*, 607, 611.

[22] CR–APO, Vol. 4, *4th Council*, d. 4, 187–8.

project was then taken forward by Father Henrique Henriques.[23]

Besides the *cartinhas*, the catechisms, and the other books, Father Gaspar Barzeus' *Regulae collegii goani* from 1552 provides an insight into other Ignatian pedagogical practices. According to Barzeus, children came to school not merely for instruction: there was also a bell that called them to Church, to which they went with a cross and a candle in their hands. Both practices, schooling and church-going, were metaphors of the passage from darkness and ignorance to the world of light and knowledge. In the chapel, to the sound of *Laudate pueri, Domine* and *Veni Creator*, they received a habit and were embraced by classmates. Subsequently, they chanted the *Salve Regina*. Only after this rite of passage did learning of the alphabet and the doctrine begin. Lessons involved simultaneously teaching a couple of virtues, in particular obedience. Learning to read and write were thereby an essential step in the instruction of Christian doctrine. Two "*acuzadores*", whose role was to monitor those who studied and who did not, aided the teacher. If the students were inattentive or fought among themselves, their punishment was exemplary, on the grounds that "the love of children causes dissolution, and this is due to lack of reason" – meaning that since children did not comprehend the language of love as a response to their misbehaviour, punishment was necessary. The Jesuit method was attentive to the needs of every age group.

Barzeus was also sensitive to the role that students could play in the diffusion of precepts learned at school. After being taught by the Jesuits, they were to teach the slaves in their homes. That they believed – or at least wanted to believe – in the efficacy of the method is confirmed by a statement of Father Baltazar Costa from 4 December 1562: he recounted that at night one could hear children teaching the doctrine to "the slaves and servants in their house!"[24]

[23] Schurhammer, *Orientalia*, 744–5; Lach, *Asia in the Making of Europe*, Vol. I, 279; Moraes, *History of Christianity*, Vol. II, 411; Županov, "Esperimenti linguistici", 44–61.

[24] See the *regulae* of Barzeus and the letter of Baltazar Costa in DI, Vol. 5, 595, 600.

Orphans were not a part of such groups. They helped with the liturgy. Depending on their reading and writing skills, some orphans were part of the choir, others wrote, while the rest did "any other activities that dealt with Church matters." As for punishments, everything was done to avoid violence, since being "older, what [they] need more than fear is love."[25] The belief was that little children understood punishment better than love, whereas once older they were better able to understand the language of persuasion and love.

The role that pedagogy could play in the construction of the subject, and through it the establishment of a Christian society, and the central role that the Jesuits ought to occupy in this society, were matters of substantial discussion by the early Jesuits.

Seven years before the Council of Trent dealt with these matters, Poulanco was confident that the education the children were getting was "the best possible". He insisted that the fathers should invest more in early identity formation, and in fact the education of the young quickly became an Ignatian *ex libris.*[26] The massive amount of correspondence on conversion success stories of native children lent weight to Poulanco's perception. Like Nunes and later Valignano, Poulanco hoped that the children and grandchildren of such converts would be born Christians and thus unaware of local "superstition".

"With time they can be moulded and make up for the lack of workers we [currently] have."[27] This declaration by Valignano encapsulates the expectations concerning early education and

[25] On this, see *Regulae Collegi Goani* of Gaspar Barzeus, DI, Vol. 2, 353–4. On the specifics of the education of the orphans in the Portuguese context, see Guedes, "Os estatuto dos colégios", *passim.*

[26] See Poulanco's letter in DI, Vol. 3, 302–11. Some years later, in 1548, Nicolao Lancilloto would convey a similar idea in a letter to Ignatius Loyola: DI, Vol. 1, 341–4.

[27] Valignano, *Sumario de las cosas que pertenecen a la Yndia Oriental,* in DHMPPO, Vol. 12, 596–601, 614. On this, see, among others, Brizzi, *La formazione della classe dirigente*; Novarese, *Istituzioni Politiche.*

Christianisation: that the meaning of Christian symbols would take root in their understanding and be part of their earliest memories. Through this process of cognitive structuring, children would be ingrained into replanting the same seed, so that future generations would automatically and naturally belong to the desired cultural order. Thereafter these new subjects could be made soldiers or preachers; or become ship hands or stonemasons or artisans. These Jesuits were fulfilling Miguel Vaz's vision from the 1530s.

As much as the Jesuits – and the Franciscans in their own way – may have believed that teaching children would effect cultural change, in fact their teachings alone could not have been very effective towards that end: this is suggested by Rita Marquilhas' work on attempts to advance literacy in Portugal.[28] Barzeus himself was aware of this danger, and in a missive registered his desire that God give these children "the grace to take advantage of, in the rest of their lives, the good education that they received when young."[29]

Que vos ensina o Mestre na escola?	What does the Master teach you at school?
Ensina vos ajudar missa?	Does he teach you to aid in the Mass?
Ensina vos a doutrina?	Does he teach you the doctrine?
Sabeis la em ambas as lingoas?	Do you know it in both languages?
Vêm muitos meninos a escola?	Do many children come to school?
Andão athe sincoenta.	Around fifty.
Quantos aprendem a ler?	How many learn to read?
Aprendem até quarenta.	Up to forty.
Alguns escrevem, outros começam.	Some write, others begin.[30]

[28] Marquilhas, *A Faculdade das Letras*, 137–9.

[29] Barzeus' missive in DI, Vol. 5, 595.

[30] IAN/TT, Manuscritos da Livraria, Cod. 757– António de Saldanha, s.j., Prasse Pastoral, fls 14v., 30.

These questions and answers, part of the above- mentioned lexicon by Father Saldanha, demonstrate the interest that the religious took in the effects of teaching. They aimed to assess the knowledge of doctrine, language, mathematics, reading, and writing, etc. assimilated by the children. Other questions were intended to gain other insights into how deeply these teachings were ingrained:

Sabeis doutrina?	Do you know the doctrine?
Rezai com atenção.	Pray carefully.
Aprendei vos a confessar	Learn how to confess.
Sabei que cousa he comungar.	Learn what it means to commune.
Quando rezais?	When do you pray?
A que Santo rezais?	To what Saint do you pray?
Que rezais a Snra?	What do you pray to the Virgin for?
Ouvis missa cada dia?	Do you listen to the Mass every day?
Quanto rezais no dia?	How often do you pray in the day?
Sois devoto de Nossa Senhora?	Are you devoted to Our Lady?
Rezais lhe o seu Rozairo?	Do you pray to her with your rosary?[31]

The Jesuit objective was not just to pass on the basics of literacy and the faith, but to be sure that these practices were internalised and practised frequently with devotion and pride. The disruption of the social order in these villages ran beyond the contents of classroom lectures and lessons. The relationship between the person and society, or the role of the relationship in society, was as relevant as the transmission of the doctrine itself.[32] The songs learned, the games played, and the friendships that emerged from

[31] Ibid., fls 6, 9v., 12, 16v., 30v.

[32] Once again, Saldanha's vocabulary is insightful. It demonstrates the interest of the missionaries in clothing and appearance, with the details ranging from shoes to sandals, their design and use, and the cleanliness of shorts and shirts. The expressions used are enlightening: "I enjoy watching you appear clean [. . .] cleaning seems in order [. . .] to see something dirty is so disgusting [. . .] if you can clean yourselves, then do it": Ibid., fls 3,

these interactions threatened the reproduction of pre-existing familial bonds and through them the existing social order which rested on them.

None of this could altogether replace the need to make education the route to complete transformation. A vital example of this was the College of Santa Fé, a project which found continuity in the Jesuit College of São Paulo. As mentioned in Chapter 2, the founding of the College of Santa Fé was in tandem with various foundations that were part of the projects of the Estado da Índia, prominently associated with the Franciscan friars of Piedade and the priests Miguel Vaz and Diogo de Borba.[33] Eventually, the college fell under Jesuit administration, becoming the College of São Paulo. Besides the name, another thing changed – its initial goals.[34]

For example, António Gomes, Rector of the College of São Paulo, opposed the admission of New Christians and local converts to the college, a view that went against the ideals of its founders. Gomes' goal was above all to educate Portuguese children. His convictions seem to have been inspired by some observations of Francis Xavier, who believed that the native populations were unable to internalise and transmit the Christian faith. Consequently, by 1551, as reported by Father Nicolao Lancilloto, Gomes expelled all local children and replaced them with Portuguese. This was done, it was said, because the admission of students had been done without "any selection" and "hence [there had] occurred confusion".[35]

8–8v., 12, translation in English. This stance on clothing is related to the outfitting of a Christian identity, as against that of the Gentiles: Pelikan, *The Christian Tradition*, Vol. 3, 30–1.

[33] As mentioned earlier, this orphanage was dedicated to the education of forty orphan boys: D'Costa, *The Christianisation of the Goan Islands*, 138.

[34] The Jesuits also aspired to a monopoly on education and sought to win over the Franciscan schools, such as the colleges of Santa Fé in Cranganore and Bassein. However, it was only in 1549, under Francis Xavier, that the Jesuits took full control of the college of Santa Fé in Goa: Moraes, *History of Christianity*, Vol. II, 395; Alden, *The Making of an Enterprise*, 44.

[35] On Gomes and Lancilloto's positions, see DI, Vol. 3, 593ff.; DI, Vol. 2, 139–43.

Loyola did not like this. He insisted that the locals continue to study in the college. Diogo Lainez and Francisco de Borgia echoed Loyola's opinion. The king of Portugal also expressed disapproval when apprised of the situation. He obliged the new administration to take back the expelled students. Local students, however, had now to be subject to difficult tests to prove their faith.[36]

A register of students dating to 1556 proves that sixty-six students were locals who belonged to a variety of indigenous groups. In contrast, the number of Portuguese were forty-four. These were the "hundred children of the land and mestizos" that the king of Portugal wished to see educated, in addition to seventy-two children who were to learn the seven liberal arts and theology. Erasmus, Nebrija, Dolet, Terence, Cicero, Virgil, Horace, Ovid, Aristotle, and in particular Thomas Aquinas were some of the authors much studied.[37]

Five years earlier, however, Viceroy Dom Afonso de Noronha (r. 1550–1554) had observed that there was no college in Goa to match the one supervised by the Franciscan Friar Vicente dos Lagos in Cranganore. All the same, the Colleges of Santa Fé and São Paulo in Goa provided models for similar institutions in Bardez and Salcete. Of particular note is the Colégio dos Reis Magos (College of the Magi), of which the construction was ordered by the viceroy.[38]

[36] "I believe that the King and all of you would want in every situation and all time the hosting of the children in the colleges here, as is now being done." On these different opinions, see DI, Vol. 1, 510–15; Vol. 3, 52–60, 302–11, 587ff.; S. Gonçalves, *Primeira Parte da História*, Vol. I, 464. See also, in this context, Mello, *The Recruitment and Formation*, 165; Alden, *The Making of an Enterprise*, 262–3.

[37] Register of 1556 and other documents on this subject in *Catalogus Puerorum Seminarii Goani*; Letter of Father Aires Brandão, 1556; Letter of Father Pedro Fernandes (Mercado), s.j., 1564, DI, Vol. 3, 483–8, 564–84; Vol. 6, 284.

[38] On the college of Cranganore, one of the first in the Estado da Índia, see BPADE, CIX/2–3, Mç. 3, nº 25 – "Carta de Frei Vicente a ElRey, dandolhe conta do Collegio", 1 Jan. 1549; IAN/TT, Corpo Cronológico, Part I, Mç. 80, nº 7.

Noronha was perhaps closer to Franciscan spirituality, and probably its patron. It was he who initially divided the parishes of Salcete and Bardez between the Jesuits and the Franciscans, a decision later approved by the subsequent viceroy, Dom Pedro de Mascarenhas (r. 1554–1555).[39]

The *Estatutos Generales de 1583* established that every Franciscan province should have at least three houses devoted to education. In 1636 Friar Paulo da Trindade mentioned colleges in Goa and Kochi that had existed since the middle of the sixteenth century. In the Kochi college, students could learn grammar and the arts, and in the Goa college theology. Such studies could begin in various monasteries and conclude at the College of Reis Magos.

Probably established in 1575 over a Franciscan residence and affiliated with the church of the same name, the College of Reis Magos functioned like a Casa dos Catecúmenos too. It admitted native students as well as Portuguese and mestizos. The goal was to teach children of the local elites as well as Portuguese children in order to make them new "apostles".[40] At the turn of the seventeenth century the seminary of Saint-Jerome supplemented the College of Reis Magos and focused on shaping Franciscan missionaries in India. Its curriculum was very similar to that of the College of São Paulo. In 1604 Luísa da Madre de Deus from the Third Order of the Franciscans – which assembled lay people – donated certain houses in Pomburpa to the Franciscans. By 1628 they seem to have established a new college there.[41]

[39] Trindade confessed that this viceroy had an "extreme devotion to our fellow friars". This devotion had practical effects on the role the Franciscans would come to have in Christianising the lands of Goa: Trindade, *Conquista Espiritual do Oriente*, Vol. I, 282ff., 363.

[40] Moraes, *History of Christianity*, Vol. II, 397.

[41] Built in 1602, it was responsible for the hospitals of Monte Guirim and of Valverde. For the feast of St Bonaventura, it received contributions from 50 villages in Salcete, 41 in Bardez, and 21 in Tiswadi, Dívar, and Chorão: A.P. Lobo, *Memória Histórico-Eclesiástica*, 53; Moraes, *History of Christianity*, Vol. 2, 397–8; Telles, "Ordens religiosas", 96–7.

Higher education for the Franciscans took place in the College of Saint-Bonaventure. This institution was established at the beginning of the seventeenth century and began life in 1618. Over their first three years students had first to undergo instruction in the arts, after which they had to pass an exam in Logic, Physics, and Metaphysics, before being permitted to take the four-year course in Theology. The main focus of their Theology years was on the four books of John Duns (or Duns Scotus, 1266–1308) and Peter Lombard, the *Magister Sententiarum*, "without obliging [the students] to read other authors . . . They also read the arts and theology in this college, as well as the language of the land." According to Trindade, "in conformity with our Statutes" theological studies revolved around the works of Duns Scotus. Friar Manuel de Monte Olivete was the main instructor.[42]

Meanwhile the Jesuits continued to petition the Crown to establish new colleges. The foundation of the Colégio do Espírito Santo (College of the Holy Spirit) in Margão in Salcete, after the death of Francis Xavier, is evidence of one of their successes.[43]

Emulating each other in the course of simultaneously competing in Bardez and Salcete, the Jesuits and Franciscans sought to transform Goa into a Christian space. Even if they shared many institutional arrangements – schools, colleges, hospitals – and methods such as preaching, education, and charity, in daily life their approaches were different.[44] There were, all the same, Jesuits who identified more with the affective Franciscan strategy, as there were Franciscans who adopted the intellectual path, showing

[42] *Estatutos Generales*, 16–16v.; Trindade, *Conquista Espiritual do Oriente*, Vol. 1, 263ff.

[43] Marques, "A evangelização da Índia", 248.

[44] The Dominicans and Augustinians, like the Jesuits and Franciscans, had their own educational institutions. The Dominicans ran the College of St Thomas Aquinas, situated in a suburb of the city of Goa, where they provided elementary and higher levels of education. The Augustinian school, Nossa Senhora do Pópulo, was only built in 1633, while the Nossa Senhora da Graça school was transferred from Neura to the city of Goa.

that the approaches of these orders were not always separate or internally consistent.[45]

One of the principal differences between the two orders was how they dealt with language skills.[46] Despite some passages in *Conquista Espiritual do Oriente*, Paulo da Trindade was unable to deny the accusation that the Franciscans did not speak the local languages fluently. Other passages prove that these skills had little place in the Franciscan methods of conversion and Christianisation. For example, Trindade refers to the first Franciscan publication in the *lingua canarim*, the *Flos Santorum*, written in 1607 by Friar Amador de Sant' Anna. Trindade also pointed to Friar João da Vila do Conde of the Province of Piedade, who was famed for his impressive local-language skills.[47]

By insisting on an affective path to conversion which sought to touch hearts rather than persuade minds, the Franciscan ethos thus did not seem to call for the acquisition of skills in local languages. Additionally, Portuguese imperialism began by assuming that the Indians would learn Portuguese and not the other way round. This awareness encouraged their disinvestment in learning the local languages.[48]

In 1641, in *Vida evangélica dos frailes menores*, Friar Miguel da Purificação explained that whether one knew the local languages, or indeed whether one followed other methods of conversion, was irrelevant to the fact of conversion. What was critical was that the natives see, interact with, and imitate the missionaries who lived in their villages. Evangelical poverty was the primary tool the Franciscans could fall back on. It is within this context that

[45] On these models and how they were expressed in narratives on the missionary experiences, see Girard, *Os Religiosos Ocidentais*. For the Goan case, see A.M. Xavier, "A Invenção de Goa", PhD thesis, Chapter 6.

[46] The language problem is already identified in decree 5 of Action 2 of the 1st Council: CR–APO, Fasc. 4, *1st Council*, 1567, Action 2, d. 5, 10.

[47] Trindade, *Conquista Espiritual do Oriente*, Vol. 1, 80, 350.

[48] Andrès Martín, *La espiritualidad franciscana*, 466; Meersman, *The Ancient Franciscan Provinces*, 2nd part, Chapters 4 and 5.

statements included in *Conquista Espiritual* make sense too: "it is not just through books and numerous sermons and exercises in their language that their spiritual fathers can aid these poor Christians."[49]

Disagreements on how one learned Christianity distanced the Franciscans from the Jesuits, marking the future of Christianisation in Goa. Their different perspectives on preaching also differentiated them. For the Franciscans the *sermo modernus* was the ideal model of preaching; that is to say, an enunciation or translation of the divine word.[50] In some of their "identity texts" the Franciscan ideal preacher was presented thus: "His words were like flames. They touched the hearts and left all remorseful and contrite. He preached with neither eloquence nor science. It is not studying and human diligence, but rather the spirit of the Lord and divine revelation, which inspires him."[51] This description of St Francis of Assisi's sermon to the birds, found in the *Chronica* by Friar Marcos Lisboa and written and published in the sixteenth century, served as a model of the style of preaching that the Franciscans in India believed they should aspire to. God must inspire preaching, which is the result of grace, and not of learning and eloquence. Another passage of this chronicle explains that the first Franciscans did not know the local languages in their preaching locations: learning languages was not necessary since the Holy Spirit provided other channels of comprehension.

It is perhaps on account of this confidence in the role of divine grace, and because they believed that the word of God could be transmitted only in Christian languages, that the majority of Franciscans utilised a less theatrical form of preaching which was

[49] Purificação, *Vida Evangélica*, 198. This did not mean that the Franciscans of Goa were not interested in knowledge. On this, see BNP, Cod. 176 – Notícias do arcebispado de Goa, 80–93, but also M.C. Matos, "A produção tipográfica", 139–43.

[50] Baubeta, "A pregação e a sociedade medieval"; I.R. Pereira, "O ensino da doutrina cristã".

[51] Lisboa, *Crónica da Ordem*, Vol. 1, 92.

more in line with a pre-Tridentine spirit.[52] In this sense they were not overly concerned with cultural adjustments to their preaching to suit the needs and capacities of their audience.[53]

In contrast, the Jesuits adapted better to the directives in vigour in post-Tridentine Europe – as described by Roberto Rusconi – and this was very visible in Goa: the doctrinal dimension was given pride of place over the mere preaching of the gospel.[54] For the Jesuits preaching went hand in hand with teaching the doctrine through catechism and was in itself a form of doctrinal education.[55] In his sixteenth-century *Doctrina Christiana*, Father João Rebelo explained that preaching was essential to a second phase in the conversion process, leading the converted to penitence. Sermons needed to repeat the same topics to achieve this.[56] The repetition resulted in a continuous exposure that gradually yet precisely transformed the predisposition and temperamental inclination of listeners in the desired direction.[57]

The objective was to reconstruct structures of understanding. Praying supplemented the effects of preaching. Should a sermon happen to be missed, prayer could compensate. The combination of teaching the locals how to read, write, and understand the basics of the Christian faith, preaching, and praying would lead new believers to become new apostles.

Father António Criminali's description from the middle of the

[52] Morán e Andrés-Gallego, "O Pregador", 121ff.; Rusconi, *Predicazione e Vita Religiosa*, 985ff.

[53] On these needs, see the decrees of the First Provincial Council on the competences of priests and confessors: CR–APO, Fasc. 4, *1st Council*, Action 3, d. 6 and 7, 36–8.

[54] Rusconi, *Predicazione e Vita Religiosa*, 1004.

[55] Preaching was the object of a conciliar session, leading to the decree *Super lectione et praedicatione* of 17 June 1546, and to the Canon IV of the *Decretum de reformation*. Cf. Morán e Andrés-Gallego, "O Pregador", 140–1.

[56] BNP, Cod. 3616 – João Rebelo, *Doctrina Christiana*, fl. 15v.

[57] Rebelo, *História dos Milagres*. On this, see the "Advertencias que se han de hazer del púlpito todos los dias despues de los sermones": ACL, Série Vermelha, nº 208, fls 21–26v.

sixteenth century is useful for understanding the different formats of preaching. At the time there was, in the city of Goa, a rather diverse array of people visiting churches:

> Gentiles, Moors, and infidels come to the Mass, and there they remain, to listen to it, and after which many convert to Christianity upon hearing the divine services . . . But the *Rationale Divinorum Officiorum* mandates that they have to leave the church after the offertory, even the catechumens. However, here, no mind is paid, neither to the catechumens nor to the infidels, since everyone including the Gentiles and other people, even if they are Gentiles or heretics, listens to the mass whenever they please . . . Sometimes I am shocked, [and] they say that it is not necessary to be so scrupulous, but I do not understand things so crudely.[58]

From this description it would seem that it was the ceremony rather than the contents that really moved non-Christians. The songs, which competed with those used in local devotions, were essential to the success of the preaching.

For example, attendance at the Church of São Paulo dropped dramatically when Father Gomes decided to end the children's choir that accompanied the divine offices. It was for this reason that Gaspar Barzeus decided to take up the plainsong that marked Dominican masses, even if it went against the Jesuit sensibility.[59] João de Lucena, the biographer of Francis Xavier, mentions Xavier assessing Barzeus' initiatives. Barzeus organised a procession and read the Passion of Christ each Friday, during which Christians mortified themselves before a crucifix. This so moved them that when they "saw the cross in the main chapel along with the singing of the psalm *Miserere mei Deus* [many] wept and committed themselves further to penitence."[60]

[58] Letter of Father Antonio Criminali in DI, Vol. 1, 8–22.

[59] This precept emerges in the Constitutions, Part 6, Chapter 3, which sought to distance the Jesuits from practices that could keep them from fulfilling their main tasks. With time, this rule underwent changes: Alden, *The Making of an Enterprise*, 14.

[60] Lucena, *História da Vida*, Vol. 4, 77. As the most dramatic moment of the Passion of Christ, the image of the cross symbolised the fight between

Hymns, processions, and dramatisations of scenes from the Passion of Christ were part of Barzeus' preaching, which enriched the text with images. Paintings and sculptures were part of his pedagogical process, following the Tridentine decrees on their use. Images of biblical episodes improved the teachings of the sermons and theatrical rendering reinforced the process.

The combination of visual and auditory tools was aimed at enhancing the experience of believers and non-believers, leading them to a genuine Christian identity.[61] The Jesuit strategy sought to combine mind and body; the gospel was to be instilled in the memory and understanding by stimulation of the body and the senses. To move people to feel and lead them to reason at the same time was seen as the most straightforward path. At a time when the Cartesian model had not yet propounded the separation between body and mind, these techniques made perfect sense.

If these mechanisms to Christianise the local people were in fact valid, the sermons themselves certainly confirmed it. A sermon in the village of Verna, one of the principal villages in Salcete, went on at length on the advantages of conversion for its residents. The preacher explained that the village would never achieve as much glory as it might once it was Christian: conversion would make it famous throughout Hindustan. The exaggeration was intended to stress the fruits which resulted from conversion and Christianisation.[62]

Preaching was another useful tool to draw people to Christianity; in a different way, so was confession. John Bossy and Adriano Prosperi, two leading scholars on the role of confession in the

---

good and evil, and was therefore the most useful pedagogic tool for those who wished to convert: Pelikan, *The Christian Tradition*, 142. The theme of the Passion had a wide-ranging impact on spirituality at the time, and the literature which encouraged its readers to reflect on it was prolific. See Loarte, *Instrução e advertencias*; Bruno, *Meditações sobre o mistério*; and Tristão Barbosa de Carvalho, *Peregrinação Cristã*.

[61] On these uses, see Bouza, *Comunicação, Memória e Conhecimento*, Chapter 1.

[62] Gracias, *Floreal da Nobreza*, 298.

construction of Christian identity and subjectivity in the early-modern period, highlight the dimension of spiritual consolation and reintegration of sinners. The suggestion that all souls could be saved was one of the primary Catholic responses to Lutheran reform. The act of self-discovery by examining one's conscience, and self-discipline – a result of penitence – was vital in developing the consciousness of the individual Christian. Through confession it was also possible to control behaviour and prevent dissent, which made it an indispensable political tool. If in the medieval period confession aimed to pacify communities, in the modern period it was the confession of private turmoil, especially of a sexual nature, that gained relevance.[63]

While studying the Portuguese case, Francisco Bethencourt stressed the social control enabled by confession. In contrast, Maria de Lurdes Correia Fernandes highlighted the anthropological aspect, in particular the "personal" dialogue between the Church and confessing penitents.[64]

If preaching and teaching in schools and colleges constituted social moments and forms of collective communication, the confession constituted a more personal kind of schooling, a powerful method for shaping the soul of each individual. It fell to the confessor to identify what ailed the individual soul – in memory, understanding, and will – and cure it, leading the penitent towards living the exemplary life. The confession was in this sense one of the most efficient instruments for the Christianisation of individuals, essential in fact for the very constitution of Christian subjects and a truly Christian community.[65]

[63] Prosperi, *Tribunali della Coscienza*, 219ff.; Prosperi, *Il Concilio di Trento*, 122ff.; Bossy, *A Cristandade no Ocidente*, 52, 64, 150, 165; Bossy, *Dalla communità all'Individuo*, 59–85.

[64] Bethencourt, "O campo ético"; M.L.C. Fernandes, "As artes da confissão".

[65] The power to confess "reserved cases" caused jurisdictional conflicts inside the church, namely between confessors, prelates, and inquisitors. About the "reserved cases" at that time, see the treatises of Porto, *Manual*

There were differences, however, between the theory and practice of confession. Confessors combined ordinary or delegated jurisdiction and familiarity with the doctrine of the Church. They had to know theology, canon law, synodal constitutions, the difference between mortal and venial sins, the circumstances of their commission, reserved cases, and those that needed restitution. The first version of the *Manual de Confessores e Penitentes*, by Friar Rodrigo do Porto, a Franciscan of Piedade – a work subsequently rewritten by the Jesuit doctor Azpicuelta Navarro – explained this well. Used as an aid by many confessors, Porto's edition of the manual emphasised the need for empathetic listening during a confession, which helped the speaker express contrition or regret. The additions by Azpicuelta suggest a heightened awareness of the link between individual and society contained in the sacrament, and its importance in ensuring that each person performed one's social duty.[66] Azpicuelta's texts circulated widely, unlike Porto's *Manual*, and allow us insights into the ideal confessor. *Cazos Rezervados* (Reserved Cases), a compilation by Boaventura das Chagas, a Franciscan friar in India in the first decades of the seventeenth century, were intended to help Franciscan confessors. Chagas explained that the Franciscans had *omnimoda* authority; this allowed them to, among other things, "dispense absolution to the new Christians for violation of chastity," as well as "commute all the vows of the Indian converts, except those of religion and Jerusalem" and "reconcile apostates from the faith".[67]

---

de Confessores; Azpicuelta Navarro, *Manual de Confessores*; Távora, *Tratado de Avisos a Confessores.*

[66] Porto, *Manual de Confessores*; Azpicuelta Navarro, *Manual de Confessores*, 26. We are aware that one hundred copies of the *Breve Memorial de Pecados* were sent to Ethiopia; the same shipment included a thousand booklets, thirty catechisms, a hundred books of the life and passions of the martyrs, a hundred books of the destruction of Jerusalem, and a hundred books of hours of the Blessed Virgin: I.R. Pereira, "O ensino da doutrina cristã nos séculos XIII a XVI", 368.

[67] Central Library of Panaji, *Cazos Reservados*, M-29, 195.

The confessor had to confess under different circumstances in the city since the city was different from the countryside. A city on the coast was more complicated than one in the hinterland, and matters in Portugal were easier than in India. Justifying his authority, the confessor explained to the penitent the meaning of confession, taking him on with joy, advising him on cases of impediments, clarifying the gestures that he must make, and the prayers he needed to articulate. Then, providing the ten commandments as a framework, the confessor asked the penitent to account for all his sins, and whether he was aware of them as sins. For example, blasphemies were a sin against the second commandment, disrespecting one's mother a sin against the third, participation in unjust wars against the fourth. Usury was a sin against the seventh, while the eighth commandment prohibited false testimony. The inquiry concluded with questions on addictions and their manifestations, the works of mercy, and the sins peculiar to each social group. In other words, the confessor had to be able to reformulate the intricate architecture and meaning of sins and apply them to every penitent in line with their social profile. In this way he was able to localise a universal sacrament.

However, as Maria de Lourdes Correia Fernandes has noted, "the greater the ignorance of the confessors [. . .], the higher the danger of the penitent's ignorance."[68] In these situations, confessors and penitents were both unable to appreciate the actions, thoughts, and circumstances that were considered sins. This problem was multiplied exponentially in the imperial territories. Unfamiliarity with the language used was one of the reasons. How to deal with the problems that translation posed within a confession was never entirely clear. Did the locals properly understand the meaning of confession? Which confessions were accurate and complete, what conditions were considered necessary for them to be valid or acceptable?

Then there was the question of interpreters and interpretations.

[68] Fernandes, "As artes da confissão", 57.

Interpreters could transmit an erroneous representation of the sins of the penitent to the confessor. They could distort the Christian message conveyed to penitents. Exhortations and questions such as "Learn to confess", "Confess often", "Did you confess well?" could only be responded to satisfactorily after learning the local language.[69] Confessors, however, confronted the most challenging problems: How to "shape the person's inner self, his soul"; how to erase the vices of body and soul and instead inscribe the virtues contradicting them.

Correspondence on confession, starting with the third decade of the sixteenth century, is evidence of its relevance in political and religious matters. The education of the confessors, besides that of the penitents, was one of the major concerns. Consequently, in 1557, a confessional was printed in Goa.[70] Also, after 1580, the Hispanic monarchy expressed concern at the quality of confessions in the villages of Goa. The king, at the macro level, sought to intervene with regard to the consciences of his subjects – those who existed at the most micro of all levels. In a royal letter written to Viceroy Dom João Coutinho (r. 1617–1619), Count of Redondo, on 20 February 1618, the king referred to "the great inconveniences that result from confessions made through interpreters," insisting on the positioning of personnel "who understand the parishioners so that they may confess . . . and teach them the Christian doctrine in their language."[71] The use of translators during confession is attested to by successive budgets of the Estado da Índia which make provision for a *lingoa*, or translator, who was meant to teach the doctrine, or for a *clerigo canarim* (local priest) – three in the case of Salcete – "who would help confess the locals."[72]

For many, the Jesuits excelled in confessions too. Writing in response to a request by the Crown for information on the situation

[69] IAN/TT, Manuscritos da Livraria, Cod. 757 – António de Saldanha, s.j., Prasse Pastoral, fls 5v., 6, 9.

[70] A. da Silva, *Trent's Impact*, 136.

[71] See *Monsoon Books*, Vol. 4, 344.

[72] Matos, "Teres e haveres", 219ff.

of Christianity, Viceroy Dom João Coutinho complimented the Jesuits on their work in Jesuit villages. In his view they aided the dispensation of "confessions and sacraments with much zeal, [good] example, and satisfaction." He concluded that "they catechised the lands of Salcete very well, and with particular emphasis on the divine service."[73]

However, despite this viceregal praise, one must ask how capable the Jesuits, as much as the other orders, were in explaining the idea and functions of a conscience to the converted population. Were the new Christians able to memorise the virtually unending list of things deemed sins that they might commit?

The road to confession was not smooth. Sometimes the intervention of inquisitors was needed when allowing confessions of reserved cases, such as heresy. Over the sixteenth and seventeenth centuries the Goan inquisition had to deal with roughly 9000 cases of heresy. This large number was evidence that Christianisation was incomplete and that confession had failed. At bottom, many locals remained Gentile.[74]

The confession was an occasion for sin, too. For some confessors it meant more than just providing spiritual consolation.[75] Even priests who were considered saintly, as was the Jesuit Miguel de Carvalho in Chaul, were subject to proceedings by the local Inquisition for their behaviour as confessors. Carvalho confessed to the sin of solicitation. While administering the sacrament of confession, he asked women who had confessed to do sinful things with him. The Inquisition punished Father Carvalho with a mandate of "perpetual silence", but not all priests guilty of the same sin were as fortunate as Carvalho.[76]

While the Jesuits may have stood out in their conduct with confessions – as they did in making the populations literate, conveying

[73] *Monsoon Books*, Vol. 5, 168, 551.

[74] References to these situations in India are found in IAN/TT, Conselho Geral do Santo Ofício, nº 184, nº 480.

[75] Prosperi, *Il Concilio di Trento*, 131.

[76] IAN/TT, Conselho Geral do Santo Ofício, nº 184.

the Christian doctrine, and preaching – compassion and charity were the realms in which the Franciscans excelled. Charity, however, also entailed a political dimension. The politicisation of charity had led to changes that provided it with a disciplinary and ordering character. It is in this context that the story of a poor widow of Portuguese origin who died alone and desperate in Goa at the beginning of the seventeenth century is a good metaphor for the caregiving provided in this region.

"Such images cannot be said to be Gods": Miracles and Cures as Instruments of Christianisation

The story begins in the convent of São Francisco in the city of Goa. A person came to the door and asked the friars to bury a person so poor that she had no one to bury her. The guardian of the convent, Friar João de São Matias, decided to go, together with 120 friars. According to Paulo da Trindade, Friar João de São Matias was himself a "living example" of poverty. Such was the poverty practised by him that he "did not use more than the poor and patched habit; and never slept in a bed, sleeping instead over straps with a book at his head." The friars went to the widow's house, which was above the Três Boticas, a well-known area of the town. There they found the chaplain, and a brother of the Misericórdia, a well-known *fidalgo* called Dom João de Lima.[77]

Climbing up the stairs, the friars and Lima "found [a widow] on a miserable mat, in a pitiful state." The nobleman observed "that not even the vicar had come" and applauded the "honoured company of the friars for more could not have been done for the viceroy himself." Dom João de Lima ended his speech by thanking God and praising the Franciscans.[78]

[77] Trindade, *Conquista Espiritual do Oriente*, Vol. 1, 153. Friar João de S. Matias was the convent's guardian in 1609, which allows one to believe that this incident may have happened at the time.

[78] Trindade, *Conquista Espiritual do Oriente*, Vol. 1, 155–6.

What is significant about this narrative is that the woman was found alone and abandoned at a time when the city of Goa hosted several institutions dedicated to the protection of women. Besides the recently finished shelter of Nossa Senhora da Serra (Our Lady of the Mountains), there was also the Convent of Santa Mónica (Saint Monica), of which the construction had begun in 1606, and which soon after operated as a shelter for twenty nuns and several widows.[79]

Although the Refuge of Nossa Senhora da Serra gave preferential treatment to orphans of wealthy families, it also accepted for short durations the wives of Portuguese sailors in the viceroy's fleets. The Convent of Santa Mónica had also been intended to host women seeking its shelter from the violence of husbands. In practice, most of the widows sheltered in these two institutions were from wealthy backgrounds. Both aimed to protect women of Portuguese origin, but also Christians of the land, from the "great disasters that happen here every day". Other houses were concerned with "Madalenas" (fallen women) and poor women.[80]

[79] Some of the situations that could lead widows to poverty were discussed in a decree from 1612: AHU, India, Cx. 2, nº 45 – "Alvará regio em favour de Brites de Pina", 12 Sept. 1619. These situations included the husband dying, no longer receiving income from the office held by the husband, the transfer of the husband's debt to the widow, the exhausting of dowry and inheritance. A petition in 1616 by Maria de Freitas, widow of Lourenço do Carvalhal, is emblematic of this kind of situation: she asked for a pension of 300 xerafins after the death of her husband since she was poor and ridden with debt: AHU, India, Cx. 4, nº 20.

[80] In a letter dated March 1597, the king ordered the viceroy to discuss the possibility of creating refuges for "married women without their husbands": CR-APO, Fasc. 3, 726; CR-APO, Fasc. 5, Vol. 3, 1493–4. Eight years later, Archbishop Dom Fr. Aleixo de Menezes recommended that these women either marry after a year of being widowed or go to an institution so as to avoid falling into a life of disrepute: BNP, Cod. 176 – Notícias do arcebispado de Goa, 119–21. For more details on these institutions, see IAN/TT, Manuscritos da Livraria, Cod. 2238 – Diogo de Sant'Anna, Resposta por parte do insigne mosteiro de Santa Mónica. On the destinies of these women, see also Bethencourt, "Os conventos femininos", 631–52; M.J.M.

The emphasis on taking care of all varieties of Portuguese women, whether unmarried, married, or widowed, and later orphans as well, demonstrates the role and image of women in society and how the control of these women ensured social, cultural, and biological reproduction. The care of women was therefore part of a broader political context. Considering that the protection of women was crucial for the conservation of the political order, the Crown and viceregal government had issued many decrees and provisions concerning their well-being. A letter from the king to Viceroy Dom Francisco da Gama (r. 1597–1600; 1622–1628), Count of Vidigueira, was very explicit about the mercy to be shown to widows. This was a response to petitions in 1597 by fifteen widows whose husbands had served the king. Other documents also mention the concern of the Crown for Portuguese widows, principally during the Iberian Union. These letters insist that viceroys pay their pensions quickly to avoid "inconveniences against the service of God".[81]

The case raised by the Franciscan narrative, however, is a testament to the failure of these charitable institutions, a disaster of such proportions that the Portuguese ought to be ashamed, said Trindade. Although the Crown felt a sense of responsibility in providing for economically vulnerable women, the institutions charged with the task were not always able to discharge their obligations effectively.[82]

Lopes, "As recolhidas de Goa", 653ff.; Sá, "Entre Maria e Madalena"; Sá, *Quando o Rico se faz Pobre*; Coates, *Degredados e Orfãs*, 236–70; A.J. Costa, "Acção missionária e patriótica".

[81] In 1608, the monarch responded to a petition from the widows that their pensions be dispatched. Two years later, however, they had not received royal confirmation, after which they reiterated their petition. These petitions and royal letters are published in *Monsoon Books*, Vol. 1, 169–73; Vol. 3, 203–4; CR-APO, Fasc. 5, Vol. 3, 1489–92.

[82] The Crown also tried to protect society from disgraced women and situations where a "scandal" could occur. For example, the *carta régia* from 1593 on "barregueiras" (prostitutes) attempts to physically separate these

Coming back to this episode: for the Franciscans it was divine grace that allowed the friars to pay back the alms that the widow had earlier bestowed on them. The narrative underlines that, besides the manifestation of *agapê* (Greek: unconditional love) in Franciscan generosity, there was an element of justice underpinning the practice of charity.

As will be recalled, it was not just Franciscan friars who attended to dead and dying widows. At the entrance to the building, they encountered representatives of the Misericórdia. This brotherhood claimed to be the sole institution that had been permitted to accompany burials of the deceased.[83] In this instance, it only sent its banner, a nobleman, and a chaplain. Probably Paulo da Trindade used this narrative to implicitly criticise the Misericórdia, the preferred welfare institution in the cities of the empire and the kingdom,[84] whose behaviour contrasted with the Franciscan response to the distress call regarding the funeral of a poor widow. Of its 600 members, the brotherhood had chosen to send merely a few officials, whereas the convent of São Francisco had sent all its friars.

This tension between Franciscans and the Misericórdia was in part due to the nature of the initial institution of charitable institutions in the Estado da Índia. The transfer of charities to the overseas territories had been simultaneous with their reorganisation in the metropole.[85] The primary objective of welfare mechanisms established in the Estado da Índia was to assist the Portuguese, the Christians, and among them the soldiers. Welfare mechanisms focused on those who had pledged their bodies to

---

women from the *casados*, placing them in "different neighbourhoods where they will live and nowhere else": CR-APO, F. 3, 412–13.

[83] Sá, *Quando o Rico se faz Pobre*, Chapters 1 and 2.

[84] In this context see the *Portugaliae Monumenta Misericordiarum*, "Introduction", vols 3, 4, and 5. See also Sá, "A reorganização da caridade", 35ff. Sá refers to the territorial diversity of Misericórdias. She also focuses on how the Crown benefited from the presence of the Misericórdia.

[85] *Portugaliae Monumenta Misericordiarum*, Vol. 3, "Introduction".

the project of conquest. When not Portuguese, the majority of the population suffering sickness, hunger, and poverty remained practically invisible in the eyes of these primary institutions.

At the time, the criterion of proximity to the Church determined the position in the hierarchy of those who deserved aid. To be Christian was important. The nature of the relationship between the agent of charity and the person receiving it was also critical. The donor was expected to prioritise those within his family, his locality, and his region, and those of the same kingdom.[86]

This way of thinking, summarised by St Thomas Aquinas and present in many theological treatises, was materialised in concrete "charitable" exchanges. By this calculation, Portuguese soldiers were the most deserving since such men not only put their lives on the line for the expansion of Christianity, they were also Christians of Portuguese origin. The proximity of welfare institutions to these soldiers was thought significant.[87] It was in this context that the city of Goa saw the establishment of a hospital, and other places in the Estado da Índia received charitable establishments.[88]

Initially handed over to the Franciscans, the Hospital Real (Royal Hospital) was later entrusted to the Misericórdia after 1542, and in 1591 to the Jesuits, who subsequently refused to administer it. Other hospitals sheltered the Portuguese sick. These hospitals

[86] Aquinas, *La Somma Teologica*, IIª, q. 26, a. 7.

[87] Sá, *Quando o Rico se faz Pobre*, 74–80.

[88] One of the first records on the existence of a hospital in Goa dates to 1511. Another is available from 1520 in the "Regimento que o Secretario deu ao comprador do Hospital de Goa", where revenues and expenses of the hospital were tallied so as to make sure the hospital could be effectively provisioned. In 1524 there are references to other hospitals. Later, in the "Regimento da casa dos mantimentos", it was ordered that the bread of the hospital in Goa be made of the finest wheat: CR-APO, Fasc. 5, Part I, 53–4, 65–72. In 1542 the governor gives privileges: IAN/TT, Corpo Cronológico, Part I, Mss. 72, nº 84 – "Traslado do Compromisso que fez o Governador da India para o Hospital da Cidade de Gôa", 7 Aug. 1542, and so forth. On this, see also Martins, *História da Misericórdia*; V.A.F. Silva, *O Hospital Real de Goa*; Gracias, *Health and Hygiene*.

also gave rise to the first brotherhoods and confraternities, as well as provided charitable services to their members, particularly in the shape of burials.[89]

When the local populations converted, they became eligible objects of charity and poor-relief decisions. Poor Christians who benefited from the alms of the vicar of Kochi in 1509 were probably among the first to enjoy this benefit. Some years later a vicar of Cannanore handed out rice on Sundays and requested that black rice be given to the poor. Before 1519 the king gave alms to "new Christians of the land" too. An *alvará* by Dom Manuel mandated this to the Misericórdia – already established in Goa – charging this brotherhood to distribute goods to the families of the converted as they saw fit. Later it was the Franciscan Guardian António do Louro who requested aid to continue the practice: he believed it was the only way to persuade locals to convert.[90]

The word "poor" soon came to stand for "Christian of the land", demonstrating that the first conversions were among the lower castes. They were in need of financial help to be able to live with (Christian) dignity. For some authors, the Misericórdia was the leading agent of charity and poor relief in the Estado da Índia, and its foundation proved the Crown's interest in helping the poor. However, these authors tend to forget that the Misericórdias acted almost only in the urban world,[91] whereas the majority of the king's subjects lived in rural areas. This means that, in the

[89] In 1595 Alessandro Valignano supported the decision of the Jesuits to refuse the administration of the Royal Hospital to avoid the opposition and hatred of the brothers of the Misericórdia: ARSI, Goana 22, fls 159–61.

[90] BPADE, CIX/2–3, M. 3, nº 13 – "Carta de Frei Antonio a ElRey Dom Manoel sobre a conversão dos Gentios", 4 Nov. 1518; CR-APO, Fasc. 5, Part I, 41 (alvará of Dom Manuel). On the same subject, see also DHMPPO, Vol. 1, 67, 70, 371–3.

[91] Boxer, *Portuguese Society in the Tropics*. The Crown did concede increased powers and privileges to the Misericórdias, which became a model of charitable institutions. In 1616 the Misericórdias sought sole responsibility for all welfare aid. See Sá, *Quando o Rico se faz Pobre*, 46ff.

context of the Estado da Índia, the Crown–Misericórdia alliance was far from exhaustive in the welfare assistance it delivered. Dom João III's reign saw a division of labour between the Misericórdia and religious orders, between urban and rural spaces, and between soldiers and local Christians.

Vicar General Miguel Vaz also strengthened the association between charity and conversion. In the first letter he wrote to the king of Portugal, Vaz demanded that the "Christians of the land . . . be delivered to [the care of] a good man, who will be as a father of these Christians and will take special care of them."[92] The establishment of the Confraternity, College, and Seminary of the Holy Faith in 1541, and a hospital for poor Christians to which Governor Martim Afonso de Sousa donated 300 *pardaos*, was part of this effort.[93]

It was to give dignity to "miserable" local Christians, who had been "thus far so oppressed and annihilated [. . .] that they were neither visible nor even taken into consideration", that political power expanded charitable assistance. An episode – reported by Paulo da Trindade after a poor Brahman from Pomburpa was converted – included a declaration by the convert that it was Jesus "who accepted me and gave food for my children and me."[94] The charity was also extended to lower-caste individuals who wished to convert. In a village in Tiswadi, the Jesuits established a permanent fund to provide food for the poorest in times of scarcity. In other villages, as mentioned earlier, they set up granaries to loan grain to poor villagers who had exhausted their own reserves.

Nevertheless, though the poverty of the majority of the Goan population was visible, the fact is that not much had changed consequent to Vaz's initial letter. In 1546, in a determined missive to the monarch, Miguel Vaz proposed a set of protective measures for "Christians of the land". First, the king should ensure that

92 HAG, Acórdãos do Senado da Câmara, nº 7737, 72–4.

93 D'Costa, *The Christianisation of Goan Islands*, 140. On this hospital, see J.M.P. Figueiredo, "Goa Dourada".

94 Trindade, *Conquista Espiritual do Oriente*, Vol. 1, 305.

these Christians did not serve in Portuguese fleets since such service resulted in suffering and poverty within their families. Second, the locals should not be pressed to provide free labour or corvée. Vaz further suggested that, on account of their poverty, converted Christians be excused from paying tithes, at least for a period immediately following conversion. A year later, in 1547, the Jesuit Lancilloto realised that many of the conversions had happened solely for economic reasons, and three years later he too argued that imposing tithes on the "newly converted" should be avoided because of their extreme poverty – which had, at times, resulted in the sale of children by their parents. The Jesuits sometimes wondered if it was lawful to "buy" the locals in order to convert them to Christianity. Considering activity of this variety as violating natural law – as defined by the Portuguese – the king of Portugal felt morally obliged to put a stop to such practices.[95]

The Crown attempted to respond to the miserable condition of the locals, and to that of the "newly converted", with protective measures. Rights to inheritance and exemption from tithes were among several of these. The exemption from tithes was repeated in 1570, subsequently in 1581, then in 1598 and into the next century. Another way the Crown aided local Christians was by giving them land confiscated from expelled Brahmans. The provision from 1575, which decreed this transfer, referred to the impoverished state the Christians found themselves in, and the need to give them alms, clothes, and other aid. The Thomist principle that Gentiles should not govern Christians structured the decree, which prohibited non-Christians from being tenants if they had Christian labourers working for them. Many similar orders, structured on these same concepts, would follow in the years to come.[96]

[95] On this, see DI, Vol. 1, Memorial of Father Miguel Vaz, 1545, 63–89; DI, Vol. 2, Letter of Father Nicolao Lancillotto, s.j., 1547, DI, Vol. 1, 63–89; DI, Vol. 2, 123–31. See also D'Costa, *The Christianisation of Goan Islands*, 133.

[96] See some of these ambivalent orders and decisions in HAG, Livro das

Among the institutions established to support the newly converted, the Pai dos Cristãos was the most unique. Until the 1550s, sources only refer to the first Pai dos Cristãos, the layman and councillor of the municipality, Rui Barbudo. Eventually, there are references to various officials, at least one per province. The *Regimento* of 1576 by Diogo Velho outlined certain rules: the Pai dos Cristãos should be solicitous with Christians, favouring them in such a way that they saw him as a defender of their needs. He needed to know if they lived well, and he was meant to help them. He needed to settle their conflicts.[97]

The vocabulary used is enlightening: "look [after]", know "how they lived", "set them apart" – in other words, to discipline the "Christians of the land" so that they followed the Christian canon. Even though this official did not participate in the matrix of disciplinary institutions identified by Foucault, the desire for social control was a structuring principle underlying the existence of the office.[98]

The "Rules for the Use of the [Jesuit] Pai dos Cristãos", written by Alessandro Valignano in 1595, provide the best clues to understanding the scope of this office. These Rules make it evident that, at the time, the Pai dos Cristãos was not a single office any more, it was a whole institution. There was an officer who bore the title, helped by a religious brother, a solicitor, or a translator. For Valignano, the Pai dos Cristãos had to focus his energies on establishing the necessary conditions that would lead to conversion from the moment of baptism, and create a system of "support and care for the newly converted" to ensure they did not lead miserable

---

Monções, nº 39, 378; CR-APO, Fasc. 3, 870–2; Fasc. 5, Vol. 3, 1068–71; DHMPPO, Vol. 12, 276. Some of these orders replicated what had been decided in the Provincial Councils. See CR-APO, Fasc. 4, *5th Council*, 1606, Action 4, d. 9 and 10, 190ff.

[97] D'Costa, *The Christianisation of Goan Islands*, 139; a summary of the activities of the Pai dos Cristãos can be found in a document of 1576, where its salary is referred to: DHMPPO, Vol. 12, 363.

[98] Foucault, *Surveiller et Punir*.

lives. He had to help eradicate local devotional practices, in public as well as private, and monitor attendance to Christian sacraments and catechism. His job also entailed the management of the Casa dos Catecúmenos and the celebration of baptisms. It was his duty to stay informed about orphans, non-Christian slaves, and prisoners.[99]

The Pai dos Cristãos was also given judicial powers. In 1598 he could "orally judge conflicts among the Christians of the said places" if they involved small sums, and against his decision "there would be no recourse to appeal or grievance". In addition he had at the beginning of the seventeenth century the job of determining which local Christians were capable of holding office in the imperial order. Though some people disagreed with this decision and urged the bestowing of such "jobs" by other methods, the viceroys privileged the opinion of these officers, rendering them critical intermediaries between the colonial order and imperial power.[100]

In 1630 the Count of Linhares sought the support of the Pai dos Cristãos to control the rising tide of poor who arrived in the city of Goa in the context of a famine. He did this by granting the latter the right to certify "those who appear so poor that they have no option but to beg."[101] Although the task required seemed to go against the nature of the office, it indicates how important the Pai dos Cristãos had become.

Powerful as they were, some fathers among the Christians misused their authority. In 1619 the Procurador da Coroa e da Fazenda (Attorney of the Crown and the Exchequer) believed this to be true of the already mentioned Friar Simão da Nazaré, the officer in charge of the village of Sirula in Bardez. In his opinion Nazaré was responsible for oppressing people in this village. Nazaré's behaviour shows that the office he held could in the wrong hands become a locus for the exercise of arbitrary power.[102]

[99] *O Livro do "Pai dos Cristãos"*, 22.

[100] CR-APO, Fasc. 5, Vol. 3, 1083–4.

[101] CR-APO, Fasc. 6, Vol. 2, 1245–7.

[102] "The Pai dos Cristãos also destroys the lands through his commands

The Casa dos Catecúmenos was another institution of primary assistance that sought to ensure that those in the process of converting stayed out of poverty. At the time of its construction, some parts of this establishment were made in haste "since they were low houses, meant to accommodate the poor and people of the land." Later, many who converted returned to the Casa dos Catecúmenos to benefit from its assistance. There was a hospital for poor natives in front of it, and "in this manner many became Christians." When it began, the hospital was able to hold seven or eight people and was "quite clean with its mattresses, pillows, and quilts." Between 1552 and 1556 this number increased to accommodate twenty to forty patients. Pedro Afonso, who managed the hospital in 1556, highlighted the humility and charity necessary to attend to patients and provide for their needs. Some arrived at the hospital with tumours, open wounds, grave injuries, and diseases of which Christian medicine had little knowledge. They nevertheless managed to convert these patients and their families after instructing them in the basics of the faith; by the year 1563 seventy locals are estimated as having been converted in this manner. The Royal Hospital took on poor mestizos and local Christians as well as those with incurable diseases with the same purpose of conversion. No patient could enter without having confessed, which naturally excluded those who had not been converted.[103]

The triad of confraternity–college–hospital was critical to the well-being of the newly converted in the city of Goa, combining notions of religion, charity, and conversion. It should therefore

---

because Your Majesty gave him a salary of a hundred xerafins [. . .] He gives gifts to the Archbishop, Inquisitors and [other] officials, and sumptuous dinners for the viceroys when they visit Bardez (except to the Count Viceroy), and he has been able to loan the Archbishop two thousand pardaos. [. . .] He is a Franciscan friar minor, and all this [money] comes from the land, and if it comes from oppression, he does not allow it to be visible": AHU, Índia, Cx. 6, nº 29 – "Do Procurador da Coroa e Fazenda", 12 Dec. 1619.

[103] *Statuta Confraternitatis Fidei*, 1541; Letter of Father Luís Fróis, 1552;

come as no surprise that, a few decades later, Salcete and Bardez had similar complexes in the vicinity of the Colleges of Espírito Santo and Reis Magos.

According to Father Francisco de Sousa, the author of *Oriente Conquistado*, the transfer of the Jesuit hospital of the poor to Margão was because of the need to spread welfare assistance. This father remembered the injustice of some officers of the Crown who had threatened the very preservation of Christianity.[104] Even though the hospital was initially only for poor Christians, i.e. poor local Christians, as time went on it began accepting the non-Christian poor who wished to convert, either during convalescence or on their deathbed. Indeed, those who were taken care of in the hospital did not leave it without becoming catechumens, and thereby converting, often along with their families.[105]

The Franciscans in Bardez established a series of hospitals too. Friar Paulo da Trindade was most enthusiastic in his praise of Franciscan prowess in the field of charitable work. He says that in these hospitals Franciscans exercised the virtues of humility and charity.[106] Some hospitals overseen by Franciscans were established through private donations, as was the Hospital of Nossa Senhora da Saúde (Hospital of Our Lady of Health), in Valverde, founded by Baltasar de Sá in the third quarter of the sixteenth century and handed over to the care of Franciscans.[107] There was also a

---

Letter of Father Pedro Fernandes (Mercado), 1564, DI, Vol. 1, 775–90; Vol. 2, 468; Vol. 6, 284, cited in Moraes, *History of Christianity*, Vol. 2, 396. See also Gonçalves, *Primeira Parte da História*, Vol. 1, 125–6; D'Costa, *The Christianisation of Goan Islands*, 140–2; Sá, "Os hospitais portugueses", 87.

[104] Sousa, *Oriente Conquistado*; J.M.P. Figueiredo, "Goa dourada", 36; Telles, "Ordens religiosas", 136. The hospital was first located in the building that later became the House of Bom Jesus. Later, it was housed in the new college of Saint-Paul.

[105] D'Costa, *The Christianisation of Goan Islands*, 140–3.

[106] Trindade, *Conquista Espiritual do Oriente*, Vol. 1, 81.

[107] Meersman disagrees with this founding date, since he could not find references to this institution in subsequent documents: Meersman, *The Ancient Franciscan Provinces*, 138–40.

hospital in Mount Guirim, famed as the hospital of the forsaken, which later shifted alongside the church, college, and seminary of Reis Magos.

Individuals also practised charity in favour of the newly converted. Dona Ana de Azevedo, who left all her goods to the Franciscans and was the founder of the Church of Our Lady of Penha de França, asked that her funeral be attended by members of the order, but also by poor people from the parish; she left them a small amount in alms.[108] Not that the poor always enjoyed priority in the economy of almsgiving. For example, as indicated earlier, in 1604 two Portuguese women, Luísa da Madre de Deus and her mother, founded the Church of Madre de Deus (Mother of God), in Pomburpa, and next to it a hospital for the poor. The testament of Luísa da Madre de Deus led to the dissolution of the hospital and its replacement by a school for boys and catechumens. This latter institution, which was never established, was meant to be maintained by a fourth of the rents that went to the testator. Only when there were no students were the poor given preferential treatment.[109]

Any comprehensive survey of the institutions engaged in charity in Goa must also look at the brotherhoods that focused solely on the "newly converted". As Leopold Rocha's study of the confraternities of Goa demonstrates, these were an essential part of the process of Christianisation because of their ability to support the identities of the "newly converted". Each parish church hosted one or more confraternity, and many of them took on the additional services of devotion and aid. An ideal example was the Confraternity of Our Lady of Esperança (Hope) in the city of Goa, created by local Christians, which played a vital role during a fire at the Casa da Pólvora (House of Gunpowder) in the city in 1621. Although many Christians from a wide array of orders provided help to the injured and burials for the deceased,

[108] A.D.S. Costa, "A expansão portuguesa", 19–25.

[109] Shastry, "The Church and the Village", 131.

the brothers from Our Lady of Esperança provided the most substantial aid.[110]

Nevertheless, in the long term it would be in the villages that the confraternities would express their disciplinary power. Almost all the Franciscan churches in Bardez had these devotional and welfare structures, the first of them being the Confraternity of the Holy Sacrament in the Church of the Reis Magos. Another was the Confraternity of Our Lady of Remédios (Remedies), based in the church of the same name in Nerul. As early as 1616 this confraternity was the primary motor of religious life in the village. It received several donations, even from residents of the village who had decided against converting. Their contributions aided the funding of the confraternity's devotional and charitable services. Something similar happened with the confraternities of the churches of Penha de França and Our Lady of Luz (Light) in the villages of Penha de França and Pomburpa, respectively, both benefiting from private funding by the Portuguese widows Ana de Azevedo and Luísa da Madre de Deus. There were other confraternities, such as that of the Boa Viagem (Good Voyage), at the fort of Aguada. Built over a structure for a local deity, of whom local fishermen beseeched protection at sea, it is not clear how these worshippers interpreted the act of charity. The same could be said of the Confraternity of Our Lady of Milagres (Miracles).[111]

The Jesuits had confraternities in the churches in Salcete, some of which provided charitable assistance. The Confraternity of the Espírito Santo in Margão (re)distributed among the poor the alms accumulated by confreres through begging from door to door. Confraternities, however, were against the spirit of the Constitutions of the Society of Jesus and this was why Alessandro Valignano regulated them closely, only supporting those that had helped the converted to internalise Christianity.[112]

[110] Rocha, *As Confrarias de Goa*,18.

[111] Ibid., 18, 114, 119, 122, 130–3.

[112] Ibid., 119–23.

The link between political power, religious power, and charitable power was solid in the rural world, in particular from the time when conversion of the locals became a systematic process. While there were recognisable links between conversion and charity, the conversions here did not merely establish an association between the poor and the Christian faith. The association between being sick and non-Christian, as well as between not being sick and recently converted, also increased, legitimating the tutelage by Christian authorities.

Ines Županov has shown that there were links between the theory of the four humours, linked to Galenic medicine, and the regeneration of the soul through a specific set of exercises, something that Ignatius Loyola mentioned in the very first pages of his *Exercises*. Unsurprisingly, the Jesuit missionaries portrayed themselves as "nurses of the body, doctors of the soul."[113] This was to say that the process of Christianisation was not merely a process of curing the soul: it required control of the body as well as the soul. The rivalries between Franciscans and Jesuits, the Misericórdia, and the other religious orders in relation to caregiving are understandable. It was through corporeal and material care that they were all hoping to regenerate the soul.[114]

This connection between body and soul had other manifestations as well.[115] Gentile physicians could not practice with Christians; only Christians could cure and purify. Father Henrique Henriques, when writing in 1558, complained of local physicians, saying that, in addition to the remedies they used, they called

[113] See, once again, Županov, "Drugs, Health, Bodies".

[114] Rocha, *As Confrarias de Goa*, 130; Sá, *Quando o Rico se faz Pobre*, 162, 193–4; CR-APO, Fasc. 3, Vol. 1, 419–35, 483–7. It is worth noting that exactly the same arguments were used in the kingdom to justify similar demands: Abreu, "Padronização hospitalar", 147.

[115] For example, local non-Christian painters were not allowed to paint divine images and non-Christian craftsmen and goldsmiths could not build Christian statues. Summarised in the first Provincial Council, this order was regularly repeated: CR-APO, Fasc. 5, Vol. 3, 1160–1.

upon demons and magic. "May the Good Lord take this plague from the Earth." The Third Provincial Council of Goa defended the expulsion of local doctors for being "prejudicial to Christianity". At the same time, the papal bull *Unigenitii Dei filii* of 1567 allowed the Jesuits to engage in medical practice as long as they had the requisite expertise.[116]

It is perhaps no chance that the patron saints of Christian churches built their structures over local temples and often mimicked the healing roles played by the local deities they were succeeding. This was the case with the churches of Our Lady of Sáude (Health), in Margão, Sancoale and Cuncolim; Our Lady of Socorro (Succour), in Sirula, Nagoa, and Carmona; Our Lady of Remédios (Remedies), in Nerul, Betalbatim, and Cansaulim; Our Lady of Febres (Fevers), in Gonsua; Our Lady of Amparo (Refuge), in Mandur; Our Lady of Ajuda (Help), in Chimbel; Our Lady of Piedade (Godliness), in Dívar; as also Our Lady of Mercês (Mercies), in Morumbim, Colva; Our Lady of Graça (Grace), in Chorão; and Our Lady of Esperança (Hope), in Candolim and Chinchinim. One must wonder how the message – "such images cannot be said to be gods" – was understood by the indigenous inhabitants when a shrine to Our Lady of Saúde was in the very place where, a month earlier, there had been a Shantadurga with similar miraculous aspects; or when a hospital became a church dedicated to one of the substituting divinities.

How Christian was the devotion of these indigenous groups towards the images of Our Lady in these churches? Was the local population able to make the distinction between similarity and essence, as stated by Friar João Soares in *Libro de la verdad de la fe* (Book of the Faith's Truth)?[117] Who were the gods that inhabited the new "houses of God"?

Aware of the dangers entailed in these analogies, the majority

[116] IAN/TT, Armário Jesuítico, Mss 14 – Livro com vários pareceres de Pes. Jezuitas, nº 7; Cartório Jesuítico, Mss. 41, nº 7 – Breve do Papa Gregório 13 para que os jesuítas pudessem curar sendo peritos em medicina.

[117] Soares, *Libro de la verdad*, 106v.

of missionaries nevertheless chose to take the path of placing their deity atop earlier ones. The references to miracles and wonders in their descriptions, for example, witness their appropriation and Christianisation of local religious practices. They aimed concurrently to demonstrate the transformation of these territories into outposts of Christendom. In the service of this agenda, the objective was to inform European readers of their success in making these distant lands Christian.

On 22 February 1619 Pedro da Silva, a surgeon from Cannanore and a professed brother of the Franciscan Third Order, a man of "good life" and "of good character", had gone to the Church of Luz to attend mass. Upon leaving the church, and on his way to Our Lady of Guadalupe in Batim, Silva realised that the monumental cross of teak, planted by the curate Manuel Rodrigues on the hill of Bela Vista, had begun to move. The figure of the crucified Christ appeared. According to the version of Friar Cristóvão de Lisboa, Pedro da Silva went towards the cross, but when he arrived the occurrence had ceased. Still, Silva had managed to see the crucified Christ.[118]

News of the "miracle" got out immediately, and splinters from the cross, its soil, and relics "spread by the faithful began to effect many miracles through the work of divine mercy, giving health to the infirm who were in much need of remedy." A gentleman from the Order of Christ, aged and infirm, had himself transported to the hole where the cross had been positioned. He lowered himself into the hole and soon felt "completely fit". A feverish boy who had bladder problems hugged and kissed the wood, and on his way home his fever disappeared. Maria Fernandes, who had fever and diarrhoea, similarly cured herself by touching the soil of the cross. António, from Ceylon, who had a mortal case of colic, and who "not trusting doctors, drank some of the water in which the same infirm [man] had put in some of the soil from the foot of the cross," saved himself similarly. The Church of Luz temporarily

[118] BNP, Cod. 176 – Notícias do arcebispado de Goa, 301; Trindade, *Conquista Espiritual do Oriente*, Vol. 1, 176.

hosted the cross. Eventually, its keepers built a new church to perpetuate memory of the epiphany. The Archbishop of Goa assembled scholars, theologians, and physicians to discuss the validity of da Silva's vision.[119]

These episodes help us understand the level and kind of Christianisation that the local populations experienced, making clear the many meanings Christianity had for them. Although the missionaries desired the eradication of "superstition", roughly the same thing was re-experienced at certain times in the intellectual, bodily, individual, and social spheres.[120]

The ensuing chapters, which will focus on the residents of the Goan villages, will discuss a multiplicity of these experiences. As such, they will examine the pragmatic reasons for choices made in relation to conversion and Christianisation. Chapter 5 focuses on some of the reasons and the practical consequences that followed.

[119] BNP, Cod. 176 – Notícias do arcebispado de Goa, 304; Trindade, *Conquista Espiritual do Oriente*, Vol. 1, 176–8; Nunes, "D. Frei Miguel Rangel", 189.

[120] Namely, in the texts written by the missionaries: Prosperi, "Intelletuali e Chiesa", 181–2.

5

Initial Moves

Discontent, Resistance, Acquiescence

THE PREVIOUS CHAPTERS demonstrated how, over the 1530s and 1540s, the Portuguese Crown adopted a strategy aimed at converting the spaces under its dominion in Goa into Christian territories. The Crown saw this as the best way of securing these territories and defending their populations. In 1548 Cristóvão Fernandes, judge of the court of appeal in Goa, used a metaphor to express this in a letter to the king: Goa, he said, "would always be protected from enemies, because of the silver roots [. . .] planted here."[1]

The process was gradual, starting with the destruction of discernible and indiscernible signs of the previous sacred order, followed by substituting temples and places of worship containing deities with Christian images, and the replacement of local priests by a Christian clergy. The large number of the regular clergy established in the villages of Goa – many of them with papal dispensations allowing them to accumulate mission and parish – as well as secular and some medical faculties, structurally modified the nature of Portuguese domination in these areas. In the medium term the new religious presence challenged the

[1] IAN/TT, Corpo Cronológico, Part II, Mç. 241, nº 89 – "Carta de Christóvão Fernandes, Desembargador da Relação de Gôa", 3 Sept. 1548. "Silver roots" (*em prata*) seems to imply roots of value and solidity.

very foundations of the local order, of the position and status of former intermediaries, of the local elites and the *casados,* and of the balance of power that had existed in the preceding decades.

As against the notion espoused via certain tenacious Orientalist tropes, the territories of Goa were far from homogeneous.[2] They were marked by dynamic configurations with variable levels of cohesion and social harmony. The villages of the territory had not always been under the dominion of the same political power, nor were they recipients of the same migratory flows. Even if they were shaped by a shared and collective history, each of them also had its own specific history.[3] In short, they were not identical.

Nevertheless, the majority of the families that constituted these villages organised daily life around their relation to the land (floodplains, palm groves, or other types of husbandry), the products they were able to extract, and sometimes trade.[4] Their lives depended on the position that they occupied in the village community, the activities that they carried out within it, and the nature of their participation in a religious organisation that conferred meaning to the political and social order. Through participation, resistance, or indifference these families and their ancestors had over time been subjects of varieties of domination, to

[2] The historiography on these places rests largely on Orientalist assumptions, from more general histories of India, such as Mahajan, *History of India*, to the works of Robert Lingat and A.S. Altekar about the political and administrative organisation of "classical India": Lingat, *The Classical Law*; Lingat, *Royautés Boudhiques*; Altekar, *State and Government*; and of D.N. Majumdar and B.G. Gokhale on the socio-cultural organisation of the Indian territory: Majumdar, *Corporate Life*; and Gokhale, *Bharatavarasha*.

[3] See on this Arild Engelsen Ruud's comparative study of two "similar" villages in contemporary Bengal. Ruud argued that Subaltern Studies rarely accounted for the multiplicity of political behaviour that could emerge in these places: Ruud, "The Indian Hierarchy".

[4] The village included the houses, gardens and backyards, tanks and fences, cattle, wastelands, arable land, small plots of lands, the forests of the neighbourhood, the temples and their land, roads, as well as their populations: see Thapar, *A History of India*, 176.

which, by way of taxes, tributes, and armies, they had contributed and helped maintain.

Were the situations in Goa analogous to those that have been studied for other regions of India, albeit with different chronologies and scales? Did Goa represent a scenario in which distinct social structuring principles coexisted within the same territory? If so, did local social organisations express the tensions deriving from such a situation? Did some social groups enjoy hegemony over others? That is, did they have the ability to impose specific models to the detriment of others? Did they have the capacity to make subaltern groups accept and reproduce these models?[5] How did this local order, i.e. the different villages and their people, perceive the new imperial situation?

In Goa certain social groups that represented themselves as descendants of Brahmans or Kshatriyas sought to impose their model and attendant social hierarchy as the constitutive template for social order. These groups had allies in the course of forging many aspects of an order frequently characterised as possessing a timeless character.[6]

How was this hegemony built within a territory that had known different migrations and dominations in the centuries preceding the Portuguese presence? What sort of distribution of power operated in Goa's villages in the early-sixteenth century, and what were its implications for the *design* of the Portuguese imperial order?

The historicity and spatiality of the caste system, and of what has been called the system of Comunidades, as well as its chronology in Goa framed the experiences of the residents of Goan villages. The same applies to the type of "Hinduism" existing therein.

[5] Similar questions were addressed in Das, *Structure and Cognition*; Dirks, *The Hollow Crown*; Subrahmanyam, Shulman, and Rao, *Symbols of Substance*; Subrahmanyam, *Penumbral Visions*.

[6] In this context I follow, in general, the proposals in Susan Bayly's *Caste, Society and Politics*. David Ludden's observations on the relationship between social groups, territory, and social categories in India are also very useful: Ludden, *An Agrarian History*, 76ff.

Goan appropriations of these three "systems" underlay their experience of conversion and Christianisation.

The majority of the literature on the system of Comunidades in Goa is almost entirely Orientalist in nature. All the same, the historical sources used in such writings do offer the possibility of alternative readings. One of these sources, already mentioned, is *Foral de Usos e Costumes*. Considered by many a description of the institutional regime that operated in the villages of Goa, or even as an "indigenous constitution", relativising and locating the descriptive potential of this document is crucial if we are to access the dynamics of the institutional and political organisation of the villages of Goa.[7] The *Foral* was the result of an inquiry conducted by the Portuguese Crown to enable it to exercise dominion, so it had privileged some interlocutors over others. Moreover, the information collected had entailed, sometimes strategically, sometimes unconsciously, problems of transcription and translation.

In contrast, the religious experience of these territories before the Portuguese arrival has not been studied thoroughly.[8] Unfortunately, for the Goan case there are no *Relaciones Geograficas* (Geographic Relations) of the type that the Spanish monarchy elaborated for their new world, nor anything like the *Ain-i-Akbari* of Abu'l Fazl Allami, his report on the twelve *subahs* (territorial divisions) of the Mughal empire.[9] The absence of such historical documentation compounds the scarcity of surviving pictorial and recorded material by local contemporaries. There are, however, a few historical sources by the Portuguese that give us access to the religious landscape. These sources offer a synchronic view of Goan

[7] A.E.A. Azevedo, *As Communidades de Goa*; Felipe Xavier, *Bosquejo histórico*; Baden-Powell, "The Villages of Goa"; Kosambi, "The Village Community"; D'Souza, "The Village Communities"; Scammell, "Indigenous Assistance".

[8] Some of the studies on this context are R.G. Pereira, *Goa – Hindu Temples*; idem, *Goa – Gaunkari*; Shirodkar, "The Influence of Nath Cult"; Mitragotri, *Socio-Cultural History*; Kamat, "Syncretic Shaktipitha".

[9] Mundy, *Mapping of New Spain*; Allami, *The Ain-i-Akbari*, Vol. 2, 129ff. On this, see also Guha, "The Politics of Identity".

villages, making it possible to see more specifically whether or not the Goan religious landscape was in line with the Brahmanisation that was taking place in early-modern South India – with the subsequent reorganisation of the local religious pantheon. Scholars have shown that during this process in South India, Brahmanic deities came to occupy a superior place within the pantheon, with local deities frequently presented as Brahmanic deities.[10] To what extent was this happening in the Goan territories? What impact did this have on the processes of conversion and Christianisation?

It is in the context of this more general picture, developed in greater detail elsewhere,[11] that I situate a microanalysis of an event on the island of Chorão in the middle of the sixteenth century. This analysis is divisible into two parts: a description of Chorão's social organisation, and an analysis of the behaviour of its population when facing conversion and the Christianisation of the island.

The Social and Religious Landscape of the Island of Chorão

On 12 November 1559 Domingos Fernandes wrote a letter from Chorão to the Jesuits of Portugal. Having settled in the village four years earlier, this Jesuit brother was involved in the conversion of around 500 inhabitants of the island on the feast day of St Bartholomew, 24 August, that year. Fernandes' missive provides a detailed description of the conversion of that multitude. However, as is common in Jesuit letters, he begins by describing the landscape and character of the place.

According to his description, Chorão was extensive, verdant, and never lacked for water. The majority of its population lived on the banks of the river and was divided into two groups: the Brahmans and "another species of men" that Fernandes designates Chaudarins.

[10] Inden, *Imagining India*; Lorenzen, "Who Invented Hinduism?"; Thapar, *A History of India*, Chapters 13 and 14; S. Bayly, *Caste, Society and Politics.*

[11] A.M. Xavier, "A Invenção de Goa", Chapter 4.

The Brahmans were obdurate and on account of "idolatrous" and "superstitious" customs resisted conversion. They washed their bodies before eating, threw water in various directions, and then over their heads. They invoked the notion of their greater purity so as not to share food and drink with foreigners and strangers. They placed a deity in front of their homes but worshipped several gods. They were generally engaged in agricultural activities.

The members of the second group are not described in the same detail by the Jesuit, except for a psychological trait which, in his opinion, was very positive: the Chaudarins were "more domestic" than the Brahmans and therefore easier to convert. In addition to these groups, another Jesuit letter refers to the existence of fishermen.[12]

Brahmans, Chaudarins, and fishermen – these three categories do not encompass the social landscape, which was far more complex than recorded by the Jesuits. Their inquiries were of a different nature: the Jesuits had their own protocols of inquiry because they were interested in specific things; therefore, the descriptions in their letters capture other parts of the social reality. It becomes necessary, therefore, to set aside the Jesuit approach and find other ways to access the social organisation of Chorão and the peculiarities of the conversion process on the island. The inventories of rents received by the Portuguese and the lists of the properties that belonged to the temples and deities of Goa are good starting points.

These documents inform us that the island of Chorão had two villages, one of which, with about 6000 inhabitants, was Chudamani or Chorão.[13] The second appeared under the names of Care, Carepa, and Caraim. The island had two *passos* (crossings) – Santinti and Ambelim[14] – the latter hosting the residences of fisher-

[12] See Letter of Domingos Fernandes, s.j., 1559; Letter of Father Lourenço Peres, s.j., 1563; DI, Vol. 4, 306–13; DI, Vol. 6, 118.

[13] António Bocarro provides higher numbers for the seventeenth century: 14,000 inhabitants, among whom 6000 were soldiers.

[14] *Passos* were river crossings between the island of Goa and other territo-

men and soldiers, local Naiks, and *peões* (sepoys) in the service of the Portuguese Crown.[15] Despite Chorão being less important than Tiswadi, it was still a strategic territory for the Portuguese, contributing about 15 per cent of the taxes paid by the thirty-three villages of the province of Tiswadi, which made it fiscally consequential.[16]

The principal economic activity on the island was agriculture. The local elites were the groups that controlled the land (landowners and tenants), and among these were to be found the best lands (the floodplains, but also palm groves). This group included not just the *gaunkars* of both villages, but also the *culacharins,* the *adventícios*, temple officials, and artisans. Fishing was commonplace until the arrival of the Portuguese but subsequently prohibited because the techniques used endangered the boats engaged in patrolling and defending the coasts facing Bijapur territory.

The *gaunkars* of the village of Chorão claimed to be of Brahman lineage and had the surnames Porobo and Malle. Although later sources refer to them as socially degraded Brahmans – because some of their remote male ancestors had married women outside the Saraswat community – they had not fallen entirely out of favour.[17] They saw themselves as the descendants of ten of the ninety-six Brahman families, belonging to ten *gotras*, settled by

---

ries under Portuguese rule which allowed for communication with Bijapuri territory.

[15] This was an attempt to reproduce in the overseas territories the system of ordinances established in the kingdom since the reign of João III. The introduction of this system in the Estado da Índia was certainly influenced by Dom João de Castro.

[16] *Tombo da Ilha de Goa,* 41–5, 50–2. These taxes did not include the Passo of Samtinty where the fishermen were obliged to stop fishing. Fishermen plying on the other side of the island had to pay taxes.

[17] The *Sahyadri-Khanda* recounts that the Saraswat Brahmans of Chorão had married with non-Saraswat Brahmans, which is why the Saraswat called them *kramavant joshi*: Mitragotri, *Socio-Cultural History*, 51; Cunha, *The Sahyadri-Khan*. On the Saraswat, see Conlon, *Caste in a Changing World.*

Parashurama in Goa. In this mythical version, Chorão, like some of the other villages of Goa, hosted one of the most important *tirthas* (pilgrimage centres) of this region.[18] The second village, Caraim, was different. Its *gaunkars* called themselves Daivadnya Brahmans, but many people considered them Vaisya or Sudra. The family name was Chatim, which seems to identify them with a group of successful merchants who were descendants of ancient emigrants from the Malabar or Coromandel coasts and bore this name.[19]

These elites were mediators between the imperial and local orders. An excellent illustration of such mediation is their participation in a meeting with the vedor da Fazenda Fernão de Castelo Branco in 1541. As remarked earlier, this negotiation was over the transfer of rents belonging to the demolished temples. Among the witness signatures to the transaction are those of Malle Porobo and Goinda Porobo, representatives of the island of Chorão.[20] Voluntarily – as suggested in the document that emerged from the meeting – or not, these *gaunkars* collaborated in one of the acts of great practical and symbolic importance for the emerging imperial order.

However, Malle and Goinda Porobo were not solely involved in the political and administrative processes overseeing the construction of the Portuguese imperial order; a *gaunkar* of Caraim, Virupa Chatim, was another central figure in the process. He was the *mocadão* (head) of the goldsmiths of the city of Goa, one of the wealthiest economic corporations in the city.[21] This Virupa

[18] Cunha, *Konkani Language*, 9; *Tombo da Ilha de Goa,* 187; Feio, *As Castas Hindus*, 22; Mitragotri, *Socio-Cultural History,* 54–8.

[19] The word "chatim" was used to identify the merchants of the Malabar and Coromandel coasts; while the word "baniane" referred to the merchants of Gujarat. Such migrants started to settle in these places from the eighth century on: Feio, *As Castas Hindus*, 75; P.D. Xavier, *Goa: A Social History,* 35–6; Mitragotri, *Socio-Cultural History*, 54.

[20] *Tombo da Ilha de Goa,* 184; Feio, *As Castas Hindus*, 21.

[21] *Tombo da Ilha de Goa,* 187.

was the son of the Muslim chief goldsmith Raulu Chatim, and the brother of his namesake who travelled to Lisbon between 1518 and 1520 to make jewellery for the Portuguese royal family. Virupa's family had visible links to the Portuguese Crown, as attested by letters of privilege they received in 1519 which show that the Crown depended on them as well.[22]

Although they are usually referred to as Brahmans, as is the case in the illustration dedicated to them in the *Codex Casanatense*, in the letters of privilege they received these Chatims also appear as "Moors". These multiple designations seem to reveal the continuing confusion of the officials of the Portuguese Crown in face of the social diversity of Goa. They also demonstrate that among the residents of Goa there continued to be Muslims.

By 1547 and 1548 Virupa Chatim had initiated a judicial conflict with the Portuguese Crown by disputing the increase in taxes paid by goldsmiths. During these years of the government of Dom João de Castro, ambitious projects were developed for building fortresses and for the effective integration of the provinces of Salcete and Bardez. These were aimed at territorialising Portuguese power and necessitated new sources of funding.[23] While the goldsmiths of the city were undoubtedly not the only group identified as a source of funding, they were affected by this policy on account of their prosperity.

The "headmen of the villages" included groups in addition to the *gaunkars* of Chorão and Caraim. As in other villages, among the elites of Chorão were other families interested in the future of the villages. In this group are to be found many of the families belonging to the *culacharins*. They were descended from the second wave of migrants established in the villages, after the *gaunkars*.

[22] IAN/TT, *Gavetas*, nº 20, Mç. 2, nº 21; Corpo Cronológico, Part II, Mç. 80, nº 20 – "Cópia da Carta de Privilégios concedido a Relaxatim", 13 Feb. 1519; nº 91 – "Copia da Carta de Privilegio concedido a Relaxatim", 5 March 1519. See, in this context, the catalogue *A Herança de Rauluchatim*.

[23] BA, Cod. 51-VII-19 – "Mandado de Rui Gonçalves de Caminha, vedor da fazenda da India", fls 232–3.

While being central to the maintenance of the local order, the *culacharins* did not enjoy the same rights. They did not have the right to vote in the *gaunkari*, and they did not control decision-making in relation to the use of land. However, some *culacharin* families were as wealthy or even better off than those among the *gaunkars*. Although the ratio of these two groups to each other is not known, there were probably more *culacharins* than *gaunkars*, which disturbed cohesion in the village. The *culacharins*, when they belonged to another varna, constituted a genuine threat to the power of the *gaunkars*.

Something similar happened with populations that had settled more recently on the island. These participated in another institutional category, which the Portuguese called *adventícios* (newcomers). The families that constituted this group had distinct ethnic origins, and their connections to the village were diverse. Some resided in the village, others had acquired land or other economic interests – shops, or some form of small trade. Among these, some were *cuntocares*, which placed them in the position of creditors of the *gaunkars* of the village. Like the *culacharins*, they wanted to be part of decisions restricted to the *gaunkars*.

The most important officers of the temples were among the local elites too. They were responsible for the realisation of sacrifices and collective worship, as well as of rituals that the members of the *dvija* varnas ("twice-born") had to perform to maintain their status and the symbolic supremacy they claimed to possess. These officials were, in fact, essential for maintaining the cohesion of the local order, and their support was required by all who nursed power ambitions.

Although they were part of the same group – landowners and tenants – the artisans of these villages constituted an in-between group. They were part of the landed elites because they also exercised control over some parcels of land which represented payment for services they had provided to the village. However, they were elements of a polity in which economic prosperity was just one among various factors of power; so the fact that they controlled land was not necessarily a determinant of their pre-eminence. The functions they performed that were perceived as pure or impure in the village – as labourers or intellectuals, and as dignified or petty – could be as significant as landownership. Other criteria pushed the majority of the artisans into disadvantaged groups. The most emblematic case is that of the *farazes*, the most "untouchable" – not a word known or used at the time – among the inhabitants of Goa. They received land for services they had performed, and yet were recognised as among the most impure groups. They had therefore to live on the periphery of the village and were subject to every form of discrimination. No one, apart from the *farazes* themselves, dared suggest that the *farazes* belonged to the local elites.[24]

Those who controlled institutional power, prime land, and religious networks in the two villages on the island employed the landless. Landless groups comprised not merely the Chaudarins mentioned above, but other disadvantaged groups as well. The word *chaudarim*, which frequently appears in Portuguese documents, identifies the workers of the palm groves, or those responsible for the extraction of *sura* (palm oil). They claimed to be descendants of Kshatriyas. In later descriptions of the social groups of Chorão, the word *chaudarim* disappears, giving way to the designation Charodo (hereafter Chardo).[25]

Since the palm groves were among the most important crops on the island of Chorão, it is not difficult to imagine that the work of

[24] The inventory of lands and rents that belonged to the deities of Chorão refers to a rice paddy that belonged to the pagoda of the *farazes*: FU, 11-2-3, fl. 47. On the *farazes* of Goa, see Feio, *As Castas Hindús*; and Perez, *et al.*, *Histórias de Goa*.

[25] Feio, *As Castas Hindús*, 22. In the mid-seventeenth century, Antonio Ardizzone Spinola refers to "bramanes e charaddos" in the island of Chorão, and, among the "rustic" population, the *farazes*, the fishermen, the malabars, and the *cafres*: BNP, Cod. 58 – Breve relação das principaes ordens, fl. 12. On the emergence of this group, see Pissurlencar, "Contribuição ao estudo etnológico".

the Chaudarins was fundamental to village subsistence. However, even this group was not homogeneous. Some, called *manducares*, had the role of supervising the work of others.[26] Most Chaudarins, however, worked the land in the strictest sense of the term.

Just like other largely agricultural villages in India, those on Chorão island reproduced the more typical social and labour division identified by M.N. Srinivas. Some groups controlled the best lands, the "landowners", and the tenants. They represented themselves as part of the higher castes and linked themselves, whenever possible, to the first three varnas of the Vedic order. Other groups were either contracted or controlled by the former to carry out much of the agricultural work. They were perceived by those in control as belonging to the lower castes.[27]

It was of course possible for other groups to live in these villages. In addition to the Chaudarins, other Sudra groups worked on their lands. Also, with Chorão there arises the generic designation of *canarins*. Probably not identifying with the Chaudarins, some of these *canarins* worked in the floodplains of the villages.[28] Some of these and other such groups were residents, while others may have had other sorts of interests in the village. Their existence, their interstitial position – and eventually their economic power – could threaten the social order. In this sense, such groups may have played a key role in triggering and resolving certain local conflicts.

In contrast with what is posited in classically Orientalist depictions, it was heterogeneity more than homogeneity that characterised the populations of these villages. This social heterogeneity could result in a diversity of perceptions on power distribution within the village. Recognition of the supremacy of the best-positioned groups was not unquestionable, and the "horizontal" ties established among the most disadvantaged groups were not

[26] BA, Cod. 46-XIII-31 – Collecçoens das ordens reaes antigas, e modernas, fl. 16.

[27] Srinivas, *India: Social Structure*, 8–20.

[28] AHU, Índia, Cx. 6, nº 30 – "A cauza porque as rendas de V. Mge. na yndia vierão a tanta deminuição".

necessarily peaceful. Reciprocity was the result of negotiation as well as location in the local group hierarchy. Social cohesion depended on distinct interests, expectations, alliances, rivalries, conflicts, and, finally, a capacity for adjustment. If a journey back in time were possible, one would ask different families from each of these groups about their past – as Bernard Cohn did for those in Senapur.[29] The versions they would recount would probably be dissonant, demonstrating that the existing social order was the result of historical construction, and that new horizons of possibility might signify, for some, a social order more adjusted with their perception of reality.

In Chorão the Chaudarins were self-represented as Kshatriyas but perceived as Sudras by the Brahmans. The Daivadnya Brahmans claimed they were Brahmans but were considered by many to be Vaisyas or Sudras. It would not be surprising to hear the Chaudarins explaining their past and present position differently from these Brahmans. And what of the versions given by the *gaunkars* of Chorão (thought of by others as degraded or fallen Brahmans) and those of Caraim (Daivadnya Brahmans, usually wealthier than the former, but of a lower status)? Which of these would have asserted most satisfaction with their social status at the time the Portuguese arrived?

Amongst the various memories of past and present social tensions and future conflicts, one that has survived in a diary from the second half of the seventeenth century is particularly suggestive. Written by a Franciscan friar of Madre de Deus, it records an episode of a few centuries earlier on the island of Chorão.[30] At that time, says the diary, Brahmans and *farazes* divided the island, with power in the hands of the Brahmans. They lived amicably enough until the population of the *farazes* significantly surpassed that of the Brahmans, upsetting the demographic equilibrium. Having reproduced more rapidly, the *farazes* began asking Brahmans

[29] Cohn, "The Pasts of an Indian Village", 21–30.
[30] BNP, Cod. 846 – *Viagens pela India*, fl. 117v.

for their daughters in marriage. Their audacity scandalised the Brahmans, who sought the aid of those in Sirula to put an end to the ambition of the *farazes*. They proceeded to kill many *farazes*, their wives, and their children, restoring Brahmanic power in the village.[31]

Quite apart from its historical reliability, and reference to the established binary of pure/impure and Brahman/untouchable, this compelling narrative seems undoubted evidence of the complexity of the social scenario of Goa's villages. Was the decimation of the *farazes* of Chorão the result of their "audacity"? To what extent was their social dissatisfaction able to constitute a significant threat to order at a time when new powers, such as the Portuguese in the sixteenth century, had begun emerging?

Very likely, not all residents of Chorão shared the same expectations and goals. The social harmony frequently invoked by elites was the product of a discursive strategy directed towards the consolidation and defence of their supremacy. Explanations produced in the religious domain and made material during the performance of rituals legitimated such a narrative. In this version of history, gods, devotions, and rituals articulated notions of hierarchy that contributed to the maintenance of the existing order of things. The aim was the interiorisation of a particular version of history and the reproduction of a specific balance of power.

Was this replicated in Chorão? Or was this village marked by the coexistence of religious explanations that were not always convergent? Did religious representations and ritual practices provide sublimation, in some form, of real conflicts and thereby help pacify discontent, legitimising thereby the village's social equilibrium?[32]

To identify the existence of such patterns in Chorão, it is imperative to observe the connections between the religious universe,

[31] The institutional memory of this conflict persisted in a rent that the *gaunkars* of Chorão paid to those of Sirula from that time.

[32] Many of these questions are related to those discussed in Fuller, "The Hindu Pantheon", 19–39; idem, *The Camphor Flame*; and Prakash, ed., *The World of the Rural Labourer*, 282ff.

social balance, and political power. Let us return, therefore, to the meeting on 28 June 1541. Malle Porobo and Goinda Porobo, *gaunkars* of Chorão, participated in this meeting, which sought to negotiate future rents accruing to recently demolished temples.

The Porobos' presence at the meeting unravels the hierarchical relationship established between the villages of the island: the village of Chorão constituted the "head", and its *gaunkars* were those with whom the external authorities communicated.[33] Their presence in this meeting sanctioned the formulation of a crucial normative document which significantly altered their religious future. Indicating that the *gaunkars* "were content to render to His Highness the service of two thousand *tangas brancas* as the rent for every one year of the said lands of the Pagodas," the vedor da Fazenda assented to the agreement.[34] The *gaunkars* of Chorão were two among those who "gladly" signed on.

Some illustrations of the religious complexity of the island, and its intersections with the power, land use, and social groups that constituted the locality, help us appreciate the impact of these changes.

The village of Chorão had twelve deities, and Caraim had two. Devaki-Krishna, Narayana, Bhagavati, Chandeshwar, Canteshwar, Ravalnath, Ganesha, Mallinatha, Baukadevi, Santa-Purusha, Dadd-Sancol, and Barazan were the deities of the principal village, and to its temples and officers belonged vast lands and incomes. Each deity enjoyed unequal parcels of land, its wealth reflecting adjustments between social groups, categories of deities, and their functions.

This set of deities suggests social diversity on the island. For example, the presence of Matsyendranath (a *siddha nath*) in the form of Mallinatha probably expresses the adherence of some families of the island to the Nath cult. The cult dates back to the

[33] The Jesuit letters argued that the decisions of these *gaunkars* were followed by the rest of the population: see, for example, DI, Vol. 6, 118.

[34] CR-APO, Fasc. 5, Vol. 1, 161–70.

twelfth century and had a big following in the Old Conquests.[35] Devaki-Krishna, another equally important deity, was probably introduced by devotees who adhered to the Vaishnava reform proposed by Madhavacharya (*c.* 1199 – *c.* 1278).

Apart from these examples, which testify to the gradual constitution of the pantheon, we cannot forget the other standard practices of families that had established themselves over the centuries, and who usually travelled with their deities. The diversity is also visible when the deities are classified according to their category. Some were explicitly Brahmanic, like Narayana, Ganesha, and Devaki-Krishna.[36] Others referred to local cults, often presented as minor forms of the Brahmanic deities. The most popular were Ravalnath, Bhaukadevi, Dadd-Sancol, and Barazan. These latter deities made the Brahmanic deities simultaneously universal and local.[37] In Chorão, Ravalnath and Baukadevi illustrate this situation well. They simultaneously represented the cults of the old goddess (Bhaukadevi often appeared as the wildest form of the benign goddesses Bhagavati and Devaki-Krishna), the heroic cults (Ravalnath as the expression of Rahul), and cults to the guardians of the superior deities. Although elsewhere Chandeshwar and Ganesha were the favourites of the great goddess,[38] on the island of Chorão it was Ravalnath who best combined various identities.

In other parts of India this plurality was part of a hierarchical system of deities where Brahmanic deities (Sanskritic, of textual origin) were located at the top, and the Dravidian deities (of Dravidian origin but transmuted into Brahmanic deities) were situated in a subaltern position. However, this hierarchy was not linear in

[35] Mitragotri, *Socio-Cultural History*, 115–16; Shirodkar, "Influence of Nath Cult"; Gopal, "Kadamba Patronage"; Chauhan, *Vaishnavism of Goud Saraswat*. It can safely be said that the Nath cult was quite widespread.

[36] The Brahmanical deities were probably linked with those located in the pilgrimage centre of Divar, which also contained temples to Narayana and Bhagavati.

[37] Fuller, *The Camphor Flame*, 39.

[38] S. Bayly, *Saints, Goddesses and Kings*, Chapter 1; Fuller, *The Camphor Flame*, 40ff.

Chorão. Ravalnath was the most represented male deity – albeit not necessarily the most powerful – in the territories of Tiswadi, Chorão, Dívar, and Bardez, in contrast with Salcete, dominated by Narayana. In Chorão, Ravalnath was the deity with the highest number of floodplains and other lands, thus standing out as the most powerful deity, possibly the chief deity of the village. To what extent does the economic pre-eminence of Ravalnath illuminate a new interpretive path? Is it possible that the process of Brahmanisation on the island of Chorão was exceptional?

Often considered a simplified manifestation of Shiva (Rahul), one of the images of Ravalnath was of a man standing upright and with four hands – one with a sword, the other with a chalice of nectar, yet another with a trident, and the last holding a drum. Dressed in a dhoti, and sporting a long moustache and necklace made of skulls, he looks a warrior and guardian. The portrayal is very similar to that of other male guardians in various locations in the Indian South. A similar representational trajectory is evident in relation to all these deities.[39] Initially subordinate to the deities they defended, these gods tended to usurp the place of the deity they protected and required constant sacrifice and devotion.[40] In addition to having trodden a probably similar path in Chorão, Ravalnath presented two antagonistic personalities: sometimes he was Shano Ravalnath, the intelligent, at other times he appeared as Pisso Ravalnath, the wild. Both these manifestations were linked to one of the neighbourhoods inhabited by Vaishnavite Brahmans, the Gaunvaddo and Pandavaddo wards. However, the relationship between this antagonism, these families, and the neighbourhoods in which they resided is still unclear.[41]

[39] See S. Bayly, *Saints, Goddesses and Kings*, 31ff.; Fuller, *The Camphor Flame*, 39ff.; Gune, *Ancient Shrines*, 16. Khandoba, for example, is described as Khandanatha, Malhari, Mailal, Martanda-Bhairava, Yella-Koti-Mahadeva, Mallukan (worshipped as a linga), or Saumya Bhairava.

[40] Initially, the deity of the lower social groups, Ravalnath, was integrated in the Brahmanical pantheon during the fourteenth century.

[41] Mitragotri, *Socio-Cultural History*, 168. In the village of Carambolim, for

Ravalnath had become a *gramadevata* (village deity) in the fullest sense of the word. His two personalities had to be placated by a Sudra priest who annually performed the impure sacrifices that worship to Ravalnath required, namely, the sacrifice of goats and roosters in the month of Ashvina (September–October).[42] These sacrifices were generally forbidden to Brahman priests specialising in the purer varieties of puja. That is, Ravalnath's satisfaction required transactions between groups with Brahman (usually vegetarian) devotions and groups with devotions that were not Brahmanic – these could include animal sacrifices.

If the cult of Ravalnath in the village of Chorão raises some unanswered questions, the same can be said of the cult of Devaki-Krishna, probably the goddess whom Ravalnath defended and protected. In Chorão it was Devaki-Krishna who performed rituals in honour of Ravalnath, not the other way round. Did Devaki-Krishna appreciate the protection that had been granted by Ravalnath? In these regions the choice of village goddess was often motivated by her association with the earth.[43] Is it possible that Devaki's relationship with Ravalnath sublimated events that had occurred in local life? What was the nature of this oblation, this transfer of gifts?[44]

Knowing that the image of Devaki-Krishna was of a mother with her son, could it be that this dialectic evoked the period

---

example, there was an explicit reference to the Ravalnath of the *chaudarins*: HAG, nº 7604 – Foral das Ilhas de Goa, 1553–1562, fl. 40.

[42] For its description, see A.B.B. Pereira, *Etnografia da Índia Portuguesa*, Vol. 2, 225, 234.

[43] The simultaneous presence of these deities in the same complex of temples possibly meant transactions between superior (vegetarian and pure) and inferior (non-vegetarian and impure) deities. See Fuller, *The Camphor Flame*, 44.

[44] On this, see also the critique of Gloria Goodwin Raheja's *The Poison in the Gift* by Gérard Toffin. Toffin questions the argument of this anthropologist, who argued that the gift economy in India was related to the need for getting rid of impure substances: Toffin, "Hiérarchie et idéologie".

when the *farazes* of Chorão threatened the power of the Brahmans under their numeric dominance? Although it is impossible to answer these questions, they are helpful in interrogating meanings expressed in the pantheon of Chorão, as well as their role in the symbolic resolution of social conflicts.

For this reason – and this concludes our short probe of the village pantheon – our analysis needs to rely on another deity, the goddess Bhaukadevi, also associated with biological and social reproduction.[45] Usually installed near burial grounds, Bhauka, like Ravalnath, required blood sacrifices and obscene songs. These sacrifices were performed by a Gauda priest, probably on the new moon of the month of Vaishak (April–May). The belief was that on an inauspicious day Bhauka's sexual abstinence could result in a destructive explosion affecting her surroundings. She was known for having neither husband nor children, which made her a sexually frustrated goddess whose pent-up energy represented the constant threat of a detonation of rage and anguish. To calm the enraged goddess it was necessary to create situations more bloody and obscene than she herself had been nurturing. The rites performed were similar to those in Tantrism.[46]

Besides the anthropological interest inherent in the identification of these latter rituals in Goa, what is essential to bear in mind is the antagonism between Bhauka and Devaki-Krishna – possibly reflecting that between Sudras/*farazes* and Brahmans.[47]

This method allows us to recover equally intriguing relations between other cohabiting gods, goddesses, and social groups on the island. At this point, however, these examples suffice to illustrate

[45] Mitragotri, *Socio-Cultural History*, 138ff.

[46] The rituals and other devotional forms present in the village were related with two reformist dynamics: an earlier Vaishnava movement and a subsequent reform within Vaishnavism by Madhavacharya: Shirodkar, "Evangelization by Missionaries", 24–5; idem, "Socio-cultural Life in Goa", 9ff.

[47] At the base of the pantheon we could find Dadd-Shankar and Barazan. Dadd-Shankar evoked the presence of malign spirits while Barazan referred to the sacred places and cults among Sudra communities.

the purpose of such analysis. Although it is difficult to resurrect its multiple meanings, the pantheon of Chorão was related in complex ways to the social order and historical experiences of the island's inhabitants.

These plural social and sacred landscapes framed, filtered, and refracted the experiences of inhabitants after 1540. It is therefore unsurprising that the consequences of such an encounter – images, perceptions, and senses that were then mobilised, adjusted, re-created – were not linear either. Ancient or recent, these devotions and practices, and the meanings people attributed to them, were not easily erased from collective memory in the way that temples and painted or sculpted images had been. The multiplicity and complexity of the local pantheon certainly relativised the Christian presence among the local populations. Perhaps they saw the Christians and their god(s) as new immigrants, even if this initial perception did not survive the violence that followed.

In sum, the historical experiences – religious, social, and other – of families in the island villages could either be of benefit or an impediment to the success of the missionary project. They benefited missionaries by facilitating the implanting of new religious structures. They hindered and impeded mission because the very concept of conversion was, in a sense, incomprehensible within an existing religious structure that was integrative, cumulative, and flexible.

To observe the details of this process, it is necessary to return to the island decades before Domingos Fernandes wrote his letter.

Dreams and Threats: Facing the Jesuit Presence

The first news of the Portuguese intervention in Chorão dates to the year 1511, a year after the conquest of the city of Goa by Afonso de Albuquerque. By this time some of the *gaunkars* of Chorão had crossed the river and taken refuge in lands under the dominion of the Sultanate of Bijapur.[48] However, a large segment

[48] Telles, *Os Franciscanos no Oriente*, 61.

of the local elites collaborated with the new project of domination, probably just as they had done earlier. "They are men full of novelties," Albuquerque told King Dom Manuel I, referring to their capacity to adapt to new situations. He added that "if they find Portuguese captains who allow them to sail freely and pay money, they can gather a hundred thousand sepoys with them instantly."[49] It was probably to show appreciation for such help that in 1512 the king of Portugal offered silk tapestries to the Naiks of Chorão.[50]

Other references to the island of Chorão appear in *Foral de Mexia* (1526); in the meeting of 1541; and subsequently, when the Jesuits received lands and revenues previously those of the temples of Tiswadi. Their presence shows that the majority of the elites of Chorão preferred to keep their privileged positions and properties rather than forsake them by disagreeing with the new imperial power.

Complementing the new institutional and legal order – symbolised by the companies of soldiers established at the river crossings, and by the regular visit of a *tanadar* to collect taxes – missionaries arrived to settle on the island of Chorão. Initially, there were two alternative models of Christianisation. The first aimed at converting the residents and simultaneously erasing the existing devotional order. Vicar General Pero Fernandes Sardinha proposed a second model whereby non-Christians of Goa would be disallowed in the islands of Chorão and Dívar. However, the model applied was

[49] BP-APO, IV-1, Part I, 406. In another letter, Albuquerque explained that the local Christians and Gentiles of Goa with whom he interacted were people with "little riches". This made them more open to the Portuguese proposals: IAN/TT, Corpo Cronológico, Part I, Mss. 66, nº 79 – "Carta de Bartholomeu Pires reprezentando a ElRey", 7 Jan. 1540; Mss. 81, nº 59 – "Carta de Fr. Antonio do Porto, dando parte a ElRey que os convertidos à Fé Catholica padecião muitas necessidades", 7 Oct. 1548; Part II, Mç. 26, nº 31 – "Ordem do capitão-mor de Goa", 10 April 1511; Mç. 48, nº 92 – "Mandado de Afonso de Albuquerque", 23 June 1512; Mç. 53, nº 2 – "Mandado de Afonso de Albuquerque", 8 Nov. 1514; nº 24 – "Mandado de Afonso de Albuquerque", 11 Nov. 1514.

[50] BP-APO, I-3, Part 1, 406–29, 459, 604.

the first of the two, making Chorão, from the perspective of the Portuguese, a model of Christianisation.

Chorão aimed to have the first entirely Christian neighbourhood of Goa. In 1541 it had a chapel. Three years later began construction of the Church of Our Lady of Graça (Grace) on the southern shore of the island, in a quarter called Maddel.[51] In the early 1550s the governor offered a field near the church for the construction of a neighbourhood. This was subsequently inhabited by poor Christians, on behalf of whom the Jesuit Gaspar Barzeus petitioned for some privileges.[52] At the same time, wealthy Portuguese folk established themselves on the island. They built leisure houses surrounded, where feasible, by palm groves and verdure in other shapes. These Portuguese became part of the group of the *adventícios* of Chorão. One of them assumed the function of the Pai dos Cristãos. A Jesuit priest visited the island every Sunday to celebrate mass. He was supported by a beadle whose task was to persuade residents of the village to attend church. Itinerant forms of preaching inching towards more stable resident forms characterised the apostolic mission of those initial years.[53]

Although the island was large, the probability of encounters between old residents and newcomers was high. Older residents are unlikely to have been indifferent to the changes in the landscape, namely, construction of the Church of São Bartolomeu (St Bartholomew) and the chapel of São Jerónimo (St Jerome), which, standing side by side with earlier deities, represented new gods, new rites, and a new priesthood.[54]

[51] Later, the Jesuits claimed this church as theirs: DI, Vol. 5, 553–5.

[52] Catão, 'subsídios para a História", 28–30.

[53] In 1562, for example, the Count of Redondo gives a paddy field to Rodrigo Monteiro; some years later, Dom Francisco de Mascarenhas offers the trade of the island to a Portuguese man: *Tombo da Ilha de Goa,* 57. On the changes in Chorão, see also Letter of Fernão Mendes Pinto, 1554; Letter of Father António Quadros, 1555; Letter of Father Aires Brandão, 1556; DI, Vol. 3, 145–6, 350, 577.

[54] In this period there were few converts. Fernandes refers to thirty in the

The power of the newcomers increased steadily. The Tombo of namoxins – lands dedicated to deities and temples – indicates that the Jesuits became powerful landowners. In 1574 Alessandro Valignano referred to the island of Chorão as belonging to the Jesuits *in temporalibus* and *in spiritualibus* (temporally and spiritually).[55] Chorão probably first experienced this type of association – also seen in Brazil and Bassein – in the context of the Portuguese empire. However, the power the Jesuits enjoyed in Chorão was less considerable than in the Brazilian *aldeamentos* (villages). Nevertheless, over three decades they had transformed their position on the island: from the periphery, the banks of the river, they wound up controlling its centre – or so they believed.

Valignano's letter was only possible because by 1574 there were so many converts in Chorão. It is therefore crucial to understand the mechanics of conversion that led to this change. Domingos Fernandes' description helps us reconstitute many dimensions of the process. It refers to the events that led to the collective conversion of the residents of Chorão between 1557 and 1560.

Fernandes explains that, when he arrived on the island between 1555 and 1556, Chorão had very few Christians. The obligation of caring for all things relating to local Christians rested on him alone. Fernandes obviously exaggerates his burden. As previously noted, the island had weekly visits from another Jesuit who preached and converted. Besides, there were other Jesuit brothers and priests who went to the island to rest, some biding their time till their next mission. Among the few Portuguese who lived there, the Pai dos Cristãos shared the tasks Fernandes claimed as his. He was undoubtedly less lonely than he claimed to be.[56] The greater

---

beginning of 1550, but Aires Brandão argues that in 1556 there were 300 Christians: DI, Vol. 3, 577.

[55] Valignano's letter of 1574 in DI, Vol. 9, 505–6.

[56] See Fernandes' letter of 1559 in DI, Vol. 3, 350, and the letter of Aires Brandão to Francisco Rodrigues of November 1556 in DI, Vol. 3, 564–84. In the letter Brandão refers to the presence of many Jesuit missionaries in Chorão.

likelihood is that he was keen to embellish his importance within the process of Chorão's conversion. Perhaps this ambition explains why he collapses two different episodes into one.

The first of the episodes alludes to the collective conversion of the Chaudarins of Chorão; the second, a year later, refers to the conversion of local Brahmans. This sequence illustrates the stages of the conversion process on the island – first the poor, second the elites – as well as the implicit differences.

Defying the ban imposed by the Portuguese, a marriage took place between non-Christians on the island of Chorão.[57] A local Christian concealed his presence at the wedding and denounced it. The marriage could not be completed, requiring the bride and groom to celebrate it again. Between the first marriage and the second, another royal decree prohibited the celebration of Gentile ceremonies in Christian lands. Nevertheless, the locals decided to celebrate the second marriage according to their rites. The same Christian again denounced the second celebration to Domingos Fernandes. Together with another Jesuit and some judicial officers, Fernandes arrested some of the participants.[58] Five hundred people, he said – a number that included the guests, but also residents of nearby villages – were marched off to prison. Eventually, Fernandes said, these prisoners converted voluntarily.

Two days later Father Luís Fróis communicated different details of the same event. He explained that the Jesuits had long been trying to convert the residents of Chorão. After the locals had violently and systematically refused conversion, persisting in their idolatry, the Jesuits resorted to other methods, such as imprisonment. Better educated than Fernandes, Fróis knew that missionary methods could be both mild and violent. He probably knew, too,

[57] For a detailed description of the wedding ceremony – though it is not clear whether it refers to Goa or to the coast of Malabar – see S. Gonçalves, *Primeira Parte da História,* Vol. 3, Chapter 13.

[58] This refers to the royal decree of Dom Sebastião of March 1559, which established a punishment for all who engaged in local rituals: CR-APO, Fasc. 5, Vol. 1, 388–90.

the texts of Francisco de Vitoria and Bartolomé de las Casas. These Spanish Dominicans had advocated coercion as a last resort, and only when resistance to missionary attempts was extreme. Fróis was also aware of reprimands directed at the Jesuits of Coimbra regarding their rigour. These two ways of action – one softer, the other rigorous – were present from the very inception of the Society and would continue through its history. Coimbra's position, represented in Goa by António Gomes, was the opposite of Loyola's. Fróis' reference was to these two methods, on display in Chorão too.

If Fernandes referred to 500 converts, Fróis registered only 30 to 40, all residents of the neighbourhood of Our Lady of Graça. Another difference: in Fróis' account many of the residents of the neighbourhood had fled in their attempt to hide from the Portuguese. However, like Fernandes, Fróis described the judicial inquiry in which one of the oldest residents of the island voluntarily proclaimed his desire to become Christian. The rest followed suit.[59]

These descriptions allow us access to some of the attitudes of the residents of Chorão. It becomes clear that some embraced Christianity from the very first years of the Christian presence. In one account, the majority of Indian peasants during this period were extremely poor.[60] Goa was no exception in this respect. For many, as already discussed, Christianity offered a way out of poverty. Conversion was for some perhaps also an oblique expression of dissent against the dominant social order. In Chorão the first to convert were the poor granted privileges and lands near the church. Perhaps among them were the *farazes* and other disadvantaged groups.[61]

[59] Letter of Father Luís Fróis, 1559, in DI, Vol. 4, 328ff.

[60] Srivastava, *Society and Culture*, 146. The same image is replicated in Chandra, "Standards of Living – Mughal India", and Fukazawa, "Standards of Living – Maharastra and Deccan".

[61] Gauri Viswanathan provides an excellent analysis of this type of strategy in British India: Viswanathan, "Religious Conversion and the Politics of Dissent"; Viswanathan, *Outside the Fold.* This type of attitude was also identified

As mentioned, the converted were well placed to take over lands confiscated from those who resisted conversion. They could similarly occupy offices held by those who had refused conversion. The converted also kept rights over their orphans and their inheritances.

The missionaries were conscious of the exercise of choice in favour of Christianity as a form of pragmatism. Valignano assumed the locals saw conversion not as metaphysical but as a plainly practical improvement of their life. This Jesuit added that the locals wanted either to escape worldly punishment or receive gifts from priests, captains, or viceroys.[62] The first to choose Christianity became the earliest allies of the missionaries, enabling them to more effectively infiltrate the local order. Jesuit narratives also refer to other attitudes: many of the residents of Chorão hid or fled from the Portuguese, while others continued to practise their rites clandestinely even after they had been prohibited. When faced with the threat of arms, some put their lives at risk. Others opted to abandon their homes and lands.[63]

The conversion of other groups generally followed conversion of the poor. In Chorão this was so with the conversion of elites. These latter conversions restarted the process, this time round from top to bottom.

How did this happen on the island of Chorão?

If one believes Fernandes' narrative, the collective baptism took place on 24 August. "Purified" and baptised with great pomp, the

---

in other studies on other imperial experiences in India, such as the Mughal empire: see Guha, "The Politics of Identity and Enumeration", 155ff. About its effects on the fixation and dissolution of caste identities, see Dirks, "The Conversion of Caste".

[62] Valignano, *Sumario de las cosas que pertenecen a la Yndia Oriental*, in DHMPPO, Vol. 12, 475.

[63] For example in 1510, at the time of the conquest of Goa by Afonso de Albuquerque, the destruction of the fields and the subsequent famine led to the migration of the starving population in search of food: Disney, *O declínio do império da pimenta*, 258.

converts participated in Christian rites, dressed, ate different foods, and openly transgressed some of the old norms.[64] The Christian significance of the event was explicit. A legend said that the Apostle St Bartholomew went to India and was responsible for the conversion of Indians in the first century of the Christian era. The celebration of baptism on that day linked it to Biblical times, transforming Jesuits into true apostles. The natives, in turn, became equivalent of the pagans of antiquity. In the same week there was the Ganesha festival, one of the deities on the island. Shortly afterwards, the commemoration of the birth of Krishna culminated with ceremonies of purification on the Khandebar River.[65] In other words, this Christian baptism became symbolic because it was superimposed over other events, thus encapsulating several meanings.

To succeed, this cultural mobility had to rely on the collective collaboration of local populations. By acting as informers and denouncers, the newly converted could undermine the strategies of resistance of those who had chosen to remain Gentile. Life became increasingly difficult for those who persisted with their traditional religion. Hiding or fleeing was a less and less secure option since there were few places on the island without Christians; Christian surveillance soon became inescapable.

[64] On this, see Letter of Father Aires Brandão, 1556; Letter of Domingos Fernandes, s.j., 1559; Letter of Father Cristóvão da Costa, 1560; Letter of Poulanco, s.j.,1563: DI, Vol. 3, 577; Vol. 4, 309ff. and 709ff.; Vol. 6, 68–9. Some of these new Christians may have defended Christian interests against the interests of their former lords: see, for example, Letter of Father Luís Fróis, s.j., 1557 and Letter of Poulanco, s.j., 1558, in DI, Vol. 3, 709–10 and Vol. 4, 132.

[65] Robinson, *Conversion, Continuity and Change*, 135. The celebration of Diwali between the end of October and the beginning of November (the month of Kartik) was related to the marriage of Krishna. The festival of Ravalnath was, surely, another of those moments when, as suggested by Fuller, there was a "collective ordering of experience": Fuller, *The Camphor Flame,* 7. On this "ordering of experience", see Luhmann's argument in *Religious Dogmatics and the Development of Society.*

After the conversion of the Chaudarins, the local elites of Chorão faced a problem. The Chaudarins were the labourers in the palm groves, one of the primary sources of income of the *gaunkari*. As with the other converts, their occupations could not be carried out by others: what if they refused to do them? What if the Chaudarins were among those who, as Father António Quadros suggested, harboured "a better opinion of themselves" and declined their old functions? What were the ground-level effects of this new perception of the self, of personal status, of group status, in the order of the village?

For the local elites, this new self-awareness was threatening because it could imply the loss of their status which was dependent, to a large extent, on services performed by lower groups. As part of the Christian order, such groups could now refuse traditional obligations, specifically cleaning the houses of Brahmans and the village itself. Brahman social identity was, as always, dependent on ensuring the internalisation by other groups of their inferiority and on their continuing to perform the "impure" functions the Brahmans themselves were forbidden to perform.

Given these new circumstances, local elites probably discussed alternative scenarios. Sebastião Gonçalves' *História* offers an insightful account of a similar process in the village of Carambolim, on Tiswadi, in the same years. This description, referred to by other authors,[66] allows us to imagine the dilemmas faced in Chorão too. Carambolim was one of the main villages of Goa and had a vote in the Câmara Geral (General Assembly). Its elites participated in the same events as did those of Chorão. In 1559 a *gaunkari* deliberated on conversion and arrived at three different opinions: some argued for abandoning their lands and resettling in Bijapur territory; others argued awaiting Viceroy Dom Constantino de Bragança's departure from Goa, their expectation being that his successor would ease the pressure to convert; and a third group said the second alternative was hopeless since the Jesuits would

[66] Robinson, *Conversion, Continuity and Change*, 52.

continue "by all means" to "make Christians". One of the oldest *gaunkars* of Carambolim concluded that "it was better to become Christians soon, for sooner or later they would be." His opinion won the day, leading to the collective conversion of the village of Carambolim.[67]

Christianity's gradual increment via conversion inducements and reductions of political and economic rights for those resisting conversion bears out the validity of this last opinion. The choices were basically three: first, active resistance (abandonment of "homeland and lands"; rebellion); second, passive resistance; and third, accommodation (conversion; fence-sitting).

In Carambolim some families decided to abandon hearth and home. Studies of analogous situations include Michael Adas on forms of protest in colonial and pre-colonial South East Asia. His argument is that fleeing was the last choice after all forms of resistance and protest had been exhausted. He shows that this behaviour was more typical among the populations of rice-cultivating regions, which were traditionally more sedentary, as against those in drier regions, where lifestyles were more mobile. Others such as David Ludden argue that sedentary agriculture was not fully established in the early-modern period, meaning that farmers too were highly mobile. Ludden's view is borne out by frequent cases of land abandonment in the Mughal empire for fiscal reasons, and in the territories of Goa even before the arrival of the Portuguese for reasons unconnected with conversion.[68] That said, it seems generally probable that fleeing was always the last choice in Goa too.

Desertion of land and home was not always a result of the conversion policy. It was also the result of a guerrilla war with Bijapur between 1540 and 1570. Destruction of cultures, the invasion of temples by soldiers, and death characterised the everyday in these villages. Conversion pressures only made matters worse, rendering

[67] S. Gonçalves, *Primeira Parte da História*, Vol. 2, 355–6.

[68] Adas, "From Avoidance to Confrontation"; Ludden, *An Agrarian History*, 67; Finer, "The Indian Experience", Vol. 3, 1251–2.

life impossible for many villagers. Some scholars of Goa go so far as to argue that half of the population of Goa – the number seems an exaggeration – had fled to the Sultanate of Bijapur between the sixteenth and seventeenth centuries on account of conversion pressure. These fugitives carried their gods with them, with many of their deities finding a home in the temples of Ponda, financed mostly by Brahmans.

It is difficult to pinpoint for that troubled time the most important reasons for a whole population fleeing – conversion (spiritual conquest), or war (territorial conquest). Although this theme is significant and relevant, historical sources for that period – namely the *olas* (palm-leaf manuscripts) housed in some of the temples of Kerala and Karnataka – need very careful scrutiny to ascertain their stories and the number of fugitives to which they allude. Usually referred to by the "translators" of such *olas*, some of these sources are involved in what is commonly called identity politics.

In any case, it is unquestionable that flights during this period were numerous. Portuguese sources refer to the desertion of many regions of Goa. Such flights were dangerous for reasons connected with both fiscal and military insecurity.[69] K.N. Chaudhuri refers to them when recalling that "pushed to its limits, mass coercion depopulated entire agricultural districts and resulted in peasants absconding, destroying the state itself in the process."[70] In 1561 Viceroy Dom Francisco Coutinho said he found Goa "very depopulated", "the villages lost", "the paddies flooded", "the river clogged", and "residents absent, and unwilling to repopulate". Countermanding the existing laws, Coutinho decided that those who returned to their villages would get back their lands. In other words, the government modified its behaviour in line with changing circumstances. [71]

Fleeing, of course, was not the principal option for the majority

[69] CR-APO, Fasc. 5, Part I, 109–202; Part II, 602–3, 841–2.

[70] Chaudhuri, *Asia before Europe*, 79.

[71] CR-APO, Fasc. 5, Part I, 489.

of the population resident in Goa. Some sought to reconcile their traditional forms of worship with Portuguese domination. Aware of the experiences of conversion of the New Christians and their strategies to cope with it in Portugal,[72] some local elites proposed similar solutions to the Portuguese government. They offered to pay a fee in exchange for the right to maintain their faith and promised to celebrate their rituals outside the territories of Goa. According to a later text, this proposal was discussed in Lisbon and accepted by Cardinal Dom Henrique. Later, Dom Philip II of Spain (Dom Philip I of Portugal, r. 1581–1598) revoked it, responding to a request by Father Alfonso Pacheco (who, shortly after, was killed in the Goan village of Cuncolim). Pacheco had warned the king's counsellors of the disadvantages of these concessions and returned to India with many orders conducive to conversion.[73] Still, at the beginning of the seventeenth century Jesuits did receive money in exchange for Jesuit acquiescence to non-Christian practices, and the payments included permissions for passages to the mainland to perform non-Christian ceremonies.[74]

These cases illustrate the pragmatism of much of the process. The same pragmatism induced some families to request that the Jesuits state they had compelled their conversion because such a proclamation would allow them to retain caste privileges. Such a demonstration would enable converts to evade the punishments that their caste tribunals decreed against them. Simultaneously, it would secure them from the contempt of relatives and other villagers. The belief that Portuguese domination would not endure long lay behind many of these requests. For villagers who

[72] See, in this context, Cunha, *A Inquisição no Estado da Índia*, on the persecution of the New Christians of Estado da Índia, which takes place precisely in the decade of the 1550s.

[73] DI, Vol. 4, 190. This proposal was refused. Similar practices were present in some Muslim polities, especially those not concerned with proselytism. This was the case with the sixteenth-century Ottoman Empire: Goffman, *The Ottoman Empire*, 170. For Pacheco's position, see also *Admirabile Vida*, 175.

[74] CR-APO, Fasc.1, Vol. 2, 91–110.

assumed the regime was transitory, this was a case of temporarily suspending their interdicted identity, an eventual return to their previous status being believed as inevitable.[75]

As against what these individuals and families believed or desired, the Portuguese presence lasted centuries, so that the counsel of the old *gaunkar* of Carambolim was wise – "it was better to become Christians soon, for sooner or later they would be". He was prescient about the durability of Christian power.

The violence of the second stage contributed to the success of later conversion. Viceroy Dom Constantino de Bragança, who some said performed "the role of the bishop", proposed extreme punishment for those who refused to convert and great rewards for those who converted. [76] The use of "*meos humanos*" (human resources) was the result of the initial refusal of the majority of the residents of Chorão to convert. They were a kind of legitimate or "just" form of war, as Fróis insinuated, and as the humanist Diogo Teive pronounced in the Portuguese court. Also familiar with the debates taking place in neighbouring Castille, Teive explained the preferences of Dom João III in the "war of conversion": the king deeply desired "that these barbarian peoples are led willingly to the sweet yoke of Christ." He believed that "with all kinds of benefits, they would integrate with the community of the kingdom." However, when they did not want to "spontaneously accept negotiations," repudiating "legitimate and sensible embassies to enter the community," they could be "dragged by the force of arms."[77]

If many Jesuits followed Bragança's decisions, others did not. Father Herédia compared António Quadros, Francisco Rodrigues, and Melchior Carneiro to judicial officers and said they had entered the houses of locals to accuse them of practising forbidden ceremonies and of harbouring hidden deities. Later, they had listed

[75] See the letters of Melchior Carneiro, 1557, and Domingos Fernandes, 1559, DI, Vol. 4, 5–13, 307–13; also of Father António Quadros, 1561, and the report of Father Henrique Henriques of 1561: DI, Vol. 5, 63–7, 160–88.

[76] S. Gonçalves, *Primeira Parte da História,* Vol. 2, 355–6.

[77] Costa, *Discurso de Diogo do Teive,* 108.

the options available to them: imprisonment in the galleys, or conversion and mercy. Fugitives fleeing conversion, he said, had been picked up by priests with guns and spears who had been guarding the crossing. Some, throwing themselves into the river, had died by drowning. Others had starved to death. Snakebite had accounted for several who hid in the forests. Finally, those who opted for Christianity, said Herédia, did so out of fear.[78] Focusing on the attitude of the local populations, the impression is that pragmatism and contingency lay behind the majority of conversions. Few had signed on with the Christian project for non-pragmatic reasons.

The most disadvantaged groups had converted "voluntarily" and pragmatically. Some, like the Paravas on the southern coast of Tamilnadu, were known as "rice Christians", having joined the Christian order in exchange for the guarantee of a food ration, which is to say conversion was their means to a subsistence that represented some improvement over their desperate situation. In the long run, some among these grew into genuine Christians.

After the conversion of these disadvantaged groups, the "intermediate groups" could hardly remain satisfied with the social order in which they continued. The set of privileges offered to those who converted was all too appealing. Naturally, these groups frequently chose the option that offered benefit and material advantages. Aware that they could hardly maintain the social status quo without converting, higher groups converted pragmatically too. Their supremacy now existed only in relative terms. For many among these upper-class or upper-caste converts, the privileges offered by the new political order did not really improve their position. On the other hand, the disadvantages they faced by remaining Gentile were enormous. As non-Christians they would end up on

[78] Letter of Father Herédia, 1561, in DI, Vol. 5, 192–202. The suspicions would continue, as is demonstrated in another letter, dated 1580, in which is written: "the devil used many inventions in order to destroy this work, disseminating in the town that we made Christians by force": DHMPPO, Vol. 12, 711.

the margins of a polity in which they had traditionally occupied the centre. It was perhaps for this reason that men like Loqu or Virupa Chatim, who had known better days in the imperial order pre-1530, converted to Christianity.[79]

Others, however, converted only nominally, remaining Gentiles at heart. For them Christianity would continue to be substantially an exterior form, or at best a new devotion integrated into a pantheon of divinities that was cumulative. Among these were families that continued to celebrate their rites clandestinely.

How could the Christian order satisfy such disparate and competing desires?

Reconstituting the Village Order: Crosses, Churches, and Rituals

Father Gomes Vaz, who had criticised the conversion of the fishermen of Chorão, indicated some years later that the island was thoroughly Christianised and under the rule of "our own". There was a new order, and it was the law of the Christians. Better still, Vaz continued, Chorão had become a centre of conversion, attracting Gentiles from the mainland. Nevertheless, some remained obstinate and continued in their efforts to harm priests and converts. The latter, this priest recounted proudly, responded by assaulting the former and robbing their lands and cattle.[80] The war of conversion continued, except now it was the locals themselves who took up arms to defend Christianity.

Although many other letters contain similar perceptions, both about Chorão and other villages in Goa,[81] it would be erroneous

[79] These examples propose an interpretation that differs slightly from the traditional, which holds that the local elites had from the start converted mainly through the action of the Jesuits. On this, see Thomaz, "O Cristianismo e as religiões pagãs"; idem, "Goa: uma sociedade luso-indiana".

[80] Letter of Father Gomes Vaz, 1578, DI, Vol. 11, 275–6.

[81] In 1557, Father Fróis says the people of Chorão fought with weapons against certain Muslims who had attempted to burn the church, killing and

to believe that this was the dominant form of behaviour among the new Christians. The exemplary function of these narratives is well known: more than simply describing the ground reality, they intended to persuade readers that Christianity taken root in Goan hearts. This was oblique propaganda calling for more and more priests, inviting them to embark on the adventure of conversion, enabling fantasy to become reality. Descriptions of local people invading villages to destroy temples and gods there, and of others who denounced and persecuted unconverted friends and relatives, were part of the same narrative strategy.[82]

By contrast with these descriptions, the majority of the converted were peaceful, indifferent, or reactively oppositional. The dominant image in the correspondence of the Jesuits is of general contentment, at least over the first decade after the conversions. As early as 1563, Lourenço Peres pointed out that the *gaunkars* of the village of Chorão were good Christians. They governed the island politically and morally according to Christian norms. Six years later Father Sebastião Fernandes reported that they had expelled two young men from the most distinguished families of the island, both relatives of the *gaunkars*. The reason for this was their frequenting of brothels. The *gaunkars* explained that such immoral and scandalous behaviour was unacceptable.[83]

The virtuous example of elites, as well as of women – perceived as the vehicles of biological and cultural reproduction – was critical to the success of Christianisation too. They were as fundamental

---

beheading them. This Jesuit concludes by saying that "in these parts even the religious arm themselves so as to be able to serve God": DI, Vol. 3, 709–10. See also the letter of Melchior Nunes Barreto of 1564 in which he explains the relevance of converts for the military defence of Goa: DI, Vol. 6, 705.

[82] These descriptions can be found in several Jesuit letters: see, among others, Letter of Father Melchior Carneiro, s.j., 1557; Letter of Father Manuel Teixeira, s.j., 1558; Letter of Domingos Fernandes, s.j., 1559; Letter of Father Jerónimo Fernandes, 1561, in DI, Vol. 4, 11, 173, 309–10 and Vol. 5, 310.

[83] Letter of Father Sebastião Fernandes, 1569, DI, Vol. 8, 68. With respect to this, see Borges, "Christianization of the Caste System".

as catechesis, preaching, confession, hospitals, and confraternities. While praising the *gaunkars*, Peres extolled the exemplary behaviour of the women of the island. Some, for example, had refused to leave the island to join husbands who had fled to the mainland. Peres was highlighting one of the characteristics of Goan Christianity – its feminine aspect.

The women were apparently so devout that they asked the priests to provide them relics and sacred objects that might aid their prayers. There was a tenuous boundary between these local devotions and what Martin Azpicuelta defined as sinning against the first commandment – idolatry.[84] What meanings were attached to such relics? Were they different from that of the woman who, in 1578, painted a crucifix on her breast "using witchcraft" and who was later denounced to the Inquisition?[85]

Other converts expressed their emotions through the sick and the dying. Parents wanted to baptise their sick children, and if the priest could not reach in time to perform the ritual, they would sprinkle the child with holy water themselves. Even people as recalcitrant as fishermen had been known to turn over a new leaf and ask for a "raised cross" in their neighbourhood. Such a cross was decorated profusely and carried in a procession with much ceremony and great joy. Years later, they put a cross in another quarter of Chorão. This second cross had cannibalised wood from a destroyed temple.[86] A century later a Franciscan noted that Christians raised crosses in place of the traditional *tulsi*.[87] In the third quarter of the sixteenth century this substitution was not regarded with suspicion.

[84] Azpicuelta Navarro, *Manual de Confessores*, 73.

[85] BNP, Cod. 1119 – Repertorio . . ., "Casos Notáveis".

[86] Letter of Father Gomes Vaz, 1566, DI, Vol. 7, 68. This habit of having crosses on house fronts where families gathered together and prayed was frequent in the villages with new Christians. Concerning this, see the expressive letter of Father Pina: DI, Vol. 5, 548–53.

[87] BNP, Cod. 846 – *Viagens pela Índia*, fl. 246. *Tulsi*, a local variety of basil, was connected with Vishnu worship and is considered sacred to this day.

Father Peres also noted the active participation of converts in Christian festivals. Several ceremonies marked the Easter period, ranging from a procession with cilices to a sermon about the Passion and the Resurrection. Peres explained that the feast of the Resurrection had been grand, with many candles, "Portuguese" dances, and other entertainments "in their way". Similar words were used to describe the transfer of the bones of those buried into church spaces.

These cases were ranged alongside others to show that the remaining Christians of the island were "friendly to the things of God". Peres believed in the annihilation of the old superstitions and attributed success to social control exercised among the "newly converted". Social control was not the expression used by this priest but was undoubtedly the meaning implied when he said "they are so careful to accuse one another that they dare not move!"[88]

If these last examples reveal how Jesuits perceived and described – often mistakenly – the behaviour of Christianised populations in the second half of the sixteenth century, a letter by Sebastião Fernandes is an exaggeration. Fernandes says that Christians had much affection for "crosses, veronicas (religious icons), relics, holy water," and liked to confess so much that they claimed it was a better remedy than any form of medicine. If not an outright invention, this is at the very least an error of interpretation. Accustomed to believing that exterior gestures corresponded to an inner order, priests like him did not contemplate the possibility that meanings attributed to gestures, crosses, veronicas, and relics had little to do with Christianity. On the contrary, they could be seen as dissembling in order to resurrect older rituals.[89]

[88] Letter of Father Lourenço Peres, 1563, DI, Vol. 6, 111–19.

[89] There are many references to the persistence of local relics. For example, in 1633 a provision of the viceroy, the Count of Linhares, tells us that there were local priests arriving in Goa "bringing with them beads, and other things like relics, that they give to those Christians that are weak and new in their Christian faith. They look for them, too, in the time of their death,

What was the significance, for example, of the formulae "Jesu Suami" and "Suamya Devari" taught by missionaries to the local populations? Designating Jesus Christ and the Virgin Mary, these were translations of Christian concepts into the local language – but whom did they really invoke?[90] What manner of divinity was Jesu Suami in a world within which there were thousands of divine forms? Who was the Jesu Suami of Goa? What was the meaning of the practice of sprinkling holy water on new converts? Did the old order and its religious reality resurface with these new practices? Or were converted villagers aware that in performing such rites they were expressing a genuine Catholic belief? What consciousness underlay such gestures?

Burdened by doubt, it was not long before the missionaries reversed their opinions. Instead of recounting exemplary behaviour, their letters began recording transgressive situations. Chorão, the refuge for Christians, eventually became an intersection for miscreants – those who were escaping justice, fleeing slaves, smugglers of weapons and other forbidden objects. In the final decades of the sixteenth century the island would also become known for cases of indecency.[91] At more or less the same time, similar behaviour gradually began to be identified everywhere. The records of the Provincial Councils of Goa and the Inquisition suggest the persistence of "Gentileness". Initially directed against New Christians, the accusations of the Inquisition were now increasingly oriented against converts. The rising number of *autos-de-fé* carried out by the Inquisition of Goa – thirty-five between 1561 and 1623, more than one every other year – are evidence of these changes.[92]

---

remembering their pagodas." On these processes, see DI, Vol. 8, 66–7; CR-APO, Fasc. 5, Vol. 3, 1399–1402; DUP, Vol. 2, 251.

90 IAN/TT, Manuscritos da Livraria, Cod. 757 – António de Saldanha, s.j., Prasse Pastoral.

91 CR-APO, Fasc. 5, Vol. 2, 869–70; CR-APO, Fasc. 5, Vol. 3, 973; DI, Vol. 11, 449. Similar worries persisted till the end of the century: CR-APO, Fasc. 6, Vol. 2, 768.

92 ARSI, Goana 9, 16; Dellon, *Voyages de Mr. Dellon*, t. 1, 400; BNP,

Was it the combination of successive disappointments that produced a reversal from optimism to pessimism amongst most missionaries? For some, such as Valignano, local populations were never Christian; he saw them continuing to believe and behave as if they were not, as if the new order were no more than another form of the previous one.[93] For seventeenth-century missionaries, the Goans saw and interpreted in Christian signs and rituals what they were habituated to seeing from an earlier time. "The fishermen make an offering of fish to a stone with a rounded base, and pyramidal top, lodged in the sea, whenever they come in with their loaded boats. This stone is next to Our Lady of the Cape, at the port of Goa." This offering was a sign of an imperfect conversion, said the Franciscan friar recording the example.[94] He was probably right because the stone he described was apparently nothing other than a Sivalinga, the phallic representation of Siva.

For European missionaries who were used to binary logic, these attitudes could have only one meaning. As an indignant and insightful author from the seventeenth century put it, the Indians "shamelessly admit two contradictions".[95] Which is to say, the fishermen were guilty of believing simultaneously in the protective powers of a Sivalinga and Our Lady of Cabo (Cape).

Cod. 1119 – *Repertorio*; IAN/TT, Conselho Geral do Santo Ofício, nº 462; nº 184 – Livro de Visita 1632. About the Goan Inquisition, see Baião, *A Inquisição de Goa*; Priolkar, *The Goan Inquisition*; Cunha, *A Inquisição no Estado da Índia*.

[93] Eric Cohen defended a similar hypothesis in relation to certain situations in Thailand, calling it the indigenisation of Christianity: Cohen, "Christianization and Indigenisation", 33ff. See, more generally, Kaplan, ed., *Indigenous Responses to Western Christianity*, for the modalities of appropriation of other religious systems. For the Goan case, Robinson argues that the Christian Goans "appropriate symbols and attributes associated with the new order, but perceive them through the web or grid of the existing culture and religion": Robinson, *Conversion, Continuity and Change*, 18.

[94] BNP, Cod. 846 – *Viagens pela Índia*, fl. 246.

[95] BA, Cod. 51-VII-27 – Breve noticia dos erros, que tem os gentios do Concão na India, fl. 88.

As mentioned earlier, the representation of the Virgin Mary was another such case. Local populations had experienced a vast multiplicity of female deities with distinct forms and expressions that were sometimes contradictory. This referential grid facilitated the inclusion of Christian "goddesses" – in this case of the different expressions of Mary and other female saints – and the attribution to them of already existing meanings and functions.[96] It was a process of translation which ensured that neither the goddesses nor Mary retained their original or intended meanings.

This cumulative capacity ultimately refers to the encounter not only between languages but also between distinct systems of representation which did not coincide in their forms of classification. Moreover, this flexibility in logic became a fundamental trait of the syncretic Christianity that emerged in Goa. It led to broad acceptance of the view that the locals would only internalise a simplified version of the Christian faith.

Even so, most of the missionaries were unable to accept that many of these "misunderstandings" were the result of the encounter between different systems of representation. Instead, there was a growing fear that the local Christians were simulators, malicious and duplicitous.[97]

A proclamation of Viceroy Dom Duarte de Menezes forbidding non-Christians from constructing objects of Christian worship emanates from this way of thinking. It came as a response to a petition from the Pai dos Cristãos denouncing non-compliance with the decrees of the Provincial Council of Goa of 1567.[98] The pronouncement prohibited local artisans from working on

[96] For the Goan case, see again Robinson, *Conversion, Continuity and Change*; but also, for what concerns South India in general, S. Bayly, *Saints, Goddesses and Kings*; and David Mosse, "Catholic Saints and the Hindu Village", 301–22.

[97] The arts of duplicity, simulation, and dissimulation could have dangerous consequences if used by the "wrong" people: see, in this context, Villari, *Elogio della dissimulazione*; Zagorin, *Ways of Lying*.

[98] CR-APO, Fasc. 4, 45.

Christian images on account of treating them with "irreverence and contempt" and "for the hatred that they had". Non-Christians could not, from this time on, paint either images of Christ and Mary or images of the saints, and in fact of all things Christian. The fines were high: fifty cruzados for the first offence, a hundred for the second, and the galleys for the third.[99]

A law of Philip II of Spain on marriages between Christians of the land is enlightening too. These festivities lasted "ten to fifteen days with banquets that are given from both sides" and emptied the purses of those that paid for them. Worse, "they imitate Gentile ceremonies". The king required that these feasts be restricted to a single day, as were marriages celebrated in Iberia.[100]

Firmness with this type of legislation accompanies the rediscovery of idolatry in the Goan territories. The archives of the Inquisition of Goa had several books outlining the offences of Goa/Tiswadi, Salcete, and Bardez, as well as file cabinets designated for each of the territories, indicating a spatial sensitivity among those recording them.[101] To the horror of the Archbishop of Goa, the missionaries, and the inquisitors, idolatry reared its ugly head

[99] CR-APO, Fasc. 5, Vol. 3, 1160–1. There is still legislation on these issues in the first decade of the seventeenth century. This renewal shows that the legal framing of the sixteenth century was not really efficient.

[100] CR-APO, Fasc. 3, 659–60. The decrees of 1613, 1620, and 1622 show that the problem persisted: CR-APO, Fasc. 6, Vol. 2, 964–5, 1200–2, 1222–3. A synthesis of the reform of marriage after the Council of Trent can be found in Prosperi, *Il Concilio di Trento*, 133ff.; and in Fernandes, *Espelhos, Cartas e Guias*, Chapter 6.

[101] IAN/TT, Conselho Geral do Santo Ofício, nº 462 – Inventário, "Denuncias e Apresentações". See also the few records of trials of the Inquisition of Goa that have survived, besides the ones that exist, in Rio de Janeiro: IAN/TT, Tribunal do Santo Ofício, Inquisição de Lisboa, Processos nº 3672, 8916, 13347, 13348, 13349, and 13352; Inquisição de Évora, Processos nº 7545 e 7717. From that moment on, the literature on Gentileness and the ways of identifying it increased: IAN/TT, Conselho Geral do Santo Ofício, nº 1776; BNP, Cod. 607 – *Divindades do Gentilismo da Índia*, Film 3622; BPADE, Col. Manizola, Cod. 29 – Pe. Manuel Barradas, s.j., *Tratado dos deuses gentilicos de todo o Oriente e dos ritos e ceremonias que usam os Malaba-*

in the most unlikely places. This discovery contributed to the expansion of melancholy in relation to conversion. The sentiment pervades the letters written by the regular clergy at the beginning of the seventeenth century. It also contributed to the diffusion of an anthropological pessimism that would justify widespread recourse to strategies elaborated by the Inquisition – apparently these were thought of as the only efficacious methods for uprooting and eliminating idolatry.

In parallel, converts developed a "kind of absence" – to use an expression coined by Veiga Coutinho – on account of the quotidian experience of signs, realities, and obligations proper to the Christian order, and the equivalent obliteration of the preceding one.[102] Local elites adapted the norms of caste to the basic requirements of the Christian faith. This allowed them to maintain their pre-eminent position within the new order, a good relationship with the Christian clergy, and the power to influence the social system.[103] In the medium and long term, however, they engaged in a kind of collective amnesia, refashioning their history and memory to suggest they had always been Christian.[104]

Partly because of the secrecy they adopted, other groups developed, instead, a culture of dissimulation, and a sort of collective schizophrenia. Among converts the most tragic predicament was again that of the disadvantaged groups. They had to postpone their

---

res, 1618; Cod. 594–6 – *Filosofia secreta da gentilidade*; BA, Cod. 51-VII-27: Breve noticia dos erros, que tem os gentios do Concão na India. For the American space, this process has been described by Serge Gruzinski in *La Colonisation de l'Imaginaire*. Similar conclusions can be found in Kenneth Mills, in what concerns the Christianisation of Peru: Mills, "The Limits of Religious Coercion". On the debates about idolatry and Gentileness in India, see Županov, *Disputed Mission*.

[102] V. Coutinho, "Cuncolim".

[103] For example, the *fabricas* of the main churches were controlled by these groups, as well as the most important confraternities.

[104] About these political identities, see Rubinoff, *The Construction of a Political Community*; also Fuller, "Kerala Christians".

earlier expectations of social redemption. At first – at the time when missionaries availed of these first converts, Ines Županov suggests, as "Trojan horses" within their communities[105] – their utility to the Christian project was high.[106] At this point converting to Christianity was a rational choice.[107] However, in the second stage the missionaries' attention was directed at the local elites. The consequence was a resumption of the previous social hierarchy: the disadvantaged were dethroned from their temporary position of privilege and returned to their previous subaltern status – different because of their conversion, perhaps, but still at the base of the social pyramid.

Elite or subaltern, all these groups were obliged to *see* other things. The landscape to which they were accustomed and of which they were part now had other signs – sacred constructions, pillories, Christian crosses. Eventually, the accumulation of these other signs would forever transform their experience of the world.

At any event, conversion did not fully satisfy any of the actors or groups involved – neither missionaries confronting the rediscovery of idolatry, nor the local people facing a new god. The locals, in one way or another, never really saw the expectations they had placed in the future Christian order bear fruit. These effects were the natural consequence of the confrontation between a complex and diverse local order and the Christian community. In both cases it led to a structural melancholy that invaded and constituted the new order – the Goan order.

[105] Županov, "Esperimenti linguistici", 53.

[106] To use these concepts does not imply, however, the total reduction of the process of conversion to mere pragmatism. My perspective is linked to the arguments developed by political scientists and anthropologists such as Scott in *Weapons of the Weak*; Rafael, "Confession, Conversion and Reciprocity"; Viswanathan, "Coping with (Civil) Death"; idem, *Outside the Fold*; Webb Keane, "From Fetishism to Sincerity".

[107] Some of these were already embedded in egalitarian worldviews, such as in the Nath cult. With respect to this, see the summary of this discussion in Robinson, *Conversion, Continuity and Change*, 45ff.

Not that the new situation left such groups and subjects entirely discontented either. Misunderstandings in perception and communication were partially responsible for the conservation of the imperial order. Had understanding of it been perfect, the order may never have been sustained for as long as it was.

Perhaps this flawed awareness explains why the endeavours of the Italian Theatine Father Ardizzone Spinola in the mid-seventeenth century – captured in his published sermons – ran into so many obstacles. Knowing that very few Christians in the land received holy communion, Spinola outlined a strategy which, he said, would allow them to enjoy the eucharistic effects at least once a year, at Easter time.

The strategy began in the parish of Our Lady of Guadalupe in the village of Batim in Tiswadi. In the course of Lent in 1645, Spinola realised that many local Christians did not receive communion on Easter Sunday. Pitying them, he resolved that in the following year only the impious would not receive it. He took the "most blessed Sacrament" to "their own houses, and even to poor and limited huts." He wrote that "as the contrary obtains in India with the natives, it is a mortal sin for which Parish priests and Curates will have to render a strict account to God at the time of their death." In Guadalupe the clergy resisted his proposals, while the Christians reacted with great joy (in Spinola's telling, of course). According to him, confession increased with "the desire of each person to effectively clean his conscience well from past sins, with firm intentions of never again offending God, since they had received Him in their hearts."[108]

This project faced stiffer resistance in the remaining parishes of Tiswadi, despite Spinola having been formally authorised by Archbishop Francisco dos Mártires to implement it. Some said that taking Christ to rude huts was indecent. Others found it strange to be doing something that had never been done before in those territories. To transform the previous *status quo* was not

[108] BNP, Cod. 58 – *Breve relação das principaes ordens*, fls 5–5v.

necessarily good. Ironically, it was the native clergy that occupied the parishes of Tiswadi – in the early-seventeenth century, eleven of the seventeen parishes – who most significantly resisted his proposals. In contrast, the Jesuits of Salcete and the Franciscans of Bardez welcomed his programme with enthusiasm.

Did the Italian intend to overturn the positions recently acquired by the "indigenous clergy" in the parishes of Tiswadi? Was this another form of discrimination against local populations, in this case their "elites"? Or did these parish priests, by their ignorance and complacence, or perhaps even by choice, not perform their duties well? Was their resistance related to caste problems? Did they want to avoid visiting the "humble houses and huts" – which many of them dared not even approach? [109]

It is not possible to answer these questions at this point in time, but they illustrate the interpretive possibilities opened up by a text like Spinola's. Although one cannot discover the motivations underlying the writing of the text, one thing seems certain: inertia seems to have been more powerful than the will to change.

There were moments when the misperceptions generated by the clash of distinct logical and behavioural systems challenged this balance. Based on Chorão, this chapter has identified attitudes to the process of conversion, both among the agents of Christianisation as well as in the local population. The next chapter looks at the open and explicit resistance to imperial domination, focusing on the martyrdom of Cuncolim and other forms of resistance.

[109] That this was not a minor matter is evidenced by the many petitions sent to *Mesa da Consciência e Ordens* in which "canarim" clerics were constantly deprecated: IAN/TT, Mesa da Consciência e Ordens – Aranha, *Meza das Tres Ordens Militares*, Vol. II, fls 79–85v.

6

The Martyrs of Cuncolim and Other Episodes of Resistance

IN 1583 IN CARDIFF (Wales), Richard Stephens received an awaited letter from his brother Thomas, a Jesuit missionary in India who was to become famous there with his texts *Doutrina Cristã em língua concana* and the *Christapurana*. The mail being slow, news from Thomas was infrequent. In his letter, Thomas Stephens acknowledged receipt of an earlier missive from his brother. In it, Richard had referred to the persecutions of Catholics in England and to the 1581 martyrdom of Jesuits, including Edmund Campion, hanged at Tyburn. Giving an account of the challenges to Christendom in Goa, specifically in the territories of Salcete, Thomas' letter in reply to Richard's was less enthusiastic than his brother's to him had been. Tormented by the hostility of non-Christians – "*bellicosi omnes* [. . .] *a fides christiana maximi abhorrentes*" (warlike people . . . the most hostile enemies of the Christian faith) – the Jesuits, he says, had faced martyrdom in the village of Cuncolim on 15 July 1583. Some of the local Christians who had helped the priests in their mission to the village had been killed too. After their deaths the local Christians had preserved parts of the garments and hair of the dead, whom they had immediately acclaimed as martyrs. Their hope was that a lush Christianity would sprout from the blood spilt on that day.[1]

[1] Letter of Father Thomas Stephen, s.j., 1583, DI, Vol. 12, 817–26.

Two months later, identical news appeared in a letter by Father Duarte Sande. Like Stephens, Sande expected Christianity in Salcete to yield fruit after the testimony of martyrdom in Cuncolim. Sande did not describe the event in detail because, as he put it, "Father Provincial wishes to communicate this in particular to Your Paternity [Claudio Acquaviva, General of the Jesuits] so that it may be communicated abroad." The decision of the strategist Alessandro Valignano is understandable: for missionary purposes it was vital that the events in Cuncolim be disseminated throughout the European world, not least because one of the Cuncolim martyrs was a nephew of Acquaviva. The flow and deployment of information were therefore essential.[2]

Four days passed before Valignano's account of the events in distant Goa were sent to Claudio Acquaviva. Composed of several pages and written in Spanish, Valignano's version has lengthy comments on the perversity of the local population and the kindness and charity of Christians. The letter provides a detailed and almost hour-by-hour account of events leading up to the martyrdom. Cuncolim was an expression of the struggles that Christians faced in their battles within the large and universal war against "paganism" – and therefore Cuncolim was now a part of universal history.[3]

Until the 1609 report of Father Sebastião Gonçalves, the Jesuits' historian in India, Valignano's version circulated as the primary record of this event. It constituted one of the sources of a heroic poem written by Father Francesco Benci for the annual letter, printed and compiled by Nicolao Orlandino,[4] and was also the source for another work, the official chronicle entitled *Ásia* by Diogo do Couto, who refers to these events in his text which is a continuation of the account by João de Barros.[5]

[2] Letter of Father Duarte de Sande, s.j., 1583, ibid., 902–4.

[3] Report of Father Alessandro Valignano, s.j., 1583, ibid., 916–32.

[4] The Jesuits published an annual letter with a synthesis of what had happened that year in their various missions around the world.

[5] *Relatione della felice morte de cinque religiosi.*

The Jesuits in Portugal awaited Gonçalves' version too. They expected it to add information favouring the process of beatification of the deceased Jesuits already under way. Gonçalves added new information and details, purging his narrative, however, of some of Valignano's more aggressive comments.[6]

In addition to their role in the discursive constitution of this event, these missionary letters contributed to moulding local memory. Until the nineteenth century, they confirmed the narrative of religious martyrdom. When reading a pamphlet written in 1884 by Phylotheio d'Andrade, a Goan Christian, one encounters the same information systematised three centuries earlier by the Jesuit priests: martyrdom, martyrs, good Christians, wicked Gentiles. Although d'Andrade's pamphlet was a response to an article by Menezes de Bragança, another local intellectual, it is telling that the publicist used the Jesuit narratives as if they were accurate descriptions of events.

Menezes de Bragança saw the missionary letters no differently. His narrative of the event too accepts them as reliable descriptions of martyrdom. However, Bragança used the same sources to justify precisely the opposite. Reacting against the beatification of the five Jesuits (which happened only in 1883), he questioned who the real martyrs were. For Bragança these were the residents of Cuncolim, put to death by the Portuguese powers when they tried to defend their culture and their faith, or what Bragança calls their "identity".[7]

Bragança's reading made visible the political nature of the events of 1583 to the average Goan. For the nativist "Goan" narrative, of which Bragança was one of the founders, 1583 was a manifestation of local resistance to Portuguese rule, anticipating future resistances. It is no surprise, then, that his version has often been revived,

[6] Archbishop Dom Frei Aleixo de Meneses initiated the process of recognising Jesuits as martyrs. Despite successive attempts before the pontifical tribunal, the beatification took place only in 1883, in quite a different context: Županov, "Drugs, Health, Bodies", 10.

[7] D'Andrade, *Os Santos Martyres*; Dolvy, *Cuncolim*.

resurfacing in the local press. At the end of the twentieth century, Veríssimo Coutinho wrote in the *Navhind Times* that "Cuncolim was a predecessor of the struggle for freedom in Goa." This Goan columnist added that "the first movement of non-cooperation had been organised by the population of Cuncolim against the Portuguese 400 years before Mahatma Gandhi launched his non-cooperation movement against the British settlers of India."[8] The exaggeration (and error) of the comparison and the suggestion of a genealogical link between a sixteenth-century event of local resistance and contemporary resistances is obvious. There was no "Goan" political consciousness in the sixteenth century, nor was there any linear continuum between the dissent of the people of that period and those at the dawn of the new millennium.

These interpretations have no equivalent in the historiography. For an extended period, historians more or less forgot the Cuncolim episode. The most recent studies also summarise it in a few paragraphs, reproducing the Jesuit letters with differing interpretations. This absence is telling, especially considering the profusion of studies on forms of resistance to imperial domination in other contexts, predominantly the British.[9] The Portuguese historiography on resistance and revolts in Goa is sparse, and the Goan interpretations of the occurrence that exist tend to be nationalistic – as for instance Pratima Kamat's important book *Farar Far.*[10] Revisiting Cuncolim is therefore necessary.

There is no doubt that the incident at Cuncolim represented an open revolt against Christian domination, and that the exemplary punishment suffered by those involved instituted what James Scott has called the "memory of repression", the intent of such repression being to prevent future recurrences of defiance.[11] At

[8] V. Coutinho, "Cuncolim".

[9] Among others, the classic study by Guha, *Elementary Aspects*.

[10] Although she resorts to a language that evokes the Subaltern Studies school, Kamat's work is also part of a tendency of Goans to exalt themselves: Kamat, *Farar Far*.

[11] Scott, *Weapons of the Weak,* 40.

the same time, Cuncolim offers contours connected with ritual, suggesting that the conflict also had characteristics absent in the proto-nationalist and nationalist narratives.

What follows below is divided into three parts. First, I focus on the political situation of Salcete in the second half of the sixteenth century, in particular within the village of Cuncolim and the surrounding villages. I then focus on the occurrences in the days before, during, and immediately after the event. Finally, I look into other "revolts", or attempts at revolt, in other villages of Goa during the sixteenth and seventeenth centuries. This chapter does not discuss other questions arising from these descriptions, one such question being their role in the construction of models of sanctity and their deployment in the imperial geography of martyrdom.[12] Nor does it discuss the uses of discriminatory vocabularies, such as "barbarian", "barbarism", and "black" by the various authors of the narratives, or differences between Italian and Portuguese missionaries in the use of those words.

The Village of Cuncolim Before 1583

When discussing the political dimensions of the events of 15 July 1583, one needs to consider the relationship between these villages and regions outside the Portuguese dominions, namely, the sultanate of Bijapur and the Vijayanagar empire, which had controlled the area before the Portuguese. The circumstances through which the village of Cuncolim and the other villages involved came under the jurisdiction of the Portuguese Crown, their geographical location, and their political-administrative status are relevant when analysing this situation.

Cuncolim, Velim, Veroda, Ambelim, and Assolna were five villages in the territory of Salcete, situated between the Sal and Oudh rivers towards the southern end of this region, and bordering

[12] This is with reference to other martyrdoms occurring in the context of the Portuguese imperial order: see, for example, Alves, "Os mártires de Achém"; Županov, "A História do Futuro".

the neighbouring territory of Bijapur. Along with Margão and Verna, Cuncolim was one of the largest villages in Salcete, and in that sense the head of this group. During the Bijapur (and earlier Bahmani) overlordship, many landowners in Salcete grew into petty warlords who bore arms and were responsible for collecting taxes at the local level, which reinforced their status. In addition, the Adil Shahs of Bijapur usually recruited soldiers for the forces they had in the region from the five villages near the River Oudh. This explains the existence of a military or paramilitary tradition amongst residents.[13] The elites of Cuncolim were part of these groups.

Cuncolim was situated on a long road that linked towns along the Malabar coast, ultimately connecting Goa with Kochi. It also served as a staging post for runners who ensured communication links between these distant places. Its position as a stopover explains the concentration of military forces in the region. The protected information that circulated via this route was particularly relevant for the preservation of political order in the vicinity. At the same time this circulation of information, and the passage of runners, opened the residents to different and varied influences.

As with the island of Tiswadi, Salcete was formerly a part of the sultanate of Bijapur and still a bone of contention between the forces of the Adil Shahs and the Portuguese. For the Adil Shahs, possession of Salcete could permit a future reconquest of the city of Goa. For groups opposed to the Shah inside the sultanate, the capture of Salcete by them was, from their perspective, an act of sedition against him. Tensions between the troops of the Adil Shah, stationed in the villages of Cuncolim and its vicinity, and those of the military governor of Belgaum, Asad Khan Lari, his subordinate, exemplified this. For the Portuguese, Salcete (as well as Bardez) constituted a buffer and a means of reinforcement for the military protection of the city of Goa. These territories also

[13] Velinkar, *India and the West*, Chapter 2; Velinkar, "Evangelization Methods in Salcete".

helped create a territorial continuum to enable future territorial expansion. Furthermore, their incorporation meant a reinforcement of the Crown's fixed income in a period of growing strain on its budget.

Although Salcete had theoretically been won for the Portuguese Crown in 1510 and 1511 through the conquests of Afonso de Albuquerque, formal incorporation of these territories into the dominion of the Crown dated only to the 1540s. Between these two periods the Portuguese made several attempts to establish administrative structures there, but, as mentioned above, there were many conflicts in which the Portuguese opposed the forces of the Adil Shah. At a certain point, the Portuguese allied with Asad Khan, who permitted them – Gaspar Correia suggests – to settle in Ponda and build a small fort in the village of Rachol in Salcete.[14]

The death of Ismail Adil Shah of Bijapur in 1534 saw the succession of his son, Ibrahim. Meanwhile Asad Khan, hostile to Ibrahim Adil Shah, had ceded the territories of Salcete and Bardez (which came under his jurisdiction as Governor of Belgaum) to the Portuguese. Later, he came under the vassalage of Ibrahim Adil Shah and was required to recover both territories. The Portuguese naturally refused to return what were now their possessions, and their refusal resulted in skirmishes in the region of Verna. The Portuguese reinforced the fort of Rachol with about 200 soldiers, in addition to Naiks (local chieftains) and sepoys. Vessels patrolled the vulnerable stretch of the river. Despite this Asad Khan, who was now supported by Ibrahim's forces against the Portuguese, destroyed the fort in 1538.[15]

The formal annexation of Salcete and Bardez to the Portuguese Crown was an outcome of these conflicts. As a consequence of intrigues between Governor Martim Afonso de Sousa and Ali bin Yusuf Adil Khan, uncle of Ibrahim Adil Shah (and also a candidate

[14] Correia, *Lendas da Índia,* Vol. 3, 462–3. The same version appears in the chronicle of Francisco de Andrada, ed., *Crónica de D. João III*, 608. See also Velinkar, *India and the West*, 32.

[15] Andrada, ed., *Crónica de D. João III*, 609ff.

for the throne of the sultanate), the Portuguese were eventually able to wrest control of these territories. Four years later, during the government of Dom João de Castro, the conflict was reignited and ended in favour of the Portuguese.[16]

In the islands of Tiswadi, Divar, and Chorão the implanting of Christianity happened after a period marked by a kind of indirect rule. In contrast, incorporation of the territories of Salcete took place during a period in which the Portuguese Crown's policy towards local populations involved forced conversion. Unsurprisingly, the population of Salcete perceived Portuguese domination very differently from the inhabitants of Tiswadi in the early-sixteenth century.[17]

Tax evasion, the refusal to allow the right of passage to royal officers, and open conflicts with agents of the Crown were some of the ways in which Cuncolim and the surrounding villages resisted attempts by the Portuguese authorities to establish their presence. In Salcete, the Christians and the Portuguese were perceived as the new enemies that village communities needed to fight.[18]

For their part, the Christians perceived these manifestations of resistance as expressions of confrontation and open conflict, describing

[16] IAN/TT, Corpo Cronológico, Part I, Mç. 77, nº 52 – "Carta de Pedro Fernandes dando parte a ElRey", 20 Dec. 1545; Mç. 74, nº 46 – "Carta de D. Garcia de Castro dando conta a ElRey que o Mouro, que recebeo em Gôa o entregou a Idalcão", 29 Dec. 1543; and nº 60 – "Carta de António Cardozo dando parte a ElRey estar o Idalcão seis legoas", 23 Dec. 1545; Mç. 78, nº 94 – "Carta de Miguel Rodrigues, dando parte a ElRey da cauza porque o Idalcão rompeo as Tregoas", 24 Nov. 1546. In addition to the letters of Dom João de Castro to his sons and to the king himself, other correspondence was sent to Lisbon with information on the local situation. V. IAN/TT, Corpo Cronológico, Part I, Mç.79, nº 139 – "Carta de D. Diogo de Almeida dando parte a ElRey", 10 Dec. 1547; Part II, Mç. 241, nº24. Martim Afonso de Sousa also referred to these events in his "autobiography": Albuquerque and Caeiro, *Martim Afonso de Sousa: Cartas*, 78.

[17] A *carta régia* from this period is very explicit about this: CR–APO, Fasc. 5, Vol. 3, 967–9.

[18] Elias and Scotson, *The Established and the Outsiders*, "Introduction".

them with recourse to the tropes of persecution of Christians by the godless.[19] It was at the time of the Viceroy Dom Constantino de Bragança that "our priests [began] to enter that savage jungle (*aquel mato tan bravo*)." Missionary narratives are clear that the local populations were far from receptive to them: "from the beginning they armed themselves heavily against the fathers, wanting to undo what they had done and to sustain the idolatry that was so deep-rooted in the land." This animosity was reason enough to justify war and legitimise the harshness of the Portuguese reaction.[20]

This reaction contributed to a growing opposition to the political and religious presence of Christians in these territories, leading eventually to the events of 1583. Resistance to agents of the imperial order grew apace: a Portuguese courier coming from Kochi was thrashed when transiting the village of Cuncolim. In instructions given to a Portuguese official charged with collecting tributes due to the Portuguese Crown, the vedor da Fazenda requested information about the villages that had refused to pay, suggesting resistance to taxation in some of the villages.[21] Daniello Bartoli's description of Cuncolim in this period indicates that it rendered tribute only when the local *feiticeiro* (sorcerer) permitted payment. If this information is accurate, the local religious order was intervening in the resolution of administrative issues, making it a

[19] Michael Adas points out, precisely, the non-differentiation – in certain acts – of the dimension of "refusal" and the dimension of "confrontation", one more passive, the other clearly active: Adas, "From Avoidance to Confrontation", 91–7.

[20] From the decade starting in 1560, Portuguese political power would show an effective interest in Salcete, dating from as early as the first installation of Jesuits in that province. On the perception of local reactions, see A.S.D. Costa, "A expansão portuguesa"; Junqueiro, "Afonso de Albuquerque"; Coxito, "O problema da 'Guerra Justa'"; Bebiano, "A guerra: o seu imaginário". One of the inspirations was Th. of Aquinas, O.P., *Somme contre les Gentils*.

[21] CR–APO, Fasc. 5, Part I, 615–22. Francisco Rodrigues, who was responsible for the collection of revenue from the temples that the Jesuits had in Salcete, was also killed on 15 July: DI, Vol. 12, 928.

menace to Portuguese power.[22] To oblige locals to pay, the Portuguese Crown assigned the task to a small army consisting of three Naiks and thirty foot-soldiers. A mid-seventeenth-century document says the populations of Salcete had risen "many times against the Estado da Índia not wanting to pay and killing some of the King's officers that went there to collect on his behalf."[23] In sum, the memory of the Portuguese Crown in relation to these territories was of dissension.

The Christian parishes came to be established along with the already difficult creation of the political administration. In 1566 the erection of new temples and repair of existing ones were prohibited in Salcete and Bardez. The objective was that "by taking away the sumptuous buildings of their idols, and the worship and superstition of idolatry" the local population would be predisposed to conversion. In the following year Diogo Fernandes nicknamed "the Strong" gained fame for having contributed to the "conversion of the infidels and Gentiles of the said lands" by demolishing 300 temples and mosques and adding the rents of these properties to the treasury of the Crown.[24]

These acts went against the treaty signed between Ali bin Yusuf Adil Khan and Pedro Mascarenhas in 1554 and confirmed the following year. The treaty postulated that in Salcete and Bardez "they would not order the destruction of the mosques and pagodas which had been made in that land, nor would they oblige them to abandon their law [*sua ley*: here, religion] by use of force, but only receive those who, of their own will, desired to become Christians."[25] Twelve years after this treaty, the policies of the Portuguese Crown had changed dramatically, violating some of its clauses.

The viceroy, Dom Francisco de Mascarenhas, confirmed that all the revenues of the temples and deities of Salcete should revert to

[22] Bartoli, *L'Asia, parte prima,* 630.

[23] ARSI, Goana 22, fl. 93.

[24] CR–APO, Fasc. 5, Vol. 2, 613–14, 872–4.

[25] CR–APO, Fasc. 5, Part I, 267–78. Three years later, a *provisão régia* confirms the situation: CR–APO, Fasc. 5, Vol. 2, 694–8.

the Society of Jesus. The decree explained that the Jesuits should use these funds "for the ordinary expenditure of churches, menial servants, and bailiffs, hospitals and to clothe catechumens." The remaining rents went to the Casa dos Catecúmenos in Goa. Leading figures of the village of Margão, the main village of Salcete, provided information about the revenues and properties of the temples of Salcete, in line with what had occurred in Tiswadi earlier.[26]

The majority of the villages in Salcete were acquiescent. Unlike Tiswadi, where conversions did not begin with the elites, here many among the local elites accepted the new circumstances, initiating a top-down conversion dynamic. Several churches were built after 1567, though soldiers had to protect all of them. However, by contrast with the conformists, the villagers of Cuncolim reacted by leading a revolt which culminated in the destruction of Jesuit residences and churches.[27]

The missionaries believed that local Brahmans, in alliance with the forces of the Adil Shah, were behind these acts of violence. Governor Dom António de Noronha (r. 1571–1573) charged Santopá Naique (Shantappa Nayak), a captain in the recently constructed fortress of Honavar (south of Goa), with having "gone over to the Moors, and risen against my service by fighting, and taking arms against Christians." Subsequently the priests rebuilt the churches and the residences. According to Sebastião Gonçalves, the number of Christians in Salcete then went up to about 10,000 by the end of the 1570s. However, we are also informed that a good part of "the land was all in an insurrection", and that consequently, the *vangana* (floodplains), the most productive lands of Salcete, were frequently difficult to give out in revenue-farm,

[26] See Annual Letter, 1577; Letter of Father Gomes Vaz, s.j., 1578; "Assento que se tomou sobre os ritos dos gentios", 1579; Letter of Archbishop Dom Henrique de Távora, 1579: DI, Vol. 10, 942; Vol. 11, 262, 563–9, 692; CR–APO, Fasc. 5, Vol. 1, 825–31; Vol. 2, 841–2.

[27] For an overview of the military organisation of the Estado da Índia, see V. Rodrigues, "A guerra na Índia".

whether to a *gaunkar* or a member of the scribal group. However, there were some exceptions, and these included Mormugão, Sancoale and Cuncolim, which did yield some revenues.[28]

During the third quarter of the sixteenth century, the five villages of southern Salcete, headed by Cuncolim, continued to be frequently in revolt. They refused to pay tributes, Cuncolim rebuilt its main temple and added four or five smaller temples "alongside it" (the *panchadevata*), and non-Christian ceremonies and festive celebrations took place. The resisters also sought a licence from the king of Portugal to practise their cult devotions freely, but without success. This incited increasingly violent reactions from the Christians, who continued to see these practices as the persecution of Christians by impious heathens.[29]

There were also intra-regional and internal rivalries. The main villages of Salcete competed with each other to establish primacy in the region, and Cuncolim was among them. So, disputes, betrayals, and alliances were a part of the quotidian within the villages.

Over the sixteenth century these situations provided the backdrop for the expectations and alliances of local populations and, at least theoretically, afforded some of them scope for negotiation. In Cuncolim, however, this combination worked differently.

Setting the Stage for Martyrdom

The first exemplary punishments took place in 1577. The Portuguese Crown wanted to secure the political integration of these territories and permit an increase of the Portuguese military apparatus in the area. In this context, "the blacks [*sic*] were punished in the following manner": Gil Eanes de Mascarenhas, Captain Major of the Malabar Coast, entered the Cuncolim region via the Sal River. He did "whatever damage he could in those villages," burning and razing "whatever he found before him . . . cut down

[28] CR–APO, Fasc. 5, Vol. 2, 489n.; Vol. 3, 993.

[29] Adas, "From Avoidance to Confrontation", 99. From the perspective of the missionaries, the Brahmans were the principal adversaries of Christianity.

the palm groves of the enemies, destroyed the gardens and rice fields, and in order that the blacks might understand that he intended to remain there some time, he built stockades in which he gathered all the people."[30] At the same time, two priests – Pietro Berno and Manuel Teixeira – killed a cow and defiled village lands with its entrails.

With this the local elites promised the Portuguese never to revolt again, honouring the viceroy with brocade robes. However, according to Valignano's version of these moments, the silence and the truces, obtained through the intercession of priests, concealed plans of revenge. The attack in 1581 by the troops of Ibrahim Adil Shah of Bijapur (r. 1580-1627), helped by residents of Cuncolim, had thus probably been brewing for a time. Jesuit churches and Christian houses were desecrated and destroyed once more. On this occasion only the hospital escaped the mob's fury, the locals seeing it as a place of protection and healing; a missionary wrote that "this Hospital is called, by the Gentiles, a House of God." In response to the attack the Jesuits recruited about 200 local Christians to protect themselves, many of the recruits being from the village of Orlim.[31]

Over the same years the Jesuit Rudolfo Acquaviva had returned from an embassy to the Mughal emperor Akbar and become rector of the college at Salcete. In a Jesuit gathering in the villages of Cortalim and Verna, Acquaviva discussed "the most suitable methods to finish converting Salcete and to induce many to convert and be baptised." He decided to visit the houses of the Jesuits in the villages and look for places to erect new crosses. On account of its past history of violence, a particular effort was made to convert the residents of Cuncolim. [32]

On 14 July 1583 the Jesuits sent a message to residents of Cuncolim informing them that they would arrive at the village for a missionary stint the following day. The villagers replied saying

[30] Report of Father Alessandro Valignano, s.j., 1583: DI, Vol. 12, 919–21.

[31] *Admirabile Vida,* 178; Bartoli, *L'Asia, parte prima,* 630.

[32] Report of Father Alessandro Valignano, s.j., 1583: DI, Vol.12, 923ff.

there were problems in the village: one of the village's most important *gaunkars* had been killed in an ambush. This violent death seems to indicate further that Cuncolim was not, as was later depicted, entirely harmonious – an instance in fact of what Victor Turner called "social drama".[33] Pre-existing tensions were part of the local contexts that stimulated the subsequent events.

An account by Francisco de Sousa provides further information on these tensions. He writes that, before the priests had left for Cuncolim, Father António Francisco asked some Christians from Orlim – perhaps Baltasar Serrão, Pedro de Mascarenhas, or Diogo de Castro, all already Christian – to proceed to Cuncolim and build a camp there.[34] The aim was to construct a shelter against heavy rain. The arrival of the Christians from Orlim was not welcomed by the villagers of Cuncolim and this began a conflict which increased with the arrival of the missionaries.

It is possible that Cuncolim's families had different notions of Portuguese domination from those of Chorão and Sirula (in Bardez). One villager, at least, already converted to Christianity, was an ally of the Portuguese: Martim Garcia protected one of the missionaries during the bloodiest moment of the subsequent events, and thanks to him the missionary survived.[35] From this it appears that internal controversy preceded the onset of violence.

In the previous chapter it was shown that, for some of the local inhabitants in Goa, collaborating with the Christian authorities seemed the best strategy for preserving their existing positions, or even improving them. It certainly protected them from the systematic destruction of their fields, the drying up of income, and exemplary punishment. The refusal of dialogue or active revolt, equally, served the interests of those families desiring reintegration into the territories of the Bijapur Sultanate. For such families a revolt might result in the termination of the Portuguese domination and a re-establishment of the earlier status quo. This was

[33] Turner, *The Ritual Process*, 69.

[34] *Purabhilekh-Puratatva,* Vol. 9, 36–8.

[35] HAG, nº 7583–5 – Foral de 1622, 933.

so for the majority of the population of the village of Cuncolim and for the surrounding villages of Velim, Veroda, Ambelim, and Assolna. The tensions between the Portuguese Crown and these villages, combined with their internal tensions, created an explosive situation on the rainy morning of 15 July 1583.

When the missionaries entered the village, the Jesuit Francisco Aranha announced that they aimed to construct a Christian church. The missionaries were accompanied by fifty people, some Portuguese, the rest Christians of local origin. They were received by a *gaunkar* who told them that a *gaunkari* assembly was taking place to try resolving a conflict that had pitted two of its leading figures against each other. Eager to bring about peace, the missionaries summoned the two parties, convinced that they would be able to settle the conflict. Only one of the parties appeared, Calgo Naique, who reacted violently towards the missionaries. The surname Naique (or Naik) was common to thirteen other residents of Cuncolim. Many of them, like Calgo, would later be identified as rebels and executed by the king's officers. Did the Adil Shahs of Bijapur give them this title, Naique? Were these people still loyal to Bijapur? Besides reacting against the missionary presence, Calgo also refused to speak to his opponent, a man called Chatim, without first discussing the matter with his own family. Like Calgo Naique, Chatim was a rebel, possibly from the family of the Santu Chatim family (or Santu Chatim himself).[36] The Portuguese Crown also executed him after the bloody events.

Once Calgo Naique refused to talk, a "sorcerer (*feiticeiro*)" apparently started a dance. While dancing he screamed like a "madman", the Jesuits wrote, inciting the locals to "go to the battle" and announcing that "the time had come". Who was this sorcerer? What was his status in the village? What was his relationship with the temples of the village?

Like other villages, Cuncolim had a vast and complex religious organisation. Historical sources show that Dravidian and Brahmanic

[36] Th. Aquinas, *Cuncolim is a Historical Village.*

deities were part of this organisation, as in Chorão and Sirula. Cuncolim also had temples dedicated to the founders of lineages. The names of temples in the village reveal alliances and negotiations between the groups settled there, either resulting from previous domination or a different migration dynamic. And, as in the other villages of Goa, the religious structure of Cuncolim mirrored to an extent its social structure, alliances, conflicts, negotiations, and specific history.[37]

According to an inventory of lands that belonged to the temples of Cuncolim, the village had a temple dedicated to Mahadeva which was destroyed by the Portuguese in 1567. Rebuilt by the locals, this temple hosted a Shivalinga Rameshwar in the sanctum, donated by Vitthaldas Vitthoji, a resident.[38] A temple of Shantadurga was paired with this Mahadeva temple. Shantadurga, who later substituted Santeri, combined traces of a Dravidian Durga with Shanta. The first was the goddess of blood and power who possessed the divine energy that allowed her to combat impure spirits, the second was a goddess inclined in the direction of peace. The goddess' double-edged character – similar in some ways to that of Ravalnath of Chorão – is central to understanding the devotional organisation of Cuncolim and the beliefs of its people at the time.

Another temple was that of Santeri, located over an anthill. That devotion to this anthill temple was active in early-modern Goa is made clear by Paulo da Trindade, who says Santeri was "that land that they worship and consider to be sacred." Father Pietro Berno had destroyed this temple during the earlier campaign of Gil Eanes de Mascarenhas.[39]

[37] HAG, nº 7583–7585, Foral de 1622, 932v.

[38] Pereira, *Goa – Hindu Temples*, 96.

[39] Trindade, *Conquista Espiritual do Oriente*, Vol. 1, 339. Did the people of Cuncolim also perceive the anthill (Santeri) as being constituted by souls, perhaps of ancestors of the community? There were also three Vaishnava temples – one to Rama, another to Krishna, and a third to Narayana Ramanatha; and temples to the lineage deities Golcho-Paik, Goddeamata, Sat-purusha, Siddha-purusha.

The anthill devotion, incomprehensible to Berno, also evoked an exemplary story compiled in the *Brahmavaivarta Purana*. In this narrative Indra, the Vedic god, was visited by Vishnu, dressed as a young Brahman. Vishnu saw a trail of ants passing by and laughed. "It was the ants that made me laugh," Vishnu said, but "do not ask me why." Indra asked Vishnu to explain himself. Vishnu answered: "O Indra, I saw the way the ants paraded in a grand procession. Each one was, in another time, an Indra. Like you, each one, by pious actions, acquired the title of King of the Gods. Nevertheless, now, after a multitude of rebirths, they have returned to the form of ants. This army is an army of ancient Indras."[40]

However, a female warrior, one of the representations of Santeri, is seen beside a lion and a mangled demon. This guardian goddess of the village could be a source of terror too. Unsurprisingly, her temple faced south, from where dark spirits were usually supposed to come. Like Shantadurga, Santeri had the power to confront and soothe earthly evil. This alliance, prevalent in South India, is also present in Parvati combined with Durga. Similarly, the combination of vegetarian and animal (and human) sacrifices, also practised in the village of Cuncolim, is evidence of a diverse sacred landscape.[41]

Sebastião Gonçalves' comment and Linschoten's observation that "they sacrificed men and committed other similar abominations" suggest devotional practices involving blood. Bloody sacrifices of roosters and sheep were frequent in territories bordering seventeenth-century Salcete, Bardez, and Tiswadi. Some of the Portuguese later condemned by the Inquisition participated in these rituals.[42] Many of these sacrifices happened in moments perceived as representing a danger to the cohesion of the village.

[40] Zimmer, *Mitos e símbolos,* 19.

[41] Heras, "Pre-Portuguese Remains", 19.

[42] This had been the case of Francisco Rangel, sentenced for having sacrificed a lamb in a local temple: v. IAN/TT, Tribunal do Santo Ofício, processo 8916.

In these situations, the guardian deities became more violent than the enemy, dismembering and destroying adversaries, regaining dominion over the physical and symbolic space under their jurisdiction.[43]

How did Cuncolim's pantheon represent the different lineages of its dominant families? The Naiks were associated with military activities, while the surname Prabhu referred to "intellectual" ones. However, the Naiks were dominant. The villages of Ambelim, Assolna, Velim, and Veroda – all satellites of Cuncolim – had people named Naik too, and the same Shaivite and Dravidian deities.[44] These similarities indicate that there were religious networks of temples associated with some lineages that transcended the limits of a village and translated into regional solidarity. Srinivas has emphasised the importance of such regional solidarities in other regions of India. Possibly this was the case with these five villages too, which were evidently regionally cohesive.[45]

Besides Naiks and Prabhus, the elites of Cuncolim included families whose surname was Chatim. As mentioned, the Chatims usually belonged to merchant groups established in the villages at a later date.

What were the relative social and political positions of these families? What was the hierarchy of their temples and religious practices? To what extent did the discord between the Chatims (merchants?) and the Naiks (warriors?), mentioned in missionary letters, reflect internal tensions? Did they reveal changing local lifestyles before the arrival of the Portuguese? Did these tensions also explain the bloodshed?

[43] On the relationship between violence and the sacred, see the inspiring study by R. Girard, *Violence and the Sacred.*

[44] In Veroda and Ambelim, Mahadeva and Durgadevata were among the main deities. Also, the surname Naik identifies the main families of these villages. In Velim and Assolna, Santeri was the main deity.

[45] The devotion to these deities of blood and power expanded to other villages too, in a devotional system that could link several villages: S. Bayly, *Saints, Goddesses and Kings*, Chapter 1.

A closer look at the role of the sorcerer may be revealing. The missionaries did not understand his functions in the context of the local order, but his role was certainly clear to the village population. According to Daniello Bartoli, the man's name was Pondu Naique, and he was a sorcerer and diviner.[46] Bartoli probably intended to seduce European readers with the "exoticism" of this figure. His colourful description apart, Bartoli transmitted reliable information, namely that the man belonged to one of Cuncolim's Naik families.

His gestures deserve closer analysis. The fact that he shook his hair loose, accompanied by uncontrolled movement, suggests the return to a state of nature, as was usual in certain rituals. In this state, passions and movements were free, evoking the transposition of a ritual and symbolic combat to a terrestrial stage. The gestures of the sorcerer and the others involved may assume religious overtones when interpreted within the context of local cultural codes.

Mahadeva, the main deity of Cuncolim, was an image of Shiva, and Shiva was also Nataraja, the lord of dance, a "pantomimic dance" that sought to "transform the dancer into the demon, god or terrestrial existence that was being interpreted." Heinrich Zimmer has suggested that "A war dance, for example, transforms those who dance it into warriors, arousing their bellicose virtues, converting them into intrepid heroes."[47] Veena Das corroborates this bellicose and heroic interpretation, affirming that actions such as loosening the hair, body, hands, and feet in more or less wild movements were gestures attributed to individuals in a liminal state. Many entered this state voluntarily, as in the case of warlocks, sorcerers, and seers. The textual descriptions of the sorcerer of Cuncolim indicate that his dance was probably part of this kind of performance.

Anthropological research on manifestations of goddesses linked to blood and power in South India – in regions proximate with the territories that constitute the modern-day state of Goa – confirm

[46] Bartoli, *L'Asia, parte prima,* 633.

[47] Zimmer, *Mitos e símbolos,* 156ff.

the continuing existence of such performances. Similar gestures heralded the unleashing of social disorder.[48] Initially, this behaviour mimicked animal postures, evoking wild aggression and imitating the bellicose fury of a military group. In a second phase, more elegant movements evoking a cosmic dance followed. They represented the body on the battlefield raised to a state of ecstasy and then to liberation. Both these rituals – the cosmic dance of Shiva and the possession of the goddess – fit missionary representations of the raging madness of the sorcerer Pondu.

The crescendo of violence that took place on 15 July 1583 suggests an extreme situation in Cuncolim which required extraordinary forms for restoring order. For Victor Turner the mechanisms used to resolve these sorts of social drama differed according to their nature and effects. They could range from mere advice to the performance of public rituals – which could involve sacrifices to exorcise an evil that had affected a village and to pacify the wrath of the gods.[49]

When dancing, Pondu Naique cried: "War! War, now is the time! Here you have them bound!"; and "this is a good gift and of many heads"; and cries to the effect that the demons wanted five roosters as a sacrifice. What did these cries indicate? The sacrifice of roosters was locally common, and the five roosters here probably substituted – i.e. represented – the undesirable humans who had to be done away with. It would seem plausible to assert that on that day the sorcerer-priests had access to the actual sacrificial offering, not just its representation. "By their actions of language and bodily attitudes, they express an intimate emotion saturated with collective intentionality, which is spatially marked just as the voluntary behaviours are governed by rules commonly accepted in a locality."[50] Applying Jackie Assayag's argument to our context,

[48] Assayag, *La colère de la déesse*.

[49] Turner, *The Ritual Process*.

[50] This forms part of a set of "ethnographic" records collected by Jackie Assayag and Gilles Tarabout in South India, with the objective of restoring this network of relations: Assayag and Tarabout, *La Possession de la Déesse*, 430ff. See also the interesting study by Brenda Beck, *Peasant Society in Konku*.

Pondu Naique may have been expressing feelings "saturated with collective intentionality". The missionary presence was an appropriate occasion for the execution of a ritual sacrifice, of which Pondu Naique would be the initiator. The sacrifice would reinforce not only internal cohesion in the village but also indicate its preeminence to the four dependent villages.

The five Jesuits killed were Rudolfo Acquaviva, a Neapolitan; Pietro Berno, a Lombard; Alfonso Pacheco, a Galician; António Francisco and Brother Francisco Aranha, both Portuguese. Other casualties included two Brahman children converted to Christianity, three adult Brahmans, and one Portuguese. Also wounded were some of the fifty who had arrived at the village.

The decapitations and mutilations of the Jesuits corroborate the idea that the killings were a ritual act. Gashes on top of Pietro Berno's head, a mutilated ear, and castration followed by stuffing into the victim's mouth his own sexual organs were known forms of defiling the bodies of enemies before killing them. Such mutilations were frequent in political and religious conflicts in other villages of South India during this period.[51]

The dying Brother Francisco Aranha was subjected to other rites, apparently standard in the interaction of Muslims with delinquents. The locals dragged him to their idols, then made him stand on one foot and bow down to them. Aranha's response was to say he was "unlike them, not a beast who worshipped sticks and stones." The narratives add that they covered "the body with wounds and arrows [making him] into another new and glorious martyr Sebastian."[52] After this killing, the residents of Cuncolim are believed to have made manifest their great sacrificial glee, smearing their victim's blood on the village's chief deity. This state of exhilaration continued until the handing over of all the bodies. The narratives say that "they were still like man-eating tigers, licking the blood of the ministers of the Gospel."

A few days after the event the viceroy of Goa, Dom Francisco

[51] S. Bayly, *Saints, Goddesses and Kings*, 53.

[52] Afonso, *No tempo em que todos eram santos,* 581–3.

Mascarenhas (r. 1581–1584), punished sixteen local residents identified as leaders of the rebellion. These men, termed "traitors", lost their lives and all their properties. The Crown extinguished the *gaunkaris* of the five villages and their territories were taken over by the Portuguese Crown. The Crown then gave the villages of Cuncolim and Veroda to Dom João da Silva, and on the same day the other villages – Ambelim, Assolna, and Velim – were handed over to Dom Pedro de Castro, who then donated them to the Jesuits.[53]

Vicente Villalobos, the Portuguese captain responsible for Salcete, carried out the punishment, impaling the heads of the sixteen in the centre of the village.[54] "The *curumbins* [i.e. *kunbis*, rural labourers] and other humble folk of the said Villages", however, escaped retribution. They were apparently needed to cultivate the lands. According to accounts of the time, other residents of Cuncolim fled to neighbouring lands, where they remained.

The Crown's intentions were clear. Punishing the elites was necessary to prevent others "at any other time to commit similar actions". Simultaneously, soothing the population working the fields guaranteed the Crown its revenues.

It is apparent that after this episode Cuncolim entered into a state of impoverishment that was visible even in 1722, when an eighteenth-century account notes that, unlike the Christian villages of Salcete, its lands were sterile. A plague of rats had destroyed crops in a field facing a chapel that stood on the ground where the events of 1583 had taken place. Rented by non-Christians who wished to sow sugarcane there, the land had proven barren. Local villagers had begun going to Christian churches instead, and thereafter the rat infestation came to an end.[55]

Cultural stigmatisation supplemented the political and economic punishment.[56] An official report of 1722 which sought to describe the state of various villages in Goa mentions many of

[53] IAN/TT, Cartório Jesuítico, Mss. 89, nº 21 – "Traslado da doação de D. Pedro de Castro".

[54] *Admirabile Vida,* 224.

[55] Budrioli, *Segni maravigliosi,* 108–13.

[56] I use this concept as articulated by Erving Goffman's *Stigma.*

the residents of the village remaining non-Christian. The Jesuits were in Salcete for more than 150 years but failed when it came to converting Cuncolim. Legends also attest to the Gentile condition of the village, while another eighteenth-century description says a family of Cuncolim communicated with each other via gruesome sounds that sounded like canine howling. This family was apparently descended of a dog that had, in 1583, discovered the decaying body of one of the missionaries. Consequently, the family had lost its ability to speak and sought refuge in a forest. This trope of vocal and auditory devastation echoes descriptions included in Megasthenes' third-century BCE account and reproduced by Pliny, Isidore of Seville, Mandeville, and others. The accounts narrate the existence of beings with the body of a man and the head of a dog. Readers of these texts were well aware of such representations and probably associated the hapless villagers with a bestial world.

Physical deaths, a political death, discursive relegation, diminution in status, economic impoverishment: the 1583 incident changed the status of these villages for centuries. From the Christian point of view, Cuncolim was an exemplary case. During the seventeenth century, memory of the repression did its work.[57] Forty years later, residents of Cuncolim were the first to resist attempted entry by the forces of the Bijapur captain of Ponda. "The residents of that village took up arms, and successively pushed them out of there," requesting military support from the governor – which was forthcoming – to prevent entry of the forces of the Adil Shah. The governor's aim was to avoid "them being discouraged and deserting the village [and instead] occupy themselves only by monitoring and guarding our lands against any attempt which might be made against them." The governor naturally wished to ensure that the Crown did not "provide any reason or occasion for disruption".[58]

[57] Scott, *Weapons of the Weak*, 40.

[58] Pissurlencar, *Assentos do Conselho de Estado*, Vol. 1, 185–6.

Christians began remembering Cuncolim primarily for 1583. The *Chronologia* of the Goan priest Sebastião do Rego glorifies an ancestor of the founder of the Congregation of the Oratory of Goa because he was one of the local Christians killed in Cuncolim alongside the Jesuit missionaries. In this way martyrdom was linked to the history of a recent congregation of local Brahmans, ennobling their Christian lineage in the process.[59] Missionary accounts said that the blood spilt on these lands fertilised a veritable "garden of Christianity". After the killings, other Christians in Goa were said to want to go on pilgrimage to Salcete to touch the bodies of the missionaries. "They were all given licence to pass and to avenge willingly, in those villages, the death of the priests," says one description. A group of about thirty left for this pilgrimage from the city of Goa. In Rachol and Margão – the centres of conversion in Salcete – many people awaited the bodies.[60] According to other Portuguese sources, after these events about 1500 locals converted to Christianity. In 1586 and 1587 another five villages converted, as did four in 1588. At this time, there were 1900 baptisms and 2000 catechumens. They imbibed Christian learning "with great joy, and to the utter amazement of the Faithful." This amazement was the greater since this region "was particularly obstinate in its idolatry . . . If someone talked about becoming a Christian it meant being immediately killed."[61]

The enthusiasm for converting to Christianity resulted, the missionaries said, in a further 3850 baptisms in 1590. The conversions continued apace and those that did not wish to convert had to leave. This was the case in Chorão: Christianity came to occupy the centre of the local order, with the expulsion of non-Christians to the margins. Exclusion and ostracism were the destiny of those who did not conform with the new social and religious mores.

[59] BA, Cod. 51–VI–33 – Miscellanea Civil, e Ecclesiastica por hum Religioso d'Alcobaça, 69.

[60] Report of Father Alessandro Valignano, s.j., 1583: DI, Vol. 12, 929.

[61] Budrioli, *Segni maravigliosi,* 40–1.

The martyrdoms of Cuncolim were the result of confrontation between forms of imperial domination and the interests of local communities. As mentioned, Christian domination began to interfere in areas such as access to power, prestige, honour, land, and women. These interferences changed quotidian village life. It is not surprising, therefore, to encounter situations of more intense resistance in places such as Cuncolim, where the military might of the Crown of Portugal was less pronounced and the proximity to Bijapur loomed large. By contrast, in places closer to the heart of the Portuguese government, as in Chorão, there was greater acquiescence among the elites.

The events at Cuncolim reveal the violence entailed in the process of conversion and Christianisation of the population of Goa, especially when the localities involved were on the borders of Portuguese dominion. They offer a clear example of the difficulty faced by the Portuguese Crown in getting a hold over the populations of villages that were only about thirty kilometres from Goa, capital of the Estado da Índia, to conform politically and militarily, and to convert. Twelve years after the Bijapuri siege of Goa (1570–1), these events represented a severe threat to the Portuguese Crown, making clear the fragility not only of the Portuguese geopolitical situation but also of the power of the Crown of Portugal. To the north of the River Mandovi, that is, in parts of Bardez, the situation was not significantly different from that south of the Zuari.

Periphery and Resistance

"It has been learnt that in Bardez, in the territories of the king of Portugal on the mainland, some Brahmans have shown contempt for a cross. They beat a friar of St Francis, who lived in a house there and left him almost dead. They feared that this friar had destroyed some pagodas, which are idols and devils."[62] Brother

[62] Cristóvão Luís' report was published in DHMPPO, Vol. 8, 485.

Cristóvão Luís thus summarised the situation of Bardez in 1561. In the 1560s many villagers forearmed themselves (or resisted) against Christianisation. The regular clergy was quite aware of this. Nevertheless, in 1566 Viceroy Dom Antão de Noronha (1564–1568) published a decree of prohibition that extended to Bardez as well against the repair of temples and deities, the intent of the viceroy being their absolute destruction and substitution with churches and Christian saints, which is what eventually happened.[63]

As with Salcete, the Adil Shah of Bijapur tried to maintain his influence over these villages. Skirmishes between Christians and non-Christians were frequent in Bardez. In 1576 a treaty of peace with Bijapur, after the so-called "war of Gorca Prabhu", was intended to settle the situation. This "war" started with the setting on fire of the Church of Nagoa by Gentiles and soldiers of Bijapur encamped in that village. Some *gaunkars* of Nagoa supported the people of Bijapur, while others denounced their presence to Portuguese agents. Portuguese soldiers entered the village and fresh skirmishes were the result.[64]

The incident in Nagoa is emblematic of local conflicts because of the Portuguese presence in Bardez. As in Salcete, in many villages here a section of the villagers resented the Portuguese imperial presence, preferring to be ruled by Bijapur.

Fernão Martins, *gaunkar* of Sirula, and André Furtado, his cousin, also a *gaunkar* of the same village, both nominally Christian, were part of the new revolts. According to a report of Friar Simão da Nazaré, Fernão Martins "rose in the war of Gorca Prabhu against the state and burned our Church of Nagoa." As punishment "he served fourteen years in the galleys."[65]

Sirula, as mentioned before, was the principal village of Bardez.

[63] Decree of Dom Antão de Noronha, 1566: CR–APO, Fasc. 5, Vol. 2, 612–14.

[64] On this, see also CR–APO, Fasc. 5, Part I, 823–31.

[65] IAN/TT, Manuscritos da Livraria, Cod. 1777 – "Relação de papeis autênticos jurados", 43v.

Even if its territories did not include the lands of Nagoa, the *gaunkars* of Sirula had connections with the *gaunkars* of other villages. Apparently, the *gaunkars* of Sirula joined those of Nagoa in the context of an agreement on mutual aid and assistance of other sorts. As in Cuncolim, the "war of Gorca Prabhu" was fought on a regional scale.

The disquiet in the villages of Bardez continued into the second decade of the seventeenth century. A report of 12 February 1619, written by the Procurador da Coroa e da Fazenda, suggests agitation in Bardez. He states that the "poor there were greatly harassed and pressured, all because of the force and tyrannies used by the tax collectors as well as the carelessness of the Pai dos Cristãos and the ambition of the Rectors."[66] Although this complaint by an officer seeking to defend the interests of the Crown against other jurisdictions is typical, the information registered coincides with the situation between Simão de Nazaré and the Crown authorities.

Information on the case is relatively abundant. It ranges from declarations on the efficacy of the Pai dos Cristãos in the conversion of Bardez to negative references in the *Livro de Visita* (Book of the Visit) of the Goan Inquisition, dated 1632.[67] The Visitor accused Friar Simão de Nazaré of many ill deeds. The same is evident in a set of papers from 1621, part of a lawsuit against Nazaré.[68] These documents provide a synchronic view of the conflicted atmosphere in Bardez over the first decades of the seventeenth century. The Archbishop of Goa praised Nazaré for "helping to clean up the lands of thieves, and evildoers, and others, and executing those guilty of visits to their goddess." His activities resulted in "bringing peace, after driving away from [these lands] many thieves, and raiders." In 1611, for example, when a

[66] AHU, Índia, Cx. 6, nº 29 – "Do procurador da Coroa e Fazenda", 12 Feb. 1619.

[67] AHU, Índia, Cx 5, nº 34 – "Carta de frei Simão da Nazareth", 24 Jan. 1618.

[68] IAN/TT, Manuscritos da Livraria, Cod. 1777 – "Relação de papeis autênticos jurados", and Inquisição – Livro da Visita, 1632.

ship from Malindi (in East Africa) had run aground on the shore in Bardez, the Portuguese authorities arrested many residents of Anjuna, Calangute, and Arpora for robbing the ship (apparently because of information provided by the friar). Another victory of Nazaré involved the expulsion of a rebel named Arnaique, "freeing the residents of the said Bardez as well as the neighbouring lands." Besides the bandits, thieves, and raiders that these documents reveal, they suggest that residents of one village were pitted against another, that some villages opposed others, and that yet other villages resisted the Portuguese presence.[69]

The opposition to Nazaré's activities and to those of other Franciscans was predictably considerable. One local faction sought to get rid of the Franciscans while retaining their temples and devotional practices. According to the Christian *gaunkars* of Candolim, another chief village of Bardez, Calangute was the centre of such opposition. Its leader was Sante Prabhu, a *gaunkar*. The faction was against Nazaré, "inviting other people to follow them". They aimed to remove Nazaré "from the post he occupied [and] which was damaging to them". In 1621 this *gaunkar* of Calangute openly accused Nazaré of being responsible for the death of one of his nephews. These accusations resulted in Prabhu and other residents of Calangute ending up in the galleys, after having been flogged and their beards shorn.[70]

In the course of this case many locals assembled accusations against Simão da Nazaré and documents to prove them. They handed these to the Portuguese nobleman Diogo de Sousa Menezes, asking him to forward them for inspection by the commissar general of the Franciscans. The *gaunkars* threatened to kill him if he did not. They also threatened to flee to the land of the "Moors", for

[69] IAN/TT, Manuscritos da Livraria, Cod. 1777 – "Relação de papeis autênticos jurados", fls 2–6; CR–APO, Fasc. 6, 1006. See also a letter of 1616 from the Archbishop of Goa to the king, cited in Araújo, "O 'Pai dos Christãos'", 322–3.

[70] IAN/TT, Manuscritos da Livraria, Cod. 1777 – "Relação de papeis autênticos jurados", 20–1.

"they had no life in the said lands with the said priest." The situation in Bardez was so tense that it led António Calado, councillor of the Câmara de Goa, to declare that "they were all mutineers in Bardez."[71]

Nazaré's erratic activities, which involved him in local politics and shifted his support across various groups, need to be studied in depth to understand the filigree of relationships established between imperial agents and local populations.[72] However, the resistance against Nazaré was not so different from that against other Franciscan parish priests in Bardez or against the priests of Tiswadi and Salcete. A decree of the Mesa da Consciência e Ordens dated 23 December 1630 recognised that "there were complaints that the parish priests of India mistreated their parishioners, and vexed the new converts with work." This description converges with the statement of the Procurador of 1619. He also accused parish priests of keeping Christians "in their service as if they were slaves".[73]

The tensions between parish priests, officials of the Crown, and the villagers were part of a generalised context of conflict. There were also conflicts between the Crown and religious orders, between the secular clergy and the regular clergy, amongst the regular clergy, and between the laity and the rest. Awareness of these tensions by local elites could help them in the pursuit of their self-interest. Denunciations made against enemies were enabled; the words of the Procurador are telling – he said that in Salcete "the oppression is very great, but even the Portuguese and officials do not speak about it in order to survive, since they do not want to be their [the Jesuits'] enemies fearing their writings." His critique gives legitimacy to complaints by the local people against parish priests as well. [74]

[71] Ibid. fls 24v.–25.

[72] IAN/TT, Inquisição, Livro da Visita, 1632.

[73] IAN/TT, Mesa da Consciência e Ordens, nº 303, Aranha, Meza das Tres Ordens, Vol. II, fls 38, 40.

[74] AHU, Índia, Cx. 6, nº 29 – "Do procurador da Coroa e Fazenda", 12 Feb. 1619. In the first half of the seventeenth century, the conflicts between the Franciscans of Portugal and the Franciscans of India, for example, were

The excesses of these parish priests were sometimes zealous excesses. One case in Anjuna persisted in collective memory because of the excesses of the rector of the church there. In 1609 the vicar and the friars of Anjuna obliged locals to become Christians "by force" – so the villagers complained. Two decades later the new rector of Anjuna ordered a pregnant woman to register her son in the parish immediately after his birth. The non-Christians of the village rebelled against his warning. The priest threatened them with secular force in order to oblige the woman to obey. The villagers then beat him brutally. This is yet one more case showing local opposition to the missionaries, especially in villages close to the borders with Bijapur. The continuous petitions, complaints, and petty revolts against a range of issues – from custody over orphans to the excesses of priests, missionaries, and Christians– suggest that the peripheries were actively resisting conversion.[75]

Resistance was also continuous in the villages on the banks of the River Chapora in north Bardez. This river separated the lands of the Portuguese Crown from those of the Sultan of Bijapur. Unsurprisingly, the populations of these villages remained much closer in spirit to Bijapur. It was stated by one viceroy that their location on a "sandy plain" made them more vulnerable to conquest. The people of Aldona, in the interior of Bardez, abandoned homesteads and fields but returned in 1605 at the insistence of the central power. A document of 1722 says the Crown accused them of ill deeds, without specifying their nature.[76] A Jesuit treatise concerned

intense: BA, Cod. 47–VIII–6 – Decreta s. congregationis episcoporum & regularum, 23, but also 47–VIII–7 – Decreta s. congregationis episcoporum & regularum, 660–98.

[75] The petition of Gangay, wife of Quelma Chatim, resident of Calangute, stated that she had sons and daughters that the missionaries wanted to take away. See also the petitions of Bellu Chatim against Manuel de Moura, judge of the orphans, in 1594; of Ratna Naiquinny, 1609; of Vitula Porobu and Goinda Porobu of the same year; of Goinda Chatim and of Gunnavanta Chatim; of Ramay, 1632; of Bapuni Sinai, 1652: BA, Cod. 46–XIII–31 – Collecçoens das ordens reaes antigas, e modernas, fls 18v.–23.

[76] HAG nº 44 – Comunidades (Aldona).

with the rights of Jesuits in the villages of Salcete says that, on account of revolts, other villages of Bardez "were taken from the *gaunkars*, and given to individuals." According to this document, the heirs of Vidal Bravo possessed Chapora, and António Francisco Moniz held Adsolim.[77]

Occasionally, missionaries even helped villagers to resist and revolt, acting as a counter-power and mobilising local populations against the interests of the Crown, the local government, and some Portuguese elites. This alliance between missionaries and local populations vs colonists/Crown has been studied for places outside Goa but is a dimension practically unexplored in relation to the Goan experience.

Signed by Miguel de Moura in the name of Philip II and sent to the viceroy of India in January 1596, a letter says that "many of the Religious of the Company [of Jesus] gain places in India not only in the government and management of everything . . . [but have] secretly advised some residents of Chaul that, with a good conscience, they can resist the creation of a customs-house and the payment of duties that they rightfully owe there." The Jesuits had questioned whether the artillery was the property of the monarch, arguing that the penalty of excommunication could not extend to those who stole artillery. The secretary invited the viceroy to enquire secretly into the matter with the archbishop, and then call on the provincial of the Jesuits to be chastised for "such a careless and imprudent case". He needed to be told to "deal only with the ministry that is their business, and [that they] should not interfere in other areas in which they should not explicitly be involved, neither as religious nor as prudent people." Similar situations developed in Bassein and Thana.[78]

These examples illustrate the complexity of the forms of resistance and revolt in the Estado da Índia. Social interaction was dominated by the opposition between Christian and non-Christian, coloniser and colonised. Nevertheless, one also sees the transversal

[77] IAN/TT, Cartório Jesuítico, Mss. 86, nº 19 – Escrituras de bens e doações de terras.

[78] CR–APO, Fasc. 3, 583–95.

networks of interests, the grouping and realignment of strategies, sometimes rather unexpected.

The preceding pages have shown that there was a geographical pattern in the resistance against the Portuguese, and that this was more frequent and explicit when the villages were distant from the city of Goa. They were more common in Bardez and Salcete, which were closer and contiguous to Bijapur territory, than in Tiswadi, which was not only the "Portuguese" heart, as it were, but effectively an island and easier to defend. The peripheral villages continued to be the first to join external forces – the Adil Shah's and later the Marathas – which sought, at various times, to invade the territories of Goa and expel the Portuguese. The Christianisation of the imagination did not in many of these villages replace collective memory of the past. They remained keenly against the Portuguese. However, exemplary punishments and the "memory of repression" that they entailed, helped curb revolts similar to those of 1583. Nevertheless, revolts both small and not insignificant continued throughout the period.

Everyday forms of resistance here were as crucial as revolts elsewhere. The persistence of prohibited religious practices even at the end of the seventeenth century is evidence of the cultural resistance to Christianisation. A document by a Pai dos Cristãos says the villagers of Goa spent large sums on festivals and pilgrimages to the temples located in Bijapur territory. These temples housed the deities that had fled their villages. The document says one particular individual spent 14,000 xerafins on building a temple, another 8000 xerafins for a ceremonial dance, and 4000 for a tank. A few years later, in a letter to Dom Pedro II in 1700, the viceroy of Goa mentioned the presence of dancers coming in from Bijapur to participate in Christian processions. They did not uncover their heads during the passage of the saints, while others refused to listen to Christian doctrine.[79]

[79] BA, Cod. 46–XIII–31, Collecçoens das ordens reaes antigas, e modernas, fls 25v.–26, fl. 90.

By 1716 it seems from the evidence that many villagers continued to flee to the interior. In Salcete the Jesuits made up a list of all non-Christians, which contributed to a fresh abandoning of lands and proved extremely detrimental to the finances of the Crown. A document argued against the Jesuit intention to renew sixteenth-century decrees justifying recourse to coercive conversions. By this time theological debates concluded that neither the king nor the Church should exercise power over the consciences of non-Christian vassals. Both institutions feared upsetting the political balance.

The fragility of Portuguese domination in these territories explains some eighteenth-century decisions. The loss of crucial fortresses to the Dutch (and to a lesser extent the English), the sieges of Goa, and the territorial ambitions of the Marathas weakened Portuguese power. In this context, Father Manuel de Sá pointed out that it was critical to avoid great commotion. He remembered the events in France, where revocation of the Edict of Nantes had led to the abandoning of territory by thousands of Protestant heretics. Friar Manuel da Natividade, a theologian who had lived in India for thirty-five years, held a similar opinion. He argued that *epikeia* (dispensing with the law in the name of the common good) justified the idea that the Crown should not proceed along confrontational lines.[80]

The ambiguity inherent in certain forms of resistance, and the multiple possibilities of interpretation and political uses that these polysemic practices could entail, also characterised the practice of compromise and collaboration. A memorial of 1627 evaluating the power of the Portuguese Crown in India asks whether the Portuguese Crown should allow "the entry [into Goa] of all the miserable Gentiles of the land of the Adil Shah." The author argues that "if they are already Christians, there would be a reason to receive them." The same did not apply, however, to those that remain "idolaters". The Crown should then impede their entry,

[80] Ibid., fls 91–110.

the document said, since "they would serve only to infest the land and consume foodstuffs so that the Christians have them for a higher cost." It concluded that the Crown should take its decision based on Realpolitik, or "Reason of State".[81]

This document is also interesting because it reveals an opposite flow: of populations living under the dominion of Bijapur trying to enter the Estado da Índia. Just as the territories of Bijapur were attractive to discontented subjects of the Portuguese Crown, the territories of Goa were apparently enticing to some of the subjects of the Adil Shah. The great famine of 1630–2 would have been an additional reason. Later, there were the uprisings of the Marathas against Bijapur, which disturbed several areas.[82] Perhaps some of these immigrants knew that certain inhabitants of Goa had thrived under the Portuguese imperial order, with many who had agreed to conversion being transformed into genuine Christians despite earlier being labelled Gentiles.

These issues are discussed in the last chapter.

[81] BA, Cod. 51–VII–30, "Memorial sobre o poder que o rei tinha na India, 1627", fl. 120. Similar situations had already been identified in the previous century: D'Costa, *The Christianisation of Goan Islands*, 135ff.

[82] The criticisms against the excessive presence of Gentiles in the territories of the Portuguese Crown date from the late-sixteenth century. On this, see *Monsoon Books*, Vol. 1, 153-154; CR–APO, Fasc. 1, Vol. 2, 77–83; Fasc. 5, Vol. 3, 1397–8; Fasc. 6, Vol. 2, 1245–7. On the instability also experienced by the neighbouring territories of Goa, see Gordon, *The Marathas*.

7

The Defence of the "Genuine Nobility"

Conflicts of Memory, Identity, and Power

THE EARLIER CHAPTERS have suggested that the processes of conversion to Christianity and Christianisation of the inhabitants of Goan villages were crucial to preserve the Portuguese empire in the region. Christianisation was the route to constituting a distinct cultural and political identity for people and territories. However, the process was not linear. Tension and conflict, as well as varying choices and attitudes, were evident.

As much as adherence to Christianity, everyday forms of resistance and open revolts such as the martyrdom at Cuncolim were aspects of these attitudes. Local people reacted variously to the colonisers, as one might expect, since they were "the established", that is, those to whom the territories of Goa "belonged". This history was the history of their region; the colonisers were outsiders. In such interactions, the "outsiders" usually adopted the rules of those who had established themselves, and not the other way round.[1] Yet the Portuguese colonisers, truly believing in their right to rule the territories of Goa, were also transforming themselves into the "established". Their belief referred to a political culture

[1] This interpretation recalls the theoretical framework of Elias and Scotson, *The Established and the Outsiders.*

with Aquinian roots which had long affirmed that Christians were meant to govern non-Christians.

The conflict of perceptions had multiple expressions. Two of the most interesting were the processes of Indianisation of some colonists, the classic move of "going native", and the reverse process of "going Portuguese" of many among the colonised. Both processes resulted in a not-always-welcome proximity of colonisers and colonised Christians. Many inhabitants of Goa, however, remained impervious to the transformations of the physical, social, and cultural landscape. The indifference was an expression of their refusal to adapt to the new political and cultural order.

The reasons for these different outcomes were also diverse. The local populations harboured different memories of the past and diverse receptions of experiences since 1510. There were also distinct ways of life in the villages of Goa. The variety is also evident within families, and, in the most dramatic cases, within the same individual.

From a particular moment on, Christian signs started to populate the memory of certain groups. Their consciousness of social position and identity had, from this time on, a central connection with Christianity. Children learned Christianity from early childhood, as well as the Portuguese language and the cognitive and expressive system it entailed. As Father António Collaço put it, schools were useful "for war and the government of the Republic, and also for the family itself."[2] Furthermore, wearing Christian clothes, changing food habits, and Christianisation of the landscape contributed to the internalisation of the Christian model.

For many families that had initially adhered to Christianity for pragmatic reasons – as a way of preserving their social position in the medium and long term – the Christian model became a point of reference. Eventually, old memories and practices were recalled, integrated, or excluded in the functioning of the new norms. This change established in Goa what Paulo Freire has defined as

[2] IAN/TT, Cartório Jesuítico, Mss. 56, nº 56 – "Parecer de Lopo Mendes".

"a culture of silence". Those in the new culture were increasingly unable to relate with the earlier history, yet also had difficulties in communicating with the new history to which they now belonged.[3]

Christianisation did not obliterate pre-existing rivalries between the various Goan groups, whether at the social apex or the base. Some of these conflicts had ancient roots, pre-dating the arrival of the Portuguese. Others had emerged with the arrival of new elites subsequent to the Portuguese presence. All this had happened alongside increasing tensions between colonists and colonised elites.

The nineteenth-century *Esplendor do Oriente, Genealogia das famílias mais ilustres da Índia* (Splendour of the Orient, Genealogy of the Most Illustrious Families of India), and later the *Nobiliarchia Bracmana* (Brahmanic Nobiliarchy) by Filipe Nery Xavier, and the later genealogical compilation *Luso-descendentes* by Jorge Forjaz, exemplify these struggles, which continued well into post-colonial times.

In the ensuing pages, I identify the emergence of specific interpretations of history defending the positions of some of these groups. Maintenance of their social power depended on their ability to forge individual historical narratives. These included either the history of "mankind" or the history of "community", and their position within them. This chapter focuses, therefore, on battles for memory. It privileges three treatises, written in Portuguese and published in the metropole, which represent the voices of Portuguese creole elites, the Brahmans, and the Chardos of Goa. They are all precious sources for social meanings within a discursive dynamic.

First, I recall some moments in the sixteenth and seventeenth centuries that led to conflicts between the colonists and the colonised, focusing on a treatise written by a Portuguese creole. Then, in the second part of the chapter, I focus on texts produced by

[3] See, again, Clignet, "Damned if You Do, Damned if You Don't", 84.

some of the colonised which argued in the main that their noble status was higher than that of their local rivals.

Institutional Routines, Social Alignments, Discursive (Re)inventions

"*Puo essere per ventura pericoloso*" (it could be dangerous): Cardinal Oriulzi read these words in a letter written on 8 June 1630 and sent from Lisbon. In this letter the Collector of Portugal – the official of the Papacy authorised to collect the rents of the Papacy in Portugal and its empire – explained his fears at the social situation of the College of Reis Magos in Bardez. The college taught Portuguese and Indian boys to become missionaries in the various parts of India. Fifty years earlier the Jesuit Father Melchior Carneiro had prophesied that the young "will be the true apostles of this land, and [members of] the religious orders their curates." Similar thinking had led to the founding of this Franciscan college. However, the Collector said, the Franciscan friars had underestimated the intellectual capacities of the local populations. They had considered them unfit for the sacred orders and had only entrusted them with minor tasks, such as being acolytes in religious ceremonies. In a second letter that the Collector of Portugal wrote to Oriulzi on the same day, he praised the skills and intellect of the people of India and their capacity for missionary work. Besides, he said, they knew the local language and culture and had a natural affection for the people.[4]

The Collector's description of the College of the Magi represents the situation of other colleges too. The imperial agents differentiated between the Portuguese and Indians. Although at the end of the sixteenth century the Dutch traveller Linschoten wrote that in Goa the smallest was equal to the greatest and there was no distinction between them, the truth is that the Dutchman had not grasped the complicated order of distinctions that operated

[4] ASCPF, Scritture Originali, nº 98, fls 77, 85.

in Goa among people of Portuguese origin. There were multiple distinctions between the Portuguese, namely those coming from the metropole and those settled in Goa. Linschoten had however noticed a clear hierarchy between the Portuguese and the locals.[5]

In the last quarter of the seventeenth century Giovanni Careri wrote in his *Giro del Mondo* (Voyage around the World) that Jews and Muslims lived separately in Goa and could not practise their religion publicly.[6] Had Careri travelled earlier he would have noticed that non-Christians also lived in separate quarters. Other texts of the same period expose a web of distinctions which operated in the Goan region. The organisation of the city of Goa was distinct from that of the villages of Salcete, Bardez, and Tiswadi. Goa had multiple communities, ethnicities, and religions. Despite the continued presence of non-Christians in these villages, they were becoming Christian. The spatial organisation of the village expressed this goal: the centre of the village, with a church, was called the *povoação* (settlement). Christians usually lived within this area.

The closest to a photographic image of Goa available for the first half of the seventeenth century is in the works of António Bocarro, who tells us that in the fortress of Reis Magos in Bardez, near the Franciscan college and seminary, the *casados* had farms, palm groves, floodplains, and houses of stone. At least three slaves assisted them. Many military people lived there: 1647 musketeers, 1140 cavalrymen, and 157 archers. This fortress and church apart, there were more than sixteen churches with Franciscan parishes in Bardez. These received revenues that had accrued to destroyed local temples; two others had private funding. Unfortunately, Bocarro says nothing about local peoples' housing.[7]

In Tiswadi, Bocarro's gaze lingers on the village of Panjim (or Panaji), the future Nova Goa (New Goa). This was a residential zone of the Portuguese comprising about thirty single-storeyed and two-storeyed houses. This architectural style characterised the villages and towns of Goa. On this, the French traveller Charles Dellon

[5] Linschoten, *Itinerário*, 150.

[6] *Viaggiatori del 600,* 701ff.

[7] Bocarro, *Década 13 da História da Índia*, 211–12.

says the Portuguese houses of Chorão were "about the same as the Parisians' . . . in the villages around Paris."[8] Venturing a little further east, Bocarro gives us a glimpse of the Ribandar Bridge, a testament to Viceroy Count of Linhares. On the border with Bijapur territory the river crossing of Naroa boasted a small castle, the houses of the captain and his family, and, as in Reis Magos, whitewashed houses where the Portuguese lived. The convent of Madre de Deus was at another river crossing. The captain and *tanadar* of Dauguim lived in large two-storeyed houses. Social hierarchy was also in evidence on the banks of the Mandovi River and visible in the dimensions and styles of dwellings and populations established there – the two-storeyed or single-storeyed houses. The same held good at the crossing of St Lawrence, from where the road to Salcete began.

Bocarro's voyage ended in the southernmost region of Salcete. Primarily interested in evidence of the means of defence, he refers to the forts of Mormugão and Rachol. The Rachol fort was a significant stronghold on the river, alongside large two-storeyed houses and the residence of their captain. In Salcete, there were 13,840 men-at-arms, besides other Portuguese and the Jesuits. The rest of the population was of local origin.[9]

Although an exceptional document, Bocarro's description of the built landscape is focused solely on the colonisers. The colonised are only referred to when they perform a military function. Bocarro does not give an account of the multiple social realignments that were occurring under the institutional routines he so magnificently depicts. For example, it is impossible to work out if some of the houses of the local populations resembled those that Bocarro recognises as Portuguese, and whether the latter's dwellings sometimes also reproduced local typologies.[10] Such hybridisms, or forms of miscegenation, are not visible in this type of documentation.

[8] Dellon, *Voyages de Mr. Dellon*, 278, 377–8, 402.

[9] Bocarro, *Década 13 da História da Índia*, 211–12.

[10] About these typologies and their transformation, see Silveira, *A Casa-Pátio de Goa*.

The colonisers did, we know, increasingly feel the need to establish criteria that would hierarchise the different varieties of Christians within the new imperial order. For example, only those of Portuguese descent were to enjoy the "privileges and freedoms of the city". Even though the converted populations were legally the equals of the "old Christians",[11] new criteria of distinction emerged to reduce the legal privileges to which the newly converted were entitled.[12]

Bocarro's description does not refer to the policy of exclusion of foreigners in either the kingdom or in the Estado da Índia. Partially resulting from the same grid of norms, this policy was articulated both in relation to the geopolitical scenario of the Estado da Índia – namely, the confrontations between the Iberian monarchy, and the Dutch and English East India Companies – as well as social situations internal to the imperial space.

This policy manifested itself in successive *cartas régias* against foreigners who had availed of the benefits of Portuguese laws and petitioned for naturalisation, against people who went to India and the other conquests, and against those who remained there without permission.[13] The policy resulted in the valorisation of all those who, in the eyes of the Crown, had naturalised themselves by legitimate means. This legitimate naturalisation applied to local converts to Christianity. Under the rule of equivalence between *generatio* and *regeneratio*, they were *pleno iure* (i.e. with full rights) subjects of the king of Portugal. A royal letter of 1617 associates the benefits of this policy to the war against the Dutch and the English. To keep the peace – and to preserve the Estado da

[11] This situation was similar to the Spanish empire, analysed in Herzog, *Vecinos y Estranjeros.*

[12] Linschoten, *Itinerário*, 150.

[13] Norms of this type can be found in *Monsoon Books*, Vol. 1, 47–8; Vol. 2, 195–7; Vol. 3, 7, 318; J.A. Figueiredo, *Synopsis Chronologica*, Vol. II, 274; Ribeiro, *Indice Chronologico*, Part 1, 24, 62; Part 5, 37; but also, CR-APO, Fasc. 3, 92–7. The Portuguese settled in the Spanish overseas territories suffered the same type of pressure: Gould, "Los extranjeros", 63ff.

Índia – "it is not practical to divide the forces nor to displease the natives, but rather to keep them calm and confident, using all possible devices to bring about hatred between them and the foreigners."[14]

This calm and confidence could be achieved, for example, by the granting of privileges, conceding to local elites the offices of governance which they had been denied until then, and allowing this class of people to meet some of the needs – in terms of human resources – of the imperial administration.[15] Because foreigners were very detrimental to "that Estado on account of the information they gathered regarding its affairs and communicated to those of their nation," the doors were increasingly closed to this group who, a century earlier, had helped the Portuguese Crown establish itself in these same places.

Even as the Crown imposed restrictions on foreigners, there was growing awareness among the local native elites that this strategy favoured them.[16] It is necessary to revisit the beginnings of the settlement of the Portuguese in these places to access the multiple meanings of these scenarios.

In the initial decades, and for a short period, the king of Portugal encouraged the settlement of Portuguese citizens through marriage with local women and the establishment of households in the Indian territories. Several *cartas régias* refer to "the many services we have received from the inhabitants of our city of Goa," and the royal interest in "conceding them grants and benefices . . .

[14] *Monsoon Books,* Vol. 4, 109–17.

[15] See the *carta régia* of João III of 1642: CR-APO, Fasc. 2, 120, and the decrees in favour of the integration of local Christians in the labour market: CR-APO, Fasc. 5, Vol. 2, 933–4; DHMPPO, Vol. 12, 406.

[16] The letters between the Câmara de Goa and the Crown of Portugal are very suggestive of the social environment of the Estado da Índia. See, as illustrations, IAN/TT, Corpo Cronológico, Part I, Maço. 31, nº 83 – "Carta da Câmara de Goa, dando parte a ElRey, chegar o Conde da Vidigueia áquella Cidade", 31 Oct. 1524; Maço 68, nº 85 – "Carta da Câmara de Goa a ElRey sobre os aggravos que recebêra do Vice Rey", 20 Nov. 1540, and a letter of 1595 published in CR-APO, Fasc. 1, Vol. 2, 5–22.

as it is right for kings and princes to do to those who serve them well." The preference for generational ties – under the aegis of the *pater* – over conjugal ties legitimised the marriage of Portuguese men with local women since these marriages did not disqualify Portuguese men and their children.[17] Which is to say that Afonso de Albuquerque believed his marriage policy did not threaten the preservation of the "Portuguese nation", as understood at the time. Initially, as is clear from a letter of 25 December 1510, Albuquerque believed that "the very tillers [of the land] shall be the Portuguese." Some years later he warned Dom Manuel I that he might have to "cast out the natives of the island", instead giving their lands and fields to the Portuguese settled there. But ultimately, issuing the orders promoting the marriages of the Portuguese in India and the creation of Christian families seemed the only way to "make settlements " and "create fresh households".[18] To establish a household, to build a house, to "brush, plough, and plant trees" appeared to be the best way of rooting the Portuguese, as well as of creating the conditions for establishing a local Western *civitas*.[19]

The intention was to transform the city of Goa into a colony in the classical sense of the term, i.e. in line with the colonies of

[17] Hespanha, "A família", 273–4.

[18] BP-APO, I–3, Part 1, 152, 406; CR-APO, Fasc. 2, 120ff.; Fasc. 5, Part I, 12–16.

[19] For this reason, marriages of local men converted to Christianity were encouraged, as well as settling in these places. There are many royal orders and local decisions between 1511 and 1514 encouraging such unions. However, hierarchy was the ruling principle behind this policy too. On this, see, among others, IAN/TT, Corpo Cronológico, Part I – Mç. 16, nº 65 – "Carta de Afonso de Albuquerque", 25 Oct. 1514; Part II – Mç. 25, nº 53 – "Mandado de Afonso de Albuquerque", 12 Feb. 1511; Mç. 26, nº 24 – "Ordem de Afonso de Albuquerque", 9 April 1511; nº 49 – "Ordem do capitão–mor de Goa", 12 April 1511; Mç. 28, nº 13 – "Mandado de Diogo Mendes de Vasconcelos", 20 August 1511; Mç. 35, nº 58 – "Mandado de Afonso de Albuquerque", 5 Nov. 1512; nº 174 – "Mandado de Afonso de Albuquerque", 30 Nov. 1512; Mç. 36, nº 54 – "Mandado de Afonso de Albuquerque", 24 Dec. 1512"; nº 69 – "Mandado de Afonso de Albuquerque", 28 Dec. 1512.

the Greeks and Romans. It is therefore not surprising that the Portuguese colonists, the *casados*, became the most privileged among those who resided in the territories of Goa, for it was on them that the imperial foundations primarily rested. At the time, it was believed that the sustainability of the city of Goa and of its hinterland depended on them.

From the moment that baptism (the *regeneratio*) began to replace *ius sanguinis* (*generatio*) as the main criterion of inclusion and exclusion in the Portuguese imperial order, other feelings of belonging emerged among the Portuguese. In order to preserve their privileged status and economic well-being, the Portuguese in the Estado da Índia recalled the relevance of their nationhood, articulated now in a different way. For many, belonging to the Portuguese nation was not limited to *ius sanguinis*, to *gens*, and blood lineage.[20] Belonging to the Portuguese nation implied combining several elements of distinction: linguistic competence, a history of allegiance to the Christian religion, place of birth, colour, intellectual capacity.[21] This combination justifying the Portuguese established in the Estado da Índia continued to apply in the offices of imperial and local governance and in maintaining the relationship between coloniser and colonised in its initial forms.

Who were these Portuguese? Since 1517 Dom Manuel I had granted the privilege of all offices of governance, justice, and revenue collection to the *casados* "wherever they fit well", a privilege reiterated several times throughout the sixteenth century.[22] Since

[20] Geneviève Bouchon underlined, years ago, the increase of endogamy within the Portuguese community from the mid sixteenth century: Bouchon, *Afonso de Albuquerque*, 89ff.

[21] On the elements that favoured the continuity of an ethnic identity, see Smith, *The Ethnic Origins of Nation,* 96–7; Dirks, ed., *Colonialism and Culture*, "Introduction".

[22] That same year, the king explained that the governing positions in the municipality were reserved for "the casados and their inhabitants that are of Portuguese nation and descent, and they should not be given to anyone of other nation, descent and quality": CR-APO, F. 2, 10–11, 115–16.

then, a significant number of such offices had been controlled or occupied by members of this group. It was only at the end of the sixteenth century, under the Iberian Union, that threats to this primacy began to emerge from several quarters.

By examining correspondence exchanged between the municipal councils of Goa and Lisbon it becomes possible to access the dominant feelings of the first generations of colonisers. Their criticisms of 1585, which reached a high degree of hostility in 1596, express their opposition to foreigners (including "*homens de nação*", or "men of the nation", that is to say New Christians and the "newly converted".[23] The content of this correspondence conveys an insistence on the preservation of privileges that the municipal council had acquired. Although the councillors did not oppose the granting of benefits to the "Christians of the land", they were unwilling to accept a situation in which such advantages meant an equalisation of the status of the two groups.[24] Their reputation was at stake, because some had compared the descendants of the Portuguese with the New Christians. "I am informed that the [female] orphans who go from this kingdom by my order to those parts do not marry immediately. When they marry, they do so with people of poor quality, New Christians, and mestizos", read a royal letter of 1608. In it the king asked the viceroy to marry orphans with persons of quality, that is to say, those without either Indian or New Christian blood.[25]

The case of Gonçalo Velozo, born in Goa of Portuguese descent, exemplifies the situation. Though he was the Vicar General of

[23] On these criticisms, see *Monsoon Books*, Vol. III, 9–11, 413–14; CRAPO, Fasc. 1, Vol. 2, 31, 140–60, 168–98; Fasc. 5, Vol. 3, 73–97; Fasc. 6, Vol. 2, 1011–13.

[24] Some of these criticisms were already present in the mid-sixteenth century: IAN/TT, Corpo Cronológico, Part I, Mç. 68, nº 85; Mç. 71, nº 10.

[25] *Monsoon Books*, Vol. 1, 191–2, 126–8. In this context, it is worth remembering Diogo do Couto's commentary, in his *Soldado Prático,* concerning the marriages between Portuguese soldiers and women of "linseed colour": Couto, *Soldado Prático*.

Goa, he was unable to reach the position of Deacon of the Cathedral of Goa because he was of the "race of [New] Christians". This decision contradicted that of the Mesa da Consciência and is evidence of the ambiguous status of the *casados*. The Crown increasingly excluded them from the royal definition of "possessing quality", and consequently having access to certain benefits. The same discourse informs the "Inquiries regarding the attributes, and qualities, which persons [in India] will have to have" in order to enter the Orders of Christ, Saint James, and Avis, set out in 1602. They prevented those who had "Moors, Jews or Gentiles" among their ancestors or "were reputed to do so" from acquiring these distinctions, thereby excluding the majority of *casados* who were of Indian descent. In 1620 the same principle applied to bar access to many ecclesiastical offices.[26]

The dominant discourses on nobility and lineage informed these decisions. These discourses claimed that "ancient" nobility "began with a person, and continued and extended from children to grandchildren, to constitute a set of relations or lineage."[27] Moreover, European astronomical and geographical knowledge had over time hierarchised the world. Temperate Europe and its inhabitants were, of course, at the centre, and tropical India – propitious to human degeneration – was not.[28] The *casados* did not fit well in either discourse.

[26] A decree of Mesa da Consciência e Ordens refers, precisely, to the caution needed in relation to these issues: IAN/TT, Mesa da Consciência e Ordens, nº 302–6, Aranha, *Meza das Tres Ordens*, Vol. 3, fl. 16; 53v; CR–APO, F.6, 739.

[27] I use here the of 1655 definition of Manuel Severim de Faria, cited by Nuno Monteiro: see Monteiro, "Casa e Linhagem", 44.

[28] These experiences should be compared with those, in the same period, in the American territories of the Spanish monarchy. Also, there the first generation of colonisers were experiencing a process of downgrading. See, among others, Gruzinski, *La Colonisation de l'Imaginaire*; Bernand and Gruzinski, *Histoire du Nouveau Monde,* Vol. II, Chapter 6; Cañizares Esguerra, "New World, New Stars"; Cañizares Esguerra, *How to Write the History;* Elliott, *Empires of the Atlantic World*, Chapter 8.

Several works, including Jean Bodin's *Methodus ad facilem historiarum cognitionem*, François de Belleforest's *Histoire Universelle du Monde*, Pierre Charron's treatise *La Sagesse*, and Giovanni Botero's works *Relazioni Universali* and *Della ragion di stato* argued that the three geographic-climatic areas of the world determined the nature of their inhabitants.[29] The temperate zones included Europe, the northern parts of Asia, and Western America. Their inhabitants were deemed the most proficient. The cold zones included the Arctic and Antarctic. The third were the tropical zones, including Africa and Ethiopia, the south-western coast of India, the Moluccas, Java, and Taprobane (contemporary Sri Lanka). The inhabitants of these regions – the theory postulated – were unable to govern themselves.[30]

In his celebrated sixteenth-century text *Colóquios,* Garcia de Orta explained some of the effects of a tropical climate on people's illnesses.[31] The reception and appropriation of his text (as distinct from its actual contents) confirmed the argument that a tropical climate was not well suited to the human body. It stimulated sensuality, carnality, vicious desires, and a corruption of the natural order of things. Given its "continual heat", Valignano wrote, India "is very contrary to the spirit, and debilitates and weakens bodies and spirits." For these reasons, the Italian Jesuit wanted missionaries "well mortified in their passions", for only then might they survive the bodily challenges that climate posed.[32] Valignano was

[29] Botero said that the "intermediate peoples, being in a place between the North and the South, consequently govern themselves righteously, through justice and reason, and were therefore inventors of laws, illustrators of politics, and masters of arts of peace and weapons": Botero, *Da Razão de Estado*, 43. See also Gossiaux, *L'Homme et la Nature,* 140–2, 159; Hogden, *Early Anthropology*, 279ff.

[30] In Valignano's words, "it seems, as Aristotle said, that their nature is to serve": Valignano, *Sumario de las cosas que pertenecen a la Yndia Oriental,* in DHMPPO, Vol. 12, 475.

[31] Barreto, *Descobrimentos e Renascimento*; Županov, "Drugs, Health, Bodies".

[32] Valignano, *Sumario de las cosas que pertenecen a la Yndia Oriental,* DHMPPO, Vol. 12, 575–6.

producing a particular reading of Orta as well as echoing Bishop Dom Duarte Nunes.

He was also echoing the *Soldado Prático* of Diogo do Couto. Couto had argued that Indian soil was by its very nature bad. Men there were infernal by inclination, causing him to rage that here in India "good thoughts and desires change in a manner that is astonishing." Other parts of the *Soldado Prático*, however, evoke the image of a natural paradise as characteristic of these places. Here, Couto says it was the Portuguese who had been responsible for the corruption of this paradise:

> The purest, most excellent airs of the world, the best and most healthy fruits and waters from sources and rivers of all the earth are in India. [One finds] bread, barley, all the vegetables, all the greens, cattle large and small, that can sustain the world, and all these are most wonderful. The worst is that we have ruined such a marvellous land with our lies, falsehoods, mockery, trickery, covetousness, injustices, and other vices of which I will not speak.[33]

It was a common belief in this period that climate and humours were interlinked, moulding bodies and souls. These beliefs had naturally influenced or prejudiced the *casados*. Blood, place of birth, and cultural hybridisation seemed to devalue their very being. If the argument that Christians should govern those who were not Christians justified their initial supremacy,[34] in a new cultural context there was simultaneously this twist of fate diminishing the *casados* and those descended of them.[35]

[33] Couto, *O Soldado Prático*, 37, 104, 215.

[34] Aquinas, *Somme Contre les Gentiles*. See Hespanha, *Panorama da História Institucional*, 30; Clavero, *Derecho Indígena*, 5–6, 13ff.

[35] The institution that represented them – the Goa Municipal Council – was increasingly the object of Crown interference. This was met with growing unease, as mentioned earlier. See, among others, Corpo Cronológico, Part I, Mç. 66, nº 1 – "Traslado de Aggravo que entrepozeram os Moradores da Cidade de Gôa, do Vice Rey D. Garcia de Noronha", 11 Oct. 1539; Mç. 71, nº 10 – "Carta de Thomé Rodrigues Soares, 17 Nov. 1541; AHU, India, Cx. 3, nº 19 – "Da câmara de Goa, para o rei", 22 Jan. 1615.

This devaluation militated against a legal decision at the beginning of the seventeenth century stating that he "who is born and lives in Goa or Brazil, or Angola" is as Portuguese as he who "lives and is born in Lisbon". Contradicting this were the differences of social status manifest in the consolidation of the categories *reinol* (born in the metropole) as opposed to *indiático* (born in India), *brasílico* (born in Brazil), and *angolense* (born in Angola).[36]

A royal letter of 25 March 1688 exemplifies the situation. This missive refers to a previous order of the Count of Alvor, by which it had been decided that the Portuguese who held offices and rents of the Crown could have their daughters inherit these only "if they [were] married to noble Portuguese born in the kingdom." The consequence was a reduction in the economic power of the *casados* and their male descendants. Power was weighted in favour of the *reinóis,* over whom the Crown had greater control.[37]

This decision of the Count of Alvor provoked immediate reactions from the *casados*. They argued "that they were equally Portuguese, and many of them *fidalgos.* Even though they had been born in India [they were] descended from fathers and grandfathers who had come from the kingdom. In this way, they would become poor and helpless. They would not find women to marry and reproduce. This would cause them hunger and need. "[38]

The claim of being as Portuguese as the *reinóis* reveals the stigmatisation of the *casados*. Giovanni Careri also noticed that Indian women disdained the Portuguese born in India and sought those arriving from the kingdom. He says this was because those born in the subcontinent had an inferior status.[39]

[36] BA, Cod. 51–VI–54, "Relação sobre a precedência q/ se deve dar ao consº da India", fl. 73. For the "brasílicos", see among others Kantor, *Esquecidos e Renascidos*; Kantor, "Do Dilúvio Universal ao Pai Tomé"; and for the "angolenses", Madeira Santos, "De antigos conquistadores a angolenses".

[37] The discussions in the Conselho Ultramarino throughout the 1640s and early 1650s reflect precisely this tension and the difficulty in managing the demands of the various groups established or about to be established in the state of India: Barros, *O Conselho Ultramarino*, 177ff.

[38] *Apud* Lobato, "Sobre os prazos da Índia", 465.

[39] *Viaggiatori del '600,* 700.

One of the views that best represents the problems of the *casados* is to be found in the writings of Friar Miguel da Purificação. The son of Portuguese parents, Purificação was a native of Tarapur (near Mumbai) in India, a Franciscan of the Province of São Tomé, custodian of the same Province, and its Procurator General. With this status he pursued the former Viceroy Dom Miguel de Noronha to the court of Felipe IV (r. 1621–1640) in Madrid. Purificação alleged that in Madrid Noronha sought to destroy the reputation of the Franciscans of India. He aimed to put an end to Noronha's plans. While in Madrid, this Franciscan friar had various meetings to solve the problem. On this leg of his journey he was received by Felipe IV. Later in Rome he even kissed the hand of the pope.[40]

In 1640 Purificação published a little treatise in Barcelona called *Relacion Defensiva dos filhos de S. Tomé.* He dedicated the treatise to Friar Paulo da Trindade, author of *Conquista Espiritual do Oriente*. The treatise magnificently articulates the systems of distinction that operated in Goa and is an excellent supplement to Bocarro's description. An advocate of the Portuguese community which resided in the Estado da Índia and saw itself as the "first conquerors", Purificação affirmed that

> the sons of the Orient, of such an inferior place, are very capable of government. Their birth in the Orient should not mean exclusion from the honours and dignities. For that reason, those who had qualities, letters, merits, and virtues should be highly esteemed and admitted to all honours and dignities. They should be equated with Eve who was formed in Paradise, that is, with all that are born in high, sublime, and honourable places.[41]

[40] Purificação, *Relação Defensiva.*

[41] Ibid., fls 31v., 57v.

[42] In 1636, the Mesa da Consciência e Ordens had ordered the Franciscans not to elect friars born in India as prelates. In 1640, one consultation pointed in the opposite direction, but another from 1643 reveals that it was not successful: IAN/TT, Mesa da Consciência e Ordens, nº 302–6, Aranha: *Meza das Tres Ordens*, Vol. 2, fls 69–9v., 71–2. Besides the conflict between "indiáticos" and the "reinóis", Purificação was also involved in the

Miguel da Purificação's immediate goal was that *indiáticos* be nominated to superior positions in the Province of São Tomé. This included the position of commissioner general of the two Provinces that had been settled in India, São Tomé and Madre de Deus. Purificação intended to prevent those who were "Indians by blood" and the Portuguese born in Portugal – and professed in the Province of Portugal – from obtaining these positions. His treatise, however, represents much more than the Franciscan position.[42] The Franciscan and *casado* aspirations were similar, with different expressions in time and space.[43] Purificação aimed to guarantee, simultaneously, the primacy of the *casados* in relation to the *reinóis* as well as to the Brahmans and Chardos of Goa. He played on two stages: that of rivalries within the colonisers, and conflicts between colonisers and the colonised.

Agreeing with the climatic theories circulating in Europe, Purificação began by assuming that the Orient was inferior, different from Europe with its "high, sublime, and honourable places". However, he differentiated the "quality" of the *indiáticos* from the "quality" of their place of birth. That is, regardless of where they were born, their "qualities" should be the first criterion to admit them "to all honours and dignities". On folio 33 the Franciscan suggests that works and virtues – merit – were the marks of genuine nobility, not lineage and place of birth. Hence, those who had "attributes, letters, merits, and virtues" were to "be equated with the Eve formed in Paradise". A set of exemplary biographies of "the children of India", i.e. the descendants of the Portuguese – "which

jurisidictional conflict that opposed the Observant Franciscans of India to those of Portugal and to the Recollects of India. This latter conflict is clear in a plea sent to the pope in 1658, in which violent accusations were made against the friars of the Mother of God: BA, Cod., 47–VIII–6 – Decreta s. congregationis episcoporum & regularum, 651–77; BA, Cod., 47–VIII–7, Decreta s. congregationis episcoporum & regularum, 660–98.

[43] A similar situation is the attempt by the "mestizo Dominican Friars" to form a Dominican Province separate from that of Portugal, an initiative which was impeded by Rome: IAN/TT, Mesa da Consciência e Ordens, nº 302–6, Aranha: Meza das Tres Ordens, Vol. III, fl. 69.

is my intent, and not the Indian natives" – completed this part of the argument. Purificação concluded that *casados/indiáticos* were valorous soldiers, hard-working, virtuous, of illustrious blood, proud and brave captains.[44]

Despite his praise of virtue and good works, Purificação's main argument was different. Later, he explains that letters and virtues, value and bravery, were associated with an invariable quality: blood. The "sons of India" were "of clean blood" and not "black, as the opposing party says, nor even mestizos, but well-born, of Portuguese mothers and fathers, and nobles by birth."[45] Their noble place of birth, the earthly paradise, only added to their other virtuous qualities.[46]

The social hierarchy prevailing in Goa was, in his understanding, the following: The well-born were the *indiáticos,* sons of Portuguese mothers and fathers, nobles and hereditary *fidalgos;* after them came the *castiços* and mestizos who had grandparents or parents from one side, who were Indian/Gentile; finally, the Indians. *Castiços*, mestizos, and Indians all had some Indian blood. Therefore, they were low-born. The difference between a well-born and a low-born was an "infallible consequence" after the experience through a "sensible medium" – this sensitive medium being the vision which allowed experiencing the difference between a Portuguese born in India and an Indian. Such a vision proved the absolute separation between two bodies born in the same place. To demonstrate his view, Purificação took with him to Rome an "Indian Negro" so that everybody could see what his treatise had argued. The image – he himself with the "Negro" – and the caption (i.e. the treatise) rounded off his delineation of the concept.[47]

This treatise by Purificação did not resolve the tensions between

[44] Purificação, *Relação Defensiva,* fl. 13.

[45] Ibid., fl. 22v. About the semantic relationship between purity of blood and nobility, and its consequences in the Iberian experiences in the overseas territories, see Zuñiga, "La voix du sang", *passim.*

[46] Purificação recalls an already outdated medieval topos that Paradise was probably located in India: Delumeau, *História do Paraíso*, 107ff.

[47] Purificação, *Vida Evangélica*, 196.

indiáticos, *reinóis*, and local elites. Another treatise, *Libra Oriental*, written sometime before 1656, discussed the same topics.[48] In the eighteenth century Viceroy Dom Luís Xavier de Menezes apparently initiated the genealogy called the *Esplendor do Oriente* (Splendour of the Orient). Ended in 1806 by João Lobo da Silveira, this genealogy intended to untangle families born in India who were genuinely Portuguese from those who had mixed blood but passed themselves off as Portuguese.[49]

While the Portuguese born in India felt harassed in the new political and social contexts, the elites of local origin who had converted to Christianity aspired to better positions.[50] Legal benefits offered to converts by the Portuguese Crown from 1540 on were taken seriously by them. The royal decrees of 1542 were emblematic. One assigned to residents of the city of Goa a status equal to those of Lisbon. Another extended the benefits of the *casados* to everyone Christian who married and settled in Goa city. Although the *Ordenações* of the kingdom required a specific period for the newly converted to enjoy the rights of "settlers" as well as the privileges and liberties associated with them, these decrees created a new political order within which converted Indians settled in the city of Goa were legally equal to the Portuguese. Later, the second decree was expanded to all territories of Goa (Salcete and Bardez included) and confirmed in 1557, 1559, and over the ensuing decades.[51]

Offices in the municipality were among the most desired on account of their high prestige. These offices offered significant

[48] ARSI, Goana 34, fls 526–30.

[49] IAN/TT, Manuscritos da Livraria, Cod. 1952 – *Esplendor do Oriente, Genealogia das Famílias mais ilustres da Índia.*

[50] It is important to remember that because of their privileged status as financial supporters of the Estado da Índia, there were still non-Christian families settled in territories under Portuguese direct rule throughout the sixteenth and the seventeenth centuries: Pearson, *The Portuguese in India*; Ames, *Renascent Empire?*

[51] CR-APO, Fasc. 2, 48–69, 120–2; Fasc. 5, Part I, 386–7; Vol. 3, 979, 983–4, 987, and 1157–8.

political and material advantages. According to the *Ordenações Filipinas,* aldermen were "to have charge of all the governance of the land, so that the land, and the inhabitants thereof may prosper";[52] to resolve judicial cases (violations of market regulations, property disputes, injuries); and to assist ordinary judges. The councillor had an obligation to make a general inspection of the city. The procurator was to defend the cases and interests of the municipality *vis-à-vis* the government of the viceroy and the "citizens". The viceroy periodically consulted them for their opinion on more general decisions involving the life of the city. Other offices amplified and executed the powers inherent in the higher offices. A treasurer was required to collect the regular taxes for the municipality, which also had the right to fines and rents, to the leasing of shops and the market square, and to other municipal taxes. The city also employed a clerk, a superintendent of public works, a judge, inspectors of the market, an accountant, a tax collector, an appraiser of houses and rural property, and village judges.[53]

The applicability of these two decrees was limited, however, by another decree of the same year, 1542. This decree explained that the offices of the municipality were exclusive "to those *casados* and residents of the City, who are Portuguese by nation and by ancestry, and not to any others of any other nation, ancestry, and quality whatsoever." Only the first were "people who know well how to rule and govern".[54] In the middle of the sixteenth century the Portuguese Crown did not contemplate candidates for administrative positions other than those of Portuguese descent. As Charles Boxer noted, a few exceptions apart, this principle applied until the eighteenth century.[55]

[52] Cited in Hespanha, *As Vésperas do Leviathan*, 161.

[53] Souza, *Goa Medieval*, 131–4.

[54] Similarly, two days after Queen Dona Catarina of Áustria confirmed the equal status of the Portuguese and the Christians of Goa in 1559, another law restricted the advantages that conversion could bring to those enslaved: CR-APO, Fasc. 2, 115–16; Fasc. 5, Part I, 390–2.

[55] Boxer, "A Note on Portuguese Missionary Methods".

In sum, the inclusive, assimilating, and equalising horizon of some laws could be reduced by recourse to legitimate legal and institutional means, thereby impeding the legal equalisation of Goa's social groups.[56] The legal categories "Christians of the land", "Christians of India", and "newly converted", which were recurrent in royal decrees and laws, ensured the continuity of the difference.[57]

The local populations, especially their elites, did not welcome the reduction of rights entailed in the initial decrees of 1542 and started to complain.[58] The Crown's response to such petitions was to reiterate the promises in its decree. A *carta régia* of King Dom Sebastião dated 1572 referred to some of these petitions. The locals said that their privileges "not only were not maintained" but that Portuguese agents imposed "many injustices and tyrannies". These attitudes "brought much loss to their properties, and danger to their lives."[59] In order to prevent the injustice, the king was committed to satisfying some of their aspirations. A decade later another *carta régia* was about the appointment to offices and positions of the "Christians of the land" if they "had the attributes and requirements". This letter explicitly defended the position that capable "Christians of the land" could participate "in the governance

[56] This case offers interesting parallels with what was happening in the kingdom with the New Christians of Jewish origin. While theoretically identical to the other inhabitants of the kingdom since 1507; in practice, after that decree, there were many restrictions that hindered this equalising impetus.

[57] See, for example, CR-APO, Fasc. 5, Vol. 2, 512–13. Also relevant is the law of November 1601 that prohibited insults to the local converted people, namely by using the word *Cristão-Novo* (New Christian), Marrano, Jewish, or any other such insult: A. Figueiredo, *Synopsis Chronologica*, Vol. 2, 288–9; IAN/TT, Livro 2 de Leis, fl. 53v.

[58] IAN/TT, Corpo Cronológico, Part I, Mç. 58, nº 7; AHU, India, Cx. 3, nº 40 – " Carta dos gentios Pomdia e Goimda, ao rei"; Cx. 9, nº 43 – "Carta do Conde Almirante ao rei sobre uma petição feita pelos gancares de Loutolim", 2 March 1626.

[59] This letter of Dom Sebastião is published in DHMPPO, Vol. 12, 252. See also CR-APO, Fasc. 5, Vol. 2, 748–9.

of the said lands, in public positions and offices, in which the Portuguese serve." The king believed that "with this favour, the conversion of the Gentiles would be further augmented."[60] Accordingly, Viceroy Aires de Saldanha (r. 1600–1605) rewarded António Rodrigues as he had "converted to our holy faith and always helped the fathers of the Company in the festivals of conversion, where infinitely many Christians were made. He has not received any reward or favour of the Crown until now. Because he was penniless and with wife and family . . ." The viceroy assigned him lands which had been forfeited by the heirs of Diogo Fernandes "the Strong".[61]

The fragility of the Estado da Índia after the English and Dutch put it under attack also explains some of these concessions to local elites. This is attested to by the proposal of 1615, according to which the viceroy "ought to have some [villages] distributed to the *Lascarins* who serve me [the king] with fidelity, so that with this [document] they may be confirmed in it. You will order, that they be very well taken care of, so that with these allowances for their sustenance, they will remain secure in their loyalty. They would be obliged to my service, and rejoice in taking part with all punctuality."[62]

By 1633 a petition from the converted people of Salcete requested the Crown for possession of lands and farms that were vacant because they belonged to fleeing non-Christian countrymen. The terminology of the petition is enlightening. It referred to "poor Christians, widows and orphans", underlining the paternalist nature of the process of conversion.[63] As elaborated in earlier

[60] This other letter is in CR-APO, Fasc. 5, Vol. 3, 989.

[61] Similar documents can be found in *Monsoon Books*, Vol. 1, 244–5 and 313–18; Vol. 2, 66–7; Vol. 3, 355–6. On land transactions, see HAG, nº 824 – Provisões do Colégio de Rachol, 1596–1680, fls 31–51.

[62] *Monsoon Books*, Vol. 3, 270.

[63] The petitions of "poor widows" increased from the second half of the sixteenth century onwards. A royal letter of 1607 warned against the power of the widows, but others of 1608 and 1614 point towards the opposite

chapters, the poor, the widows, and the orphans, like everyone in need of guardianship, had a privileged status under Portuguese law. The semantic parallels between them and the "newly converted" opened up a new path of political negotiation that was exploited by some of their number.[64] Nevertheless, the Portuguese Crown declined the requests in the petition of 1633.[65]

More than supporting one or other social group, the Portuguese Crown invested in a social and political balance conducive to the preservation of its rule. In the case of the Estado da Índia, the Crown supported some of those who sought power, trying at the same time to ensure that none of these groups enjoyed excessive power. It conceded favours and offices according to convenience and opportunity, that is to say, for reasons of state.[66]

A *carta régia* of 1607 expresses this economy of prudence. This document shows a concern for the priests of the parishes of Goa. The king established a hierarchy of preferences combining function, appropriateness to function, and group identity. The *carta régia* sets out that these offices are to be occupied, first, by secular clerics who know the language; then by the religious with *officium parocchi* (parish care) as long as they master the local tongues; and, in the absence thereof, by "native *canarins* of the land". This was in effect to say that the locals only had access to these offices when the "Portuguese" regular clergy ran into some insuperable

---

direction: *Monsoon Books*, Vol. I, 118–19, 160–73; Vol. 3, 203–4; CR-APO, Fasc. 5, Vol. 3, 1489–1492–4. See also the cases referred to in Foral de Salcete, copy of 1585, HAG, nº 3071, fls 546–55; in Foral de 1622, HAG, nº 7583–5, Vol. 1, fls 10v, 25v, 32, 45–45v, 49, and 50–2; Vol. 3, fls 932–3; in Foral de Salcete of 1622, summary of 1635, HAG, nº 7604, fls 8–62; Foral Antigo de Bardez of 1649, HAG, nº 7587, 49ff.; and Assentos do Conselho da Fazenda, HAG, nº 1160, fls 114 and 267–267v.

[64] This agreed with the legal doctrine that argued that the "poor" had access to judicial offices, as well as ecclesiastic offices: Velasco, *De Privilegiis Pauperum*, I, q. 6 and q. 7.

[65] CR-APO, Fasc. 5, Vol. 3, 1403–4n.

[66] Botero, *Da Razão de Estado*, 119; *Monsoon Books*, Vol. V, 374–5.

difficulty. Access to priestly positions by the "native clergy" was another focus of tension. Even in the late-seventeenth and early-eighteenth centuries the local elites were continuing to complain on the issue.[67] At the end of the eighteenth century this sense of dissatisfaction was one of the driving forces in the "revolt of the Pintos" of 1787, the most significant upheaval against Portuguese metropolitan power in the territory.

If there was a limit on local access to religious offices, so was it in relation to offices of justice. In 1608 a decision specified that the office of *catual* (i.e. *kotwal*, police officer, jailor) was not to be awarded to "men of the land, and many newly converted, in whom there is always little truth." The judge of the orphans could, however, be a native subject.[68]

These decrees show the difficulties of responding to the demands of local elites. The Crown relied on the Pai dos Cristãos, to whom was delegated the selection of "Christians of the land" most capable of exercising imperial offices according to "their quality and merits and services".[69] The Brahmans Jordão and Guilherme Pereira were among the lucky. They obtained positions as clerks at the Conselho da Fazenda.[70]

A final example relates to lawsuits and the expertise demonstrated by local lawyers involved in them. The *gaunkars* of Salcete accused Diniz and Jerónimo Mendes of committing various tyrannies. They took "many lands and grounds" of the villages of Curtorim, Benaulim, Utordá, and Davorlim, as well as "many

[67] *Monsoon Books*, Vol. I, 84, 157–61, 359–60; CR-APO, Fasc. 6, Vol. 2, 1118–19. The situation changed in 1618, when the "canarins" were prevented access to the secular clergy: *Monsoon Books*, Vol. 4, 344–5; CR-APO, Fasc. 6, Vol. 2, 1159–60. On the reasons for this situation, see "Colecção de Papeis varios, que dizem respeito ao Governo Ecclesiastico, & Secular do Estado da Índia", ACL, Série Vermelha, nº 34.

[68] *Monsoon Books*, Vol. 1, 203–10.

[69] CR-APO, Fasc. 5, Part 2, 911–12. See also CR-APO, Fasc. 5, Part 2, 913fn., 914fn.

[70] HAG, nº 8779, Cartas, Provisões e Alvarás Régios, Regimentos e Leis, L. 1, fl. 146.

farms of private individuals" in Margão, Camorlim, and other villages. They did not pay their labourers. Moreover, they robbed "ash and salt and pairs of oxen to farm their farms without pay", and "evildoers, thieves, and sorcerers" lived on their land. In addition, these men terrorised villages and abused the women in them. Finally, as if these tyrannies were not enough, Diniz and Mendes moved lawsuits against all those who denounced them and won the suits with the use of false testimonies. In this way they were "getting into said lands, taking other people's farms and *gaunkaris*, without the descent to be a *gaunkar*."[71]

This manner of exploitation of the interstices of the legal system characterised seventeenth-century Goa, most clearly by manipulative uses of the language of domination. Local converts deployed the idiom for a single purpose: to improve and optimise their position within the imperial order. After complaining about the poverty of the Portuguese, Diogo do Couto referred to the undesirable rise of the "Indians . . . The Brahmans, who become Christians, soon learn this doctrine of ours and soon become fraudsters and cheaters, and they know the order of judgment better than the prosecutors themselves, that this is what we have been teaching them."[72] The Crown also said that they regularly committed irregularities "in the criminal and civil lawsuits, which they initiate, either personally or through intermediaries, and against the Portuguese residents of the said city and islands."[73] It noted that they had won many of these suits.

From the middle of the sixteenth century the participation of locals in judicial processes had increased significantly. The increase in conflicts justified the nomination of a Judge of the Christians of the Land in 1581.[74] The following decade saw the amendment

[71] *Monsoon Books*, Vol. 3, 320–4. See also, CR-APO, Fasc. 3, 361–2; Fasc. 5, Part 3, 975–6, 991–2.

[72] Couto, *O Soldado Prático*, 149.

[73] HAG, nº 9530 – Assentos do Conselho de Estado, 1618–24, fls 182v.–183; CR-APO, Fasc. 5, Part 3, 1374–5, 1420–6.

[74] CR-APO, Fasc. 5, Part 3, 974–5.

of some of the processual rules involving situations of conflict. The new rules stipulated that judicial proof use the Portuguese language. Moreover, the court had to confirm the documents of the donations referred to in the plaint "under pain of not being admitted". Excluded from the matter of proof were the old *olas* (palm-leaf manuscripts) written in the Kannada language, which was a severe blow to local judicial practices.[75] Until then palm leaves had been the primary medium for recording the most crucial information concerning land distribution, payments of tax, and the various transactions carried out within the village and between villagers. Henceforth, by contrast, the Portuguese courts would only accept paper documents in which the pages had to be countersigned by a Portuguese officer. It was in this period, too, that the decisions of the *gaunkari* started to be recorded in books made of paper.[76] The imposition of a particular vocabulary, judicial procedures, and "Portuguese" paper was part of the process of westernisation of the territories of Goa.[77] However, reiterations of this type of legislation revealed its ineffectiveness – generating tensions between colonisers and colonised – as well as the difficulties faced by the Portuguese in imposing their way of doing things.[78]

The perplexity and indignation with which many Portuguese

[75] CR-APO, Fasc. 5, Part 3, 1323–4. In this way, the Crown reserved the right not to recognise certain powers and situations, which could ultimately revert in its favour. Something similar happened in relation to the tax administration: HAG, Conselho da Fazenda, Assentos, nº 1160, fl. 229.

[76] See, in this context, the information included in the first pages of the codex HAG, nº 10226, Comunidades – Cortalim, 1614.

[77] Goody, *A Lógica da Escrita*, 1987, 134ff.; Cohn, *Colonialism and its Forms of Knowledge*, 57ff.

[78] CR-APO, Fasc. 3, 659–60; Fasc. 5, Vol. III, 1430–3; HAG, nº 8780 – Relação de Goa – Índice dos Assentos & registo, fl. 271; HAG, nº 8779 – Relação de Goa – Assentos, fl. 83. Also HAG, nº 1160 – Assentos do Conselho da Fazenda, fl. 63, fls 229v.–231; HAG, nº 3041, Conventos Extintos, Papéis, 1549–1693, fl. 324; HAG, nº 470, Livros de Cartas Patentes, Provisões & Alvarás, 1611, fls 261–2; HAG, nº 824 – Provisões do Colégio de Rachol, 1596–1680, fls 13v.–17.

contested the efficiency of local lawyers, eventually denouncing their attitudes as "falsehoods and conspiracies", was part of a loss of innocence. The growing suspicion about the sincerity of local converts also explains that the "books of *gaunkaris*" were locked in the sacristy of the village church. A Christian clerk loyal to the Portuguese had to attend the *gaunkari*. These decisions were intended to prevent the change of the *nemos* so that "Portuguese judges may have more certain information and clarity in their doubts." The "capacity" of the locals to interpret Pegas, Pinheiro, and other Portuguese barristers had enabled them to win many cases and was the subject of criticism.[79]

This supposed capacity of the local inhabitants was also a result of the Portuguese system of education. Already in 1562 at the College de S. Paulo there were mock trials involving "an altercation between two students, one from India and another from the kingdom." In these disputations students voiced opinions in favour of their respective homelands. The judge was "a student from India".[80] Unsurprisingly, it turned out that the Christians of Goa were not as submissive as the political and religious agents had made them out to be.

The changes in local contexts, the dependence of the Portuguese Crown on local populations, the geopolitical fragility of the Estado da Índia, and new policies under the Iberian Union fuelled the aspirations of local elites within the imperial order. In 1640 the possibilities of an alliance between the populations of the different colonial territories multiplied once again.[81]

Some groups aimed to regain their previous status within the new order. Others tried ways of improving their position. Both took advantage of the ignorance of local history among the Portuguese elites, and their innocence in accepting narratives provided

[79] BA, Cod. 46–XIII–31 – Colleccoens das ordens reaes antigas, e modernas, fls 2–4v., 10–16, and 19v.–23; CR-APO, Fasc. 5, Vol. 3, 1382–3, fn.; 1420–6, and 1430–1, fn.

[80] Letter of Father Balthasar da Costa, 1562, DI, Vol. 5, 593–4.

[81] See Barros, *O Conselho Ultramarino*, 2004, 104ff.

by their informants. The native elites also took advantage of the Portuguese discourse on nobility, seeking to move from the margins of political life to its centre.[82] Ironically, however, every time they recognised the legitimacy of the Portuguese Crown as an arbitral power, these groups effectively contributed to the consolidation of imperial domination.[83] By striving for social equilibrium in the imperial order and recognising it, they ensured its durability. The treatises, the subject of the next section, are part of the same process.

Brahman Nobility or Chardo Nobility?

The *Aureola dos Indios* by António João Frias (1664–1727), published in Lisbon in 1702, and the *Promptuario de diffiniçoes indicas* by Leonardo Paes (1662–1715), a response to Frias' treatise, published in the same city in 1713, are excellent illustrations of the relationship between institutional routines, social alignments, and discursive construction in a colonial context.

It is not possible to designate this field "the first Goan writing" since there are no clear linking themes in this literature; read as a body they do not suggest the sense of a Goan identity as much as provide a sense of local rivalries and represent, most accurately, the ongoing negotiations of a kind of social contract between colonisers and some of the colonised. Other treatises in this discursive endeavour, such as the *Aureola*, defend Brahman aspirations. These treatises include *Espelho de Brâmanes* (Mirror of Brahmans) by Mateus de Castro; *Tratado Apologetico contra varias calumnias impostas pela malevolencia contra a sua Nação Bracmana* (Apologetic Treatise against Various Malicious Calumnies Spread against Our Brahman Nation) by Father Francisco do Rego; *Defensa da Nobiliarchia Bracmana* (The Defence of the Brahman Nobility)

[82] On that discourse, see Monteiro, *O Crepúsculo dos Grandes*, 25ff.

[83] Benton, "Colonial Law and Colonial Difference", 563–4; Hunt and Wickham, *Foucault and Law*, 48–9. These authors call attention, precisely, to these normalising practices.

by the same António Frias; and *Chronologia da Congregação do Oratório de Goa* (Chronology of the Congregation of the Oratory of Goa) by Sebastião do Rego.[84] Another, *Espada de David, contra o Golias do Bramanismo* (The Sword of David Against the Goliath of Brahmanism) by João da Cunha Jacques defends, like the work by Leonardo Paes, the nobility of the Chardos of Goa.[85]

The participants in this debate were native converts to Christianity who were well positioned in the local order. Dissatisfied with their position, they sought to affirm their primacy relative to members of the other groups. In some ways this debate was analogous to the one among the elites of Portuguese origin. Also, as in the other case, some of the differences here culminated in a war of words. In the earlier debate, this war had used old topics to defend the primacy of *casados* in the imperial order. Something similar now transpired among the local Christian elites. The Brahmans and Chardos (who often coincided with the *gaunkars* of the villages) wished to convince the imperial power that they were the genuine Indian nobility and therefore best suited as intermediaries between Portuguese rule and the Goan order. Both believed that, sooner or later, they would replace the *casados* in the prerogatives the latter had hitherto enjoyed.

A starting moment of this discursive battle was the nomination of Mateus de Castro, a Brahman of Dívar, as Bishop of Crisópolis and apostolic protonotary of the Propaganda Fide to Japan and the territories of Bijapur.[86] Born on the island of Dívar in 1594, Mateus de Castro was the son of Brahmans who had converted to Christianity. He studied Humanities at the College of Reis Magos, where he faced all kinds of obstacles when he proposed pursuing

[84] BA, Cod. 51–VII–33 – Rego, Sebastião do, *Chronologia da Congregação do Oratorio de Goa.*

[85] The only known manuscript version is in BA, Cod. 49–II–9 – Jacques, João da Cunha, *Espada de David contra do Golias do Bramanismo.* On this treatise, see A.B. Xavier, "David contra Golias".

[86] On this, see Mello, *The Recruitment of Native Clergy*; Sorge, *Matteo di Castro.*

an ecclesiastical career. The description he offers of this period – "imposition upon imposition", "they ply us with false information", "if one wants to be religious, they ask for the permission of the pope, if one wants to be a clergyman, they ask for the permission of the king" – is consistent with the letter of the Collector of Portugal to Cardinal Oriulzi. The Collector may have been informed of discrimination in the College of the Magi by Castro himself or by Friar Manuel de Ataíde, who denounced a similar situation through a libel presented in Rome in 1629.[87]

Castro left Goa for Rome in 1621, arriving four years later. In the Baroque Rome of Bernini and Borromini, the newly created Roman Congregation of the Propaganda Fide sought to centralise the missionary process, challenging the framework of the rights of patronage of the Iberian Crowns. In the Oratory of Rome, Castro studied Philosophy and Theology, paid for by Propaganda Fide and protected by Ingoli, the powerful secretary of the Congregation. He became a priest around 1627 and doctor in Philosophy and Theology in 1631. In Rome, Castro defended the priesthood of the Brahmans of Goa. He contested the criticisms made against them, namely the idea that they were intellectually inferior and prone to drunkenness.[88]

Castro returned to India in 1633 after having transited through Madrid and Lisbon. The arrival in Goa of a titular bishop of Indian blood with the purpose of overseeing the Portuguese missions was not welcomed. Castro's arrival generated a flurried exchange of correspondence, anticipating his return to Rome. He returned to India as an apostolic vicar in the lands of Bijapur as Bishop of Crisópolis. Facing continued opposition by the Goan ecclesiastical hierarchy, Castro decided to settle in Bijapur, where he built some Christian churches. There he established a kind of Oratory with some Brahmans of Goa whom he ordained.[89]

[87] ARSI, Goana 34, II, fls 459–73; Trindade, *Conquista Espiritual do Oriente*, Vol. 1, 291, fn. 3.

[88] ARSI, Goana 34, II, fls 459–73.

[89] Thekkedath, *History of Christianity*, Vol. 2, 417ff.

It was then that Castro and his followers were accused of conspiracy against the Portuguese Crown, as can be seen in the "*Auto que o ouvidor geral mandou faser* [. . .] *contra Andre Ferrao*" (Complaint which the chief magistrate made [. . .] against Andre Ferrao).[90] Though this document does not provide the true motivations of these men, it shows that what was at stake was mainly a disagreement over the geometry of powers in the Goan imperial order rather than resistance against Portuguese domination. For those involved in the so-called conspiracy, the Portuguese had mistreated the Brahmans of Goa: this was the argument of Castro's manuscript *Espelho de Bramenes,* copied by André Ferrão and Nicolau Dias and circulated in Salcete and Bardez.

Castro began his treatise by invoking a group of older authorities who had recognised Brahmanic superiority in order to refute the criticisms hurled at Brahmans. To support his case, Castro invoked Francis Xavier and a group of ecclesiastical authorities from Goa who pronounced in his favour. António Faria Machado of the Goa Inquisition was one of these authorities. Two others were a judge of the same tribunal and the Deacon of the Cathedral of Goa.[91] Their reports – as demonstrated by Carlos de Mercês de Mello – favoured the ambitions of the Catholic Brahmans whom the Bishop of Crisópolis represented.

This intent is also stated in the "*Carta que o Bispo Dom Matheus de Castro escreveo a cidade de Goa* . . ." (Letter by Bishop Dom Matheus de Castro to the city of Goa . . .) In this letter Castro says the locals were treated as "slaves", not as "vassals". However, since they were Christians, they had to "lay down their lives for the defence of the faith of the Magisterium of JESUS." This had prevented, for example, the triumphant entry of the forces of Bijapur into the territories of Goa. However, if Bijapur opted to entice them "using honours", and "with promises of grants, agreeing not to build mosques, or send Moors and Gentiles there", the

[90] ARSI, Goana 34, II, fls 459–73.

[91] IAN/TT, Inquisição – Livro de Visita, 1632, fls 43, 58–92, 117ff.

inhabitants of Salcete and Bardez "might once again become the vassals of His Highness" (i.e. the Adil Shah of Bijapur). All this was the result of the social situation in Goa.

> What do we care about the king of Portugal, or Goa, for he tyrannises us, and treats us as slaves, deprived of all goods and positions, and benefits, honours, and dignities, and more that are listed in my treatise, so that a native cannot even become bailiff of his own affairs? On top of all this, they lay on us imposition upon imposition. They ply us with false information. If one wants to become a member of a religious order, they tell you that you need a licence from the pope. If one wants to be a clergyman, they ask for a licence from the king, saying there are many clergymen of the land, when in fact there are no more than 299, the Christian natives being close to 900,000. The Portuguese inhabitants of Goa number only 400. The priests and friars number more than 1200. Each time one of these is ordained, offices are made available to him. Whereas they do not ordain those who are of Goa, saying this is of no benefit to them. They want to make us slaves.[92]

For Castro, the Crown needed to treat local inhabitants as vassals and respect their privileges: the "native clergy", in particular the Brahmans, ought rightfully to be the parish priests of Goa. To achieve this, the Franciscans and the Jesuits needed to abandon their parishes. In order to reinforce this argument and discredit the religious orders, Castro recounts the case of a Jesuit who had defected to a neighbouring court, writing "two large volumes against our Holy Faith in favour of the Mohammedan sect . . ."

For Catholic Brahmans, an ecclesiastical career emerged as the first step in the process of accessing the higher offices of imperial governance. As Purificação for his "sons of India", so Castro here provides a series of examples which, in his understanding, provide evidence of the superiority of Brahmanic groups. Despite this the Brahmans, he says, are treated "as if they were captives on the Barbary coast". Castro recalled the cases of Rama Queni and

[92] ARSI, Goana 34, II, fls 459–73.

Baba Queni, "the richest merchants of all the Orient". They were "dragged to the gallows and butchered through the Holy Office," and "millions in gold were seized from them." Questioning the power of the Inquisition to do this, Castro asks sarcastically: "How could Gentile unbelievers be accused of denying the articles of the faith [which they did not profess]?" Castro's assertiveness is absent in the treatises of Frias, Paes, and Cunha Jacques, though they pursued similar objectives: justifying the giving of offices of local governance to members of the groups to which they belonged.[93] If Castro's strategy was to point out contradictions in the imperial order, the cases hereafter under analysis follow a different strategy. To achieve their desired aims, they adopted the imperial idiom, adhering to debates on the nobility of arms vs the nobility of the letters, of Christian nobility vs civil nobility, of lineage vs household.

Nuno Monteiro has demonstrated that after the Restoration of 1640 there was "a devaluation of lineage in favour of the [noble] household". Lineage, hitherto the most recurrent criterion in definitions of the nobility, which encompassed above all chivalry and military exploits, was now challenged by another discourse that also valued the actual virtues and manifestations of service to the king, not necessarily involving the use of weapons. It was through the "state" and the "household" that this virtue, this service, this honour was recognised. In this sense the discourses around lineage and household were becoming "competing criteria of classification and hierarchy".[94] However, both criteria could coexist in the same argument. For example, a better noble was one who combined both titles, that is to say, the intrinsic nobility reproduced by lineage and the extrinsic nobility of merit.[95]

Each discourse refers to distinct modes of relationship with memory and group identity. The discourse of lineage evoked a

[93] On this, see A.B. Xavier, "David contra Golias".

[94] Monteiro, "Casa e Linhagem", 45; see also Hespanha, "A nobreza nos tratados jurídicos".

[95] Hespanha, "A nobreza nos tratados jurídicos", 32.

more or less crystallised primordial identity which was transmitted over time and was relatively impervious to the challenges of time. Alternatively, the discourse of the household included the variability of the performance of the subjects and families in different historical contexts. It was, so to speak, more permeable to historical dynamics, although it subsequently also tended towards a fixing of the acquired ethos.

How did the Christianised native elites engage in these debates, how did they interpret them, and how did they adapt them to their context? Which, among these groups, linked themselves to the model of an intrinsic nobility? Which groups adhered to the idea that the Crown was the source of extrinsic nobility, acknowledging and rewarding services rendered in the court and administration?

The pages that follow reflect on some of these questions. First, they analyse the formal apparatus that organises the treatises of Frias and Paes, their literary genre, the textual structure adopted, the authorities cited, the recourse to sonnets and other affective modalities, the people to whom they were dedicated. Next, I discuss the definitions of nobility presented by Frias and Paes, relating them with the discourses mentioned above as well as the local socio-political contexts.

The books by Frias and Paes use Portuguese in an exemplary way.[96] It is also likely that their authors already had the language as their mother tongue because both use linguistic structures as well as vocabulary and concepts that suggest ingrained habit. Instead of being shared by all Goans, as João de Barros had once wished, the Portuguese language had become a mode of expression among the local elites.[97]

Mastering the Portuguese language, Frias and Paes chose distinct

[96] Both these authors had attended the College of São Paulo. Leonardo Paes even praises one of the Jesuits who had been his teacher in Aristotelian Physics.

[97] Similar linguistic situations from the same period can be found in other parts of India: see, *in genere*, Guha, "Transitions and Translations", and bibliography.

literary genres to defend their arguments. The *Aureola dos Indios* is a kind of genealogical treatise while the *Promptuario de diffiniçoes indicas* presents itself as history, even if its title points towards the category of grammars and dictionaries.[98] Their literary choices could result from their stylistic preferences, their perception of the status of these discourses in the context of the intellectual production of the time, as well as the expectations of their different audiences. Perhaps Paes addressed the learned because they were the least sensitive to his arguments, while Frias addressed members of the lineages who were most recalcitrant with regard to the nobility of the Brahmans.[99]

The treatises included applause sonnets, elaborate indexes, prefaces and prologues, dedications, and above all a list of authorities that was likely to feature in treatises written by a Portuguese. These compilations were aimed at inserting Frias and Paes in the Christian and Western communicative fields.[100] They cited Aristotle and Plato, Ovid and Virgil, and Pliny and Strabo with respect to the classics. The Books of Genesis, Ecclesiastes, the Book of Kings, the prophets Ezekiel and Isaiah, St John and St Matthew, St Paul, St Augustine, St Jerome and St John Chrysostom, St Isidore of Seville and St Thomas were among their theological references. The more recent authorities cited included Jerónimo Osório, João

[98] Sanjay Subrahmanyam has analysed three forms of writing the collective memory of power in early-modern South India, and the different sources (oral and written) that they used. See Subrahmanyam, *Penumbral Visions*, Chapter 6, *passim*; and also, Subrahmanyam, Shulman, and Rao, *Symbols of Substance*.

[99] See, in this context, Burguière, "La mémoire familiale", *passim*.

[100] Ambrosio Calepino, Aristotle, Dionysius of Halicarnassus, Ovid, Pliny, Quintus Curtius, Strabo, Martial, Cicero, Virgil, for the classics; Genesis, Ecclesiastes, Book of Kings, Ezekiel, Joshua, Isaiah, St John the Evangelist, St Matthew, St Paul, St Augustine, Eusebius Caesarea, St Gregory Nazianzus, St Jerome, St John Chrysostom, St Isidore of Seville, Ludolph of Saxony, St Thomas Aquinas, for the patristic and biblical culture; Jerónimo Osório, João de Barros, Luís de Camões, Damião de Góis, Diogo do Couto, Saint Francis Xavier, Horácio Turselino, Father João de Lucena, Soror Maria de Jesus, Friar Manuel dos Anjos, and Manuel de Faria e Sousa for the Iberians.

de Barros, Luís de Camões, Damião de Góis, Diogo do Couto, Friar Manuel dos Anjos, and Manuel de Faria e Sousa.[101]

In contrast, both explicitly disqualified local sources of knowledge. Although Frias and Paes refer to them, even mentioning them in the titles of their treatises, they play second fiddle to the main argument. Frias explains that he prefers foreign writers to the writings of the Brahmans so that the proof of his treatise is seen as irrefutable.[102] Paes says he used "serious Authors" not only for "their authority" but also for the truth of their books. He adds that there were in India those who wrote "books and histories of their nobility" without knowing how to do so. They neither quoted authorities nor used a method that involved proving the veracity of their arguments.[103]

If the Western apparatus authorised the contents of their books, the offices that Frias and Paes held helped authorise their views. Leonardo Paes had a degree in the Sacred Canons and was a parish priest in the village of Gandaulim, Vicar of the Church of São Tomé, as well as an apostolic protonotary and pontifical notary. He also claimed he was descended from the family of the kings of Sirgapor (Sirgapur). António João Frias was a master of arts born in the village of Talaulim. He was an apostolic protonotary too, Notary of the Bull of Santa Cruzada, judge of the qualifications of the military orders, *fidalgo* chaplain of the king, and Vicar of the parish Church of Santo André of Old Goa.

The dedications in their works were also critical to the securing of authority. Frias, who wrote earlier, dedicated his book to the Marquês de Marialva, Dom Pedro Luís de Menezes, *mordomo-mor* (steward) of the king of Portugal, one of the two most important offices of the Royal House. One of the reasons for this dedication was service on the part of his family to this Peer of

[101] The *História Universal* of Friar Manuel dos Anjos of the mid seventeenth century was a scholastic *summa* used in the education of clerics: Anjos, *História Universal.*

[102] Frias, *Aureola dos Índios*, "Prologo ao Leytor".

[103] Paes, *Promptuario de Difinniçoes Indicas*, "Prologo ao Leytor".

the Realm. Paes, on the other hand, dedicated his treatise to the monarch himself, Dom João V (1706–1750), recognising him as the principal dispenser of benefits. While the first highlighted the Marquês de Marialva's role as a defender against those denying the nobility of the Brahmans, the second wanted the king's support in his struggle against the envy of the Brahmans.

The table of contents in the work by Paes reveals the motivation underlying his choice of genre. It intended to establish the truth of the argument, moving gradually from the universal to the particular. Paes opted to begin his treatise at the moment of divine creation, referring to the most critical stages of Christian history. It was apparently in India that "God created Paradise . . . the Most Holy Virgin Mary was born . . . and Christ, our Lord, died and was marvellously resurrected." To this area Noah sent Indo, his descendant. Then there was the River Phison, one of the four rivers of Paradise, transformed into the Ganga by a brother of Indo. This transformation explained the sacred status of the Ganga. The rites of cleansing, and the preservation of Ganga water in houses were similar to what "Christians do with holy water". Paes goes on to describe the space and its insertion into various moments in Christian history, moments which constituted India into a territory that was pre-Christian and Christian for a long time.[104]

After locating the territory and its links to Biblical times, Paes describes its political history, tracing a genealogy of the royalty of India, its divisions, and its geographical spread. Returning to the patriarch Noah and the descendants of his son Shem, Paes links them to the history of the Chardos. Treatise III was specifically dedicated to the "people of India". Combining the Portuguese corporate representation of society with the varna theory, Paes explains that at the head of the Indian system were emperors and kings (the Kshatriyas), at its heart the prophets and the sages (the Brahmans), while at its feet lay plebeians (the Sudras). A treatise called *Jadelgatutan*, or *Pomar das Castas* (Orchard of Castes), written

[104] Ibid., 5, 14.

by the Brahmans, accepted this hierarchy too, Paes argued.[105] This treatise also explained that the Chardos were the noblest among all the nations of India. They were descended from kings and were the traditional keepers of temporal power.[106] In this way Paes tried to counter some of the discourses that aimed to disqualify his group. One of these discourses presented the Chardos as descendants of mere soldiers. Others said that the name Chardo derived from the combination of the word *charo*, which meant salary, with the verb form *di* (to give): *Charo* + *di* = *charodi*. From repeated utterances of this request had resulted the name Chardo.[107] Another version explained that an ancient king of India had adopted some Chardos and that this was the origin of their hypothetical royal linkage (not by blood, but by adoption). After refuting these theories, Paes was concerned with countering Brahmanic primacy and their version of history. Since Paes' treatise was an explicit response to Frias' book, it becomes necessary to ask: what version of history did Frias' book present?

By its textual organisation Frias' narrative recalled the structure of the treatises of lineage and nobility that had circulated within the kingdom of Portugal. He refers first to "the founder, and its propagator" because "the lustre of any family consists in the dignity and excellence of its derivation."[108] More than a genealogical history of "India", Frias was interested in explaining the history of the Brahmans of the South. In this context he evoked Cheriperimal (Cheraman Perumal), king of Malabar, who had lived in the first century of the Christian era. He explained that this founding king

[105] Ibid., 155–78. There is a reference to the same treatise with a Tamil title – *Câtikal tottam* – in an earlier text by Agostinho de Azevedo. This treatise indicates that "the first caste is that of the rayas which is a very noble nation from which all the kings of Canara proceed. They are as old and famous in the [use of] arms in these parts as are the Goths of Europe": DUP, Vol. 2, 260.

[106] This function converged with the varna theory: Das, *Structure and Cognition*, 7.

[107] Paes, *Promptuario de Difinniçoes Indicas*, 154, 167.

[108] Frias, *Aureola dos Índios*, 20; see also, Monteiro, "Casa e Linhagem", 44.

of the Brahmanic nation was none other than Gaspar, one of the Magi who had paid homage to the newborn Christ. By arguing that the origin of the Brahmans was a king who shared Christian history, and who had already paid homage to the Christian God, Frias grafted the Brahmans into Christian history. It is true that, in the course of his argument, Frias contradicted some of his own theses, also affirming that there were Brahman kings in Malabar before Cheriperimal, but this twist did not affect – at least for him – his main argument. The royal origin of the Brahmans later declined into those who exercised priestly dignity, but it could only have been attained by "those who proceed from the Royal Blood". Kings and priests, then, were initially Brahmans, and were situated inside the head of Brahma, being "the Arms of the Ghetris" (Kshatriyas).[109] The rest of the Frias treatise follows a similar pattern, combining chapters that insert the history of Brahmans into Christian history, with others that are more analytical and that describe the virtues of the Brahmans: their antiquity, lineage, and science. Finally, some chapters complement the argument with a history of the present, merging past and present to assert a single argument: Brahmanic supremacy.

Although both authors claimed superiority for their group, one of the most relevant differences between the two treatises was their definition of nobility. Although Frias explicitly wrote a genealogical treatise, it was Paes who referred to the criterion of lineage as the main (and perhaps only) way of acquiring nobility.

Presenting himself as a descendant of the kings of Sirgapor, Paes argued that genuine nobles were those whose ancestors sprang from a royal family, which is why it was necessary to correctly establish the genealogy of each lineage: it would enable one to know the antiquity of each nobleman and the legitimacy of his status. In Goa, and according to Paes, only the Chardos were descended from royal blood and therefore had legitimate claims to nobility.

[109] Frias, *Aureola dos Índios*, 27–33.

For Frias, on the other hand, the noblest were those who combined various types of nobility: lineage, sciences, wealth, arms, virtue, merit: "hereditary nobility is always more illustrious because it is natural; and if this were joined together with virtue, science, and value, it would make these virtues more pronounced, and bring whoever possesses them greater glory."[110] It was not the Chardos, but the Brahmans, of course, who best combined these different virtues.

While both authors sought to establish their superiority *vis-à-vis* each other, they also attempted to demonstrate that they were nobler than most of the Portuguese settled in Goa – certainly nobler than the *casados* by antiquity and purity of blood, as well as by the exercise of virtue. Highlighting the nobility of the founders, the antiquity of their foundations, and the endogamy of the group was of the utmost importance. Even in nineteenth-century Portugal it was said that the old nobility was "that which came from the King Dom Afonso V, or further beyond."[111] Anticipating this, both Frias and Paes traced their noble origins back to Biblical times.

Frias affirmed that the Brahmans had descended from one of the Magi.[112] Besides linking Brahmanic descent to historically proven royalty, he integrated it into Christian memory, combining at the same time the two sources of nobility defined by Jerónimo Osório: civil nobility and Christian nobility. This inscription, this marking, and this appropriation of Christian memory combined as a consciously strategic gesture. By saying that the founder of the Brahmans was one of the Magi, Frias also sanctified an activity associated with the Brahmans – the magic arts – invoked frequently by the Holy Office to condemn members of this group. This had also been a central argument in João da Cunha Jacques' treatise *David contra Golias*, which sought to downgrade the Brahmans of Goa.

[110] Ibid., 9.

[111] As expressed by the Count of São Lourenço, cited by Monteiro, "Casa e Linhagem", 44.

[112] Frias, *Aureola dos Índios*, 20–4.

Taking for granted the identification between Cheriperimal and Gaspar, and between the Magi and Brahmanic science, Frias proposed a historical reconstruction of Gaspar's life in India. He repeated some narratives that had circulated among the Christians of St Thomas – stories that were familiar to the Portuguese public as well. Among these events, the baptism of Cheriperimal by St Thomas stands out. It was assumed, at the time, that this coincided with Gaspar's renunciation of the throne, which had resulted in a division within the royalty and the start of the royal house of Calicut, from which had descended its present Samudri. These myths also suggested that Gaspar had built a Christian church in Calicut, subsequently transformed into a temple which Vasco da Gama had entered, there recognising an image of the Virgin and the Magi.[113]

After establishing the filiation between the Brahmans and King Cheriperimal, in a subsequent chapter Frias sought to prove that the Brahmans combined nobility of arms with episcopal nobility, even to the point of maintaining they were responsible for some of the first missions outside India. Finally, he concluded that the Brahmans had shown themselves "the noblest, and foremost among the Indians, not only for their natural nobility inherited from their progenitors, but also for others acquired by their behaviour: making them deserving of everyone's praise, and qualifying them for the attainment of eternal glory."[114]

Responding to Frias, Paes located the paternity of the Chardos in an even more distant past. Indo, the grandson of Saba, the son of Shem, one of Noah's sons, was the progenitor of the Rajas, or Rajput Kshatriyas, or, in the Goan language, Chardos. The Emperor Pondo, mentioned in the Gentile scriptures, was a descendant of Indo. His royalty had left many vestiges in the territories of "India" where there were "houses & palaces of said Emperor", like the "many subterranean palaces" of Salcete in Goa. The

[113] Ibid., 25–7, 37–9.
[114] Ibid., 47–54, 57, 70.

caves in the village of Aquém were ruins of one of these palaces, Paes said. The Chardos of Goa had also descended from another Kshatriya emperor, the mythical Poro (or Porus) whom Alexander had fought in his campaigns in North India. Although his kingdom was in Punjab, one of his descendants, Raja Satespor, had settled in the village of Colvale in the lands of Bardez. A great tank and a rock lay adjacent to his palace. This rock, with Gentilic inscriptions, narrated "the excellences of this king". Declaring himself a descendant of kings, Paes concluded that "in India, he has never heard of a king that was not of the origin of the Royal nation of the Razeputrus Qhetris", deducing, in this way, that the genuine nobility of Goa were to be found only among the Chardos.[115]

Paes also felt the need to associate a Kshatriya king with St Thomas. This king was Sagamo, who, according to Paes, was the first to give the apostle the wood with which to build the first Christian church in India. Later, "this king was martyred by the unbelievers, and was buried in the same pious temple." Additionally, Paes refuted the Brahman Frias' arguments: contrary to what Frias had affirmed, the Brahmans were descended from Magog, the grandson of Noah, who was also the ancestor of the Jews. Just as the Jews had murdered Christ, the Brahmans had murdered St Thomas: "the Brahman priests, magi of the Gentiles of India, seeing the miracles of the glorious Apostle St Thomas, and that their cult of idols, and their credit, and sustenance were being lost, determined to take his life since they could not in sight of his miracles [continue with the] use of their deceptions."[116] Worse still, Paes pointed out that the same King Perumal, to whom the Brahmans attributed the identity of King Gaspar, was a descendant of the very Brahmans who had killed the apostle, and who had only been around as late as the twelfth century – Paes was

[115] Paes, *Promptuario de Difinniçoes Indicas*, 63, 69. An archaeological survey argued, instead, for the existence of a palace of the sultans of Bijapur in this village: Heras, "Pre-Portuguese Remains", 19. Paes' interpretation, however, was more convenient for his argument.

[116] Paes, *Promptuario de Difinniçoes Indicas*, 70–1, 243.

referring to Perumal, the Kadamba king of Goa – and could not therefore have been a contemporary of St Thomas. Moreover, the Samudri of Calicut who had introduced Islam into India was descended of Perumal, and had died, according to legend, on his way to Mecca.[117] It was futile, Frias maintained, to assert that the Brahmans had killed the apostle.

The Brahmans were like St Paul, said Frias. Initially, they were "blinded in the errors of their idolatry" and "zealous observers of it". After becoming Christians, they were the most ardent defenders of the Christian faith. In the martyrdom of 1583, for example, at least three Brahmans died alongside the Jesuit priests.

In listing examples of Brahmans and Chardos who had proved their virtue, António João Frias and Leonardo Paes were following in the footsteps of Miguel da Purificação and Mateus de Castro. Paes invoked Timoja and Mel Rao, who had helped the Portuguese conquer Goa. Other Chardos had been extremely useful in the process of achieving Christian domination. The Crown had rewarded some with titles and honours. This was the case with Heman Naique, known as Baltasar Noronha, "whom His Majesty, for services rendered by his father, made a *moço da Camera* [chamberlain], and later elevated to an *Escudeiro fidalgo* [squire], and finally to a *Cavalleiro fidalgo* [knight], with large residences." Paes' ancestors too had interceded for Bishop Mateus de Castro in the Bijapur court, acquiring from the Adil Shah the concessions which had enabled the construction of churches in Bicholim, Banda, and Virgula. Other cases were those of Agostinho Correia, a native of Nerul, and Lourenço Gonçalves, from the village of Santa Bárbara, martyred; the people of Orlim, who had barricaded themselves within the Church of São Miguel when the forces of the Adil Shah had taken Salcete, "flying the flag of the magnanimous king of Portugal, and defending it with great value, spirit, and gallantry for six months."[118] And finally, Zaitagy Rane, who for having accompanied

[117] Ibid., 142.

[118] Ibid., 125–30, 163, 171, 173–4.

the Portuguese in the war of Ceylon had received the villages of Nadora, Revora, and Pirna, confiscated from their previous *gaunkars* who had revolted. "As compensation, those who converted from the said family to our Holy Catholic Faith had been given the title of *Dom* and the surname Lisboa."[119] What better insignia than these could manifest the reliable connection established between the Chardos and the Portuguese Crown?

Frias and Paes were well acquainted with discourses legitimising the nobility that circulated in the Portuguese kingdom, as well as the intended audience of their treatises. Both used a similar strategy to defend differing contents: a combination of the criteria of lineage, and through it an intertwining of the history of India and their nation in Christian history; and with the criterion of service to the king; and further with the possession of those elements that critically defined the concept of "household" – feudal privilege, "palatine" office, title.

Affirming his descent from kings, Paes did not doubt that his family, as well as the rest of the Chardo families of Goa, were best placed to take on the offices of government. Even though Frias did not renounce royal descent, his argument nevertheless privileged the service which priests had, from time immemorial, rendered to the kings, services that gave them precedence in government. Since the Brahmans valued wisdom, science, and letters more than arms, Frias had no doubt about the primacy of the Brahmanic group.

Both Paes and Frias were also aware that the varna system could be compared with the three-fold classification that characterised the three estates model. As in Portugal, however, these social classifications could conceal "enormous ambivalence" and a "great diversity of appropriations".[120] That is, they could conceal their social dynamic, essentialising group identities and presenting them as timeless in order to guarantee the fixing and reproduction of a status which could in fact have been acquired – as was

[119] Ibid., 177.

[120] Monteiro, *O Crepúsculo dos Grandes*, 19.

sometimes the case – quite recently.[121] Furthermore, the social conflict between Brahmans and Chardos that had persisted in these territories before and during Portuguese domination, and which was explicitly evoked in these treatises, was not resolved by these books. They did not guarantee the future primacy of either of these groups.

The construction of identity that these treatises entailed had expressions at other levels too, instances being the houses of Goa, the forms of courtesy, the confraternities and brotherhoods of the locals, the new and old rituals, and apparel.[122] All these cultural signifiers were part of the resources employed by Miguel da Purificação, Mateus de Castro, António Frias, Leonardo Paes, and many others.

The fact that their treatises were produced *extra territorium* by people of mixed descent and "native Indians" gives them a unique status. The distance from Portugal facilitated certain types of conceptualisation. They entailed a poetics of distance, an aestheticisation of the contents, removed from their context, discursively isolated and reconstructed. In the case of the treatises by Frias and Paes, both contributed to the construction of the identity of Christian Brahmans and the Chardos of Goa and, thus, to Goan identity itself. In the process they omitted some of the constitutive elements of the earlier memory of these same groups, while underlining others more current and more effective, transforming the whole into an "immemorial memory". In reality, these discourses sought to impose themselves, as Paul Connerton might

[121] Similar processes have been identified by Christopher Bayly, *Indian Society*; Susan Bayly, *Caste, Society and Politics*; and Guha, "Lower Strata, Older Races", in the context of British imperial experiences. The ways in which Indian elites used their ideological resources to their own advantage have been particularly highlighted.

[122] In 1630, for example, the members of the Confraternity of Our Lady of Remédios of the Church of São Tomé "of the naturals of the land and descendants of Gentiles" petitioned the king successfully for the right to use the robes of the confraternity in the processions: IAN/TT, Manuscritos da Livraria, ns. 302–6 – Aranha, *Mesa das Tres Ordens*, Vol. III, fls. 64–64v.

say, "as history".[123] The "western" and "Christian" contents of this group's memory/history thus point to levels of adherence to the Portuguese imperial order, constituting these elites as critical pillars of Portuguese rule at the local level.

The fixing of a set of more or less coherent topics in books that were eventually published adds to their importance. This fixing reveals a new sensitivity to the processes of preservation and transmission of memory that operated in the imperial world. Frias said that writing precluded forgetting. The format, the language chosen, the authorities cited, the narrative structure, revealed in both cases an internalisation of Christianity. Both offer evidence of an increasing Christianisation of the imagination, of the relation between the real and memory, and of the preponderance of topics and images that were more Christian and western than local. The privileging of texts produced in the context of Portuguese domination, and the disqualification of sources of local origin – referred to as a category of "fables" by both Frias and Paes – indicate an interiorisation of the imperial idiom. The consequences of this were significant not only for local life but also for the permanence of Portuguese domination.

Similar situations were occurring in territories neighbouring Goa. In *Caste, Society and Politics*, Susan Bayly demonstrates that an intensification in the representation of Indian societies as polities consciously organised around varnas was contemporaneous with the decline of the Mughal empire and multiplied through the eighteenth century.[124] She states that two processes which converged in this period informed this dynamic: on the one hand an affirmation of royalty associated with priests and ascetics; on the other the recognition of Brahmans as scribes and merchants. These processes were already visible in the sixteenth-century Vijayanagar monarchy, reappeared in the figure of Shivaji in the second

[123] Connerton, *How Societies Remember*, 13ff.

[124] S. Bayly, *Caste, Society and Politics*. See also C.A. Bayly, *Indian Society*, 25.

half of the seventeenth century, and spread from there throughout India.[125] The growing tendency to claim the status of Kshatriyas was part of the same process. This happened with the Rajputs of Rajasthan, as well as with those who claimed to be their descendants, such as the Chardos of Goa.[126] In the eighteenth century, as Nicholas Dirks demonstrates in his analysis of the construction of the Palaiyakkarar royalty in the Tamil country, there were many commissions of "dynastic chronicles" which sought to affiliate elites with mythical and religious, i.e. Kshatriya, origins. In *Symbols of Substance*, Subrahmanyam, Shulman, and Rao have identified something similar in the Nayaka kingdoms, as well as the attempt at the fixing – through writing – of political identities. David Ludden has also highlighted how the very mobility that ensured urbanisation and constant migration facilitated the development of strategies of ascension, manifest in the repositioning of certain groups within a mythical, timeless hierarchy, above all in spaces within which the previous status of such groups had been ignored.[127] Veena Das had already identified the historicity of these processes, showing that in Gujarat many of the texts produced by Brahman and Baniya groups were associated with the need for these groups to mark their social difference within Muslim domination.[128] Finally, the work of Sumit Guha reiterates the existence of varied identity dynamics in India, namely in regions that were adjacent to territories dominated by the Portuguese.[129]

The circumstances of elites in the villages of Bardez, Salcete, Tiswadi, Chorão, and Dívar are also part of these Indian experiences. The *Mahabharata* and the *Ramayana* that circulated in Goa at the

[125] On the relevance of Shivaji for the local political imagination, see Gordon, *The Marathas*.

[126] Paes, *Promptuario de Difinniçoes Indicas*, 32.

[127] Dirks, *The Hollow Crown;* Subrahmanyam, Shulman, and Rao, *Symbols of Substance*; Subrahmanyam, *Penumbral Visions*; Ludden, *India and South Asia*, Chapter 2.

[128] Das, *Structure and Cognition*, 13–14.

[129] Guha, "The Politics of Identity"; idem, "Transitions and Translations"; idem, "Lower Strata, Older Races".

beginning of the sixteenth century, possibly authored by Krushnadas of the village of Quelossim,[130] had adjusted the Valmiki version of the *Ramayana* to local interests. The handwritten form of both texts allowed manipulations and adjustment to local circumstances. In the Goan *Ramayana* – and something similar happened with the *Mahabharata* – a new episode explained that a demon had brought Rama, still a child, from Ayodhya to Goa, to the village of Cola, where Vasishtha, Rama's guru, was meant to find him. Meanwhile a rival, Indrajit, Ravana's son, had taken Rama to Mormugao, from where Vasishtha would rescue him. He and Rama encountered the *gaunkars* of Majorda, Utorda, and Chicolna in Salcete, before finally returning to Ayodhya. This episode does not coincide with another myth circulating in Goa, at least since the eighteenth century. While in the epic poem the villages of Cola, Majorda, Utorda, and Chicolna had direct contact with the hero, in the myth of Parashurama, as described in the Goan version of the *Sahyadri-Khanda*, it was the village of Benaulim that was chosen by the gods. Although they were all, relatively speaking, neighbouring villages of Salcete, these versions are a testimony to the multiplicity of historical explanations that continued to coexist in the Goan space, and to the modalities of Brahmanic consciousness that developed there at least from the fifteenth century.

It is also possible to establish links between these experiences of Goa with those in other parts of the Hispanic monarchy. For example, the *Titulos Primordiales* (Primeval Titles) studied by Serge Gruzinski for Spanish America documented the indigenous millenarian discourses that emerged as a form of resistance, in which local memory was rewritten and inscribed within Christian history. Written by mestizos, these histories inserted the history of the Incas, Aztecs, and Mayans into global history.[131] Moreover,

[130] Gomes, *Old Konkani Language*, "Introduction".

[131] Gruzinski, *La colonisation de l'imaginaire*, Chapter 3; Zuñiga, "La voix du sang"; Cañizares Esguerra, "New World, New Stars". Nancy Shoemaker analyses a process somewhat similar and which took place in North America

Garcilaso de la Vega, the Inca, dedicated the first edition of his *Commentarios Reales,* published in Lisbon in 1609, to Duchess Catarina de Bragança. Although the Goan case – evidently a micro situation as compared to the territorial and cultural dimension of the American spaces of the Spanish empire – does not offer situations identical to those that gave rise to the *Titulos,* there are also mestizo histories, such as the *Relação Defensiva*, and reconstructions of memory that deploy Christian history. Establishing these types of links between both experiences – which have been explored above all by Serge Gruzinski – can provide exciting avenues of analysis.[132]

Finally, the observations condensed here challenge some aspects of other broad explanations. In *Imagined Communities*, Benedict Anderson suggested that the decline of the sacred community, of the idea of *respublica christiana*, constituted one of the cultural conditions that, in the long run, was responsible for the emergence of the concept of the nation as an imagined political community. This rupture was associated with European expansion and a simultaneous decrease in the knowledge of Latin as against the expansion of vernacular languages. That is, the emergence of the nation was correlated with the process of secularisation. In the Goan case, however, the resurgence of the idea of *respublica christiana*, of *civitas dei*, stimulated a novel articulation of the concept of "Portuguese nation" and, above all, the concept of "*pátria*" (homeland). The Brahman nation, the Chardo nation, and finally the Goan nation were also conceived alongside the Portuguese nation, all of them presenting themselves as privileged parts of the greater *pátria* which was Portugal.[133]

---

in the first half of the eighteenth century: Shoemaker, "How the Indians Got to be Red". And at the start of *Penumbral Visions*, Subrahmanyam mentions the connections that can be established between the "American" and "Indian" historical processes: Subrahmanyam, *Penumbral Visions,* Chapter 1.

132 Gruzinski, *Les Quatre Parties du Monde.*

133 Anderson, *Imagined Communities,* Chapter 2.

It was the confessional dimension of the Portuguese empire – the alliance between politics and religion – which in the first place strengthened the identitarian redefinition of these Goan local elites. It was not secularisation but confession (of religion) that stimulated a new "imagined community". In this sense, the results of the present study converge more with the argument of Peter van der Veer in *Conversions to Modernities* – which argued that the colonial era allowed new imaginations of community, and that it was in the religious domain that these imaginations occurred in the first place.[134] Given the nature of their imperial experiences, the Iberian cases can be analysed from this perspective.

[134] Van der Veer, ed., *Conversions to Modernities*, 7.

Conclusion

THIS BOOK STARTED with some of the assertions in a treatise, *Aureola dos Indios* by Father António João Frias, in Goa at the end of the seventeenth century. Frias' opinions and constructions led us in turn into larger discussions of some core questions about Portuguese imperialism in Goa, its consequences, and its contradictions.

Frias' work and career is a good metaphor for the process by which Europe and Europeans were accepted as rationalising agents in other parts of the world and by their populations. In Goa this process was associated with Portuguese and Christian imperial expansion. Frias can also be seen as personifying in many ways the process of transition from pre-modern political systems to modern ones. One of the expressions of this transition is the capacity of political power to invent or mould society and individuals within it. A major argument of this book is that these two processes converged in the project of conversion and Christianisation of the populations of Goa. That Frias behaved as a Portuguese, and felt he was Portuguese even though he was an Indian, is an excellent example of the efficacy of the tools used to assert Portuguese authority. Frias' personality and work epitomise Portuguese rationalising power and transformative capacity *vis-à-vis* local populations in the imperial project of integrating people within its rule.

In the Introduction I also asked whether the group of people that Frias represented, i.e. local elites of Indian origin, were not only symbolic of the success of these two processes but also proof of the tensions and contradictions within the Portuguese empire. While feeling and acting Portuguese, and claiming the legal equality promised by the official discourse, did Frias and others of his ilk also disturb the hierarchy of the imperial order? How did early-eighteenth-century claims by such people challenge the relationship between colonisers and colonised that had developed since the mid-sixteenth century?

This book tries as a whole to understand, therefore, the extent to which these processes contributed to a hegemonic imperial presence in which the colonised were also able to reinvent themselves and transform their condition using the language and cultural codes of the coloniser. It aims to explain how this hegemony was constructed and its characteristics. To what extent did it embrace the entirety of the population? Did the narrative provided by the colonisers and internalised by some of the colonised develop as the only available narrative? Was this the narrative that Goans used to locate themselves in relation to their inner selves, the sacred realm, and the world? Which segments of the Goan population came under the Portuguese hegemonic narrative?

My book tries to show that Goa – i.e. the imagined Goa, the constituted Goa, the constructed Goa – was invented as much by the agents of Portuguese imperial domination – whether established *in loco* or residing in the metropole – as by the populations that lived within these territories. The imperial order established an unequal social balance which, while obviously not satisfactory to all groups, enabled their coexistence. A reduction of the distance between colonisers (or colonists) and colonised was critical to this equilibrium. Sometimes, this reduction created the illusion that the distance had disappeared – as in the case of the reception by the local populations of decrees from the time of Dom João III, and subsequently in the second half of the eighteenth century via the Pombaline legislation. Local elites believed, or wished to believe, in this possibility, and in various ways the metropole fed them beliefs about equality.

These elites, both the pre-existing elites as well as those who were constituted and reinvented in the context of imperial domination, were the social groups over whom Portuguese hegemony was most effective. In contrast with what Gianbattista Confalonieri predicted in 1593 about the relationship between the metropole and the colony, in Goa communication and affection united many of these new subjects to the metropole.

The participation of local populations in the political configuration of the territories where they lived from 1510 until 1961 has been my central focus. The colonised were agents of their history, even if they did not ultimately achieve all that they had aspired to achieve. Their actions, choices, and words did however actively intervene in the historical process of their formation, a process which ended in the politically formal sense on 18 December 1961. Their designs, memory, and history continue however to constitute contemporary Goa.

The role of the colonised in the construction of a collective memory and history of Goa is captured by the voices of the priests in the preceding chapter. With their printed books they contributed to the new encyclopaedia which had been in the process of being crafted since 1510. Through a westernisation of the physical and mental landscape, local historical sources and local intellectuals antedating the Portuguese arrival were marginalised in this encyclopaedia until nineteenth-century Orientalism. However, records of the new cultural hierarchy imposed on the earlier social order enable us to appreciate the emergence of some of the nuances of Portuguese imperial rule in Goa.

This process was initiated in the sixteenth century and within it the episodes in Sirula, Chorão, and Cuncolim are symptomatic. They show that conversion and Christianisation were the only ways in which local elites could secure effective dominance.[1] When writing to Cardinal Dom Henrique, Father Melchior Carneiro plainly expressed the view that the converted needed to maintain "among themselves their ranks of honour".[2] Some years later the Jesuit Alessandro Valignano suggested that local Jesuits turn a blind eye to the behaviour of upper-caste converts who continued to

[1] See, in this context, Bloch, *How We Think They Think*, esp. the chapters "Internal and External Memory" and "Autobiographical Memory and the Historical Memory of the More Distant Past".

discriminate against those from the lower castes.[3] Such Jesuits explained that the social sphere and its distinctions on the one hand, and the local religion on the other, were not interdependent, allowing the maintenance of pre-existing social inequalities – namely, caste distinctions.[4] In other words, converting the rural elites was necessary to bend the requirements of Christianity to those of the local hierarchy.[5]

The relationship between Christianisation and the conservation of the power of local elites constitutes one of the features of Portuguese imperial experience in these territories. Portuguese imperial hegemony was articulated primarily by those who had power at the local level or who aspired to power. It turned out, however, that in the long term the internalisation of the metropolitan idiom by these groups went against the maintenance of this hegemony.

If Portuguese imperial domination was tendentiously hegemonic among these elites, the same could not be said of the rest of the colonised, and especially of the socially marginalised. The Christian presence did not significantly change the lifestyles of these groups. Initially, they demonstrated a desire to stay with the Christian order, given the possibilities it offered as an alternative to their social difficulties. They thereby reproduced the attitudes expected of resident peasants in flatlands and irrigated agricultural areas – such people have frequently demonstrated great flexibility.[6] Later, however, when the methods of conversion changed and the conversion of elites became a priority, the investment of the

[2] Cited in Rocha, *As Confrarias de Goa,* 276; also 9–10 and 16; and Pearson, *The Portuguese in India,* 127.

[3] Valignano, *Sumario de las cosas que pertenecen a la Yndia Oriental,* in DHMPPO, Vol. 12, 600.

[4] See Županov, "Le repli du religieux"; idem, *Disputed Mission.*

[5] This is similar to what had happened in the Chinese territories, where Christianity and Confucianism had to face off against each other: Hsia, "Entre chrétien et chinois", 243ff.

[6] On this type of behaviour, see Bloch, *How We Think They Think,* 75ff.; Connerton, *How Societies Remember*; Ludden, *An Agrarian History,* Chapter 1.

imperial order in the total cultural conversion of these social groups diminished considerably.

Some of the institutions launched in the context of the imperial Christian order, such as primary education from childhood, had a slighter impact on these populations. This was because of the perception of the inferior "quality" of these social groups, and the fact of limited resources which prevented encompassing everybody. The practical needs of the local and imperial order, as of members of the religious orders – whose well-being depended in good part on the labour of these populations – also militated against their being provided an education that might elevate their status.[7] Charity and poor relief were thought sufficient and remained two of the most important vehicles in the Christianisation of the subaltern social groups.

Despite many local actors adhering to the Christian visual order, the fact that they often could not sufficiently master the required linguistic idiom also proved an impediment in their being able to present themselves as Portuguese, emphasising the separation that existed, de facto, between Portuguese and Indians. The confusion of the seventeenth-century author who recollected that the local populations "shamelessly admit two contradictions" is also telling. This capacity to accumulate contradictions – i.e. the existence of a local system of logic in which some facts were not necessarily contradictions – may also have contributed to the conservation of imperial power among these groups.

For example, the analogies established between Christian charity, medical practices, and a set of local social and cultural practices explain how the local system continued to survive even as Christianity rooted itself firmly in the Goan context. While local elites maintained ancient symbols and practices and attributed new meanings to them, groups lower down continued to interpret

[7] While this question was being discussed in the kingdom, the colleges in Goa were reduced, being considered harmful to the "Conquests": IAN/TT, Manuscritos da Livraria, ns. 302–6 – Aranha, Mesa das Tres Ordens, Vol. III, fl. 67.

the new symbols through their "old" encyclopaedia. These lower groups did not internalise the totalising character of Christianity, often supplementing it with local devotions and remaining centrally immersed in earlier systems of reference and action. For such reasons these populations continue even today as a receptacle of cultures and practices that existed locally before the arrival of the Portuguese.

This happened *in loco*, against the metropolitan desire to Christianise and westernise all inhabitants under Portuguese rule. The totalitarian project of Christian political universalism inspired the formulation of imperial tools, and of the practices of many agents of the Portuguese Crown, described through the chapters of this book. It has been shown as well that efficient power, i.e. administrative mechanisms and their efficacy, were insufficient to embrace such a multitude. As Ernest Gellner has pointed out, institutional and human agents are never entirely able to prevent the colonised from interpreting and conceiving their imaginaries differently.[8] This also happened among the Christianised local elites, those most vulnerable to the imperial idiom. Even for those among them – such as Frias, his contemporaries, and their descendants – the physical, geographical, cultural, and personal distance inherent in these appropriations transformed them into a kind of poetics, an intellectual experience which, for this very reason, had a reality distinct from the reality of the metropole.

In short, the cultural conversion of the local order was never complete and had distinct consequences, depending on the imperial agents, their period in power, the adequacy of their power, and the specific situation of the groups that were Christianised. Christianisation with heightened westernisation with the larger part of the local elite, and Christianisation with little westernisation with the demographic majority, were simultaneously parallel and convergent and always incomplete. It was their coexistence – and the social modalities of their coexistence – which guaranteed the

[8] Ruud, "The Indian Hierarchy", 718.

permanence of Portuguese imperial power and the gradual constitution of a distinct political and cultural identity later recognised as Goan.

Besides the diversity of local populations and their forms of appropriation of Christianity, an explanation of this failure of the complete Christianisation of Goa was the absence of unanimity among the agents of the Portuguese Crown on how to develop the process. They rarely spoke in a single voice, either in the metropolitan context or in the imperial territories. Recent historiography that focuses on agents of the imperial bureaucracy stresses the existence of multiple opinions pertaining to ways of colonising.[9] As discussed over the course of this book, missionaries were also very divided on the methods to be used to convert and Christianise. It is also worth pointing out that even if imperial agents had been unanimous and capable, Portuguese imperial power was insufficient, or simply not strong enough to be able to impose its rule as thoroughly as it wished.

Fortunately, an absolute colonisation of the imagination and a complete colonisation of consciousness proved to be unrealisable Portuguese utopias. Given the incommensurable re-creations, reinventions, and reimaginings of reality by the appropriations, selections, recombinations, and reinterpretations by living beings – colonisers and the colonised – involved in these processes, the outcome was always likely to be more diverse than the design.

This conclusion does not imply any exculpation of the colonisers, nor any implicit diminution of the violence and inequality that characterised the imperial experience in Goa. Military, political, and cultural violence was unceasing and manifest in either everyday or momentous forms, given that colonisers of Portuguese origin were involved in a continuous effort to regulate their distance from the colonised and guarantee their own supremacy in the local imperial order. A good section of them found space within the category of the *casados* – the colonisers established *in loco* and

[9] In this context, see the essays included in Gouvêa, Fragoso, and Bicalho, eds, *O Antigo Regime nos Trópicos*; Monteiro, Cardim, and Cunha, eds, *Optima Pars*; Bicalho and Ferlini, eds, *Modos de Governar*, and bibliography.

resident in Goa.[10] These were mostly officials of the established imperial architecture of the region. However, temporary officials, the *reinóis*, occupied the principal offices in imperial governance. In line with what was ongoing in Europe, these metropolitan *reinóis* asserted themselves as more authentically Portuguese, and therefore as superior to those born in the imperial territories. This assertion structured another type of hierarchy within the imperial order, that between the metropole and the colony, the *reinóis* and the colonists.

Colonial elites of Portuguese origin, the *casados*, refused this discrimination, evolving strategies for arguing – not always successfully but always with discursive intensity – for their own political importance and social status. Even soldiers, in the liminal position attributed to them, reflected on their identity, resulting in remarkable texts which await more systematic analysis. In these texts, too, the need to differentiate and exalt difference between self and other – even if not always the same difference – was constant. Each group also fought vigorously against possible reductions of their social distance from the Christianised local populations.

Though the longevity of Portuguese imperial rule suggests a reduction in distance between colonisers, colonists, and some of the colonised, the fact remains that imperial power could only survive if difference, hierarchy, and distance were maintained. Even though transfigured and visible in a variety of shapes, the distance, difference, and hierarchy remained until the end. Goa, like every other colonised region, was no exception.

Before concluding, I should like to outline the themes for further research that have emerged in the course of writing this book. While seeking to recuperate the multiple voices of those involved in the imperial experience, inaudible voices long relegated to distant corners – in part due to the nature of the historical methods generally used – have become somewhat audible. Besides the traditional subalterns – local populations, including women – the secondary location that the region's historiography usually attributes

[10] See, in this context, A.M. Xavier, "Nobres per geração".

exclusively to missionary actors such as the Franciscans, Dominicans, and Augustinians deserves attention too. These and other religious agents were actively involved in the process of conversion and Christianisation, and thus in the construction of imperial power. Like the Jesuits, they were equally relevant in the invention of Goa. The case of the Franciscans is emblematic. Less interested in writing than the Jesuits, their historical experiences fell into a penumbral zone. They are often read in the light of narratives that the Jesuits produced to suit their particular agendas, and which historians, bound down by their documentary obsession, have ended up reproducing.

Discussions in the second chapter of this book made it clear that the plans for conversion were primarily designed in the decade between 1530 and 1540, which is before the Jesuits arrived in Goa. Rather than starting off conversion and Christianisation, the Jesuits continued and transformed older ideas and tactics. Many of these had been conceived, realised, and perfected earlier, or around the time of their arrival, and were marked by Franciscan spirituality. However, it is difficult to disentangle strategies that emerged among the Observants from those specific to the friars of Piedade (subsequently integrated into the Custody of the Madre de Deus of Goa). This is especially important in light of the fact that Frei Gaspar de Leão, the first Archbishop of Goa, was not only the founder of the first Recollect convent in Goa but also the promoter of institutional events and discourses that constituted the diocese of Goa, the Provincial Councils, and the first constitutions of the archbishopric.

Localising, apart from historicising, the role of the Jesuits is necessary to provide more complexity to the historical landscape of the early-modern period. The same rationale can be applied to the role attributed to the Misericórdias.[11] This institution slowly monopolised poor relief in Portugal, enjoying more or less the

[11] See the introductions to volumes 1 to 5 of the collection *Portugaliae Monumenta Misericordiarum,* co-ordinated by José Pedro Paiva.

same position in various imperial territories. Despite the imperial relevance of the Misericórdias alongside the *câmaras*, they were practically non-existent in the rural areas of the empire. As a consequence, it was the regular clergy that took up the responsibilities of poor relief, combining material support with a spiritual ministry. Missionaries believed it was easier to capture the hearts of the local populations by this method.

Many of the happenings and trajectories in Goa were similar to those in Mexico and Peru. Despite spatial and cultural differences, the Iberian elites shared more in common than is often imagined. The friars of Piedade are an ideal case for study. The twelve missionaries who accompanied Martim de Valencia to Mexico shared the same spirituality. The integration of the histories of these three spiritual conquests is another project yet to be initiated.

In turn, other signs point towards the existence of a constellation of images that marked the central decades of the sixteenth century. The imperial model par excellence, frequently invoked when discussing the Spanish empire, was also the referential framework for the Portuguese: the Roman empire, the empire of Augustus, and the empire of Constantine. Territoriality, linguistic colonisation, religious colonisation, and juridical unification were all constitutive elements of late-Roman imperial expansion as well as a series of other elements, ranging from urbanism to communications. All these were present in the imperial imagination of the court of Dom João III. A humanist culture with Italian and Christian roots was combined with imperial ambitions, and the process of conversion and Christianisation of the populations of Tiswadi, Chorão, Dívar, Bardez, and Salcete was part of the realisation of this model. Even though it dovetails with the contemporary reigns of Charles V, Henry VIII, and Süleyman the Magnificent, the reign of Dom João III is often ignored because it is sandwiched between the reign of Dom Manuel and the battle of Alcácer-Quibir in 1578, which led to the Iberian Union.

Hopefully, my readers will also have been convinced with regard to the critical importance of varying political and cultural geographies for the shaping of imperial experiences. These contexts were not static, and their anterior and coeval dynamics should be taken into consideration. For example, the failure of linguistic colonisation and fixing of the Konkani language, in part the result of work by Jesuit missionaries, was undoubtedly also linked to the language dynamic in the territories neighbouring Goa. And the same applies, for example, to the dynamic of identity writing.[12] In short, identifying and analysing the totality of dynamics that were developed and made operational within the Portuguese empire and beyond would result in a more sophisticated history of these and other aspects of Portuguese rule in Goa.

[12] Guha, "Transitions and Translations".

Bibliography

PRIMARY SOURCES

Manuscripts

Academia das Ciências de Lisboa (ACL)

nº 34: *Colecção de Papeis varios, que dizem respeito ao Governo Ecclezias-tico, & Secular do Estado da India.*

nº 208: *Colecção de vários sermões e outras práticas devotas para o tempo de missão.*

Arquivo Histórico Ultramarino, Lisbon (AHU)

India, Caixas 12,15; 29, 30; 34; 45; 77; 109, 208.

Cx. 2, nº 45: "Alvará régio em favor de Brites de Pina, viúva de Cosme Lafeta, 12 de Setembro de 1619".

Cx. 3, nº 19: "Da câmara de Goa, para o rei, 22 de Janeiro de 1615".

Cx. 3, nº 40: "Carta dos gentios Pomdia e Goimda, ao rei, queixando-se de lhes não terem sido pagas as dívidas (. . .)".

Cx. 4, nº 20: "Petição de Maria de Freitas, viúva de Lourenço do Carvalhal . . ."

Cx 5, nº 34: "Carta de Frei Simão de Nazareth indigno frade menor do seraphico pe. nosso sao Fr.co . . . , 24 de Janeiro de 1618".

Cx. 6, nº 29: "Do procurador da Coroa e Fazenda, 12 de Fevereiro de 1619".

Cx. 6, nº 30: "A cauza porque as rendas de V. Mge. na yndia vierão a tanta deminuição (. . .)".

Cx. 9, nº 43: "Carta do Conde Almirante ao rei sobre uma petição feita pelos gancares de Loutolim . . . 2 de Março de 1616".

Archive of the Archdiocese of Goa, Panaji (AAG)

Livro 1 de Visitas Pastorais, 1747.

Archivum Romanorum Societatis Iesu, Rome (ARSI)

Goana 9, 22, 34.

Archivum Sacra Congregazione della Propaganda Fidei, Rome (ASCPF)

Scritture Originali, nº 98.

S. Congregatio Concilii – Relatio de Statu Ecclesiae Goanae ab Archiepiscopo Cristophoro de Sa e Lisboa, Goa (1621).

Biblioteca da Ajuda, Lisbon (BA)

Cod. 46-XIII-31: Colleccoens das ordens reaes antigas, e modernas sobre varios negocios pertencentes ao governo da India.

Cod. 47-VIII-6: Decreta s. congregationis episcoporum & regularum.

Cod. 47-VIII-7: Decreta s. congregationis episcoporum & regularum.

Cod. 49-I-77: Sant'Anna, Diogo de, *Cathecismo da Perfeição Evangelica que Hesu Xº Ds. & Salvador nosso insinou pera a salvação quando foi servido alumiar & Reinar o Mundo, que pello peaco tinha caído nas trevas, e captiveiro do demónio (. . .).*

Cod. 49-II-9: Jacques, João da Cunha, *Espada de David contra do Golias do Bramanismo péssimo inimigo de Nosso Senhor Jesu Christo, verdadeiro Deos e verdadeiro Homem, dedicado a S- Francisco Xavier.*

Cod. 49-II-48: Leis e Provisoes que elRey Dom Sebastiao fez, depois que começou a governar, Impressas em Lisboa por Francisco Correa, 1570 (manuscript copy).

Cod. 51-VI-33: Miscellanea Civil, e Ecclesiastica por hum Religioso d'Alcobaça em 1598/Memorias de couzas varias antigas.

Cod. 51-VI-54: "Relação sobre a precedência q/ se deve dar ao consº da India entre os mais conselhos e tribunais deste Rº", fls 69–77v.

Cod. 51-VII-19: "Mandado de Rui Gonçalves de Caminha, vedor da fazenda da India a Francisco Pires, mestre de obras d'el-rei (. . .),1547, Goa, agosto 27", fls 232–3.

Cod. 51-VII-22: "Parecer do bispo Dom Juan sobre a conversão do rei de Tanor", 197–181v.

Cod. 51-VII-27: Breve noticia dos erros, que tem os gentios do Concão na India.

Cod. 51-VII-30: "Apontamentos de cousas de mto serviço de S Magde", fls 7-10v.

Cod. 51-VII-30: "Memorial sobre o poder que o rei tinha na India, 1627", fls 116-127v.

Cod. 51-VII-33: Rego, Sebastião do, *Chronologia da Congregação do Oratorio de Goa.*

Biblioteca Nacional de Portugal, Lisbon (BNP)

Cods. 58 – Spinola, Antonio Ardizone, *Breve relação das principaes ordens com que o Illustrissimo e Reuerendissimo Senhor Dom Frey Francisco dos Martyres, Arcebispo Metropolitano de Goa, Primâs da India, tem zelado em seu Arcebispado a observancia do preceito da Sagrada Comunhão na Pascoa, e no perigo da morte, conforme a doutrina, que se trata no sermão: Da causa dellas, e seus effeitos*

Cod. 176 – *Notícias do Arcebispado de Goa.*

Cod. 607 (Film 3622) – *Divindades do Gentilismo da Índia.*

Cod. 846 – *Viagens pela India.*

Cod. 1119 – Repertorio . . . , "Casos Notáveis.

Cod. 3616 – Rebelo, João, S.J., *Doctrina Christiana.*

Biblioteca Pública/Arquivo Distrital de Évora (BPADE)

Cod. CIX/2-3, nº 9, "Carta do Bispo Dumiense ao Secretº Antº Carneiro em que lhe diz que o Arcebispo se prepara pª ir esperar a Rainha; e que elle está prompto pª fazer a viagem da India debaxo de certas condiçoens, de 5 de Outubro de 1518".

Cod. CIX/2-3, nº 10, "Carta do Bispo Dumiense ao Secretº Antº Carneiro sobre a sua viagem, e volta para o Reino de 15 de Dezembro de 1519".

Cod. CIX/2-3, nº 11, "Carta do Bispo Dumiense a Antonio Carneiro Secretario de Estado sobre os preparos de sus aviagem e sobre alguas circunstancias que lhe dizião respeto ate voltar ao Reyno de 16 de Dezembro de 1519".

Cod. CIX/2-3, nº 12, "Carta do Bispo Dumiense em que dá conta a ElRey do estado em que se acham as Pregações, Igrejas e Governo da India de 12 de Janeiro de 1522".

Cod. CIX/2-3, nº 13, "Carta de Frei Antonio a ElRey Dom Manoel sobre a conversão dos Gentios e estabeecimento dos seus Religiosos de 4 de Novembro de 1518".

Cod. CIX/2-3, nº 22, "Carta de Fr. Lourenço de Goes, Guardião do Convento de Santo Antonio de Cochim dando parte a ElRey do estado da Christandade daquella Terra de 28 de Dezembro de 1536".

Cod. CIX/2-3, nº 25, "Carta de Frei Vicente a ElRey, dandolhe conta do Collegio que edificara em Cranganor, Estatutos dos Collegiaes delle, e outas noticias daquelle Estado de 1 de Janeiro de 1549".

CXVI/1-39, nº21, "Memorias Sepulcraes da India".

Colecção Manizola

Cod. 29 – Barradas, Pe. Manuel, S.J., *Tratado dos deuses gentilicos de todo o Oriente e dos ritos e ceremonias que usam os Malabares, 1618.*

Cod. 48, nº 11 – *Das fábulas de Talmud.*

Cod 594, nº 6 – *Filosofia secreta da gentilidade.*

Fundo Rivara

r 5e 6-14: Fundação do convento de S. Francisco, Collegio de S. Boaventura e mais Igrejas desta – Provincia de S. Thome.

Central Library, Panaji (Goa)

M-4 – Graça, Fr. António da, OFM, *Breves Resoluçoens Morais.*

M-29 – Chagas, Fr. Boaventura das, OFM, *Cazos Reservados.*

Nobili, Roberto di, S.J., *Catecismo em que se explicam todas a verdades catholicas em tamil pelo Pe. Nobili. Tradusido em lingoa portuguesa pelo P. Balthasar da Costa da mesma Compª, Missionário da mesma Missão.*

Historical Archives of Goa, Panaji (HAG)

nº 470: «Cartas patentes, provisões e alvarás, 1611»

nº 824: «Provisões do Colégio de Rachol, 1596–1680»

nº 1160: «Conselho da Fazenda, Assentos»

nº 2789: «Conventos extintos, Papéis, 1619–1810»

nº 3041: «Conventos extintos, Papéis, 1549–1693»

nº 3071: «Foral de Salcete, cópia feita de 1585»

nº 4469: «Provisões, leis e alvarás, 1558–1567»
nº 7583-7585: «Foral de 1622»
nº 7587: «Foral antigo de Bardez, 1649»
nº 7604: «Foral das Ilhas de Goa, 1553–1562»
nº 7737: «Senado da Câmara – Acórdãos»
nº 8779: «Relação de Goa – Assentos»
nº 8780: «Relação de Goa – Índice de Assentos e Registos»
nº 9530: «Assentos do Conselho de Estado, 1618–1624»
nº 10020: «Azossim, Deliberações e contas correntes, 1608»
nº 10023: «Azossim, Deliberações e contas correntes, 1614»
nº 10024: «Azossim, Deliberações e contas correntes, 1615»
nº 10226: «Cortalim – Corrente, 1629»
nº 10041: «Comunidades – Carambolim, 1612»
nº 10042: «Comunidades – Carambolim, 1613–1614»
nº 10043: «Comunidades – Carambolim, 1615»

Instituto dos Arquivos Nacionais/Torre do Tombo, Lisbon (IAN/TT)

Armário Jesuítico

Mss. 8 – *Livro de Pareceres do Pe. António Soares.*
nº 14 – *Livro com vários pareceres de Pes. Jezuitas sobre varias materias resolvidas pelo Pe. Diogo de Areda.*
Mss. 18 – *Hum livro dezencadernado que se intitula Pareceres sobre a Gente da Nação, e expulsão della, remedio contra o Judaísmo* (. . .) .

Cartório Jesuítico

Mss. 41, nº 7 – "Breve do Papa Gregório 13 para que os jesuítas pudessem curar sendo peritos em medicina".
Mss. 56, nº 56 – "Parecer de Lopo Mendes, Procurador da Casa da Suplicação, acerca de uma doação para a obra pia".
Mss. 57, nº 2 – "Alvará sobre os mosteiros e outras comunidades, nam Comprarem, nem possuirem bens de raiz, na forma das Leys antiguas destes Reynos, de 30 de Julho de 1611".
Mss.57, nº 26 – Informaçam por partes dos Religiosos da C.ª de IESU sobre os bens de raiz".
Mss. 81, nº 21 – "Traslado da doação de D. Pedro de Castro feita aos

jesuítas das aldeias de Assulana, Velim, e Ambelim e notícias históricas sobre as mesmas aldeias, sendo a província a missão jesuítica de Malabar em Cochim".

Mss. 86, nº nº 19 – "Escrituras de bens e doações de terras, documentos relativos à fundação da missão da Índia Oriental, do Brasil e de Portugal".

Colecção São Vicente

L. 2 – Matérias várias do tempo do rei D. João III e da rainha D. Catarina.

L. 6 – Cartas da Embaixada do Comendador-Mor em Roma.

L. 9 – Várias Cartas e Provisões do rei D. João III e da rainha D. Catarina.

L. 10 – Cartas e papéis variados da rainha D. Catarina.

L. 19 —Cartas de Filipe IV sobre as matérias da Índia.

Corpo Cronológico

Part I

Mç. 12

nº 39: «Carta para ElRey sobre o que ordinariamente sucede na India, entre a Christandade, de 7 de Dezembro de 1512".

Mç. 16

nº 65: "Carta de Afonso de Albuquerque, de 25 de Outubro de 1514".

Mç. 23

nº 5: "Carta de Sebastião Pires, Vigario de Cochim, referindo a ElRey o estado em que se achava o Christianismo na India, de Cochim a 8 de Janeiro de 1518".

nº 133: "Carta do Commissario Guardião a ElRey sobre o Estado, em que ficava e as Cidades em que se poderião estabelecer outros Conventos, de 4 de Novembro de 1518".

Mç. 25

nº 55: "Carta do Juiz da Confraria de Nossa Senhora do Rozario de Gôa, dando conta a ElRey, que por se fazer Freguezia esta Ermida foi precizo fazer-se maior caza, e mais Ornamentos, e porque a dita Confraria está pobre, pediam ao mesmo Senhor lhe fizesse esmolla, que fosse servido. Dada em Goa a 25 de Outubro de 1519".

Mç. 27

nº 93: "Carta de Sebastião Pires Vigario Geral de Cochim, dando conta a ElRey do máo tratamento que os Capitaens davam aos que se faziam Christaons (. . .) Cochim a 10 de Janeiro de 1522".

nº 95: "Carta do Bispo Dumuense dando conta a ElRey de suas Missoens: Que as Igrejas da India estavam indecentes, principalmente a de Gôa da invocação de Santa Catharina (. . .) De Cochim a 12 de Janeiro de 1522".

Mç. 28

nº 122: "Carta de Pedro de Faria, dando parte a ElRey, que o Vigario de Goa vinha para Lisboa por ser chamado a Cochim pelo Vigario Geral por cauza de reprehender os Clerigos no seu modo de viver (. . .) De Goa a 25 de Outubro de 1522".

Mç. 30

nº 36: " Carta de Antonio Fonseca dando conta a ElRey, do rendimento que havia na India: Das Fortalezas, Hospitaes, e Navios, que lá se acharam, De Goa a 18 de Outubro de 1523".

nº 76: "Carta do Bispo de Cochim dando conta a ElRey do mao governo daquella terra; Que os Vigarios recebiam homens , que eram cazados tres vezes, e que dos Conventos ficavam muitos frades fora. De Cochim a 28 de Dezembro de 1523".

Mç. 31

nº 83: "Carta da Camara de Goa, dando parte a ElRey, chegar o Conde da Vidigueia áquella Cidade, e ser estimado de todos pela rectidão, com que administrava a justiça (. . .) de Gôa a 31 de Outubro de 1524".

Mç. 45

nº 127: "Carta de Fr. Vicente de Laguna a ElRey sobre a necessidade em que achou a Índia de ter Ministros que semeassem a palavra Evangelica, De 25 de Setembro de 1530".

Mç. 46

nº 21: "Carta de Nuno Vaz de Castello Branco a ElRey referindo o tempo em que chegou a Gôa; a armada do Turco intentar destruir a India, e o levantamento que houve em Baçaim; De 16 de Novembro de 1530".

Mç. 50

nº 40: "Carta de Pedro de Faria dando parte a ElRey do Estado das Conquistas da Ásia, e necessidade que tinha de socorro para a sua conservação, 23 de Novembro de 1532".

nº 45: "Carta de Fr. Vicente Laguna a ElRey sobre o grande descuido que havia nos Vigarios da India no cumprimento das suas obrigações, De 29 de Novembro de 1532".

nº 52: "Carta do Bispo D. Fernando, dando parte a ElRey da sua viagem para Gôa: O estado, em que tinha achado aquellas Conquistas: Os vicios, que nellas grassavam; e o que sobre este respeito tinha tratado com o Governador. De Gôa a 12 de Dezembro de 1532".

Mç. 58

nº 7: "Carta da Câmara de Gôa expondo a ElRey os relevantes serviços que seus Moradores sempre fizerão ao mesmo Senhor e muito especialmente em Salsete, e Bardez (. . .) de Goa a 15 de Novembro de 1536".

nº 23: "Carta de Frei Lourenço de Goes, Guardião de Convento de S. Antonio de Cochim dando parte a ElRey do estado do Christianismo daquella terra (. . .) De Cochim a 28 de Dezembro de 1536".

Mç. 59

nº 109: "Carta de Pedro de Faria dando conta a ElRey, que as Fortalezas de Dio, e Baçaim estavam acabadas bem guarnecidas e municionadas (. . .) De Goa a 20 de Outubro de 1537".

Mç. 64

nº 4: "Carta de Diogo Pereira a ElRey sobre o deploravel estado em que estava pela debilidade de suas Fortalezas, de 25 de Janeiro de 1539".

nº 138: "Auto de Protesto que o Bispo de Gôa mandou fazer, sobre a nova creação do Deado da Sé da dita Cidade, por Bula dizer que o seria o que estivesse servindo de Vigario, e o que actualmente existia não ter capacidade para o ser, De Goa a 6 de Junho de 1539".

Mç. 65

nº 72: "Instrumento de testemunhas que mandou tirar o Bispo de Gôa porque se provou que o Padre Diogo de Moraes Viagairo que foi na Sé de Goa era ignorante e indigno de ser Sacerdote e administrar os Santos Sacramentos da Igreja, Goa a 16 de Setembro de 1539".

Mç. 66

nº 1: "Traslado de Aggravo que entrepozeram os Moradores da Cidade de Gôa, do Vice Rey D. Garcia de Noronha por lhes não goardar os Prirvilegios, Graças, e Franquezas, que ELRey D. Manoel lhes concedeo (. . .) em Gôa a 11 de Outubro de 1539".

nº 12: "Carta de D. Garcia de Noronha Vice Rey da India ao Secretario Antonio Carneiro sobre o Governo e decadencia daquelle Estado (. . .) de Gôa a 29 de Outubro de 1539".

nº 37: "Carta de Pedro Faria reprezentando a ElRey a necessidade em que estavão as Fortalezas da Índia de socorro de gente, e mantimentos, pois deviam estar sempre promptas assim como os inimigos nunca se esqueciam de lhe fazer mal, de 20 de Novembro de 1539".

nº 53: "Inquirição que se tirou conta o Padre Diogo Moraes Vigairo que foi na Sé da Cidade de Goa. Na dita cidade a 16 de Setembro de 1539".

nº 79: "Carta de Bartholomeu Pires reprezentando a ElRey que os Officiaes da Fazenda, e Justiça naquelle Estado das Indias, feitos contratadores, só cuidavão de se asenhorear de tudo em prejuizo dos pobres, que por fome, se passavão aos Mouros (. . .) De Cochim a 7 de Janeiro de 1540".

nº 99: "Carta de Diogo Rebello dando parte a ElRey que a India estava exaurida de todo o necessario, para rezistir á invazão dos Rumes. De 24 de Janeiro de 1540".

Mç. 68

nº 85: "Carta da Câmara de Goa a ElRey sobre os aggravos que recebêra do Vice Rey falecido; o rendimento da dita Cidade, e pedindo a conservação de seus privilegios. De 20 de Novembro de 1540".

Mç. 71

nº 10: "Carta de Thomé Rodrigues Soares dando arte a ElRey, do estado em que achava a India, e violencias que os Governadores cometiam, tirando os soldos a tantos, que o tinham servido, pelo que se achaa proxima a sua ruina. De Goa a 17 de Novembro de 1541".

nº 31: "Carta da Confraria da Conversão da Fé, estabelecida em Goa, pedindo a D. João III os patrocinasse no compromisso que remetiam ao papa sobre o acrescentamento de indulgências e rendas, 14 Dec. 1541".

Mç. 72

nº 84: "Traslado do Compromisso que fez o Governador da India para o Hospital da Cidade de Gôa, com a graças e privilégios que havia de ter, Feito em Gôa a 7 de Agosto de 1542".

nº 155: "Carta do Chantre de Gôa dando parte a ElRey, que por ordem do Duque de Bragança viera a Roma, donde estava para requerer a Sua Santidade, os Privilégios da Sé de Lisboa fossem igualmente concedidas a Gôa, De Roma a 31 de Outubro de 1542".

Mç. 74

nº 46: "Carta de D. Garcia de Castro dando conta a ElRey que o

Mouro, que recebeo em Gôa o entregou a Idalcão, que queria lhe succedesse no Reino, de que ficou tão satisfeito que fez Doação ao Estado das Terras de Salsete, e Bardez (. . .) De Goa a 29 de Dezembro de 1543".

Mç. 75

nº 109: "Carta do Cabido da Sé de Gôa expondo a ElRey o grande zelo, e virtudes do Vigario Geral Miguel Vaz (. . .) De Gôa a 3 de Dezembro de 1544".

Mç. 77, nº 12

"Carta de D. João, Principe do Ceilão dando parte a ElRey ter recebido o Sacramento do Baptismo, e seu Irmão a quem ElRey seu Pay matára, e obstinadamente presseguia a todos os que se querião baptizar não obstante os Prodigios que Deos obrou abrindo Cruzes na Terra, e Ceo, e fazendo tremer a terra pela morte do dito seu Irmão, por cujos motivos todos os dias se augmentava a Christandade naquela Ilha (. . .) De Gôa, a 15 de Novembro de 1545".

Mç. 77, nº 52

"Carta de Pedro Fernandes dando parte a ElRey que Martinho Affonso de Souza contratara com o Idalcão entregar-lhe Meale (...)De Gôa a 20 de Dezembro de 1545".

nº 60: "Carta de António Cardozo dando parte a ElRey estar o Idalcão seis legoas afastao de Goa com muita gente de pé, a cavallo, pedindo-lhe cumprissem o contrato feito com Martim Affonso de Souza, sobre a entrega de Meale, sua mulher, e filhos (. . .) De Gôa a 23 de Dezembro de 1545".

Mç. 78

nº 94: "Carta de Miguel Rodrigues, dando parte a ElRey da cauza porque o Idalcão rompeo as Tregoas com o Governador D. João de Castro (. . .), De Dio a 24 de Novembro de 1546".

Mç. 79

nº 139: "Carta de D. Diogo de Almeida dando parte a ElRey os Capitães do Idalcão recuperarem a terra firme de que os tinha lançado fora (. . .) De Aguacim a 10 de Dezembro de 1547".

Mç. 81

nº 59: "Carta de Fr. Antonio do Porto, dando parte a ElRey que os convertidos à Fé Catholica padecião muitas necessidades por seus Pays, e parentes os desprezarem (. . .) De Baçaim a 7 de Outubro de 1548".

nº 62: "Carta de Thome Lobo dando conta a ElRey do grande fruto que fazia S. Francisco Xavier com a sua predica, e doutrina (. . .) De Gôa a 13 de Outubro de 1548".

nº 99: "Carta de Fr. João de Albuquerque, Bispo de Gôa, dando conta a ElRey que Fr. João de Villa do Conde vinha a esta Corte dar contas das couzas do Ceilão, sobre a conversão da Christandade, pedindo ao mesmo Snr. o houvisse por ser bom Religiozo. De Gôa a 6 de Dezembro de 1548".

nº 101: "Carta de Fr. Diogo Bermudes dando parte a ElRey do deploravel estado em que estava a Christandade nas partes da India, principalmente nas partes de Ceilão (. . .) De Gôa a 6 de Dezembro de 1548".

nº 116: "Carta de Rui Barbudo dando conta a ElRey das couzas que erão necessarias na India para augmento da Christandade de que era encarregado (. . .) De Gôa a 18 de Dezembro de 1548".

Mç. 82

nº 5: "Carta dos mestres da Casa dos Vinte e Quatro de Goa dando parte ao rei estar acabada a casa que o mesmo senhor mandara fazer para os religiosos de S. Domingos, celebrando-se a primeira missa dia de Natal, de que o povo estava contentíssimo, de 4 de Janeiro de 1549".

Mç. 83

nº 59: "Carta de Rui Gonçalves de Caminha, dando parte ao rei remeter apontamentos sobre a as liberdades e isenções que deviam ter as gentes da pescaria da Índia. Que o governador lhe encarregara o cuidado dos padres de S. Domingo a quem deram um grande chão para edificarem a igreja, dormitório e noviciado, de 30 de Dezembro de 1549".

nº 60: "Carta de Cosme Annes, Ouvidor Geral da Fazenda da India, dando conta a ElRey do deploravel estado daquella terra, que o Turco tinha feito algumas conquistas de novo, e a gente se hia auzentando persuadindo-se ser muito justo ir Governar o Infante por ser aquelle governo só para Príncipes. De Cochim a 30 de Dezembro de 1549".

Mç. 87

nº 45: "Carta de Fr. Diogo Bermudes expondo a D. Bernardo Bispo de S. Thomé o deploravel estado em que se achava a India tanto no Espiritual como no Temporal, pela pouca vigilancia do Bispo, e cuidado do Vice Rey (. . .) De S. Silvestre a 31 de Dezembro de 1551".

Mç. 95

nº 26: "Carta de ElRey ao Dezembargador da Relação da India Sebastião Pinheiro para o administrar durante a Sé Vacante, De 23 de Março de 1555".

Mç. 97

nº 27: "Carta de Baltasar Lobo pedindo à rainha rogasse ao rei mandasse fazer um recolhimento em Goa para os órfãos e desamparados, de 12 de Outubro de 1555".

Mç. 100

nº 122: "Carta de frei Estêvão de Santa Maria, religioso da Ordem de S. Domingos, em que escreve ao seu provincial dando-lhe conta da sua vida e de como o mandavam da Índia a Cochim a fundar um convento de sua ordem e o acabou com as esmolas que tirou, sem que o rei lhe desse para ele coisa alguma, com os particulares sobre a sua religião, de 25 de Outubro de 1557".

Mç. 106

nº 121: "Minuta dos apontamentos que a rainha e o cardeal haviam de dar para o bom regimen das órfãs da Índia, 20 de Fevereiro de 1564".

nº 122: "Carta de frei André Torneiro expondo à rainha o desamparo das órfãs do Brazil e Índia, que seria útil mandar a mesma senhora se dessem os oficios às pessoas que com elas casassem, revogando as provisões em contrário, de 20 de Fevereiro de 1564".

Mç. 107

nº 38: "Carta de D. Antão de Noronha dando conta a ElRey da sua Viagem, e estado em que achou a India; razoes que teve para não dar Igrejas, e aforar algumas Aldêas aos Padres da Companhia, Gôa a 30 de Dezembro de 1564".

Part II

Mç. 25

nº 53 – "Mandado de Afonso de Albuquerque para o feitor de Goa dar a sete mulheres casadas sete panos de seda, 12 de Fevereiro de 1511.

Mç. 26

nº 24 – "Ordem de Afonso de Albuquerque, governador de Goa, ao feitor Francisco Corvinel para que pague às pessoas declaradas nas ordens, as quantias expressas nestes bilhetes, procedidas dos motos de seus casamentos, 9 de Abril de 1511".

nº 31 – "Ordem do capitão-mor de Goa ao feitor da dita fortaleza em que lhe manda dar aos malabares que andam na terra de Chorão, nove fardos de arroz, 10 April 1511".

nº 49 – "Ordem do capitão-mor de Goa ao feitor da Fortaleza de Goa para dar a Pedro Mendes, casado na dita cidade, 8 mil réis para cumprimento de pago de seu casamento, 12 de Abril de 1511".

Mç. 28

nº 13 – Mandado de Diogo Mendes de Vasconcelos para Francisco Corvinel, feitor de Goa, dar 10 mil réis a Pedro Vaz de seu casamento, 20 de Agosto de 1511.

Mç. 35

nº 58 – "Mandado de Afonso de Albuquerque, capitão-geral e governador da Índia, por que ordena a Francisco Corvinel, feitor de Goa, pague a Mateus Fernandes 18 mil réis de seu casamento de que o rei lhe faz mercê, 5 de Novembro de 1512".

nº 174 – "Mandado de Afonso de Albuquerque, capitão-geral e governador da Índia, por que ordena a Francisco Corvinel, feitor de Goa, dê a Fernando de Basto 18 mil réis e uma escrava para seu casamento, 30 de Novembro de 1512".

Mç. 36

nº 54 – "Mandado de Afonso de Albuquerque, governador das Índias, por que ordena a Francisco Corvinel, feitor de Goa, dê a Pedro, cristão canarim, 2000 réis de seu casamento, 24 de Dezembro de 1512".

Mç. 36

nº 69 – "Mandado de Afonso de Albuquerque, governador das Índias, por que ordena ao feitor de Goa dê a Diogo Mendes, Henrique de Nostra Dama, Rodrigo Rebelo e Jorge de Albuquerque, naique, 3000 réis a cada um de seu casamento, 28 de Dezembro de 1512.

Mç. 48

nº 92 – "Mandado de Afonso de Albuquerque para o feitor de Goa, dar a 34 gançares da Ilha Dadivary a cada um seu pachori de mercê, 23 June 1512".

Mç. 53

nº 2 – "Mandado de Afonso de Albuquerque para o feitor de Goa dar a um bramani 1000 réis para seu mantimento, 8 Nov. 1514".

nº 24 – "Mandado de Afonso de Albuquerque para Francisco Corvinel, feitor de Goa, dar a Pedro e a Manuel que se fizeram cristãos, a cada um, 100 réis e 2 panos, 11 Nov. 1514".

Mç. 77

nº 108 – "Mandado de Diogo Lopes ordenando a Francisco Corvinel, feitor de Goa, compre para os frades de São Francisco da dita cidade 12 pipas de vinho, 1 de vinagre e um quarto de azeite de Portugal, que lhe dá de esmola, 25 de Setembrode 1518".

Mç. 80

nº 20: "Cópia da Carta de Privilégios concedido a Relaxatim, Mouro, Ourives Mór de Goa, e a seus Parentes, para não pagarem Direitos das Terras que lavrarem na Ilha de Cari, mais do que athé 4$ reis. Dada em Almeirim a 13 de Fevereiro de 1519".

nº 91: "Copia da Carta de Privilegio concedido a Relaxatim, Ourives Mór de Goa, para comprar, e vender hum Cavallo, em cada anno, sem pagar Direitos. Dada em Almeirim a 5 de Março de 1519".

Mç. 86

nº 8 – "Alvará de Diogo Lopes de Sequeira, Governador das Indias para os Palmares de que ElRey fez merce aos Moradores de Gôa, se arrendarem á gente da terra (. . .) De Gôa a 24 de Novembro de 1519".

Mç. 154

nº 47 – "Recibo de frei Francisco de Alenquer, vigário do Convento de S. Francisco de Goa por que consta ter recebido de Francisco Corvinel, feitor de Goa, 40 cotonias para vestiaria dos religiosos, 8 de Março de 1528".

Mç. 165

nº 3 – "Recibo de frei António, guardião do Mosteiro de S. Francisco de Goa, de 2 arrobas de ferro que recebeu de Francisco Corvinel, feitor de Goa, 9 de Setembro de 1530.

Mç. 221

nº 172 – "Certidão do juramento que prestou D. João de Albuquerque na sua Sagração no Convento de S. Francisco de Lisboa, De 30 de Agosto de 1538".

Mç. 241

nº 24 – "Carta de Chrisna expondo a ElRey o serviço que lhe fizera persuadindo ao Idalcão largar ao mesmo Snr. as terras de Salsete, e Bardez, sobre as quaes contratara ao depois com o Gov.or Martinho Affonso de lhe entregar por ellas a Miele, e seus filhos, o que o dito

Gov.or não cumprio (. . .) escrita de Bijapur a 6 de Dezembro de 1546".

nº 89 – "Carta de Christóvão Fernandes, Desembargador da Relação de Gôa, dando parte a ElRey chegar a Gôa na Nau Flor de la Mar a 3 de Setembro de 1548 (. . .)".

nº 90 – "Carta o Fr. João de Albuquerque Bº de Goa dando parte a ElRey bautizar hum gentio chamado Loquce, a quem pozera o nome de Lucas de Sá, sua mulher, e quatro pessoas".

Gavetas

nº 15, Nº 20.

Inquisição

Conselho Geral do Santo Ofício, nº 184, nº 462, nº 1176.

Inquisição de Lisboa, Processos nº 3672, 8916, 13347, 13348, 13349, 13352.

Inquisição de Évora, Processos nº 7545 e 7717.

Tribunal do Santo Ofício, processo nº 8916.

Manuscritos da Livraria

nº 757 – Saldanha, António, S.J., *Prasse Pastoral, Modo Breve de Catequizar os Cathecumenos adultos que se hão de Bautizar, e outra vária doutrina sobre os Sacramentos da Santa Madre Igreja.*

nº 1777 – *Relação de papeis autênticos jurados, & passados polla Chancelaria Real (. . .) em defensa da honra do padre Fr. Simão da Nazareth (. . .)*

nº 1952 – Conde da Ericeira (attrib.), *Esplendor do Oriente. Genealogia das Famílias mais Ilustres da Índia.*

nº 2238 – Sant'Anna, Diogo de, OSA, *Resposta por parte do insigne mosteiro de Santa Mónica.*

Mesa da Consciência e Ordens

Ns. 302–306: Aranha, Lázaro Leitão, *Meza das Tres Ordens Militares. Da jurisdição da Ordem de Cristo por tudo o q/ toca o Ultramar.*

Núcleo Antigo

Tombo de Simão Botelho, 1554.

PRINTED SOURCES

Admirabile Vida, y virtudes del santo martir Rodulfo Aquaviva, hijo del Excmo Señor Duque de Atri, Don Juan Geronimo Aquaviva, Vida del santo martyr P. Alonso Pacheco, Breves Noticias de los tres compañeros en el martyrio del P. Rodulfo (s.l., s.d.).

Albuquerque, Luís de, ed., *Cartas de D. João de Castro a D. João III* (Lisbon: CNCDP, 1989).

Albuquerque, Luís de, and Caeiro, Margarida, ed., *Martim Afonso de Sousa, Cartas* (Lisbon: Alfa, 1989).

Allami, Abu'l Fazl, *The Ain-i-Akbari*, trans. H. Blochmann and H.S. Jarrett (Delhi: D.K. Publishers and Distributors, 2006).

Andrada, Ernesto de Campos de, ed., *Relações de Pero de Alcáçova Carneiro, Conde de Idanha, Do tempo que ele e seu pai, António Carneiro, serviram de secretários (1515–1568)* (Lisbon: Imprensa Nacional de Lisboa, 1937).

Andrada, Francisco de, *Crónica de D. João III* (Porto: Lello, 1976).

Anjos, Manuel dos, OFM, *Historia Universal, em que se descrevem os Impérios (. . .)* (Lisbon: Miguel Deslandes, 1702) (1651).

Apresentação, Dâmaso da, OFM, *Obrigaçam do frade menor, em que se tratão as cousas que está obrigado a guardar, assim por sua regra, como por ley divina* (Convento da Carnota: António Álvares, 1627).

Aquinas, Thomas of, OP, *Somme Contre les Gentils – Contra Gentiles* (Paris: Ed. du Cerf, 1993).

———, *La Somma Teologica* (Florence: Adriano Salami, s.d.).

Aragão, Fernão Ximenes de, *Doutrina católica para instrução e confirmação dos fieis e extinção das seitas supersticiosas e em particular do judaísmo* (Lisbon: Pedro Craesbeeck, 1625).

———, *Extinçam do Judaismo e mais seitas superticiozas; e exaltaçam da fé verdadeira* (. . .) (Lisbon: Pedro Craesbeeck, 1628).

Arrais, Amador dos, *Diálogos*, OC (Lisbon: Sá da Costa, 1981) (1604).

Azpicuelta Navarro, Martim de, *Manual de Confessores & Penitentes* (Coimbra: Off. João Barreira, 1560).

———, *Relectio cap. Ita quorundam de Iudaeis, in qua de rebus ad Sarracenos deferri prohibitis, & censuris ob id latis non segniter disputatur, composita, & pronunciata in inclyta Conimbricensi Academia* (Coimbra: 1560).

Barros, João de, *Gramática da Língua Portuguesa. Cartinha, Gramática,*

Diálogo em Louvor da Nossa Linguagem e Diálogo da Viciosa Vergonha, Lisbon, FLUL (Lisbon, 1971) (1540).

———, *Ásia. Dos feitos que os Portugueses fizeram no descobrimento e conquista dos mares e terras do Oriente* (Lisbon: INCM, 1988) (1552–1563).

Bartoli, Daniello, S.J., *Dell'istoria della Compagnia di Giesu, L'Asia, parte prima de Daniello Bartoli, Terza edizione accresciuta della missione al mogor e della vita e morte del P. Ridolfo Acquaviva* (Rome: Stamperia del Varese, 1668).

Boaventura, São, OFM, *Alguns tratados do seraphico doctyor Sam Boaventura, em que se contém huma doctrina mui proveitosa, & necessaria a toda a pessoa, principalmente religiosa,* trans. João da Madre de Deus (Lisbon: António Álvares, 1602).

Bocarro, António, *Década 13 da História da Índia, publicada de Ordem da Classe de Sciencias Moraes, Politicas e Bellas-Lettras*, ed. R.J. de Lima Felner (Lisbon: Academia Real de Sciencias, 1876).

Botelho, Simão, *Textos sobre o Estado da Índia (1504–1654)* (Lisbon: Alfa, 1989).

Botero, Giovanni, *Da Razão de Estado*, Coimbra, INIC, 1992 (1583).

Bragança Pereira, A., *Arquivo português oriental* (Bastorá: Tip. Rangel, 1936, 6 vols).

Breve Relaçam das Christandades que os Religiosos de N. Padre Santo Agostinho tem a sua conta nas partes do Oriente (Lisbon: António Álvares, 1630).

Bruno, Vicente, *Meditações sobre os mistérios da paixão, ressurreição e ascensão de Cristo nosso Senhor e vinda do Espírito Santo, recolhidas de diversos santos padres e devotos autores,* trad. de Brás Viegas) (Lisbon: Pedro Craesbeeck, 1601).

Budrioli, Andrea, S.J., *Segni maravigliosi co quali si e compiaciuto iddio di autorizzare il Maritirio de' Vener. Servi di Dio Ridolfo Aqcuaviva, Alfonso Paceco, Pietro Berna, Antonio Franceschi,e Francesco Araña della Compagnia di Gesu, succedduto nell'Indie il di 15 Luglio 1583* (Rome: Antonio de Rossi, 1745).

Cardoso, João, OFM, *Jornada da alma libertada, guiada no arriscado, e tempestuoso mar do mundo, por Christo Piloto divino, na Nao da Igreja ao porto celestial da salvação* (Lisbon: Geraldo da Vinha, 1626).

Carvalho, Tristão Barbosa de, *Peregrinação Cristã que contém um epílogo da obra de Deus nosso Senhor desde a criação dos anjos, do mundo, do homem, da vida, paixão e morte do Redentor e da Virgem Senhora Nossa* (Lisbon: Geraldo da Vinha, 1620).

Colecção de São Lourenço, 3 vols, ed. Elaine Sanceau, *et al.* (Lisbon: Centro de Estudos Históricos Ultramarinos, 1973–83).

Córdova, António de, OFM, *Tratado de Casos de Consciência* (Lisbon: Simão Lopes, 1586).

Correia, Gaspar, *Lendas da Índia* (Porto: Lello, 1975).

Couto, Diogo do, *Decadas da Asia* (Lisbon: Off. de Domingos Gonsalves, ed. de 1736).

———, *Soldado Pratico* (2ª ed., Lisbon, Livraria Sá da Costa, 1954).

Cunha, J. Gerson da, ed., *The Sahyadri-Khan of the Skanda Purana: A Mythological, Historical and Geographical Account of Western India* (Bombay: 1877).

Cunha Rivara, J.H., *Archivo Portuguez Oriental*, 6 Fascicules (reprint, New Delhi: Asian Educational Services, 1992).

Dellon, Charles, *Voyages de Mr. Dellon avec sa relation de l'Inquisition de Goa, augmentée de diverses pieces curieuses et l'histoire des dieux qu'adorent les Gentils des Indes* (Cologne: Chez les Heritiers de Pierre Marteau, 1711).

Deos, Jacinto de (OFM Rec.), *Caminho dos Frades Menores para a Vida Eterna* (Lisbon: Miguel Deslandes, 1689).

Documentação Ultramarina Portuguesa, 5 vols., ed. A. da Silva Rego (Lisbon: Centro de Estudos Históricos Ultramarinos, 1960–7).

Documentos Remettidos da Índia ou Livro das Monções, publicados de Ordem da Classe de Sciencias Moraes, Politicas e Bellas-Lettras, 5 vols, ed. Raymundo António de Bulhão Pato (Lisbon: Academia Real de Sciencias, 1880–1935).

Documentos Remetidos da Índia ou Livro das Monções, Vols 6-10, ed. A. da Silva Rego (Lisbon: Imprensa Nacional, 1974–82).

Estatutos Generales OFM (s.l.: 1583).

Estêvão, Tomás, S.J. [Thomas Stephens] *Doutrina Christam em lingoa bramana canarim: ordenada a maneira de dialogo, para ensinar os mininos* (Rachol: Colégio de Rachol da Companhia de Jesus, 1622).

Figueiredo, Jozé Anastácio de, *Synopsis Chronologica de subsídios ainda os mais raros para a historia e estudo critico da legislacao portugueza (. . .)*, Tomos I – Desde 1143 até 1549 e II – Desde 1550 até 1603 (Lisbon: Officina da Academia, 1790).

Frias, António João de, *Aureola dos Indios, e nobiliarchia bracmana: tra-*

tado historico, genealogico, panegyrico, politico, e moral (. . .) (Lisbon: Off. Miguel Deslandes, 1702).

As Gavetas da Torre do Tombo, ed. A. da Silva Rego, 11 vols (Lisbon: 1960).

Galvão, António, *Tratado dos Descobrimentos*, ed. Luís de Albuquerque (Lisbon: Alfa, 1989).

Garcia, José Ignacio Abranches, *Archivo da Relação de Goa*, Parts I–II (Goa: 1874).

Goltz, Hubert, *Fastos Magistratuum et Triumphorum Romanorum ad Augusti obitum (. . .)* (s.l.: 1529).

Gonçalves, Sebastião, S.J., *Primeira parte da Historia da Companhia de Jesus na Índia* (Lisbon: 1954).

Guerreiro, Fernão, S.J., *Relação Anual das Coisas que fizeram os Padres da Companhia de Jesus nas suas Missões (. . .) Anos de 1600–1609*, 3 vols, ed. Artur Viegas (Lisbon: Imprensa Nacional, 1930–42).

Halicarnasso, Dioniso, *De origine urbis Romae (. . .)* (s.l.:1526).

Holanda, Francisco de, *Alguns dos desenhos das Antigualhas* (Lisbon: Livros Horizonte, 1989).

———, *Da fábrica que falece à cidade de Lisboa* (Lisbon: Livros Horizonte, 1984).

Jorge, Marcos, S.J., *Doutrina Christam* (Augsburg: 1616).

La Croze, M. Veyssère de, *Histoire du Christianisme des Indes* (The Hague: 1724).

Laeti, Pomponii, *De magistratibus & sacerdotijs romanorum* (. . .) (s.l.: 1515) (1501).

Leão, Gaspar de (OFM Rec.), *Desengano de Perdidos* (Coimbra: Universidade de Coimbra, 1958) (1573).

———, ed., *Tratado de Jerónimo de Santa Fé contra os judeus em que prova o messias da Lei ser vindo. Carta do primeiro arcebispo de Goa ao povo de Israel seguidor ainda da lei de Moisés e do Talmud* (Goa: João de Emden, 1565).

Linschoten, Jan Hugyen van, *Itinerário, viagem ou navegação para as Índias Orientais ou Portuguesa*, ed. and trans. Arie Pos and Rui Loureiro, 2nd edition (Lisbon: CNCDP, 1997) (1598).

Lisboa, Marcos, OFM, *Crónicas da Ordem dos Frades Menores* (Porto: FLUP, 2002) (1557–1562).

Lista das rendas e despesas da Província de Goa da Companhia de Jesus pera o Senhor Conde Viso-Rei Joam Nunes da Cunha, in Calado, Adelino de Almeida, "A Companhia de Jesus em meados do século XVII", *Studia*, nº 40, Dez. 1978, 349–67.

Loarte, Gaspar de, S.J., *Istrução e advertências para meditar a paixão de Cristo* (Lisbon: António Ribeiro, 1587).

Loyola, Inacio de, S.J., *Exercícios Espirituais* (Porto: Apostolado da Imprensa, 1983) (1548).

Lucena, João de, S.J., *História da vida do Padre Francisco Xavier* (Lisboa: Alfa, 1989) (1600).

Machiavelli, Nicolao, *Il principe* (Milan: Mondadori Editore, 1994) (1513).

Manual de las cosas essentiales a que son obligados los frayles menores (. . .) compuesto por un docto padre de la misma orden de la provintia de la Conceptio (Coimbra: Joam Barreira, 1571).

Martinez de la Puente, Joseph, *Compendio de las historias de los descubrimientos, conquista y guerras de la India Oriental, y sus Islas desde los tiempos del Infante Don Enrique de Portugal su inventor, hermano del Rey D. Duarte; hasta los del Rey D. Felipe II. de Portugal, y III de Castilla (. . .)* (Madrid: Imprenta Imperial, 1681).

Monforte, Luís de, OFM Rec. *Chronica da Provincia da Piedade* (Lisbon: Off. Manescal da Costa,1751).

O Livro do "Pai dos Cristãos", ed. J. Wicki, s.j., (Lisbon: Centro de Estudos Históricos Ultramarinos, 1969).

Pais, Leonardo, *Promptuario de diffiniçoes Indicas Deduzidas, De varios Chronistas da India, graves Authores, e das Historias Gentilicas* (Lisbon: Off. António Pedrozo Galram, 1713).

Perez de Chinchón, Bernardo, *Libro llamado AntiAlcorano: q/ quere dizir contra el Alcorano & mahoma (. . .)* (Seville: 1532).

Pinheiro, António, *Colleçam das Obras Portuguezas do sabio bispo de Miranda e de Leyria D. Antonio Pinheiro, pregador do senhor Rey D. Joam III e mestre do Principe*, ed. Bento Joze de Souza Farinha, tomo I (Lisbon: Off. Joze da Silva Nazareth, 1784).

Pissurlencar, P.S.S., ed., *Assentos do Conselho de Estado*, 5 vols (Bastorá-Goa: Tipografia Rangel, 1953–7).

Por Terras de Portugal no século XVI. Bartolomè de Villalba Estaña, Gianbattista Confalonieri (Lisbon: CNCDP, 2003).

Porto, Rodrigo do, OFM, *Manual de Confessores & Penitentes em ho qual breue & particular & muy verdadeyramente se decidem & declarã quasi todas as duuidas & casos que nas confissões soe[m] ocorrer* (Coimbra: João Barreira e João Álvares, 1549).

Portugaliae Monumenta Misericordiarum, ed. José Pedro Paiva, 10 vols (Lisbon: União das Misericórdias Portuguesas, 2002–17).

Purificação, Miguel da, OFM, *Relação defensiva dos filhos da Índia Oriental e da província do apóstolo S. Thome dos frades menores da regular observância da mesma Índia* (Barcelona: Sebastião e João Matheva, 1640).

———, *Vida evangelica y apostolica de los frailes menores en Oriente, ilustrada con varias materias y anotaciones predicables* (Barcelona: Gabriel Nogues, 1641).

Rebelo, João, S.J., *História dos milagres do rosário e de muitas e diversas devoções* (Evora: Manuel de Lira, 1602).

Rego, António da Silva, S.J., ed., *Documentação para a história das missões do padroado português do Oriente,* 12 vols (Lisbon: Fundaçâo Oriente-CNCDP, 1996).

Relatione della felice morte di cinque religiosi della compagnia di Giesù. Et di alcuni altri secolari ammazati dá Gentili per la Fede, nell'India Orientale, l'Anno 1583 (Cavata da una del Padre Alessandro Valignano . . .) (Milan: Pacisico Pontio, 1585).

Resende, Garcia de, *Breve Memorial dos pecados e cousas que pertencem ha confissam* (Lisbon: Nicolau Gazini, 1518).

Ribeiro, João Pedro, *Indice Chronologico Remissivo da Legilsção Portugueza posterior à publicação do codigo filippino com hum appendice. Parte I, desde a mesma pubblicação até o fim do reinado do senhor D. João V (. . .)* (Lisbon: Typographia da Academia, 1805).

———, *Indice Chronologico Remissivo da Legilsção Portugueza posterior à publicação do codigo filippino com hum appendice. Parte V (. . .)* (Lisbon: Typographia da Academia, 1826).

São Boaventura, OFM, *Alguns Tratados* (. . .) (Lisbon: António Álvares, 1602).

Santarém, Visconde de, *Quadro Elementar das Relações Políticas e Diplomáticas de Portugal com as diversas partes do mundo desde o princípio da monarchia até aos nossos dias,* Paris, Vols X and XIII (Paris: J.P. Aillaud, 1842).

Santo Estêvão, Antonio de, OP, *Relações Summarias de alguns serviços que fizerão a Deos, & a estes Reynos, os Religiosos Dominicos nas partes da India Oriental nestes annos proximos e passados* (Lisbon: Lourenço Craesbeeck, 1635).

Soares, João, OSA, *Libro dela verdad dela fe* (Alcalá de Henares: Juan de Brocar, 1545).

Sousa, Fr. Luís de, OP, *Anais de D. João III* (Lisbon: Sá da Costa, 1983).

Sousa, Francisco de, S.J., *Oriente conquistado a Jesu Christo pelos Padres da Companhia de Jesus da Provincia de Goa . . .* (Porto: Lello & Irmãos, 1978) (1710).

Suárez, Francisco, S.J., *Tractatus de legibus ac Deo Legislatore* (Coimbra: 1612).

Távora, Henrique de, OP, *Tratado de Avisos de Confessores* (Lisbon: 1560).

Tombo da Ilha de Goa e das Terras de Salcete e Bardez (Bastorá: Rangel, 1952).

Tratado da vida e martírio dos cinco mártires de Marrocos enviados por S. Francisco (Coimbra: João Álvares, 1568).

Trindade, Paulo da, OFM, *Conquista Espiritual do Oriente,* 4 vols (Lisbon: Centro de Estudos Históricos Ultramarinos, 1962–1964).

Valignano, Alessandro, S.J., *Historia Indica,* in Rego, António da Silva, ed., *Documentação para a história das missões do padroado português do Oriente,* vol. 11 (Lisbon: Fundaçâo Oriente-CNCDP, 1993).

Velasco, Gabriel Alvarez de, *De Privilegiis Pauperum et Miserabilium Personarum ed Logem Unicam (. . .)* (London: Horatii Boissat & Georgii Remeus, 1663).

Viaggiatori del 600, a cura di Marziano Guglieminetti (Turin: Unione Tipografico-Editrice, Torinense, 1976) (1967).

Wicki, Josephus, S.J., *Documenta Indica,* 1540–1597, 18 vols (Rome: Monumenta Historica Societatis Jesu, 1948–1988).

Xavier, Filipe Nery, *Collecção de leis peculiares das communidades agricolas das aldeas dos concelhos das ilhas de Salcete e Bardez* (Nova Goa: Imprensa Nacional, 1871).

SECONDARY SOURCES

A.A.V.V., *O Humanismo Português, 1500–1600* (Lisbon: Academia das Ciências de Lisboa, 1988).

A Herança do Relauchatim (Lisbon: CNCDP, 1995).

Abreu, Laurinda Faria Santos, "Padronização hospitalar e Misericórdias: apontamentos sobre a reforma da assistência pública em Portugal", in *Congresso Comemorativo do V Centenário da Fundação do Hospital Real do Espírito Santo de Évora, Actas* (Évora: Hospital do Espírito Santo, 1996), 137–48.

Adas, Michael, "From Avoidance to Confrontation: Peasant Protest in Precolonial and Colonial Southeast Asia", in Nicholas Dirks, ed., *Colonialism and Culture* (Ann Arbor: University of Michigan Press, 1992).

Afonso, Carlos Alberto, *No tempo em que todos eram santos. Estudos sobre o "Martirológio Nacional Português": O Agiológico Lusitano de Jorge Cardoso* (Braga: Universidade do Minho, 1988).

Aiala, Frederico Diniz de, *Goa antiga e moderna* (Nova Goa: Coelho, 1927).

———, ed., *Portugal no Mundo*, Vol. III (Lisbon: Alfa, 1989).

Albuquerque, Luís de, *Alguns Casos da Índia Portuguesa no Tempo de D. João de Castro,* Vol. II (Lisbon: Alfa, 1989).

Alden, Dauril, *The Making of an Enterprise: The Society of Jesus in Portugal, Its Empire and Beyond, 1540–1750* (Stanford: Stanford University Press, 1996).

Alencastro, Luiz Filipe, "The Apprenticeship of Colonization", in Patrick Manning, ed., *Slave Trades, 1500–1800, Globalization of Forced Labour*, Vol. 15 of A.J.R. Russell-Wood (gen. ed.), *An Expanding World: The European Impact on World History, 1450–1800* (Aldershot: Ashgate Variorum, 1996), 83–106.

Allegra, Luciano, "Il parroco: un mediatore fra alta e bassa cultura", in Corrado Vivanti, ed., *Storia d'Italia, Annali 4, Intelletuali e Potere* (Turin: Giulio Einaudi, 1981), 895–930.

Alonso Romo, Eduardo Javier, "A 'lusitanização' de S. Francisco Xavier e dos seus companheiros espanhóis (1540–1552)", *Brotéria*, 147, 1998, 565–80.

Altekar, A.S., *State and Government in Ancient India* (Delhi: Motilal Banarsidass Pub., 1997) (1949).

Alves, Jorge Manuel dos Santos, "Os mártires de Achém nos séculos XVI e XVII: Islão versus Cristianismo?", in *Congresso Internacional de História – Missionação Portuguesa e Encontro de Culturas, Actas*, Vol. II (Braga: UCP-CNCDP-FEC, 1993).

Ames, Glenn, *Renascent Empire? The House of Braganza and the Quest for Stability in Portuguese Monsoon Asia, ca. 1640–1683* (Amsterdam: Amsterdam University Press, 2000).

Anderson, Benedict, *Imagined Communities: Reflections on the Origin and Spread of Nationalism* (London: Verso, 1994).

Andrès Martín, Melquíades, "La espiritualidad franciscana en España en tiempos de las Observancias (1380–1517)", *Studia Historica/ Historia Moderna, vol. VI – Homenage al Professor Dr. D. Manuel Férnandez Alvarez*, 1988.

———, "Primeros pasos comunes de la Descalcez Franciscana en España y Portugal (1500–1523), *Primeiras Jornadas de História Moderna, Actas, Vol. II* (Lisbon: Centro de História da Universidade de Lisboa, 1986).

Antunes, José, "Acerca da liberdade de religião na Idade Média. Mouros e Judeus perante um problema teológico-canónico", *Revista de História das Ideias*, Vol. 11, 1989, 64–83.

Aquinas, Thomas, *Cuncolim is a Historic Village, 4th Century Commemorative Pub. (July 1583–1983)* (Cundhi, Salcete-Goa: 1983).

Araújo, Maria Benedita, "O 'Pai dos Christãos'. Contribuição para o estudo da Cristianização na Índia", in *Congresso Internacional de História – Missionação Portuguesa e Encontro de Culturas, Actas, Vol. II* (Braga: UCP-CNCDP-FEC, 1993), 305–23.

Asad, Talal, "Comments on Conversion", in Peter van der Veer, ed., *Conversion to Modernities: The Globalization of Christianity* (New York and London: Routledge, 1996), 263–74.

Assayag, Jackie, *La Colère de la déesse décapitée. Traditions, cultes et pouvoir dans le sud de l'Inde* (Paris: CNRS Ed., 1992).

———, and Tarabout, Gilles, eds, *La Possession en Asie du Sud. Parole, Corps, Territoire* (Paris: EHESS, 1999).

Aubin, Jean, ed., *La Decouverte, le Portugal et l'Europe* (Paris: FCG-CCP, 1990).

Azevedo, António Emílio de Almeida, *As communidades de Goa. História das Instituições Antigas* (Lisbon: Bertrand, 1890).

Baden-Powell, B.H., "The Villages of Goa in the Early Sixteenth Century", *Journal of the Royal Asiatic Society of Great Britain and Ireland*, 1900.

———, *The Origin and Growth of Village Communities in India* (London: 1908).

Ballhatchet, Kenneth, *Caste, Society and Catholicism in India (1789–1914)* (London: Curzon Press, 1998).

Baroncelli, F., and G. Assereto, "Pauperismo e religione nell'età moderna", *Società e Storia*, n. 7, 1980, 169–201.

Baroncelli, Flavio, "Contro la carità discreta. Misericordia, raziocinio e volontà di non sapere in una polemica cinquentecesca sulla povertà", *Materiali per una storia della cultura giuridica*, Vol. XV, nº 1, 1985, 3–49.

Barreto, Luís Filipe, *Descobrimentos e Renascimento. Formas de Ser e Pensar nos séculos XVI e* XVII (Lisbon: INCM, 1983).

Barros, Edval de Souza, "O Conselho Ultramarino e a Disputa pela Condição da Guerra no Atlântico e no Índico (1643–1661)", PhD thesis, Rio de Janeiro: UFRJ, 2004.

———, "*Negócios de tanta importância." O Conselho Ultramarino e a Disputa pela Condição da Guerra no Atlântico e no Índico (1643–1661)* (Lisbon: CHAM, 2008).

Bastos, Cristiana, "Medicina, império e processos locais em Goa, século XIX", *Análise Social*, Vol. XLII (182), 2007, 99–122.

———, "The Inverted Mirror: Dreams of Imperial Glory and Tales of Subalternity from the Medical School of Goa", *Etnográfica*, Vol. 5, No. 1, 2002, 59–76

Bayly, Christopher A., *Empire and Information. Intelligence Gathering and Social Communication in India, 1780–1870* (Cambridge: Cambridge University Press, 1999) (1996).

———, *Indian Society in the Making of the British Empire, Vol. II.1* in *The New Cambridge History of India* (Cambridge: Cambridge University Press, 1988).

Bayly, Susan, *Saints, Goddesses, and Kings. Muslims and Christians in South Indian Society, 1700–1900* (Cambridge: Cambridge University Press, 1989).

———, *Caste, Society and Politics*, Vol. IV.3 in *New Cambridge History of India* (Cambridge: Cambridge University Press, 1999).

Baubeta, Patricia Anne Odber de, "A pregação e a sociedade medieval portuguesa", in *Congresso Internacional de História – Missionação Portuguesa e Encontro de Culturas, Vol. 1* (Braga: UCP-CNCDP-FEC, 1993), 279–99.

Beato, Agostinho Pires, *Rodrigo Sanches, Epistolário Latino* (Master's thesis) (Coimbra: FLUC, 1991).

Bebiano, Rui, "A Guerra: o seu imaginário e a sua deontologia", in Manuel Themudo Barata and Nuno Severiano Teixeira, eds, *Nova História Militar de Portugal* (Lisbon: Círculo de Leitores, 2003), 36–67..

Beck, Brenda, *Peasant Society in Konku: A Study of Right and Left Subcastes in South India* (Vancouver: University of British Columbia, 1972).

Bergin, Joseph, "The Counter-Reformation Church and its Bishops", *Past & Present*, nº 165, Nov. 1999, 30–73.

Bernand, Carmen, and Serge Gruzinski, *De l'idolâtrie: Une archéologie des Sciences religieuses* (Paris: Éd. du Seuil, 1988).

———, *Histoire du Nouveau Monde*, 2 vols (Paris: Fayard, 1991).

Bernhard, Jean, Charles Lefebvre, and Francis Rapp, *L'Époque de la Réforme et du Concile de Trente*, tome XIV of Gabriel Le Bras and Jean Gaudemet, eds, *Histoire du Droit et des Institutions de l'Église en Occident* (Paris: Ed. Cujas, 1990).

Bethencourt, Francisco, "O campo ético no século XVI", in *Estudos de Homenagem a Vitorino Magalhães Godinho* (Lisbon: Livraria Sá da Costa, 1988).

———, "A Inquisição", in Yvette Centeno, *Portugal: Mitos Revisitados* (Lisbon: Edições Salamandra, 1993).

———, "Os conventos femininos no Império Português. O caso do convento de Santa Mónica", in *O rosto feminino da expansão portuguesa* (Lisbon: Comissão para a Igualdade e para os Direitos das Mulheres, 1994).

———, *História das Inquisições* (Lisbon: Círculo de Leitores, 1995).

———, "Configurações do Império", in *A formação do Império, 1415–1570*, Vol. I of Kirti Chaudhuri and Francisco Bethencourt, eds, *História da Expansão Portuguesa* (Lisbon: Círculo de Leitores, 1998).

———, "A Inquisição", in João Francisco Marques and António Camões Gouveia, ed., *Humanismo e Reforma*, Vol. 2 of Carlos Moreira de Azevedo, ed., *História Religiosa de Portugal* (Lisbon: Círculo de Leitores, 2000).

Bhabha, Homi, "Of Mimicry and Man", in Frederick Cooper and Ann Laura Stoler, eds, *Tensions of Empire: Colonial Cultures in a Bourgeois World* (Berkeley: University of California Press, 1997).

Bicalho, Maria Fernanda, and Vera Ferlini, eds, *Modos de Governar. Ideias e Práticas Políticas no Império Português – Séculos XVI a XIX* (São Paulo: Editora Alameda, 2005).

Bloch, Maurice E.F., *How We Think They Think: Anthropological Approaches to Cognition, Memory and Literacy* (Colorado: Westview Press, 1998).

Borges, Charles J., "Christianization of the Caste System in Goa", in B.S. Shastry, ed., *Goa through Ages (Seminar Papers)* (Delhi: Asian Publication Services, 1987).

———, "Foreign Jesuits and Native Resistance in Goa (1542–1759)", in Teotonio R. de Souza, ed., *Essays in Goan History* (Delhi: Concept Publishing Company, 1989).

———, *The Economics of the Goa Jesuits, 1542–1759. An Explanation of Their Rise and Fall* (Delhi: Concept Publishing Company, 1994).

Bossy, John, "The Counter-Reformation and the People of the Catholic Europe", *Past & Present*, 47, 1970, 51–70.

———, *A Cristandade no Ocidente, 1400–1700* (Lisbon: Edições 70, 1990) (English version: *Christianity in the West*, 1985).

Bouchon, Geneviève, *Afonso de Albuquerque. O Leão dos Mares* (Lisbon: Quetzal, 2000).

Bourdieu, Pierre, "Cultural Reproduction and Social Reproduction", in *Power and Ideology in Education*, ed. Jerome Karabel and A.H. Halsey (New York: New York University Press, 1977).

Bouza, Fernando, *Portugal no Tempo dos Filipes (1580–1668), Política. Cultura. Representações* (Lisbon: Quetzal, 2001).

———, "Comunicação, Memória e Conhecimento na Espanha da Época Moderna", in *Cultura – Revista de História das Ideias*, nº 14, 2002, 107–71.

Boxer, Charles R., *Relações Raciais no Império Colonial Português* (Lisbon: Afrontamento, 1988) (English version: *Race Relations in the Portuguese Colonial Empire, 1415–1825*, 1963).

———, *Portuguese India in the Mid-Seventeenth Century* (Delhi: Oxford University Press, 1980).

———, "A Note on Portuguese Missionary Methods in the East: Sixteenth to Eighteenth Century", in J.S. Cummins, ed., *The Mission of the Church and the Propagation of the Faith, Studies in the Church History*, Vol. 6 (Cambridge: Cambridge University Press, 1970).

———, *Portuguese Society in the Tropics. The Municipal Councils of Goa, Macau, Bahia and Luanda (1510–1800)* (Madison-Milwaukee: University of Wisconsin Press, 1965).

———, *A Igreja e a Expansão Ibérica*, (Lisbon: Edições 70, 1981) (English version: *The Church Militant in Iberian Expansion, 1440–1770*, 1978).

———, *The Portuguese Seaborne Empire (1415–1825)* (Exeter: Carcanet/ Fundação Calouste Gulbenkian, 1991) (1969).

Breckenridge, Carol A., and Peter van der Veer, eds, *Orientalism and the Postcolonial Predicament: Perspectives on South Asia* (Philadelphia: University of Pennsylvania Press, 1993).

Brito, Raquel Soeiro de, *Goa e as Praças do Norte revisitadas* (Lisbon: CNCDP, 1998) (1966).

Brizzi, G.P., ed., *La "Ratio Studiorum". Modelli culturali e pratiche educative dei gesuiti in Italia tra cinque e seicento* (Rome: Bulzoni Ed., 1981).

Buescu, Ana Isabel, *Imagens do Príncipe, Discurso Normativo e Representação (1525–1549)* (Lisbon: Cosmos, 1996).

———, *D. João III. 1502–1557* (Lisbon: Círculo de Leitores, 2008).

Burguière, André, "La mémoire familiale du Bourgeois Gentilhomme: Généalogies Domestiques en France aux XVIIe et XVIIIe Siècles", *Annales HSS*, Vol. 46, Issue 4, August 1991, 771–88.

Caetano, Joaquim, "Ao modo da Itália: a pintura portuguesa na idade do Humanismo", in *A Pintura Maneirista em Portugal: Arte no Tempo de Camões* (Lisbon: CNCDP, 1995).

———, "S. Silvestre mostrando a Constantino as efígies de S. Pedro e S. Paulo", in *A Pintura Maneirista em Portugal: Arte no Tempo de Camões* (Lisbon: CNCDP, 1995).

———, "A identificação de um pintor (Diogo de Contreiras)", *Oceanos*, nº 13, 1993, 112–18.

Caetano, Marcello, "Recepção e execução dos decretos do concílio de Trento em Portugal", *Revista da Faculdade de Direito da Universidade de Lisboa*, Vol. 19, 1965.

Cañizares Esguerra, Jorge, "New World, New Stars: Patriotic Astrology and the Invention of Indian and Creole Bodies in Colonial Spanish America, 1600–1650", *American Historical Review*, Feb. 1995, 33–68.

———, *How to Write the History of the New World. Histories, Epistemologies, and Identities in the Eighteenth-Century Atlantic World* (Stanford: Stanford University Press, 2001).

Cardim, Pedro, "O Poder dos Afectos. Ordem amorosa e dinâmica política no Portugal do Antigo Regime", PhD thesis, Lisbon: FCSH, 2000.

Carvalho, José Adriano de Freitas, "D. António, prior do Crato, Príncipe Penitente. Os Psalmi Confessionales: do Exemplum à devoção. 1595–1995", *Via Spiritus 2*, 1995, 67–129.

Carvalho, Joaquim Barradas de, *As fontes de Duarte Pacheco Pereira no "Esmeraldo de Situ Orbis"* (Lisbon: INCM, 1982).

Carvalho, Joaquim, and José Pedro Paiva, "A evolução das visitas pastorais da diocese de Coimbra nos séculos XVII e XVIII", *Ler História*, nº 15, 1989, 29–41.

Catão, Francisco Xavier Gomes, "The Reformed Franciscans and the Friary of Our Lady of the Cape, in Goa", *Indian Church History Review*, Vol. 4, No. 2, Dec. 1970, 79–92.

———, *O primeiro seminário de Goa* (s.l., 1955).

Chakrabarty, Dipesh, "Postcoloniality and the Artifices of History. Who Speaks for 'Indian' Pasts?", *Representations*, Special Issue: *Imperial Fantasies and Postcolonial histories,* nº 37, Winter 1992, 1–26.

Chandra, Satish, "Standards of Living – Mughal India", in *Cambridge Economic History of India*, Vol. 1, ed. Irfan Habib and Tapan Raychaudhuri (Cambridge: Cambridge University Press, 1982).

Chatellier, Louis, *A religião dos pobres* (Lisbon: Estampa, 1995) (1993).

Chaudhuri, K.N., *Asia Before Europe: Economy and Civilisation of the Indian Ocean from the Rise of Islam to 1750* (Cambridge: Cambridge University Press, 1990).

———, "O estabelecimento no Oriente", in Kirti Chaudhuri and Francisco Bethencourt, eds, *História da Expansão Portuguesa,* Vol. 1 (Lisbon: Círculo de Leitores, 1998), 248–73.

Chaudhuri, Kirti N., and Francisco Bethencourt, eds, *História da Expansão Portuguesa*, Vols 1–2, (Lisbon: Círculo de Leitores, 1998).

Chauhan, V.P., *Vaishnavism of Goud Saraswat Brahmins and a Few Konkani Folklore Tales* (Delhi: Asian Educational Services, 1991).

Claval, Paul, *Géographie Culturel* (Paris: Nathan, 1995).

Clavero, Bartolomé, *Derecho Indígeno y Cultura Constitutional en América* (Madrid: Siglo XXI, 1994).

Clignet, Remi, "Damned If You Do, Damned If You Don't: The Dilemmas of Colonizer–Colonized Relations", in Philip G. Altbach and Gail P. Kelly, eds, *Education and the Colonial Experience*, 2nd revised edition (New York: Advent Books Inc., 1992) (1984).

Coates, Timothy J., *Degredados e Órfãs: colonização dirigida pela coroa no império português. 1550–1755* (Lisbon: CNCDP, 1998) (English version: *Convicts and Orphans: Forced and State-Sponsored Colonizers in the Portuguese Empire, 1550–1755*, 2001).

Cohen, Eric, "Christianization and Indigenization: Contrasting Processes of Religious Adaptation in Thailand", in Steven Kaplan, ed.,

Indigenous Responses to Western Christianity (New York and London: New York University Press, 1995).

Cohn, Bernard S., "The Pasts of an Indian Village", in Diane Owen Hugues and Thomas R. Trautmann, eds, *Time: Histories and Ethnologies* (Ann Arbor: The University of Michigan Press, 1993).

———, *Colonialism and its Forms of Knowledge, The British in India* (Princeton, NJ: Princeton University Press, 1996).

Comaroff, J.L., "Images of Empire, Contests of Conscience", in Frederick Cooper and Ann Laura Stoler, eds, *Tensions of Empire. Colonial Cultures in a Bourgeois World* (Berkeley: University of California Press, 1997).

Comaroff, John, and Jean Comaroff, *Of Revelation and Revolution*, 2 vols (Chicago and London: University of Chicago Press, 1991).

Conlon, Frank, *Caste in a Changing World: The Chitrapur Saraswat Brahmans, 1700–1935* (Berkeley: University of California Press, 1977).

Connerton, Paul, *How Societies Remember* (Cambridge: Cambridge University Press, 1989).

Continisio, Chiara, "Il principe, il sistema delle virtù e la costruzione di una «Buona Società»", in Cesare Mozzarelli and Danilo Zardin, eds, *I tempi del Concilio. Religione, Cultura e società nell'Europa tridentina* (Milan: Bulzoni Editore, 1997).

Cooper, Frederick, and Ann Laura Stoler, eds, *Tensions of Empire. Colonial Cultures in a Bourgeois World* (Berkeley: University of California Press, 1997).

Copete, Marie-Lucie, and Federico Palomo, "Des carêmes après le carême. Stratégies de conversion et fonctions politiques des missions intérieurs en Espagne et au Portugal (1540–1650)", *Revue de synthèse*, 4ª S. nos 2–3, Avr.–Sept. 1999, 359–80.

Correia, Alberto C. Germano da Silva, *História da Colonização Portuguesa da Índia,* 4 vols (Lisbon: Agência Geral das Colónias, 1948–1954).

Correia, Alves, *A dilatação da fé no império português* (Lisbon: Agência Geral das Colónias, 1936).

Correia, José Manuel, *Os franciscanos em Cochim* (Braga: Ed. Franciscana, 1991).

———, *D. Francisco de Almeida: o 1º Vice-rei da Índia* (Lisbon: CNCDP, 1997).

Correia-Afonso, John, S.J., "Ignatius de Loyola, Portugal and the Indian Missions", in *Congresso Internacional de História – Missionação*

Portuguesa e Encontro de Culturas, Actas, Vol. I (Braga: UCP-CN-CDP-FEC, 1993).

Costa, Alfredo, "Orfãs d'El-Rei e as Mulheres Portuguesas vindas à India durante o século XVI", *Boletim do Instituto Vasco da Gama,* 47, 1940, 115–24.

Costa, António Domingos S., "A expansão portuguesa à luz do direito", *Revista da Universidade de Coimbra,* Vol. XX, 1962.

Costa, Avelino de Jesus, "Acção Missionária e patriótica de D. Frei Aleixo de Meneses, Arcebispo de Goa e Primaz do Oriente", *Congresso do Mundo Português,* Vol. 6 (Lisbon: 1940).

Costa, Francisco Xavier da, *Anais Franciscanos em Bardês* (Nova Goa: 1926).

Costa, João Paulo de Oliveira e, *A Missão de João de Brito* (Lisbon: Secretariado para as Comemorações dos 5 Séculos de Evangelização e Encontro de Culturas, 1992).

———, "A colonização portuguesa na Ásia", in Luís de Albuquerque, *et al.*, dir., *Portugal no Mundo, Vol. III* (Lisbon: Alfa, 1989), 158–79.

———, "A diáspora missionária", in João Francisco Marques e António Camões Gouveia, ed., *Humanismo e Reforma,* Vol. 2 of Carlos Moreira de Azevedo, ed., *História Religiosa de Portugal* (Lisbon: Círculo de Leitores, 2000).

———, and Vítor Rodrigues, *Portugal y Oriente, El proyecto indiano del rey Juan* (Madrid: Mapfre, 1992).

Coutinho, Fortunato, *Le régime paroissial des diocèses de rite latin de l'Inde des origines (XVIe. siècle) jusqu'à nos jours* (Louvain-Paris, PUL & Ed. Béatrice-Nauwelaerts, 1958).

Coutinho, Veríssimo, "Cuncolim – The Land of Freedom Fighters – I, II and III", in *The Navhind Times,* Feb. 1997.

Couto, Dejanirah, "Quelques observations sur les renégats portugais en Asie au XVIe siècle", *Mare Liberum,* nº 16, Dec. 1998, 57–86.

Couto, Gustavo, "Acção missionária dos franciscanos na Índia", in *Boletim Agência Geral das Colónias,* Lisbon, 4 (32), 1928.

Cox, Jeffrey, *Imperial Fault Lines: Christianity and Colonial Power in India* (Stanford: Stanford University Press, 2002).

Coxito, Amândio Augusto, "O problema da «Guerra Justa» segundo Frei Bartolomeu dos Mártires", in *Actas do III Encontro sobre História Dominicana,* tomo II, in *Arquivo Histórico Dominicano Português,* Vol. IV/2, 1989.

Crispim, Mª de Lourdes, "O Espelho de Cristina – Um 'Espelho' da Educação das mulheres no tempo da expansão", in A.A.V.V., *O rosto feminino da expansão* (Lisbon: Comissão para a Igualdade e para os Direitos das Mulheres, 1994).

Cruz, Maria Augusta da Lima, "Exiles and Renegades in Early Sixteenth Century Portuguese Asia", in A. Disney, *Historiography of Europeans in Africa and Asia, 1450–1800*, Vol. 4 of A.J.R. Russell Wood, ed., *An Expanding World. The European Impact on World History, 1450–1800* (s.l.: Variorum, 1995).

Cruz, Maria do Rosário Themudo Barata, *As regências na menoridade de D. Sebastião* (Lisbon: INCM, 1992).

Cruz, Maria Leonor Garcia da, "As controvérsias ao tempo de D. João III sobre a política portuguesa no Norte de África", *Mare Liberum*, nº 13, Jun. 1997, 123–99.

———, "As controvérsias ao tempo de D. João III sobre a política portuguesa no Norte de África. Compilação de documentos", *Mare Liberum*, nº 14, Dec. 1997, 117–200.

———, *Gil Vicente e a sociedade portuguesa de Quinhentos* (Lisbon: Gradiva, 1990).

———, *Os Fumos da Índia. Uma leitura crítica da expansão portuguesa* (Lisbon: Cosmos, 1998).

Cunha, Ana Cannas da, *A Inquisição no Estado da Índia: Origens (1539–1560)* (Lisbon: IAN/TT, 1995).

Cunha, J. Gerson da, *Konkani Language and Literature* (Bombay: Government Central Press, 1881).

Cunha, Mafalda Soares da, and Nuno Gonçalo Monteiro, "Vice-Reis, Governadores e Conselheiros de Governo no Estado da Índia (1505–1834), Recrutamento e Caracterização Social", *Penélope*, 15, 1995, 91–120.

Cunha, Mafalda Soares da, "Governo e Governantes do Império português do Atlântico (século XVII)", in Maria Fernanda Bicalho and Vera Ferlini, eds, *Modos de Governar. Ideias e Práticas Políticas no Império Português – Séculos XVI a XIX* (São Paulo: Editora Alameda, 2005).

Cunha, T.B., *Denationalisation of Goans* (Goa: Gazetteer Department Ed., 1955) (1944).

Cunha Rivara J.H. da, *Brados a favor das communidades das aldeas do Estado da Índia* (Nova Goa: 1870).

Curto, Diogo Ramada, "A Cultura Política", in Joaquim Romero de Magalhães, ed., *No Alvorecer da Modernidade (1480–1620)*, Vol. 3 of José Mattoso, ed., *História de Portugal* (Lisbon: Círculo de Leitores, 1993).

———, "Práticas de Identidade", in Vol. II of Kirti Chaudhuri and Francisco Bethencourt, eds, *História da Expansão Portuguesa* (Lisbon: Círculo de Leitores, 1998).

Curvelo, Alexandra Campos, "A imagem do Oriente na Cartografia Portuguesa do século XVI", Master's thesis, Lisbon: FCSH, 1996.

D'Andrade, Philotheio Pereira, *Os Santos Martyres de Cuncolim (Subsídios para a História da sua vida)* (Margão: Typographia das Ortigas, 1894).

D'Costa, Anthony, S.J., *The Christianisation of the Goan Islands, 1510–1567* (Bombay: 1965).

D'Souza, Carmo, "The Village Communities: A Historical and Legal Perspective", in Charles J. Borges, *et al.*, *Goa and Portugal: History and Development* (Delhi: Concept Publishing Co., 2000).

Daniélou, Alain, *Mythes et Dieux de l'Inde, Le Polythéisme Hindou* (Paris: Flammarion, 1992).

Das, Veena, *Structure and Cognition: Aspects of Hindu Caste and Ritual*, 2nd edn (Delhi: Oxford University Press, 1982) (1977).

De Witte, Charles-Martial, *La correspondance des premiers nonces permanents au Portugal, 1532–1553*, 2 vols (Lisbon: Academia Portuguesa de História, 1986).

Deliège, Robert, "The Myths of Origin of the Indian Untouchables", *Man*, Vol. 28, No. 3, Sept. 1993, 533–49.

Delumeau, Jean, *Catholicism between Luther and Voltaire: A New View of Counter-Reformation* (London: Burns & Oates, 1977) (1971).

———, *Uma história do paraíso – O jardim das delícias* (Lisbon: Terramar, 1994) (1992).

Deswarte, Sylvie, *Ideias e Imagens em Portugal na Época dos Descobrimentos. Francisco de Holanda e a Teoria da Arte* (Lisbon: Difel, 1992).

———, "La Rome de D. Miguel da Silva (1515–1525)", in AA.VV., *O Humanismo Português, 1500–1600* (Lisbon: Academia das Ciências de Lisboa, 1988).

———, "Francisco de Holanda: Maniera e Idea", in *A Pintura Maneirista Portuguesa: A Arte no Tempo de Camões* (Lisbon: CNCDP, 1995).

———, "Neoplatonismo e arte em Portugal", in Paulo Pereira, ed.,

História da Arte Portuguesa, Vol. II (Lisbon: Círculo de Leitores, 1995).

Dias, João José Alves, *Portugal do Renascimento à Crise Dinástica*, Vol. V of Joel Serrão and A.H. Oliveira Marques, eds, *Nova História de Portugal* (Lisbon: Ed. Presença, 1998).

Dias, J.S.S., *Correntes do sentimento religioso em Portugal (séculos XVI a XVIII)*, 2 vols (Coimbra: Universidade de Coimbra, 1960).

———, *Política Cultural da época de D. João III*, 2 vols (Coimbra: Universidade de Coimbra, 1969).

———, *Os Descobrimentos e a Problemática Cultural do século XVI* (Lisbon: Ed. Presença, 1973).

———, *Portugal e a Cultura Europeia*, in Revista *Biblos*, 1954.

———, "Cultura e obstáculo epistemológico do Renascimento ao Iluminismo em Portugal", in Francisco Contente Domingos and Luís Filipe Barreto, eds, *A Abertura do Mundo. Estudos de História dos Descobrimentos Europeus*, Vol. I (Lisbon: Presença, 1986).

Dias, Mariano José, "The Hindu-Christian Society of Goa", *Indica*, Vol. 17, nº 2, Sept. 1980, 109–16.

Dirks, Nicholas B., ed., *Colonialism and Culture* (Ann Arbor: The University of Michigan Press, 1992).

———, *The Hollow Crown: Ethnohistory of an Indian Kingdom* (New York: Cambridge University Press, 1987).

———, "The Conversion of Caste: Location, Translation, and Appropriation", in Peter van der Veer, ed., *Conversion to Modernities: The Globalization of Christianity* (New York and London: Routledge, 1996).

Disney, Anthony, *A decadência do império da pimenta* (Lisbon: Edições 70, 1985) (English version: *Twilight of the Pepper Empire*, 1978).

Diz, Simão Pires, *As classes dirigentes de Portugal e o Humanismo nas Epístolas de Cataldo*, PhD thesis, Lisbon: Faculdade de Letras da Universidade de Lisboa, 1995.

Dolvy, Lingu Roguvir, *Cuncolim, Apontamentos para a sua História* (s.l.: 1908).

Duncan, James, and David Ley, *Place/Culture/Representation* (London and New York: Routledge, 1994).

Dupront, Alphonse, "Espace et humanisme", in Alphonse Dupront, *Genése des Temps Modernes. Rome, les Réformes et le Nouveau Monde* (Paris: Gallimard Le Seuil, 2001).

Duverger, Christian, *La conversion des Indiens de Nouvelle Espagne avec le texte des Colloques des Douze de Bernardino de Sahagún (1564)* (Paris: Seuil, 1987).

Elias, Norbert, and John L. Scotson, *The Established and the Outsiders. A Sociological Enquiry into Community Problems* (London: Sage, 1994) (1977).

Elliott, John H., "Empire and State in British and Spanish America", in Serge Gruzinski and Nathan Wachtel, ed., *Le Nouveau Monde. Mondes Nouveaux. L'Expérience Américaine* (Paris: Ed. Recherche sur les Civilisations/EHESS, 1992).

———, *Empires of the Atlantic World: Britain and Spain in America, 1492–1830* (New Haven: Yale University Press, 2006.

———, *La España Imperial, 1469–1716* (Madrid: Vicens Vives, 1965) (English version: *Imperial Spain, 1469–1716*, 1963).

Farinha, António Lourenço, *A Expansão da Fé no Extremo Oriente (subsídios para a história colonial)* (Lisbon: Agência Geral das Colónias, 1943).

Feio, Mariano, *As Castas Hindus de Goa* (Lisbon: Junta de Investigações Científicas do Ultramar, 1979).

Feitler, Bruno, "A circulação de obras anti-judaicas e anti-semitas no Brasil Colonial", *Cultura, Revista de História e Teoria das Ideias*, 24, 2007.

———, *O catolicismo como ideal: produção literária antijudaica no mundo português da Idade Moderna* (São Paulo: Novos Estudos, CEBRAP, 2005).

Fernandes, Maria de Lourdes Correia, "As artes da Confissão. Em torno dos Manuais de Confessores do século XVI em Portugal", *Humanística e Teologia*, 11, 1990, 47–80.

———, "Da reforma da igreja à reforma dos cristãos: reformas, pastoral e espiritualidade", in João Francisco Marques e António Camões Gouveia, ed., *Humanismo e Reforma*, Vol. 2 of Carlos Moreira de Azevedo, ed., *História Religiosa de Portugal* (Lisbon: Círculo de Leitores, 2000), 15–47.

———, *Espelhos, Cartas e Guias. Casamento e Espiritualidade na Península Ibérica, 1450–1700* (Porto: Faculdade de Letras da Universidade do Porto, 1995).

Fernandes, R.R. Lagrange, "O «Pai dos Cristãos» nas Cristandades do Padroado Português do Oriente (1532–1840). Novas perspectivas para a história do cargo de «Pai dos Cristãos» e da Missionação dos Povos", Phd Thesis, Rome: Pontifícia Universidade Gregoriana, 1965).

Fernandez Alvarez, Manuel, *Carlos V. Un Hombre para Europa*, 2ª ed. (Madrid: Ed. Espasa Calpe, 1999) (1976).

Ferreira, Ana Maria Pereira, *Problemas marítimos entre Portugal e a França na primeira metade do século XVI* (Redondo: Património, 1995).

Ferro, Maria José, *Inquisição e Judaísmo* (Lisbon: Ed. Presença, 1987).

———, *Os Judeus em Portugal no Século XV*, 2 vols (Lisbon: Faculdade de Ciências Sociais e Humanas, 1982–1984).

Ferry, Jean-Luc, *Les Puissances de l'Expérience* (Paris: Ed. du CERF, 1991).

Figueiredo, Caetano de, *As comunidades de Goa* (Nova Goa: Imprensa Nacional, 1923).

Figueiredo, João M. Pacheco de, "Goa dourada nos séculos XVI e XVII. O Hospital dos pobres do Padre Paulo Camerte (Esboço de sua reconstituição histórica)", *Studia*, 25, 1968, 117–46.

Finer, S.E., "The Indian Experience and the Mughal Empire: 1526–1712", in Vol. III of *Empires, Monarchies and the Modern State*, in S.E. Finer, *The History of Government from the Earliest Times* (Oxford: Oxford University Press, 1997).

Flores, Jorge, "A imagem do Oriente no Ocidente Europeu: dos ecos da expansão mongol ao Portugal manuelino", *Revista da Biblioteca Nacional*, Lisbon, 2ª série, 5 (2), Jul.–Dec. 1990.

Fonseca, José Nicolau da, *An Historical and Archaeological Sketch of the City of Goa* (Bombay: Thacker & Co., 1878).

Foucault, Michel, *As palavras e as coisas* (Lisbon: Edições 70, 1991) (1968).

———, *L'ordre du discours* (Paris: Gallimard, 1971).

———, *Surveiller e punir: naissance de la prison* (Paris: Gallimard, 1975).

———, *L'archéologie du Savoir* (Paris: Gallimard, 1977).

———, *A Microfísica do Poder* (Graal: 1992).

Fragoso, João, Maria Fernanda Bicalho, and Maria de Fátima Gouveia, eds, *O Antigo Regime nos trópicos:a dinâmica imperial portuguesa (séculos XVI–XVIII)* (Rio de Janeiro: Civilização Brasileira, 2001).

Frigo, Daniela, "Tradizione aristotelica e virtù cristiane: la trattastica sulla famiglia", in Cesare Mozzarelli and Danilo Zardin, eds, *I tempi del Concilio. Religione, Cultura e società nell'Europa tridentina* (Milan: Bulzoni Editore, 1997).

———, "'Disciplina Rei Familiarae'. A Economia como modelo administrativo do Ancien Régime", *Penélope, Fazer e Desfazer a História*, nº 6, 1991.

Frova, Carla, "Discipline e ruoli sacrali nella trattatistica medioevale sull' educazione (sec. XIII – XIV)", in AAVV, *Sapere e Potere. Discipline, Dispute e Professioni nell' Universitá Medioevale e Moderna, Il caso bolognese a confronto. Atti del 4º convegno,* Vol. III, *Dalle Discipline ai Ruoli Sociali* (Bologna: Istituto per la Storia di Bologna, 1990).

Fukazawa, H., "Standards of Living – Maharashtra and the Deccan", in *Cambridge Economic History of India,* Vol. 1, ed. I. Habib and T. Raychaudhuri (Cambridge: Cambridge University Press, 1982).

Fuller, C.J., "Kerala Christians and the Caste System", *Man,* Vol. 11, nº1, March 1976, 53–70.

———, "The Hindu Pantheon and the Legitimation of Hierarchy", *Man*, Vol. 23, nº 1, March 1988, 19–39.

———, *The Camphor Flame: Popular Hinduism and Society in India* (Princeton, NJ: Princeton University Press, 1992).

Ganho, Maria de Lourdes Sirgado, "A obra *Desengano dos Perdidos* de D. Gaspar de Leão", in *Congresso Internacional de História – Missionação Portuguesa e Encontro de Culturas, Actas, Vol. II* (Braga: UCP-CNCDP-FEC, 1993).

Geremek, Bronislaw, *Poverty. A History* (Oxford: Blackwell, 1994).

———, "L'exemplum et la circulation de la culture au moyen âge", in *Rhétorique et Histoire, L'exemplum et le modèle de comportement dans le discours antique et mediéval (Table Ronde organisée par l'École Française de Rome, 1979)* (Rome: École Française de Rome, 1980).

———, ed., *Inutiles au monde: Truands et misérables dans l'Europe moderne (1350–1600)* (Paris: Gallimard, 1980).

Ghantkar, Gajanana S.S., *History of Goa through Gōykanadi Script* (Panaji: 1993).

Gil, Juan, "A apropriação da ideia de império pelos reinos da Península Ibérica: Castela", *Penélope,* 15, 1995, 11–30.

Ginzburg, Carlo, *História Nocturna. Uma Decifração do Sabat* (Lisbon: Relógio d'Água, 1985) (1989).

Girard, René, *Violence and the Sacred* (Baltimore: The Johns Hopkins University Press, 1977) (1972).

Girard, Pasquale, *Os Religiosos Ocidentais na China na Época Moderna.*

Ensaio de Análise Textual (Macau: Fundação Macau/Instituto Politécnico de Macau, 1999).

Glick, Thomas F., *Islamic and Christian Spain in the Early Middle Ages* (Princeton: Princeton University Press, 1979).

Godinho, Jno, *The Padroado of Portugal in the Orient (1454–1860)* (Bombay: 1924).

Godinho, Vitorino Magalhães, *Les Finances de l'État Portugais des Indes Orientales (1517–1635). Matérielles pour une étude structurale et conjoncturelle* (Paris: Fondation Calouste Gulbenkian-Centre Culturel de Paris, 1988).

Goffman, Erving, *Stigma. Notes on the Management of Spoiled Identity* (Englewood Cliffs: Prentice-Hall, 1963).

Gokhale, Balkrishna Govind, *Bharatavarasha: A Political and Cultural History of India* (Delhi: Sterling, 1982).

Gomes, Olivinho J.F., *Village Goa (A Study of Goan Social Structure and Change)* (Delhi: S. Chand & Company, 1987).

——, *Old Konkani Language and Literature. The Portuguese Role* (Chandor-Goa: Konkani Sorospot Prakashan, 1999).

Gonçalves, Nuno da Cunha, "Padroado", in Carlos Moreira Azevedo, ed., *Dicionário de História Religiosa de Portugal*, Vol. III, *J-P* (Lisbon: Círculo de Leitores, 2001), 364–8.

Gonçalves, Manuel Pereira, "A presença franciscana na Índia do século XVI", in Luís de Albuquerque, ed., *Portugal no Mundo*, Vol. III (Lisbon: Alfa, 1989).

Goody, Jack, *A lógica da escrita e a organização da sociedade* (Lisbon: Edições 70, 1987) (English version: *The Logic of Writing and the Organization of Society*, 1987).

Gopal, B.R., "Kadamba Patronage to Jainism and Saivism in Goa", in P.P. Shirodkar, ed., *Goa: Cultural Trends (Seminar Papers)* (Goa: DAEM, 1988).

Gordon, Stewart, *The Marathas, 1600–1818*, Vol. II-4 of *New Cambridge History of India* (Cambridge: Cambridge University Press, 1993).

Gossiaux, Pol-P., *L'Homme et la Nature. Genèses de l'Anthropologie à l'Âge Classique, 1580–1750* (Brussels: De Boeck Université, 1993).

Gould, Eduardo S., "Los extranjeros y su integración a la vida de una ciudad indiana: los portugueses en Cordoba del Tucuman", *Revista de Historia del Derecho*, nº 24, 1996, 63–112.

Graça, Luís, *A visão do Oriente na literatura portuguesa de viagens: os viajantes portugueses e os itinerários terrestres (1560–1670)* (Lisbon: INCM, 1983).

Gracias, Fátima da Silva, *Health and Hygiene in Colonial Goa, 1510–1961* (Delhi: Concept Publishing Company, 1994).

Gramsci, Antonio, *Selections from the Prison Notebooks* (New York: International Publishers, 1971).

Grimal, Pierra, *O Império Romano* (Lisbon: Edições 70, 2010) (1993).

———, *O Século de Augusto* (Lisbon: Edições 70, 2008) (1965).

Gruzinski, Serge, *La colonisation de l'imaginaire. Sociétés indigènes et occidentalisation dans le Mexique espagnol, XVI–XVIII siècles* (Paris: Gallimard, 1988).

——, *Les Quatre Parties du Monde. Histoire d'une Mondialisation* (Paris: Martinière, 2004).

———, and Nathan Wachtel, "Cultural Interbreedings: Constituting the Majority as a Minority", *Comparative Studies in Society and History*, Vol. 39, No. 2, April 1997, 231–50.

Guedes, Ana Isabel Marques, "Tentativas de controle da reprodução da população colonial: as órfãs d'el-rei", in *O rosto feminino da expansão* (Lisbon: Comissão para a Igualdade e para os Direitos das Mulheres, 1994).

———, "Os estatutos dos colégios dos órfãos: Estratégias e vivências (séculos XVI a XVIII)", *Cadernos do Noroeste,* Vol. 11 (2) – *Misericórdias, caridade e pobreza em Portugal no período moderno*, 1998, 115–46.

Guerra, François-Xavier, "L'État et les Communautés: Comment Inventer un Empire. Introduction", in Serge Gruzinski and Nathan Wachtel, eds, *Le Nouveau Monde. Mondes Nouveaux. L'Expérience Américaine* (Paris: Ed. Recherche sur les Civilisations/EHESS, 1992).

Guha, Ranajit, *Elementary Aspects of Peasant Insurgency in Colonial India* (Durham and London: Duke University Press, 1999) (1983).

Guha, Sumit, "Lower Strata, Older Races, and Aboriginal Peoples: Racial Anthropology and Mythical History", *The Journal of Asian Studies,* Vol. 57, Issue 2, May 1998, 423–41.

———, "The Politics of Identity and Enumeration in India *c.* 1600–1990", *Comparative Studies in Society and History*, Vol. 45, Issue 1, Jan. 2003, 148–67.

———, "Transitions and Translations: Regional Power and Vernacular

Identity in the Dakhan, 1500–1800", *Comparative Studies of South Asia, Africa and the Middle East*, Vol. 24, Issue 2, 2004, 23–31.

Gune, V.T., *Ancient Shrines of Goa. A Pictorial Survey* (Panaji: Department of Information-Government of Goa, 1965).

Guimarães, José Maria Teixeira, *Comunidades Indianas das Velhas Conquistas* (s.l.: 1885).

Gutton, Jean-Pierre, *La société et les pauvres en Europe (XVIe–XVIIIe siècles)* (Paris: PUF, 1974).

Habib, Irfan, *Agrarian System of Mughal India* (Bombay: Asia Publishing House, 1963).

Harris, Howard, and Alan Lipman, "Social Symbolism and Space Usage in Daily Life", *Sociological Review*, Vol. 28, nº2, 1980, 415–28.

Heras, H., "Pre-Portuguese Remains in Portuguese India", *Journal of the Bombay Historical Society*, Sept. 1932, 1–184.

Herzog, Tamar, *Vecinos y Extranjeros. Hacerse español en la Edad Moderna* (Madrid: Alianza, 2006).

Hespanha, António Manuel e Catarina Madeira Santos, "Os Poderes num Império Oceânico", in António Manuel Hespanha, ed., *O Antigo Regime (1620–1807)*, Vol. 4 of José Mattoso, ed., *História de Portugal* (Lisbon: Círculo de Leitores, 1993).

———, "A família", in A.M. Hespanha, ed., *O Antigo Regime (1620–1807)*, Vol. IV of José Mattoso, ed., *História de Portugal* (Lisbon: Círculo de Leitores, 1993).

———, "A nobreza nos tratados jurídicos dos séculos XVI a XVIII", *Penélope, Fazer e Desfazer a História,* nº 12, 1993.

———, *As Vésperas do Leviathan* (Coimbra: Livraria Almedina, 1995).

———, *Panorama da História Institucional e jurídica de Macau* (Macau: Fundação Macau, 1995).

———, *Panorama Histórico da Cultura Jurídica Europeia* (Lisbon: Publicações Europa-América, 1997).

———, "A constituição do Império português. Revisão de alguns enviesamentos tradicionais", in João Fragoso, Maria Fernanda Bicalho, Maria de Fátima Gouveia, eds, *O Antigo Regime nos trópicos: a dinâmica imperial portuguesa (séculos XVI–XVIII)* (Rio de Janeiro: Civilização Brasileira, 2001).

Hogden, Margaret, *Early Anthropology in the Sixteenth and Seventeenth Centuries* (Philadelphia: University of Pennsylvania Press, 1971).

Hsia, Ronnie Po-Chia, *Social Discipline in the Reformation: Central Europe, 1550–1750* (London and New York: Routledge, 1989).

———, "Etre chrétien et chinois: les témoignages des convertis aux XVIe, XVIIe et XVIIIe siècles", in Gabriel Audisio, ed., *Religion et Identité* (Aix-en-Provence: Presses de l'Université de Provence, 1998), 241–8.

Hunt, Alan, and Gary Wickam, *Foucault and Law. Towards a Sociology of Law as Governance* (London: Pluto Press, 1994)

Inden, Ronald, *Imagining India* (Cambridge: Blackwell, 1990).

Jordan, AnneMarie, *Retrato de Corte em Portugal. O Legado de António Moro* (Lisbon: Quetzal, 1994).

Jordan-Gschwend, Annemarie, "O Maneirismo e o retrato de corte em Portugal: as fontes, as inovações e a importação de um estilo", in *A Pintura Maneirista em Portugal: Arte no Tempo de Camões* (Lisbon: CNCDP, 1995).

Junqueiro, Maria Clara, "Afonso de Albuquerque à luz dos requisitos fundamentais da guerra justa", in *2º Seminário Internacional de História Indo-Portuguesa* (Lisbon: Edição do Instituto Luso-Árabe, 1982).

Jütte, Robert, *Poverty and Deviance in Early Modern Europe* (Cambridge: Cambridge University Press, 1994).

Kamat, Pratima P., *Farar Far: Local Resistance to Colonial Hegemony in Goa, 1510–1912* (Panaji: Institute Menezes Bragança, 1999).

———, "Syncretic Shaktipitha: The Image of the Divine Feminine as Santeri-Shantadurga-Saibin in Goa", *Purabhilekh-Puratatva*, Vol. 2, 2, Jul.-Dec. 2001, 3–31.

Kantor, Iris, "Do Dilúvio Universal ao Pai Tomé. Fundamentos teológico-políticos e mensuração do tempo na historiografia brasílica (1724–1759)", in Ângela Barreto Xavier and Catarina Madeira Santos, eds, *Cultura Intelectual das Elites Coloniais*, special issue, *Cultura-História e Teoria das Ideias*, Vol. XXV, 2007, 181–93.

———, *Esquecidos e Renascidos: historiografia acadêmica luso-americana, 1724–1759* (São Paulo: Hucitec, 2004).

Kaplan, Steven, ed., *Indigenous Responses to Western Christianity* (New York: New York University Press, 1995).

Keane, Webb, "From Fetishism to Sincerity. On Agency, the Speaking Subject and Their Historicity in the Context of Religious Conversion", *Comparative Studies in Society and History*, Vol. 39, Issue 4, October 1997, 674–93.

Khare, R.S., *The Hindu Heart and Home* (Delhi: Vikas Publishing House, 1976).

Kosambi, D.D., *An Introduction to the Study of the History of India* (Bombay: Popular Prakashan, 1998) (1956).

———, "The Village Community in the 'Old Conquests'", *Journal of the University of Bombay*, 15, 1947, 63–78.

Kriegel, Maurice, "De la «question» des «nouveaux – chrétiens» à l'expulsion des juifs: la double modernité des procès de l'exclusion dans l'Espagne du XVe siécle", in Serge Gruzinski and Nathan Wachtel, eds, *Le Nouveau Monde, Mondes Nouveaux. L'expérience Américaine, Actes du Colloque Cermaca* (Paris: EHESS, 1992).

Kukathas, Chandran, "Explaining Moral Variety", in Ellen Frankel Paul, Fred. D. Miller, Jr., and Jeffrey Paul, eds, *Cultural Pluralism and Moral Knowledge* (Cambridge: Cambridge University Press, 1994).

Kulkarni, A.R., "Marathi Records on Village Communities of Goa", in Luís de Albuquerque and Inácio Guerreiro, eds, *Segundo Seminário Internacional de História Indo-Portuguesa, Actas* (Lisbon: IICT/ CECA, 1985).

———, "Portuguese in the Deccan Politics. A Study of New Marathi Documents from Lisbon", in Teotonio R. de Souza, s.j., ed., *Indo-Portuguese History: Old Issues, New Questions* (New Delhi: Concept Publishing Company, 1985).

Lach, Donald F., *Asia in the Making of Europe*, Vol. I – *The Century of Discovery* (Chicago: University of Chicago Press, 1965).

Le Goff, Jacques, "O Ocidente Medieval e o Oceano Índico: um horizonte onírico", in Jacques Le Goff, *Para um novo conceito de Idade Média. Tempo, trabalho e cultura no Ocidente* (Lisbon: Ed. Estampa, 1993) (1977).

Leitão, Ana Maria Proserpio, "Os primordios das rivalidades entre franciscanos e jesuítas no Japão em finais do século XVI. A questão da vinda de outras congregações religiosas", in *Congresso Internacional de História – Missionação Portuguesa e Encontro de Culturas, Actas, Vol. II* (Braga: UCP-CNCDP-FEC, 1993).

Lemoine, Robert, *L'Époque Moderne (1563–1789), Le Monde des Religieux, tome XV*, in Gabriel le Bras and Jean Gaudemet, eds, *Histoire du Droit et des Institutions de l'Église en Occident* (Paris: Ed. Cujas, 1976).

Lingat, Robert, *Royautés Boudhiques. Asoka. La Fonction royale a Ceylon* (Paris: EHESS, 1989).

———, *The Classical Law of India* (Berkeley: University of California Press, 1973).

Lobato, Alexandre, "Sobre os prazos da Índia", in Luís de Albuquerque and Inácio Guerreiro, eds, *II Seminário Internacional de História Indo-Portuguesa – Actas* (Lisbon: 1985), 461–6.

Lobo, Amaro Pinto, Pe, ed., *Memoria histórico-eclesiástica de Goa* (Nova Goa: Tip. "A Voz de S. Francisco Xavier", 1933).

Lobo, Eulália Maria Lahmeyer, *Administração Colonial Luso-Espanhola na América* (Rio de Janeiro: Ed. Companhia Brasileira de Artes Gráficas, 1956).

Loomba, Ania, *Colonialism / Postcolonialism* (London and New York: Routledge, 1998).

Lopes, Fernando Felix, *Os franciscanos no Oriente Português de 1584 a 1590* (Lisbon: CEHU, 1962).

——, *Colectânea de Estudos de História e Literatura,* 2 vols (Lisbon: Academia Portuguesa da História, 1997).

Lopes, Maria de Jesus dos Mártires, *Goa Setecentista* (Lisbon: UCP – Centro de Estudos dos Povos e Culturas de Expressão Portuguesa, 1996) (English version: *Tradition and Modernity in Eighteenth Century Goa*, New Delhi: Manohar Publishers, 2006).

———, "As recolhidas de Goa em Setecentos", in *O Rosto Feminino da Expansão Portuguesa* (Lisbon: Comissão para a Igualdade e para os Direitos das Mulheres, 1994).

———, ed., *O Império Oriental, 1660–1820,* 2 vols (Lisbon: Editorial Estampa, 2006).

Lorenzen, David, "Who Invented Hinduism?", *Comparative Studies in Society and History*, Vol. 41, nº 4, Oct. 1999, 630–59.

Loureiro, Rui M., "O encontro de Portugal com a Ásia no século XVI", in Luís de Albuquerque, António Luís Ferronha, José da Silva Horta, and Rui Loureiro, eds, *O confronto do olhar. O encontro dos povos na época das navegações portuguesas. Séculos XV e XVI* (Lisbon: Ed. Caminho, 1991).

———, "O descobrimento da civilização indiana nas cartas jesuítas (século XVI)", in Berta Ares Queija and Serge Gruzinski, ed., *Entre dos Mundos: Fronteras Culturales y Agentes Mediadores* (Seville: Ed. Escuela de Estudios Hispano-Americanos, 1997).

———, "O Humanismo Português e o Oriente", in *Do Mundo Antigo aos Novos Mundos. Humanismo, Classicismo e Notícias dos Descobrimentos em Évora (1516–1624)* (Évora: CME/CNCDP, 1999).

Ludden, David, *An Agrarian History of South Asia*, in Vol. IV.4 of *The New Cambridge History of India* (Cambridge: Cambridge University Press, 1999).

———, *India and South Asia: A Short History* (London: Oneworld Pub., 2002).

Luhmann, Niklas, *Religious Dogmatics and the Development of Society* (New York: The Edwin Mellen Press, 1984) (1977).

MacCormack, Sabine, "Sin, Citizenship, and the Salvation of Souls: The Impact of Christian Priorities in Late-Roman and Post-Roman Society", *Comparative Studies in Society and History*, Vol. 39, 4. Oct. 1997, 644–73.

Machado, Álvaro Manuel, *O mito do Oriente na literatura portugues,* (Lisbon: ICALP, 1983).

Madeira-Santos, Catarina, *Goa é a chave de toda a Índia, Perfil político da capital do Estado da Índia (1505–1570)* (Lisbon: CNCDP, 1999).

———, "De antigos conquistadores a angolenses. A elite colonial de Luanda no contexto da cultura das Luzes, entre lugares da memória e conhecimento científico", in Ângela Barreto Xavier and Catarina Madeira Santos, eds, *Cultura Intelectual das Elites Coloniais*, special issue, *Cultura-História e Teoria das Ideias*, Vol. XXV, 2007.

Magalhães, Joaquim Romero de, "O enquadramento do espaço nacional", in Joaquim Romero de Magalhães, ed., *No Alvorecer da Modernidade (1480-1620)*, Vol. 3 of José Mattoso, ed., *História de Portugal* (Lisbon: Círculo de Leitores, 1993).

———, "Os régios protagonistas do poder. D. João III", in Joaquim Romero de Magalhães, ed., *No Alvorecer da Modernidade (1480–1620)*, Vol. 3 of José Mattoso, ed., *História de Portugal* (Lisbon: Círculo de Leitores, 1993).

Mahajan, V.D., *History of India, From Beginning to 1526 A.D.* (Delhi: S. Chand & Company, 1999) (1970).

Majumdar, Romesh Chandra, *Corporate Life in Ancient India* (Delhi: Cosmo Pub., 1994) (1918).

Manoel, Jeronymo P.A. da Camara, *Missões dos Jesuítas no Oriente nos séculos XVI e XVII* (Lisbon: Imprensa Nacional, 1894).

Marques, João Francisco, "A Evangelização da Índia no Epistolário de Afonso de Albuquerque e S. Francisco Xavier. Cotejo e Problemas", in *Congresso Internacional de História – Missionação Portuguesa e Encontro de Culturas, Actas, Vol. II* (Braga: UCP-CNCDP-FEC, 1993), 217–59.

Marquilhas, Rita, *A Faculdade das Letras* (Lisbon: INCM, 2001).

Martins, José Frederico Ferreira, *História da Misericórdia de Goa*, 3 vols, (Nova Goa: Imprensa Nacional, 1910–1914).

Mascarenhas, Mira, "The Church in Eighteenth Century Goa", in Teotónio de Souza, ed., *Essays in Goan History* (Concept Pub. Company, 2014).

Matos, Artur Teodoro, "The Financial Situation of the State of India During the Philippine Period", in Teotónio de Souza, S.J., ed., *Indo-Portuguese History: Old Issues, New Questions* (Delhi: Concept Publishing Company, 1985).

———, "Teres e haveres das ordens religiosas de Goa em finais do século XVI", *Studia,* nº 53, 1994, 219–28.

Matos, Manuel Cadafaz de, "A produção tipográfica da Companhia de Jesus no Oriente, entre os séculos XVI e XVII ao serviço da missionação portuguesa. Alguns dados para a História da Leitura a partir de catálogos bibliográficos macaenses (1584–1700)", in *Congresso Internacional de História – Missionação Portuguesa e Encontro de Culturas, Actas, Vol. II (*Braga: UCP-CNCDP-FEC, 1993).

Meersman, Achilles, OFM, *The Ancient Franciscan Provinces in India, 1500–1835* (Bangalore: Christian Literature Society Press, 1971).

———, *The Friars Minor, or Franciscans in India, 1291–1942* (Karachi: Rotti Press, 1943).

Mello, Carlos de Mercês de, *The Recruitment and Formation of Native Clergy in India (16th–18th Centuries*) (Lisbon: 1955).

Mendes, António Rosa, "A vida cultural", in Joaquim Romero de Magalhães, ed., *No Alvorecer da Modernidade (1480–1620),* Vol. 3 of José Mattoso, ed., *História de Portugal* (Lisbon: Círculo de Leitores, 1993).

Mendonça, Délio, *Conversions and Citizenry. Goa under Portugal (1510–1610)* (Delhi: Concept Publishing Company, 2002).

Mitragotri, V.R., *Socio-Cultural History of Goa, From Bhojas to Vijayanagar* (Panaji-Goa: Institute Menezes Bragança, 1999).

Monteiro, Nuno Gonçalo, "Trajectórias sociais e governo das conquistas: Notas preliminares sobre os vice-reis e governadores gerais do Brasil e da Índia nos séculos XVII e XVIII", in João Fragoso, Maria Fernanda Bicalho, and Maria de Fátima Gouveia, eds, *O Antigo Regime nos Trópicos: A dinâmica imperial Portuguesa (séculos XVI–XVIII)* (Rio de Janeiro: Civilização Brasileira, 2001).

———, "Casa e linhagem: o vocabulário aristocrático em Portugal nos séculos XVII e XVIII", *Penélope*, nº 12, 1993, 43–63.

———, *O Crepúsculo dos Grandes – A Casa e o Património da Aristocracia em Portugal(1750–1832)* (Lisbon: INCM, 1998).

Monteiro, Nuno G., Pedro Cardim, and Mafalda Soares da Cunha, eds., *Optima Pars. Elites Ibero-Americanas do Antigo Regime* (Lisbon: Imprensa de Ciências Sociais, 2005).

Moraes, George Mark, *A History of Christianity in India. From Early Times to St Francis Xavier: A.D. 52–1542* (Bombay: Manaktalas, 1964).

———, *Kadamba Kula. A History of Ancient and Medieval Karnataka* (Delhi: Asian Educational Services, 1990) (1931).

Morán, Manuel, and José Andrés-Gallego, "O Pregador", in Rosario Villari, ed., *O Homem Barroco* (Lisbon: Ed. Presença, 1995) (1993).

Moreira, Rafael, ed., *História das Fortificações Portuguesas no Mundo* (Lisbon: Alfa, 1989).

———, "A Arquitectura do Renascimento no Sul de Portugal. A Encomenda Régia entre o Moderno e o Romano", PhD thesis Lisbon: Faculdade de Ciências Sociais e Humanas da Universidade Nova de Lisboa, 1991.

———, "Arquitectura: Renascimento e Classicismo", in Paulo Pereira, ed., *História da Arte Portuguesa*, Vol. 2 (Lisbon: Círculo de Leitores, 1995).

———, "Cultura Material e Visual", in Kirti N. Chaudhuri and Francisco Bethencourt, eds, *História da Expansão Portuguesa*, Vol. 1 (Lisbon: Círculo de Leitores, 1998).

Moreno, Humberto Baquero, *Marginalidade e conflitos sociais em Portugal nos séculos XIV e XV. Estudos de História* (Lisbon: Editorial Presença, 1985).

———, "Exclusão e marginalidade social no Portugal quatrocentista", *Ler História*, 33 (1997), 37–51.

Mosse, David, "Catholic Saints and the Hindu Village Pantheon in Rural Tamil Nadu India", *Man,* Vol. 29, nº 2, Jun. 1994, 301–32.

Mozzarelli, Cesare, and Danilo Zardin, eds, *I tempi del Concilio. Religione, Cultura e società nell'Europa tridentina* (Milan: Bulzoni Editore, 1997).

Mundadan, A.M., *History of Christianity in India, Vol. I – From the Beginning up to the Middle of the Sixteenth Century (up to 1542)* (Bangalore: Theological Publications of India, 1994).

Mundy, Barbara, *Mapping of New Spain: Cartography and the Maps of Relaciones Geograficas* (Chicago: Chicago University Press, 2000).

Novalin, Jose Luis Gonzalez, dir., *História de la Iglesia en España, III-2º – La Iglesia en la España de los siglos XV y XVI* (Madrid: Biblioteca de Autores Cristianos 1980).

Novarese, Daniela, *Istituzioni politiche e studi di diritto fra cinque e seicento. Il Messanense studium generale tra política gesuitica e istanze egemoniche cittadine* (Milan: Giuffrè, 1994).

Nunes, Fernando Oudinot Larcher, "D. Frei Miguel Rangel e as problemáticas da missionação no Oriente do seu tempo", *Congresso Internacional de História – Missionação Portuguesa e Encontro de Culturas, Actas, Vol. II* (Braga: UCP-CNCDP-FEC, 1993).

Olival, Fernanda, *As Ordens Militares e o Estado Moderno: Honra, Mercê e Venalidade em Portugal (1641–1789)* (Lisbon: Estar Editora, 2001).

Ohlmeyer, Jane H., "'Civilizinge of those Rude Partes': Colonization within Britain and Ireland, 1580s–1640s", in Nicholas Canny, ed., *Oxford History of British Empire, Vol. 1 – The Origins of Empire* (Oxford: Oxford University Press, 2001).

Pagden, Anthony, *Spanish Imperialism and Political Imagination: Studies in European and Spanish-American Social and Political Theory* (New Haven and London: Yale University Press, 1990).

———, *Lords of All the World: Ideologies of Empire in Spain, Britain and France, c. 1500–1800* (New Haven and London: Yale University Press, 1995).

———, *Povos e Impérios* (Lisbon: Círculo de Leitores, 2003) (English version: *Peoples and Empires: A Short History of European Migration, Exploration and Conquest: From Greece to the Present,* 2001).

Paiva, José Pedro, "A Igreja e o Poder", in João Francisco Marques e António Camões Gouveia, ed., *Humanismo e Reforma,* Vol. 2 de Carlos Moreira de Azevedo, ed., *História Religiosa de Portugal* (Lisbon: Círculo de Leitores, 2000).

———, "Dioceses e Organização Eclesiástica", in João Francisco Marques e António Camões Gouveia, ed., *Humanismo e Reforma,* Vol. 2 de Carlos Moreira de Azevedo, ed., *História Religiosa de Portugal* (Lisbon: Círculo de Leitores, 2000).

———, "Inquisição e Visitas Pastorais, Dois mecanismos complementares de controle social?", *Revista de História das Ideias,* Vol. 11, 1989.

———, *Os Bispos de Portugal e do Império 1497–1777* (Coimbra: Universidade de Coimbra, 2006).

———, "Uma instrução aos visitadores do bispado de Coimbra (século xvii?) e os textos regulamentadores das visitas pastorais em Portugal", *Revista de História das Ideias*, Vol. 15, 1993, 637–61.

Palomo, Federico, "La autoridad de los prelados postridentinos y la sociedad moderna. El gobierno de Don Teotonio de Braganza en el Arzobispado de Évora (1578–1602)", *Hispania Sacra*, Madrid, 47 (1995), 587–624.

———, "'Disciplina Christiana'. Apuntes historiográficos en torno a la disciplina y el disciplinamiento social como categorías de la historia religiosa de la alta edad moderna", *Cuadernos de Historia Moderna*, nº 18, 1997.

———, *Fazer dos campos escolas excelentes: os Jesuítas de Evora e as missões do interior em Portugal (1551–1630)* (Lisbon: Fundação Calouste Gulbenkian, 2003).

Palomo, "Para el sosiego y quietud del reino. Felipe II y el poder eclesiástico en el Portugal de finales del siglo XVI", *Hispania,* Vol. LXIV/1, nº 216, 2004.

———, *A Contra-Reforma em Portugal* (Lisbon: Livros Horizonte, 2005).

Panikkar, K.M., *Asia and Western Dominance. A Survey of the Vasco da Gama Epoch of Asian History, 1498–1945* (Kuala Lumpur: The Other Press, 1993) (1953).

Pearson, M.N., *The Portuguese in India*, Vol. I.1 of *The New Cambridge History of India* (Cambridge: Cambridge University Press, 1987).

Pelikan, Jaroslav, *The Christian Tradition. A History of the Development of the Doctrine – The Growth of Medieval Theology (600–1300)*, Vol. 3 (Berkeley: University of California Press, 1978).

Penco, G., G. Battista, A.G. Mattanic, G. d'Urso, and G. Sommavilla, *Gli Ordini Religiosi. Storia e Spiritualità. Benedettini, Cisterciensi, Francescani, Domenicani, Gesuiti* (Firenze: Nardini Editore, 1992).

Pereira, António Bernardo de Bragança, *Etnografia da Índia Portuguesa,* 2 vols (Nova Goa: Imprensa Nacional, 1940) (1923).

Pereira, António dos Santos, "Intenções catequéticas e projectos de reforma administrativa eclesiástica", in *Congresso Internacional de História – Missionação Portuguesa e Encontro de Culturas, Vol. 1* (Braga: UCP-CNCDP-FEC, 1993), 345–56.

Pereira, Gerald, *An Outline of the Pre-Portuguese History of Goa* (Vasco da Gama, Goa: 1973).

Pereira, Isaías da Rosa, "O ensino da doutrina cristã nos séculos XIII a XVI", in *Congresso Internacional de História – Missionação Portuguesa e Encontro de Culturas, Vol. 1* (Braga, UCP-CNCDP-FEC, 1993), 356–70.

Pereira, Paulo, ed., *História da Arte Portuguesa*, Vol. II (Lisbon: Círculo de Leitores, 1995).

Pereira, Rui Gomes, *Goa – Hindu Temples and Deities* (Goa: 1978).

———, *Goa. Gaunkari, the Old Village Associations* (Goa: 1981).

Perez, Rosa Maria F., ed., *Histórias de Goa* (Lisbon: Museu Nacional de Etnologia, 1997).

———, *Os Portugueses e o Oriente: história., itinerários, representações* (Lisbon: Dom Quixote, 2006).

Pescatello, Ann, "The African Presence in Portuguese India", in Patrick Manning, ed., *Slave Trades, 1500–1800: Globalization of Forced Labour*, Vol. 15 in A.J.R. Russell-Wood (gen. ed.), *An Expanding World: The European Impact on World History, 1450–1800* (Aldershot: Ashgate-Variorum, 1996), 143–65.

Phal, S.R., *Society in Goa (Some Aspects of Tradition and Modern Trends)* (Delhi: B.R. Pub. Corporation, 1982).

Phelan, John Leddy, *The Millennial Kingdom of the Franciscans in the New World*, 2nd edition (Berkeley and Los Angeles: University of California Press, 1970).

Pinto, Carla Alferes, *A infanta D. Maria de Portugal (1521–1577). O mecenato de uma princesa renascentista* (Lisbon: Fundação Oriente, 1998).

Pinto, Jeanette, *Slavery in Portuguese India (1500–1842)* (Bombay: Himalaya Publishing House, 1992).

Pissurlencar, P.S.S., *Agentes da diplomacia portuguesa na Índia* (Goa: Arquivo Histórico do Estado da Índia, 1952).

——, "Contribuição ao estudo etnológico da casta indo-portuguesa denominada 'chardó', à luz de documentos inéditos encontrados no Arquivo Histórico da Índia", in *Trabalhos do 1º Congresso Nacional de Antropologia Colonial, II – Comunicações* (Porto: 1ª Exposição Colonial Portuguesa, 1934).

———, *Goa Pré-Portuguesa através dos escritores lusitanos dos séculos XVI e XVII* (Lisbon: 1951).

Plattner, Felix Alfred, *Quand l'Europe cherchait l'Asie: Jésuites missionnaires, 1541–1785* (Tournai: Casterman, 1954).

Prakash, Gyan, ed., *The World of the Rural Labourer in Colonial India* (Delhi: Oxford University Press, 1992).

———, ed., *After Colonialism: Imperial Histories and Postcolonial Displacements* (Princeton: Princeton University Press, 1995).

Priolkar, A.K., *The Goan Inquisition* (Bombay: Bombay University Press, 1961).

Prodi, Paolo, *The Papal Prince. One Body and Two Souls: The Papal Monarchy in Early Modern Europe* (Cambridge: Cambridge University Press, 1987) (1982).

———, ed., *Disciplina dell'anima, disciplina del corpo e disciplina della società tra medioevo ed età moderna* (Bologna: Il Mulino, 1994).

Prosperi, Adriano, "Intelletuali e Chiesa all'inizio dell'etá moderna", in Corrado Vivanti, ed., *Storia d'Italia. Annali 4. Intelletuali e Potere* (Turin: Einaudi, 1981).

———, "O Missionário", in Rosario Villari, ed., *O Homem Barroco* (Lisbon: Ed. Presença, 1995) (1993).

———, *Tribunali della Coscienza, Inquisitori, confessori, missionari* (Turin: Giulio Einaudi, 1996).

———, *Il Concilio de Trento: una introduzione storica* (Turin: Giulio Einaudi, 2001).

———, "'Otras Indias': missionari della Controriforma tra contadini e selvaggi", in Giancarlo Garfagnini, ed., *Scienze credenze occulte livelli di cultura* (Florence: Olschki, 1982).

Pullan, Bryan J., *Rich and Poor in Renaissance Venice. The Social Institutions of a Catholic State to 1620* (Oxford: Blackwell, 1971).

Quine, N.V., *The Roots of References* (La Sala, Illinois: Open Count Pub. Comp., 1990) (1974).

Rafael, Vincent, "Confession, Conversion and Reciprocity in Early Tagalog Colonial Society", in Nicholas B. Dirks, ed., *Colonialism and Culture* (Ann Arbor: The University of Michigan Press, 1991).

Raheja, Gloria Goodwin, *The Poison in the Gift: Ritual, Prestation, and the Dominant Caste in a North Indian Village* (Chicago: University of Chicago Press, 1988).

Rambo, Lewis, "Theories of Conversion. Understanding and Interpreting Religious Change", *Social Compass*, nº 46, No. 3, 1999, 259–71.

Raminelli, Ronald, "Império da Fé: Ensaio sobre os portugueses no Congo, Brasil e Japão", in João Fragoso, Maria Fernanda Botelho, Maria de Fátima Gouveia, eds, *O Antigo Regime nos Trópicos: A dinâmica imperial portuguesa (séculos XVI n XVIII)* (Rio de Janeiro: Civilização Brasileira, 2001), 227–47.

Ramos, Rui Manuel Monteiro Lopes, *Tristes Conquistas. A Expansão Ultramarina na Historiografia Contemporânea (c.1840–1970)* (Lisbon: Instituto de Ciências Sociais, 1997).

Randles, W.G.L., "'Peuples Sauvages' et 'États despotiques': la pertinence, au XVIe siècle de la grille aristotélicienne pour classer les nouvelles societés révélées par les Découvertes au Brésil, en Afrique et en Asie", *Mare Liberum: Revista de História dos Mares*, nº 3, Dec. 1991, 229–307.

Rego, António da Silva, *História das Missões do Padroado português do Oriente* (Lisbon: Agência Geral das Colónias, 1949).

Reinhard, Wolfgang, "Disciplinamento sociale, confessionalizzazione, modernizzazione. Un discorso storiografico", in Paolo Prodi, ed., *Disciplina dell'anima, disciplina del corpo e disciplina della società tra medioevo ed età moderna* (Bologna: Il Mulino, 1994).

Richards, John F., *The Mughal Empire*, Vol. I.5 in *The New Cambridge History of India* (Cambridge: Cambridge University Press, 1993).

Rijs, Thomas, *Aspects of Poverty in Early Modern Europe* (Stuttgart: Klett-Cotta, 1981).

Robinson, Rowena, *Conversion, Continuity and Change. Lived Christianity in Southern Goa* (New Delhi: Sage, 1998).

———, "Sixteenth-Century Conversions to Christianity in Goa", in Rowena Robinson and Clark Sathianathan, eds, *Religious Conversion in India. Modes, Motivations and Meanings* (Oxford: Oxford University Press, 2003).

Rocha, Leopoldo da, *As confrarias de Goa – Conspecto historico-juridico (Século XVI–XX)* (Lisbon: Centro de Estudos Históricos Ultramarinos, 1973).

Rodrigues, Francisco, S.J., *História da Companhia de Jesus na Assistência de Portugal* (Porto: Livraria do Apostolado da Imprensa, 1931–1950).

Rodrigues, Maria Idalina Resina, *Fray Luis de Granada y la literatura de espiritualidad en Portugal (1554–1632)* (Madrid: Universidad Pontifícia de Salamanca/Fundación Universitaria Española, 1988).

———, "Frei Luís de Granada e a espiritualidade peninsular do seu tempo", in *IV Centenário da Morte de Frei Luís de Granada, Actas do Colóquio Comemorativo* (Lisbon: Associação dos Arqueólogos Portugueses e Edições Távola Redonda, 1988).

———, "Literatura e Anti-Semitismo (séculos XVI e XVII)", in Maria Idalina Resina Rodrigues, *Estudos Ibéricos. Da Cultura à Literatura. Pontos de Encontro. Séculos XIII a XVII* (Lisbon: ICALP, 1987).

Rodrigues, Manuel Augusto, *Do Humanismo à Contra-Reforma em Portugal* (Coimbra: Centro de Estudos de História da Sociedade e da Cultura da Universidade de Coimbra, 1981).

Rodrigues, Teresa Ferreira, "As estruturas populacionais", in Joaquim Romero de Magalhães, ed., *No Alvorecer da Modernidade (1480–1620)*, Vol. 3 de José Mattoso, ed., *História de Portugal* (Lisbon: Círculo de Leitores, 1993).

Rodrigues, Vítor, "A Guerra na Índia", in António Manuel Hespanha, ed., Vol. 2 of Manuel Themudo Barata e Nuno Severiano Teixeira, ed., *Nova História Militar de Portugal* (Lisbon: Círculo de Leitores, 2004).

Rodriguez Sanchez, Angel, "Carlos V y Portugal", in *Actas das Primeiras Jornadas de História Moderna, Lisbon*, Vol. 1 (Lisbon: Centro de História da Universidade de Lisboa, 1986).

Rosa, Maria de Lurdes, "D. Jaime, Duque de Bragança: entre a cortina e a vidraça", in Diogo Ramada Curto, ed., *O tempo de Vasco da Gama* (Lisbon: Difel/CNCDP, 1998).

Rubinoff, Arthur, *The Construction of a Political Community. Integration and Identity in Goa* (New Delhi: Sage, 1998).

Rusconi, Roberto, *Predicazione e Vita Religiosa nella societá italiana da Carlo Magno alla Controriforma* (Turin: Loescher, 1981).

Ruud, Arild, "The Indian Hierarchy. Culture, Ideology and Consciousness in Bengali Village Politics", *Modern Asian Studies*, nº 33 (3), 1999, 697–732.

Sá, Isabel dos Guimarães, "Entre Maria e Madalena: a mulher como sujeito e objecto da caridade em Portugal e na colónias (séculos XVI-XVIII)", in *O Rosto Feminino da Expansão Portuguesa* (Lisbon: Comissão para a Igualdade e para os Direitos das Mulheres Congresso Internacional, 1994).

———, "Os Hospitais portugueses entre a assistência medieval e a intensificação dos cuidados médicos no período moderno", in *Congresso Comemorativo do V Centenário da Fundação do Hospital Real do Espírito Santo de Évora, Actas* (Évora: Hospital do Espírito Santo, 1996), 87–103.

———, *Quando o rico se faz pobre: Misericórdias, caridade e poder no império português, 1500–1800* (Lisbon: CNCDP, 1997).

———, *As Misericórdias Portuguesas de D. Manuel a Pombal* (Lisbon: Livros Horizonte, 2001).

Said, Edward, *Orientalism: Western Conceptions of the Orient* (London: Penguin, 1991) (1978).

———, *Culture and Imperialism* (London: Vintage, 1994) (1993).

Saldanha, António Vasconcelos e, "Conceitos de Espaço e Poder e seus requisitos na Titulação Régia Portuguesa da Época da Expansão", in Jean Aubin, ed., *La Decouverte, le Portugal et l'Europe* (Paris: FCG-CCP, 1990).

———, *Iustum Imperium*: *Dos Tratados como fundamento do Império dos Portugueses no Oriente: Estudos de História do Direito Internacional e do Direito Português* (Lisbon: ISCSP, 2005).

Saldanha, M.J. Gabriel de, *História de Goa,* 2 vols (Bastorá: Typographia Rangel, 1925–1926).

Santos, Nair de Nazaré Castro, *O Príncipe Ideal no século XVI e a obra de Jerónimo Osório* (Lisbon: INIC, 1994).

Scammell, G.V., "Indigenous Assistance in the Establishment of Portuguese Power in the Indian Ocean", in J. Correia-Afonso, ed., *Indo-Portuguese History: Sources and Problems* (Bombay: Oxford University Press, 1981).

Schallenberger, E., "Conflitos coloniais e as Missões: Uma avaliação das estruturas sócio-económicas do Paraguay", *Estudos Ibero-Americanos,* Vol. 11, 1984.

Schaub, Jean-Frédéric, *Portugal na Monarquia Hispânica (1580–1640)* (Lisbon: Livros Horizonte, 2001).

Schilling, Heinz, "Chiese confessionali e disciplinamento sociale. Un bilancio provvisorio della ricerca storica", in Paolo Prodi, ed., *Disciplina dell'anima, disciplina del corpo e disciplina della società tra medioevo ed età moderna* (Bologna: Il Mulino, 1994), 125–60.

———, "Confessionalization in the Empire: Religious and Social Change in Germany Between 1555 and 1620", in Heinz Schilling, *Religion, Political Culture and the Emergence of Early Modern Society. Essays in German and Dutch History* (Leiden-New York-Köln: Brill, 1992), 247–301.

Schurhammer, Georg, S.J., *Orientalia*, ed. László Szilas (Lisbon-Rome: Centro de Estudos Históricos Ultramarinos-Institutum Historicum Societatis Jesu, 1963).

———, *Francisco Javier, su vida y su tiempo* (Navarra: Gobierno de Navarra – Compañia de Jesu – Arzebispo de Pamplona, 1992).

Scott, James, *Weapons of the Weak: Everyday Forms of Peasant Resistance* (New Haven: Yale University Press, 1985).

Seed, Patricia, *Ceremonies of Possession in Europe's Conquest of the New World, 1492–1640* (Cambridge: Cambridge University Press, 1995).

Sen, Kshitimohan, *Medieval Mysticism of India* (Delhi: Oriental Books Reprint Corporation, 1974).

Senos, Nuno C.C., *O Paço da Ribeira, 1501–1581* (Lisbon: Temas & Debates, 2002).

Serrão, Joaquim Veríssimo, "João de Barros: entre Erasmo e o Império", in *O Humanismo Português, 1500–1600* (Lisbon: Academia das Ciências de Lisboa, 1988).

Serrão, Vítor, *História da Arte em Portugal. O Renascimento e o Maneirismo* (Lisbon: Editorial Presença, 2002).

———, "Os painéis da Igreja de Unhos, secs. XVI–XVII", Lisbon, Sep. do *Boletim da Junta Distrital de Lisboa*, n. LXXIII–LXXIV, III[a] série, 1970.

Shirodkar, P.P., ed., *Goa: Cultural Trends* (Goa: DAEM, 1988).

———, "Evangelization by Missionaries in Indian Sub-Continent. Harsh Realities", in *Researches in Indo-Portuguese History*, Vol. II (Jaipur: Pub. Scheme, 1998), 84–98.

———, "Influence of Nath Cult in Goa", in P.P. Shirodkar, ed., *Goa: Cultural Trends (Seminar Papers)* (Goa: DAEM, 1988), 8–21.

———, "Socio-Cultural life in Goa, 16-17 Centuries", in *Researches in Indo-Portuguese History*, Vol. II (Jaipur: Pub. Scheme, 1998), 24–55.

Shoemaker, Nancy, "How the Indians Got to be Red", *American Historical Review*, Vol. 102, nº 3, Jun. 1997, 625–44.

Silva, A. da, *Trent's Impact on the Portuguese Patronage Missions* (Lisbon: Centro de Estudos Históricos Ultramarinos, 1969).

Silva, Amélia Maria Polónia da, *O Cardeal D. Henrique, Arcebispo de Évora, Um prelado na viragem tridentina* (Porto: Universidade do Porto, 1989).

———, "O Cardeal Infante D. Henrique: Um prelado no limiar da viragem tridentina segundo o paradigma do «Stimulus Pastorum?»", in *Actas do Congresso Internacional IV Centenário da Morte de D. Fr. Bartolomeu dos Mártires* (Fátima: Movimento Bartolomeano, 1994).

Silva, Amélia Polónia da, *D. Henrique* (Lisbon: Círculo de Leitores, 2005).

Silva, António Delgado da, *Collecção da Legislação Portuguesa desde a última compilação das Ordenações, Vol. 1: 1750–1762* (Lisboa: Typographia Maigrense, 1830).

Silva, Vítor, *O Hospital Real de Goa (1510–1610): Contribuição para o estudo da sua História e Regimentos*, Master's thesis, Lisbon: Universidade de Lisboa, 1997.

Silveira, Ângelo, *A Casa-Pátio de Goa* (Porto: FAUP, 1999).

Smith, Anthony D., *The Ethnic Origins of Nations* (New York: Basil Blackwell, 1988).

Soares, Franklin Neiva, "A missionação na arquidiocese de Braga pelas visitas pastorais nos séculos XVI e XVII", in *Congresso Internacional de História – Missionação Portuguesa e Encontro de Culturas*, Vol. 1 (Braga: UCP-CNCDP-FEC, 1993), 313–44.

Sorge, Giuseppe e Enrico Fasa, ed., *India tra Occidente e Oriente: l'apporto dei viaggiatori e missionari italiani nei secoli XVI–XVII* (Milan: Jackbook, 1991).

———, *Matteo De Castro (1594–1677). Profilo di una Figura Emblematica del Conflitto Giurisdizionale tra Goa e Roma nel Secolo XVII* (Bologna: Clueb, 1986).

Souza, Teotónio de, S.J., *Goa medieval. A cidade e o hinterland* (Lisbon: Estampa, 1994 (English version: *Medieval Goa: A Socio-Economic History*, 1979).

———, and Charles J. Borges, S.J., *Jesuits in India: In Historical Perspective* (Macau: Instituto Cultural de Macau/Xavier Centre of Historical Research, 1992).

Srinivas, M.N., *India: Social Structure* (Delhi: Hindustani Publishing Corporation, s.d.).

Srivastava, M.P., *Society and Culture in Medieval India (1206–1707)* (Allahabad: Chugh Publications, 1975).

Strathern, Alan, "O papel da província da Piedade na evangelização dos indianos" in *D. João III e o Império. Actas do Congresso Internacional* (Lisbon: CEPCEP, Universidade Católica Portuguesa, 2004).

Stoler, Ann Laura, "Sexual Affronts and Racial Frontiers. European Identities and the Politics of Exclusion in Colonial Southeast Asia", in Frederick Cooper and Ann Laura Stoler, eds, *Tensions of Empire. Colonial Cultures in a Bourgeois World* (Berkeley: University of California Press, 1997).

Subrahmanyam, Sanjay, *Explorations in Connected History*, 2 vols (Delhi: Oxford University Press, 2005–6).

———, *O Império Asiático Português, 1500–1700* (Lisbon: Difel, 1995).

———, *The Portuguese Empire in Asia, 1500–1700: A Political and Economic History*, 2nd edn (Chichester: Wiley-Blackwell, 2012).

———, David Shulman and V. Narayana Rao, *Symbols of Substance: Court and State in Nayaka Period Tamilnadu* (Delhi: Oxford University Press, 1998).

———, *Penumbral Visions. Making Polities in Early Modern South India* (Oxford: Oxford University Press, 2001).

———, and Luís Filipe Thomaz, "Evolution of Empire. The Portuguese in the Indian Ocean During the Sixteenth Century", in James Tracy, ed., *The Political Economy of Merchants Empires. State, Power and World Trade, 1350–1750* (Cambridge: Cambridge University Press, 1991).

Subtil, José, "O governo e a administração", in António Manuel Hespanha, ed., Vol. 4 of José Mattoso, ed., *História de Portugal* (Lisbon: Círculo de Leitores, 1993).

Tau Anzoátegui, Victor, *Casuismo y Sistema, Indagación Historica sobre el espiritu del Derecho Indiano* (Buenos Aires: Instituto de Investigaciones de Historia del Derecho, 1992).

Tavim, José Alberto R.S., *Judeus e Cristãos-Novos de Cochim: História e Memória* (Braga: APPACDM, 2003).

Telles, Ricardo Michael, "Ordens Religiosas e seus Conventos", *Boletim do Instituto de Vasco da Gama*, nº 59, 1944.

———, *Os Franciscanos no Oriente e seus conventos* (Nova Goa: Tip. Rau e Irmãos, 1922).

Terra, José da Silva, "Espagnols au Portugal au temps de la Reine D. Catarina I - D. Julião de Alva (c. 1500–1570)", *Arquivos do Centro Cultural Português*, Vol. 9, 1975, 417–506.

Thapar, Romila, *A History of India*, Vol. 1 (London: Penguin, 1990) (1966).

Thekkedath, Joseph, *History of Christianity in India, Vol. II – From the Middle of the Sixteenth Century to the End of the Seventeenth Century (1542–1700)* (Bangalore: Theological Publications of India, 1994).

Thomaz, Luís Filipe, "O Cristianismo e as Tradições Pagãs na Índia Portuguesa", in *Actas do Congresso Internacional de Etnografia*, Vol. 4 (Santo Tirso: 1963).

———, "L'idée imperiale manueline", in Jean Aubin, ed., *La Decouverte, le Portugal et l'Europe* (Paris: Fundação Calouste Gulbenkian, 1990).

———, "Descobertas e Evangelização", in *Congresso Internacional de História, Missionação e Encontro de Culturas, Actas, Vol. 1* (Braga: Universidade Católica Portuguesa, 1993).

———, "A Estrutura Política e Administrativa do Estado da Índia no Século XVI", in Luís Filipe Thomaz, *De Ceuta a Timor* (Lisbon: Difel, 1994).

———, "A «Política Oriental» de D. Manuel I e as suas Contracorrentes", in Luís Filipe Thomaz, *De Ceuta a Timor* (Lisbon: Difel, 1994).

———, "Goa: Uma sociedade luso-indiana", in Luís Filipe Thomaz, *De Ceuta a Timor* (Lisbon: Difel, 1994).

———, "A Crise de 1565–1575 na História do Estado da Índia", *Mare Liberum*, nº 9, *O Estado da Índia e a Província do Norte. Actas do VII Seminário Internacional de História Indo-Portuguesa* (Goa: 1994–5), 481–520.

Thompson, E.P., *The Making of the English Working Class* (London: Victor Gollancz, 1963).

Toffin, Gérard, "Hiérarchie et idéologie du don dans le monde indien", *L'Homme,* vol. 30, nº 14, 1990, 130–42.

Trautmann, Thomas R., *Aryans in British India (*Berkeley: University of California Press, 1997).

———, "Indian Time, European Time", in Diane Owen Hughes and Thomas Trautmann, eds, *Time: Histories and Ethnologies* (Ann Arbor: The University of Michigan Press, 1993), 167–97.

Tulard, Jean, ed., *Les empires ocidentaux de Rome à Berlin,* Vol. 1 (Paris: PUF, 1997).

Turner, Victor, *The Ritual Process. Structure and Anti-Structure* (New York: Aldine de Gruyer, 1969).

Valladares, Rafael, *Castilla y Portugal en Asia (1580–1680). Declive Imperial y Adaptacion* (Leuven: Leuven University Press, 2001).

Van der Veer, Peter, ed., *Conversion to Modernities: The Globalization of Christianity* (New York and London: Routledge, 1996).

Van Oss, Adriaan C., *Catholic Colonialism. A Parish History of Guatemala, 1524–1821* (Cambridge: Cambridge University Press, 2002).

Vasantamadhava, K.G., "Gove-Karnataka Cultural Contacts from 1000–1600 A.D.", in P.P. Shirodkar, ed., *Goa: Cultural Trends* (Goa: DAEM, 1988), 22–33.

Velinkar, Joseph V., "Evangelization Methods in Salcete (Goa)", in *Congresso Internacional de História – Missionação Portuguesa e*

Encontro de Culturas, Actas, Vol. II (Braga: UCP-CNCDP-FEC, 1993), 285–90.

———, *India and the West: The First Encounters* (Bombay: Heras Institute of Indian History and Culture – St Xavier's College, 1998).

Vieira, Alberto, "As Constituições Sinodais das dioceses de Angra, Funchal e Las Palmas nos séculos XV a XVII", in *Congresso Internacional de História–Missionação Portuguesa e Encontro de Culturas, Vol. 1* (Braga: UCP-CNCDP-FEC, 1993), 455–81.

Villari, Rosario, *Elogio della dissimulazione: La lotta politica nel Seicento* (Rome: Laterza, 1987).

Villiers, John, "The Estado da Índia in Southeast Asia: Administration, Law and International Relations", in A.J.R Russell-Wood, ed., *Government and Governance of European Empires, 1450–1800*, Vol. 21: Part 1 of A.J.R, Russell-Wood, gen. ed., *An Expanding World: The European Impact on World History, 1450–1800* (Aldershot: Ashgate Variorum, 2000).

Viswanathan, Gauri, "Coping with (Civil) Death: The Christian Convert's Rights of Passage in Colonial India", in Gyan Prakash, ed., *After Colonialism. Imperial Histories and Postcolonial Displacements* (Princeton: Princeton University Press, 1995).

———, "Religious Conversion and the Politics of Dissent", in Peter van der Veer, ed., *Conversion to Modernities: The Globalization of Christianity* (New York and London: Routledge, 1996).

———, *Outside the Fold, Conversion, Modernity and Belief* (Princeton: Princeton University Press, 1998).

Von Moos, Peter, "Kirchlische Disziplinierung zwischen Mittelalter und Moderne. Adriano Prosperis *Tribunali della coscienza* aus mediävistischer Sicht, *Zeitschrift für Historische Forstung*, nº 27, 2000.

Wachtel, Nathan, *La Vision des Vaincus* (Paris: Gallimard, 1971).

Wicki, Josef, S.J., *Kânara und die dortige Jesuitenmission 1646–1648*, in *der Darstellung des P. Leonardo S.I. Honâvar Anfang 1648, Aufsätze zur portugiesieschen Kulturgeschichte/herausgegeben von Hans Flausche* (Münster-Westfalen: Aschendorffsche Verlagsbuchhandlung, 1980), 261–345.

———, *Missionskirche im Orient: ausgewählte Beiträge über Portugiesisch-Asien* (Immensee: Neue Zeitschrift für Missionswissenschaft, 1976).

———, *Problemas morais no Oriente portugues do século XV* (Lisbon: Centro de Estudos Históricos Ultramarinos e as Comemorações Henriquinas, 1961).

Xavier, Ângela Barreto, "Katholischer Orientalismus: Wege des Wissens im Goa der Frühen Neuzeit", in *Novos Mundos – Neue Welten. Portugal und das Zeitalter der Entdeckungen* (Dresden: Sandstein Verlag, 2007).

———, "'Nobres por geração'. A consciência de si dos descendentes de portugueses na Goa seiscentista", in Ângela Barreto Xavier and Catarina Madeira Santos, eds,, *Cultura Intelectual das Elites Coloniais*, special issue, *Cultura-História e Teoria das Ideias*, Vol. XXV, 2007, 89–118.

———, "Cultura Intelectual das Elites Coloniais" (with Catarina Madeira Santos), in Ângela Barreto Xavier and Catarina Madeira Santos, eds, *Cultura Intelectual das Elites Coloniais*, special issue, *Cultura-História e Teoria das Ideias*, Vol. XXV, 2007, 9–32.

———, "Itinerários franciscanos na Índia seiscentista, e algumas questões de história e de método", in *Lusitania Sacra*, 2ª série (18), 2006, 87–116.

———, "Pensare la nazione a partire dell'impero. I "nati in India" nei secoli XVI e XVII", in Aldo Mazzacane, ed., *Oltremare. Culture e istituzioni dal Colonialismo all'età postcoloniale* (Napoli: Istituto Suor Orsola Benincasa, 2006).

———, "De converso a novamente convertido. Identidade política e alteridade no reino e no império", *Cultura – Revista de História e Teoria das Ideias,* 2ª série, nº 22, 2006, 245–74.

———, "David contra Golias na Goa seiscentista e setecentista. Escrita identitária e colonização interna", *Ler História*, nº 49, 2005, 107–43.

———, "A organização religiosa do primeiro Estado da Índia. Notas para uma investigação", *Anais de História de Além-Mar*, nº 5, Dezembro, 2004, 27–59.

———, "Aparejo y disposición para criar un otro nuevo mundo. A conversão dos indianos e o Projeto imperial joanino", *Actas do Congresso D. João III* (Lisbon: CEPCEP-Universidade Católica Portuguesa, 2004).

———, "A Invenção de Goa. Poder Imperial e Conversões Culturais nos séculos XVI e XVII", PhD thesis, Florence: European University Institute, 2003.

Xavier, Filipe de Nery, *Bosquejo historico das comunidades dos concelhos das ilhas Salcete e Bardez* (Nova Goa: Imprensa Nacional, 1852).

Xavier, P.D., *Goa: A Social History (1510–1640)* (Goa: 1993).

Zagorin, Perez, *Ways of Lying: Dissimulation, Persecution and Conformity in Early Modern Europe* (Cambridge: Harvard University Press, 1990).

Zimmer, Heinrich, *Mitos e símbolos na arte e civilização indianas* (Lisbon: Assírio & Alvim, 1996).

Zuñiga, Jean-Paul, "La voix du sang. Du métis à l'idée de métissage en Amérique espagnole", *Annales HSS,* mars-avril 1999, nº 2, 425–52.

Županov, Ines G., "Le repli du religieux: Les missionnaires jésuites du 17e siècle entre la théologie chrétienne et une éthique païenne", *Annales HSS,* nº 6, Nov.–Dec. 1996, 1201–23.

———, *Disputed Mission: Jesuit and Brahmanical Experiments in the 17th Century* (Delhi: Oxford University Press, 2000).

———, "Drugs, Health, Bodies and Souls in the Tropics: Medical Experiments in Sixteenth-Century Portuguese India", *The Indian Economic and Social History Review,* Vol. XXXIX, No. 1, Jan.–March 2002, 1–43.

———, "Esperimenti linguistici dei gesuiti: le grammatiche e i catechismi tamil (sec. XVI–XVII)", *Etnosistemi,* anno IX, nº 9, gennaio 2002, 44–61.

———, "A História do Futuro. Profecias viajantes dos jesuítas: de Nápoles para a Índia e para o Brasil (século XVII)", in Ângela Barreto Xavier and Catarina Madeira Santos, eds,, *Cultura Intelectual das Elites Coloniais,* special issue, *Cultura-História e Teoria das Ideias,* Vol. XXV (2007).

Index

Adil Shah(s) of Bijapur 49, 249–50, 254, 256, 258, 266, 269, 275–7, 309, 320
Albuquerque, Juan de, O.F.M. Rec. (Bishop of Goa) 53, 66, 67, 69, 74, 77, 95, 97, 112, 141
Albuquerque, Afonso de (Governor of Estado da Índia) 18, 22, 82, 153, 158, 218–19, 224, 250, 286
Alexander the Great 19, 30, 256, 319
Ali bin Yusuf Adil Khan 145, 250–4
Ambelim 83, 125, 130, 204, 248, 258, 261, 265
Assolna 83, 125, 130, 248, 258, 261, 265
Augustinians (O.S.A.) 111, 120, 132, 336
Augustus (Roman emperor) 19, 29, 337
Azevedo, Ana de (Dona) 193–4
Azpicuelta Navarro, Martim 177, 234

Barreto, Francisco (Governor of Estado da Índia) 86, 96, 133
Barros, João de 34, 41, 157–8, 160–1, 245, 311–13
Barzeus, Gaspar, S.J. 163, 165, 174–5, 220
Bassein 43, 76, 221, 274
Bayly, Christopher 7, 139
Bayly, Susan 323
Bethencourt, Francisco 35–6, 176
Bijapur Sultanate 48, 102, 136, 138, 145, 205, 218, 226–8, 248–9, 257–8, 266, 268–9, 273, 275, 277, 283, 306–8
Bocarro, António 120, 282–4, 293
Borba, Diogo de (O.F.M. Rec.) 67, 159, 67
Borgia, Francisco, S.J. 50, 96, 168
Bossy, John 104, 175
Boxer, Charles 297
Brahman(s): beliefs 260; and conversion 94, 135, 137, 141, 187, 222, 264, 267, 302, 316, 319–20; decisions against 89–92, 308; punishments of 70, 216; religious practices 76, 79, 141, 204, 228, 268; status 135, 201, 205–7, 211–12, 217, 226, 294, 301, 305–8, 312, 314–18, 322–4
Brazil 49, 101, 221, 292

Calicut 58, 318, 320

Câmara de Goa 25, 66, 126, 272, 337
Canarim 126, 161, 171, 179, 300
Caraim 204, 206–7, 211, 213
Carambolim 133, 147–8, 226–7, 230
Carlos V 42, 337
Carneiro, Melchior, S.J. 50, 96, 103, 230, 281, 330
Casa dos Catecúmenos (also House of the Cathecumens) 71, 119, 159, 169, 190–1, 254
Casados 83–4, 94, 120, 190, 200, 282, 287, 289, 291–5, 297, 306, 334–5 (*see also* Portuguese residents)
Caste 92, 103, 136, 139, 145, 158, 186–7, 201, 210, 229, 231, 233n, 240, 243, 314, 323, 330–1
Castelo Branco, Fernão Rodrigues de 74 , 81–2, 206
Castro, Dom Pedro de 125, 129, 265
Castro, João de (Governor and Viceroy of the Estado da Índia) 47, 48, 68, 84, 95, 110, 207, 251
Castro, Mateus de (Bishop of Crisópolis) 305–10, 320, 322
Catarina of Austria (Queen of Portugal) 49, 86, 86, 91, 222
Ceylon 2, 9, 53, 197, 321
Chardo 209, 280, 294, 305–6, 314–18, 319–22, 324, 326
Chatim 206–7, 232, 258, 261
Chaudarins 203–4, 209–11, 226
Chaul 69, 72, 76, 180, 274
Cheriperumal (Cheran Perumal, King of Malabar) 315–16, 318–19
China 22, 53, 73
Chorão 3, 11, 15, 123, 125, 196, 203–7, 209–22, 226, 230, 232–4, 236, 243, 251, 259, 268, 324, 330, 337
Christianisation, agents and tools of 107–8, 120–1, 157, 159, 161, 171–2, 176, 181, 193–4, 219–20, 243, 332, 336 (*see also* preaching, schools, confession, hospitals, Pai dos Cristãos)
Christians of St Thomas 55, 318
Christians: benefits 46, 70–1, 86, 88, 187–8, 191, 288; conflicts 95, 244–5, 252, 254, 257, 269, 302; demography 55–6, 120–1, 137, 254, 258; differences among 297–8; forced 99, 273; genuine 28, 60, 97, 99, 100, 103, 106–7, 155–6, 164, 174, 182, 186, 189, 191, 231–5, 245–6, 255, 277, 308, 320; justice 134, 177, 190, 302; labour of 127, 149, 187–8, 272, 298–9, 301; land for 188, 266; prohibitions 64, 147, 167, 180, 239; sacraments for 59, 66, 242; social control of 64, 71, 91, 140, 156, 189, 236, 238; solidarity among 76, 140; spiritual health of 51, 53; teaching of 66, 71, 162–3
Christians of the land (*see* Christians)
Colleges 3, 34, 45, 71, 87, 90, 118–19, 123–5, 136, 159,

160, 167–70, 187, 191–9, 256, 281–2, 306–7, 311: Reis Magos 168–9, 192–3, 281, 282, 306; Santa Fé 123, 159, 167–8, 187; São Paulo 87, 119, 125, 160, 162, 167–8
Confalonieri, Gianbattista 17–19, 329
Confession 32, 36, 37, 103, 137, 156–7, 175–80, 234, 327
Confessionalisation 21, 27, 28, 33, 37, 39, 50, 75, 104–5, 141, 327
Confraternity of Santa Fé 71, 78, 123, 187
Constantine (Roman emperor) 29, 96, 337
Constantino de Bragança (Viceroy of Estado da Índia) 91, 96–7, 161, 226, 230, 252
Convent (*also* Monastery of São Francisco) 56–7, 67, 116, 137, 181, 184
Correia, Gaspar 18–19, 250
Cosme Annes 48, 74
Council of Trent 33, 37, 49, 75, 100, 109, 113–14, 116, 129, 161–2, 164, 173, 175
Coutinho, Francisco (Viceroy of Estado da Índia) 91, 134, 228
Couto, Diogo do 245, 291, 302, 311
Cranganore 43, 56, 58, 168
Criminali, Antonio, S.J. 149, 173
Cultural conversions 9, 15–16, 23, 60, 100, 122, 104–8, 146, 148–9, 165, 197–8, 233, 275, 278–9, 328, 330–1, 333–4
Cuncolim 16, 83, 196, 229, 243–9, 251–2, 254–62, 264–8, 270, 278, 330

Deities of Goa: Barazan 213–14; Bhukhadevi (*also* Bhaukadevi) 213–14, 217; Bhagavati 136, 213–14; Devaki-Krishna 213–14, 216–17; Ganesha 213–14, 225; Mahadeva 259; Mahakali 136; Mahalakshmi 136; Mallinatha 136, 213; Narayana 136, 213–15; Parvati 260; Ravalnath 136, 213–16, 259; Samjanato 85; Santeri 136, 259–60; Shantadurga 259–60; Somanatha 136; Vitthala 136
Diu 43, 84, 47
Dívar 3, 11, 46, 123, 197, 215, 219, 251, 324, 337
Dom Luís (Infant of Portugal) 10, 11, 52
Dominicans (O.P.) 54, 69, 107, 109, 111, 125, 132, 223, 336

Estado da Índia 14–15, 22–3, 26, 38, 43–4, 50, 65, 68, 73, 87, 100–2, 116, 129, 131–2, 157–8, 162, 184, 187, 268, 274, 283–4, 304

Farazes 208, 211–12, 217, 223
Fernandes, Domingos, S.J. 203, 221, 218, 222–3
Foral de Mexia 81, 202, 219
Franciscan Provinces (O.F.M.; O.F.M. Rec.): Arrábida 116; Madre de Deus 116–17, 294; Piedade 61, 74, 116;

Portugal 116; São Tomé 116–17, 293–4; St Gabriel 61, 67
Franciscan residencies and parishes 55, 72, 109, 111, 116, 118–19, 135, 141, 159, 169–70, 184, 192, 194, 243, 282
Franciscan spiritual tradition, models and methods 15, 55–6, 79, 100, 124, 128, 132, 137, 146, 151, 154, 156, 159–60, 165, 169–72, 177, 181, 184, 192, 237, 281, 336
Franciscans 11, 43, 53, 55–7, 59, 61–2, 67–9, 74–5, 109, 116–18, 120, 128, 136–7, 139, 141, 143, 150, 158–60, 168–72, 177, 181, 190, 192, 197, 237, 268–72, 276, 281, 293, 307, 309, 313, 336
Frias, António João (Goan priest) 1–3, 5, 11, 13, 16, 305–6, 310–13, 315–23, 328, 333
Fróis, Luís, S.J. 94, 222–4

Gaunkar(s) 81–2, 88, 133, 137, 140, 142, 147–8, 205–8, 211, 213, 218, 227, 230, 232–4, 255, 269–71, 274, 306, 321, 325
Gaunkari 133, 135, 145, 147–8, 208, 226, 236, 265, 303–4, 306
Generatio 46, 284, 287
Gentiles 56–7, 70, 76, 78, 88, 89, 91–2, 95, 98–9, 103, 130–1, 134, 141–2, 147, 149, 153–4, 167, 174, 188, 219, 225, 231–2, 239, 246, 253, 256, 269, 276–7, 289, 295, 299, 308, 319, 322; behaviour 70, 76, 78, 95, 99, 174, 232, 246, 256, 269, 276; devotions and rituals 60, 75–6, 99, 134, 141, 147, 153–4, 222, 239, 318–19; scriptures 318, 324–5 (*see also* non-Christians)
Goa: political and economic centre 4, 19, 25, 43–4, 46, 66, 102, 111, 116, 206–7, 282, 286, 297; religious and intellectual centre 62, 136, 158–9; poor relief institutions 185, 190, 193; residents of 43, 78, 81, 88, 91, 120–1, 130, 174, 284–5, 287, 296–7, 302
Gomes, António, S.J. 45, 90, 167, 223
Gonçalves, Sebastião, S.J. 106, 226, 245–6, 254, 260
Gruzinski, Serge 10, 325–6
Guha, Sumit 322
Gujarat 48, 116, 324

Henrique (Cardinal; King of Portugal) 28, 34–5, 229, 330
Henriques, Henrique, S.J. 149, 151, 160, 163, 195
Herédia, António de, S.J. 98, 141, 230–1
Hespanha, António Manuel 39
Hinduism 6, 201
Holy Office (see Inquisition)
Hospital(s) 33, 43, 46, 118, 156, 169–70, 185, 187, 191–3, 234, 254, 256; of Monte Guirim 193; of Nossa Senhora da Saúde 192; of the Poor 191–3; Real, 185, 191

Iberian Union 183, 288, 304, 337
India 24, 48, 51, 53, 104, 139–41, 143, 178, 201, 210, 214, 225, 229, 244–5, 247, 250, 260–1, 272, 276, 281, 284–6, 289–95, 298, 304, 207, 313–15, 317–18, 324
Indians 1, 3, 6, 8, 94, 177, 223, 281, 288–9, 292, 295, 302, 307, 322, 328, 331 (*see also* Gentiles and non-Christians)
Indiáticos 292, 294–6 (see also *Casados*)
Inquisition 20, 32–3, 36–7, 44, 69, 91, 129, 139–41, 180, 234, 236, 239–40, 260, 270, 308, 310, 317
Islam 24, 49, 50, 320

Japan 53, 73, 117, 306
Jacques, João da Cunha (Goan priest) 306, 310, 317
Jesuit Provinces: Goa 117; Japan 117; Malabar 117; Portugal 117
Jesuits (S.J.): differences among 98–9, 103, 170, 223, 229–30, 254, 256, 265, 274; economics 118–19, 123–7, 130–2, 165, 219, 221; identity and memory 11, 73–4, 164, 204, 225, 229, 235, 244–6, 264; models and methods, 5, 37, 45, 75, 82, 86, 98–9, 104, 107, 141, 154, 163, 172–3, 180, 187–8, 195–6, 222, 243, 276, 330–1
Jews 28, 56, 90, 91, 92, 282, 319
João III (King of Portugal) 10, 14, 20–3, 27–30, 34–6 , 40, 42, 49–50, 53, 62, 67–8, 77, 84, 88, 90, 111, 159, 187, 230, 329, 337

King Gaspar (Magi King) 316, 318–19
Kochi 53, 55, 58–9, 76, 160, 169, 186, 249, 251
Kshatriyas 201, 209, 211, 314, 316, 318–19, 324

Lancilloto, Nicolao, S.J. 94, 149, 167, 188
Language(s), local 105–6, 113, 116, 139, 160–1, 171–2, 236, 246, 281, 338
Leão, Gaspar de, O.F.M. Rec. (Archbishop of Goa) 97–8, 114–15, 137, 336
Lisbon 17–19, 24, 35, 287, 292, 307
Loqu (Goan Brahman) 78, 144–5, 232
Louro, António, O.F.M. 55–8, 66, 89, 106, 159, 186
Loyola, Ignatius de (St) 72, 154–5, 168, 223
Ludden, David 227, 324

Madre de Deus, Luísa da 169, 193–4
Malacca 18, 24, 26, 53, 63, 159
Manuel I (King of Portugal) 3, 29, 51, 62, 80, 158, 186, 219, 286–7, 337
Margão 118, 196, 249, 254, 267, 302
Martyrs of Cuncolim: Alfonso Pacheco, S.J. 264, 229;

Francisco Aranha, S.J. 258, 264; Manuel Teixeira, S.J. 256; Pietro Berno, S.J. 256, 259–60, 264; Rudolfo Acquaviva 245, 256, 264
Mascarenhas Francisco de (Viceroy of Estado da Índia) 251, 253, 264–5
Mascarenhas, Pedro de (Viceroy of Estado da Índia) 10, 96, 112, 169, 253, 257
Melo, Francisco (Bishop of Goa) 52, 53, 62
Mesa da Consciência e Ordens 33, 44, 101, 109, 114, 129, 272, 289
Mestizos 23, 57, 168–9, 191, 288, 325
Misericórdia(s) 119, 181, 184–7, 195, 336
Mughal(s) 202, 227, 256, 323
Muslims 28, 56, 59, 71, 80, 91–2, 94, 207, 229, 264, 282, 308, 324

Naik (*also* Naique) 140, 205, 219, 250–1, 253, 254, 258, 261–4, 271, 320
Nazaré, Simão da, O.F.M. 133, 139–41, 190, 269–72
New Christians 46, 49, 56, 64–6, 71, 85n, 91, 140, 156, 167, 229, 236, 288–9, 298n
new Christians (*see* Christians/ Christians of the land)
Nobili, Roberto di, S.J. 151, 161
Non-Christians: discriminatory laws towards 46, 66, 70, 76, 79, 92–3, 119, 134, 142, 144, 188, 190, 195, 238–9, 267, 279; fleeing of 224, 226–8, 266, 271, 273, 276, 299; temples, devotions and rituals of 46, 59, 90, 126, 222, 229, 255
Noronha, Garcia de (Viceroy of Estado da Índia) 25, 67
Noronha, Miguel de (Viceroy of Estado da Índia) 131, 149, 190, 283, 293
Nunes, Dom Duarte (O.P., Bishop of Ring) 55, 57, 60, 64, 89, 100, 106, 164, 291

Officium parochi 112, 117, 129, 155, 300
Order of Christ 16, 27, 51–3, 68, 197, 289
Orientalism 4, 5, 6, 10, 12, 200, 202, 210, 330
Orlim 256–7, 320
Orphans 71, 83, 86, 87, 144, 145, 155, 164, 182–3, 190, 224, 273, 288, 299–301

Paes, Leonardo (Goan priest) 305–6, 310–23
Pai dos Cristãos 64–6, 127, 133, 139, 141, 189, 221, 238, 270, 275, 300–1; António Martins 133; Rui Barbudo 66, 189
Paiva, José Pedro 35–6
Palomo, Federico 28, 37, 157, 161
Paulo da Trindade, O.F.M. 117, 136–8, 142–3, 145, 160, 169, 170–1, 181, 183–4, 187, 192, 259, 293
Pearson, M.N. 121, 137
Peres, Lourenço, S.J. 233–5
Philip II of Spain (I of Portugal) 19, 229, 239, 274

Physical separation 56, 70, 79, 89–93, 91, 106, 144, 146, 189, 219, 276, 282
Policies of conversion 39, 42, 42, 45–6, 53, 56–7, 62, 67, 70–2, 74, 76, 80, 85, 87–8, 93, 98–9, 119, 121–3, 126–7, 154, 159, 170, 173, 187–8, 191, 195, 223–4, 226, 229–30, 254, 299, 331–2, 336
Ponda 228, 266, 250
Poor relief 2, 10, 15, 156, 186, 332, 336–7
Popes, *see* Roman popes
Porobo, Goinda (Brahman of Goa) 205–6, 213
Porobo, Malle (Brahman of Goa) 205–6, 213
Portugal 11, 13, 19, 90, 178, 326
Portuguese residents 2, 4, 6, 8, 9, 16–18, 22–3, 27, 55, 58–9, 60, 62, 64, 81, 84–5, 90–1, 94–5, 106, 120, 143, 156, 167–9, 181–5, 193, 219, 222, 264–5, 269, 271, 274, 280–8, 291–7, 299, 302–6, 308, 332, 335 (see also *Casados, Indiáticos*, and *Reinóis*)
Portuguese imperial power 2, 3, 12–14, 16–9, 24, 29, 35, 39–40, 45, 47, 49–51, 63, 73, 93–4, 105, 110–11, 199, 201–2, 205–7, 221, 229, 250–5, 257–8, 265, 268–9, 273, 276–8, 285, 287, 296–7, 300, 305–6, 308, 321–3, 327–8, 331, 333–4, 338
Portuguese (language) 41, 157–62, 166, 171, 179, 303, 311, 323, 329
Preaching 1, 37, 57, 60, 67, 69, 76, 112, 150–1, 155–7, 159, 165, 170–6, 181, 220–1, 234
Propaganda Fide 129, 233, 306–7
Prosperi, Adriano 21, 37, 175
Provincial Councils of Goa 162, 196, 236, 336; 1st 87, 91, 238; 2nd 87; 3rd 88n, 93, 196; 4th 162
Purificação, Miguel da, O.F.M. 171, 293–5, 309, 320, 322

Quadros, António, S.J. 95, 98, 112, 226, 230

Regeneratio 46, 284, 287
Reinóis 292, 294, 296, 334–5 (*see also* Portuguese residents)
Resistance 6, 15–16, 61, 80, 93–8, 96, 137–8, 141, 149, 199–200, 204, 218, 222–5, 227–8, 231, 242–7, 251–2, 255, 257, 266, 268–9, 271–5, 278, 308, 325
Robinson, Rowena 146–7
Roman Empire 22, 34, 41, 84, 337
Roman popes: Adrian VI 75; Alexander VI 51; Calisto III 50; Paul III 73, 74; Paul IV 112; Pius V 65
Rome 14, 18–19, 67, 69, 116–17, 120, 129, 293, 307

Saldanha, António, S.J. 126, 135, 165–7
Schools 32–3, 46, 63, 71–2, 75, 77, 107, 117, 155–6, 158–9, 163, 165, 167, 176, 193, 279
Sebastião (King of Portugal) 28, 91, 298

Seminaries: Reis Magos 193, 282; Santa Fé 187; São Paulo 119
Simão da Nazaré, O.F.M. 133, 139–41, 190, 269–72
Sirula 135–7, 143, 145, 190, 196, 212, 257, 259, 269–70, 330
Shiva 215, 262–3
Society of Jesus (S.J.), *see* Jesuits
Sousa, Martim Afonso de (Governor of Estado da Índia) 82, 125, 187, 250
Souza, Teotónio de 4
St Thomas (Apostle) 55, 58, 318–20
Stephens, Thomas, S.J. 161, 244
Subrahmanyam, Sanjay 13, 26
Sudra 206, 210–11, 217, 314

Thomas of Aquinas, O.P. 58, 168, 185, 312, 319–20
Thomaz, Luís Filipe 4, 26, 39, 40, 232
Toscano, Tomé, O.F.M. 137, 138, 140–1
Turner, Victor 65, 257, 263
Types of conversion 66–9, 78–9, 97–9, 103–4, 137–8, 144–5, 153, 164, 171, 186, 203–4, 221–2, 225–6, 229, 231, 237, 241, 251, 254, 276–7

Vaisya 206, 211
Valignano, Alessandro, S.J. 72, 103, 104–6, 127, 137, 151, 162, 164, 189, 194, 221, 224, 237, 245–6, 290, 330
van Linschoten, Jan Huyghen 143, 260, 281–2
Vaqueiro, Fernando, O.F.M. Rec. (Bishop of Ring) 55, 61–3
Vaz, Miguel (Vicar-General) 46, 54, 62–4, 66, 70–1, 74, 76–7, 89, 165, 167, 187–8
Velim 82, 125, 130, 248, 258, 261, 265
Veroda 82, 248, 258, 261, 265
Vijayanagar 25, 48, 248, 323
Villages of Bardez: Aldona 273; Anjuna 82, 271, 273; Arpora 271; Calangute 271, Calata 84, 125; Candolim 196, 271; Chapora 273–4; Chimbel 196; Colvale 319; Mapusa 135; Nadora 82, 320; Nagoa 196, 269–70; Nerul 194, 196, 320; Pirna 82, 320; Pomburpa 169, 187; Revora 82, 320; Sancoale 196, 255;
Villages of Chorão: Caraim 204, 206–7, 211, 213; Chorão 3, 11, 15, 46, 119, 123, 125, 196, 203–7, 209–22, 226, 230, 232–4, 236, 243, 251, 259, 268, 324, 330, 337
Villages of Dívar: Dívar 3, 11, 46, 123, 197, 215, 219, 251, 324, 337
Villages of Salcete: Ambelim 83, 125, 130, 204, 248, 258, 261, 265; Benaulim 125, 300–1, 325; Betalbatim 125, 196; Camorlim 302; Cansaulim 196; Carmona 83, 125, 196; Chicolna 325; Chinchinim 125, 196; Colva 196; Cortalim 148, 256; Cuncolim 16, 83, 196, 229, 243–7, 248–9, 251–2, 254–62, 264–8, 270, 278,

330; Curtorim 84, 301; Davorlim 300; Dramapur 125; Gandaulim 313; Gonsua 196; Majorda 125, 325; Margão 118, 196, 249, 254, 267, 302; Mormugão 255, 283, 325; Navelim 82; Orlim 256–7, 320; Quelossim 125, 324; Rachol 110, 118, 125, 250, 267, 283; Seraulim 84; Utordá 84, 300, 325; Vanelim 84; Verna 175, 249–50, 256; Velim 82, 125, 130, 248, 258, 261, 265; Veroda 82, 248, 258, 261, 265

Villages of Tiswadi: Azossim 133, 147; Batim 197, 242; Carambolim 133, 147–8, 226–7, 230; Mandur 196; Morumbim 196; Talaulim 84, 125, 313

Widow(s) 85–6, 133, 144–5, 181–4, 193–4, 299–300

Women 23, 64, 76, 83, 85–6, 92, 94, 130, 141, 148, 160–9, 180–3, 193–4, 205, 233–4, 268, 285–6, 288, 292, 335

Xavier, Francis, S.J. 69, 72–4, 112, 117, 150–1, 160, 167, 174, 308

Županov, Ines G. 157

www.ingramcontent.com/pod-product-compliance
Lightning Source LLC
LaVergne TN
LVHW050146080826
844660LV00002B/97

* 9 7 8 1 4 3 8 4 8 9 1 1 7 *